Multiple Personality
Disorder

WILEY SERIES IN GENERAL AND CLINICAL PSYCHIATRY

The Broad Scope of Ego Function Assessment
Edited by Leopold Bellak and Lisa A. Goldsmith

The Psychological Experience of Surgery
Edited by Richard S. Blacher

Presentations of Depression: Depressive Symptoms in Medical and Other Psychiatric Disorders
Edited by Oliver G. Cameron

Clinical Guidelines in Cross-Cultural Mental Health
Edited by Lillian Comas-Diaz and Ezra E.H. Griffith

Sleep Disorders: Diagnosis and Treatment (Second Edition)
Edited by Robert L. Williams, Ismet Karacan and Constance A. Moore

Multiple Personality Disorder: Diagnosis, Clinical Features, and Treatment
Colin A. Ross

MULTIPLE PERSONALITY DISORDER

Diagnosis, Clinical Features, and Treatment

Colin A. Ross, M.D.

WILEY

A Wiley-Interscience Publication

JOHN WILEY & SONS

New York • Chichester • Brisbane • Toronto • Singapore

Library of Congress Cataloging in Publication Data:

Ross, Colin A.
   Multiple personality disorder: diagnosis, clinical features, and
treatment/Colin A. Ross.
       p.   cm.—(Wiley series in general and clinical psychiatry)
   "A Wiley-Interscience publication."
   Includes bibliographies and index.
   ISBN 0-471-61515-3
   1. Multiple personality.   I. Title.   II. Series.
   [DNLM: 1. Multiple-Personality Disorder.   WM 173.6 R823m]
RC569.5.M8R67   1989
616.85'236—dc20
DNLM/DLC
for Library of Congress   89-14608
                                                             CIP

Printed in the United States of America

10 9 8 7 6 5 4 3 2

Series Preface

This series of books is addressed to psychiatrists, mental health specialists, and other serious students of the behavioral sciences. It is inspired by the genius of Adolf Meyer, who introduced psychobiology to psychiatry and charted the course, recently reformulated by George L. Engel, of the biopsychosocial model. Each book may consider the importance of any level of human behavioral interaction—community, family, interpersonal, individual, psychological, psychoanalytic, physiological, biochemical, and genetic or constitutional. Each level is respected on its own terms; no book in this series will fall victim to the fallacy of reductionism.

All aspects of psychiatric disorders, including theoretical, empirical, and therapeutic, are considered. Specific research studies, with their practical applications, are also included. It is our intention that the books in this series be comprehensive, thorough, rigorous, systematic, and original.

MAURICE R. GREEN
ROBERT W. RIEBER

New York University Medical Center
New York, New York

College of Physicians and Surgeons
of Columbia University
and John Jay College of the City University of
New York
New York, New York

Preface

The purpose of this book is to give the reader a comprehensive and detailed grounding in the history, diagnosis, and treatment of multiple personality disorder (MPD). It is not to create diagnosticians or therapists *de novo* out of untrained individuals. The assumption throughout is that MPD must be treated by trained professionals and that the treatment is based on general principles of psychotherapy. Having said that, I must acknowledge that I launched into my first case without adequate training or supervision: I hope that this book will be helpful for clinicians who find themselves in a similar situation.

In August 1979 I was a third-year medical student at the University of Alberta in Edmonton. About 3 weeks into my first clinical rotation, I was assigned to do an admission history and physical on a woman with amnesia. This patient provided me my first opportunity to diagnose and treat multiple personality disorder. Although I worked with her therapeutically for only a short time, I learned that dissociative disorders were my area of subspecialty.

I submitted an account of the case to *The International Journal of Clinical and Experimental Hypnosis,* which had a history of publishing papers on MPD. By chance the editor, Martin Orne, was looking for one more paper for a special issue on MPD, and mine was accepted (Ross, 1984). This was my first experience with editorial comment from a psychiatric journal, although I had published previously in a medical journal (Ross, 1981). The detailed and helpful editing steered me more strongly into the dissociative disorders.

Since then I have received support from a number of people and institutions whose contributions to my career, and indirectly to this book, I wish to acknowledge. I would like to thank my colleagues in the Department of Psychiatry at St. Boniface Hospital. The Fee Pool of the Department has paid for a full-time Dissociative Disorders Nursing Research Assistant for three years, out of joint clinical earnings. In addition my colleagues at St. Boniface Hospital have adjusted to a significant drain on departmental resources created by work with MPD patients on the ward, in the outpatient department, and in the emergency department. Few subspecialists in dissociation have had the benefit of such support and encouragement.

The inpatient work described in these pages would not have been possible without the dedicated efforts of the nursing staff on my inpatient unit, M3. The nurses have often borne the major burden of the work, have learned a great deal about MPD, and have spent many hours in process meetings, discussions, bedside therapy, and planning meetings. This effort had to be crammed into a full work load with no direct benefit to the nurses other than the satisfaction of helping dissociative patients.

I have received two research grants from the Manitoba Mental Health Research Foundation and one from the Manitoba Health Research Council. Their support will yield more than 10 publications on dissociation. Securing research funds from major agencies for the study of dissociation has thus far been a difficult task. The other source of funding has been the B.Sc. Med. Program of the Faculty of Medicine, University of Manitoba, which has allowed medical students to complete projects under my supervision. The California Institute of Integral Studies and the University of Toronto have also contributed by approving theses by Lynne Ryan (1988) and Margo Rivera (1988), respectively, on which I was able to have input and act as an examiner.

A source of indirect support has been a number of drug companies that have employed me as an investigator on clinical trials of their products. I have diverted substantial amounts of money from these projects to otherwise unfunded aspects of dissociative research such as data analysis. The well-being of dissociative disorders as a field of study could be furthered by direct contributions from these corporate sources. MPD is common, and the investigation of its psychopharmacology is in its infancy.

Dr. Ron Norton has helped me in my research development by teaching me about statistics and methodology, and by acting as collaborator and coauthor on a number of studies. Evidence of his contribution can be found in the references. Few psychiatrists without a Ph.D. can do serious research without a Ph.D. collaborator. I am not one who could.

Two Canadian psychiatrists deserve mention because of a special contribution they have made to my work: without them I would have felt alone among psychiatrists in Canada. Collaborators with me on workshops, Dr. George Fraser and Dr. John Curtis (1988) have provided the core of a growing network of Canadian mental health professionals interested in MPD. They are the only other psychiatrists in Canada with trained nurses able to offer intensive psychotherapy for MPD. Canada is a big country; it is easy to feel very isolated as an MPD specialist.

I would also like to thank the specialists in MPD south of the border who have provided encouragement, letters, opportunities, and consultations. Drs. Richard Kluft, Bennett Braun, Frank Putnam, and George Greaves have contributed to the development of most investigators in the field, and I am no exception. Among these four, Richard Kluft has done the most, reviewing grant and scholarship applications, writing letters, editing papers, and suggesting collaborations, among other forms of support.

Two colleagues have contributed more than any others. These are Geri Anderson (Anderson, 1988; Anderson & Ross, 1988a; Anderson & Ross, 1988b) and Pam Gahan (Ross & Gahan, 1988a; Ross & Gahan, 1988b), who work with me in the Dissociative Disorders Clinic at St. Boniface Hospital. As coauthors, coeducators, and cotherapists they have been there on a daily basis. I would not have been able to do the work without their clinical skills and their direct personal support. Both are gifted therapists. Setting up and running the Dissociative Disorders Clinic has taken a great deal more time, energy, and organization than running an anxiety disorders clinic. Without Pam and Geri I would be an individual psychiatrist treating MPD patients, and there would be no Clinic. They have helped introduce residents, medical students, nurses, and many other professionals to MPD through workshops, seminars, consultations, and cotherapy. Throughout the book, when I refer to "we," it is to work done by Pam, Geri, and myself.

I would like to acknowledge joint prior copyright on material in the Appendices: Copyright on the Therapist Dissociative Checklist is held by Geri Anderson and myself, and on the Dissociative Disorders Interview Schedule by Sharon Heber and myself. I thank these collaborators for permission to include this material in the present volume.

I don't know how anyone could work intensively with MPD patients without the support of loved ones at home. I have had that, and I want to thank my wife for everything she has done, for both my professional and my personal life. Finally, I would like to thank the patients. They have been my teachers and have tolerated my errors and uncertainties. Having worked with psychiatric patients of all types, I have learned infinitely more from these courageous survivors of unimaginable childhoods than from all other patients, books, and colleagues put together.

COLIN A. ROSS

Winnipeg, Manitoba, Canada
October 1989

Contents

Multiple Personality
Disorder

Introduction

This book is meant for mental health professionals from all disciplines. Its purpose is to provide a broad yet detailed grounding in the recognition and treatment of multiple personality disorder (MPD). Why bother writing or reading such a book? Is it worth expending much effort on a rare disorder of questionable status in psychiatry? For me it would not be worth the effort if MPD truly were an exotic curiosity. I believe that MPD is actually quite common and that dissociation is a common feature of many other psychiatric disorders, just as anxiety and depression occur in many illnesses that are not primarily anxiety or affective disorders.

Working with MPD patients and consulting with nonmedical community-based therapists have taught me about the limitations of diagnostically based assessment and therapy. Because I work within the sociological structure of a hospital and have a variety of highly differentiated treatment modalities available, it is important for me to make specific psychiatric diagnoses. It makes a big difference in my setting whether I diagnose someone as suffering from panic disorder, schizophrenia, or MPD. I need to be able to make valid and reliable diagnostic discriminations between these disorders.

In a community-based agency that services disturbed individuals with counseling and psychotherapy, there is little if any need for differential diagnosis. The process of diagnostic labeling is, in fact, often counter-therapeutic in such settings. In addition, the individuals seeking the services of such agencies have often had unpleasant contacts with hospital-based psychiatry and feel strongly that the diagnostic process works against their interests, rather than in favor of them.

In general I think that an adult female who has been sexually abused as a child, whether or not she has MPD, has better odds of getting helpful treatment from a nonmedical community-based agency than from an academic department of psychiatry. I hope that therapists outside the psychiatric domain of the mental health system will be able to benefit from this book and will not be put off by its medical flavor.

The diagnosis of MPD does not imply that anything is fundamentally wrong with the person who has the disorder. There is no evidence that anything is wrong with the brains of people who have MPD. Nor does the diagnosis imply that the person is "hysterical" or in any way bad, inferior, or weak. MPD is, however, a true psychiatric disorder. It has an etiology, phenomenology, treatment, and prognosis that differentiate it from any other disorder.

MPD is based not on defect but on talent and ability. The patients have used their ability to dissociate to cope with overwhelming childhood trauma, which usually involves both physical and sexual abuse. MPD is a creative and highly effective strategy for preserving the integrity of the organism in the face of chronic catastrophic trauma. The problem with adult MPD is that, like any survival strategy gone wrong, it creates more problems than it solves. If this were not so, the person wouldn't come for treatment. The treatment involves unlearning an overreliance on dissociation and learning more varied, flexible, and adaptive ways of coping with life.

Nonmedical threrapists could easily incorporate the assessment and treatment techniques described in this book into their practices without ever having to use the term *MPD* or having to refer to the dissociated parts of their clients as "personalities." I make these remarks because I am aware that many therapists might reject a book like this on the assumption that it medicalizes the consequences of childhood abuse, labels the victims as deviant, and perpetuates a variety of social prejudices against abused children, battered wives, and women in general. I don't think that is true.

There is a big gap between hospital-based psychiatry and nonmedical community-based therapy in North America, which MPD patients might help to bridge. They do have a specific psychiatric disorder, and they can benefit from hospitalization in a unit that can deal with them effectively. Better liaison between hospital and community would work to the benefit of the mental health system and the MPD patient/client.

There is a great deal of resistance to MPD in North America, despite the exponential increase in the diagnosis and treatment of MPD since 1980. Consequently I have tried to provide a broad historical and conceptual discussion: It is important to know how to think about MPD, not just what diagnostic and therapeutic techniques to use. Once one learns to think dissociatively, the plan of action falls into place more easily. The opening historical section of the book is directly relevant to therapy.

I have decided not to attempt an exhaustive referencing of the literature on MPD for several reasons. First the literature up to 1985 is available in two bibliographies (Boor & Coons, 1983; Damgaard, Van Benschoten, & Fagan, 1985) and is further updated in reviews by Kluft (1985d; 1985f; 1987a). Compared to affective or anxiety disorders, the MPD literature is still small. By reading these references and special issues on MPD of four psychiatric journals, it is possible to get a good grasp of the field. The other major source is a journal founded in 1988 with Richard Kluft as editor-in-chief. It is called *Dissociation* and is available from the Ridgeview Institute, 3995 South Cobb Drive, Smyrna, Georgia 30080, U.S.A. The articles in this journal provide ongoing up-to-date references for dissociative disorders.

The four special issues of psychiatric journals devoted to MPD are *The American Journal of Clinical Hypnosis* (1983, 26:2); *Psychiatric Annals* (1984, 14:1); *Psychiatric Clinics of North America* (1984, 7:1); and the *International Journal of Clinical and Experimental Hypnosis* (1984, 32:2). In addition a special issue of *Investigations* (1985, 1:3-4) dealt exclusively with MPD. A number of papers from these special issues and from *Dissociation* are referenced in this book, but persons with a serious interest in dissociation will want to read all of this material.

Because I am a male hospital-based physician treating primarily female patients, I have adopted a number of conventions. Throughout I will refer to the therapist as male and the patient as female. I will refer to the recipient of the therapy as a patient rather than a client.

I have tried to clarify for the reader when my discussion has a base in clinical experience, when it is based on research data, and when it runs beyond experience and data into conjecture. I may appear, at times, to speak with unwarranted certainty about the etiology, phenomenology, and treatment outcome of MPD; I think that research and clinical findings will accumulate over the next decade supporting my views. However, I do not expect the skeptical reader to be immediately convinced by everything I say. Psychiatry has suffered from too many fads and transient enthusiasms, and I hope that MPD will not be one more of these.

MPD is not just a metaphor for guiding therapy, it is not an iatrogenic artifact, and it is not an epiphenomenon of histrionic or borderline personality disorder. It is a legitimate and real psychiatric disorder with a specific treatment. It is not just another way of describing an amorphous, heterogeneous group of people who have been called "borderline," "as if personality," and a variety of other terms.

It is true that there is a large group of disturbed individuals who do not fit into the psychiatric diagnostic system very well and for whom conventional treatments are not very helpful. These people tend to be polysymptomatic and to receive numerous different diagnoses. Only some people within this group have MPD. Those who do are fortunate because they have a chance for complete recovery if they can find a therapist and can tolerate the difficult work of psychotherapy.

As I propose in the second section of this book, MPD is a hierarchically superior diagnosis within a large cluster of symptoms and disorders. The cluster includes depression, borderline personality disorder, panic disorder, eating disorders, Schneiderian first rank symptoms of schizophrenia, substance abuse, extrasensory perception experiences, secondary features of MPD, and MPD itself. The cluster is strongly associated with severe, chronic childhood trauma.

Patients with MPD tend to have symptoms from many different areas of the diagnostic system. However, they have only one disorder. I have called this disorder chronic trauma disorder with multiple personality disorder (see Chapter 7). Chronic trauma disorder can occur in nondissociative individuals who have been severely abused as children, in which case the diagnosis is chronic trauma disorder without MPD. The study of MPD, I believe, will eventually result in a reorganization of our diagnostic system.

In discussing the relationship between MPD and other psychiatric disorders in Chapter 7, I have deliberately made no attempt to reference the literature on schizophrenia, obsessive-compulsive disorder, anorexia nervosa, and the other disorders mentioned. Readers can consult the general psychiatric literature in this regard.

MPD is an important disorder, about which all mental health professionals should be knowledgeable, because it is common and treatable, and because it illustrates with great clarity and intensity the consequences of the childhood sexual and physical abuse endemic in our society. Those are the assumptions on which I have based this account of the diagnosis, clinical features, and treatment of MPD, a disorder thought to be extinct only three decades ago.

The focus in these pages is on adult MPD as it presents in clinical settings. I have no experience with MPD in old age and there is only one paper on this topic (Kluft, 1988d). Although I discuss forensic, childhood, and polyfragmented MPD, these are special areas with little supporting literature; therefore, I have not said much about them. Likewise I have not dealt at any length with cult-abused MPD patients because, although there is much clinical concern and discussion about them, I have only a little direct experience, and again there is little solid published material.

Another area I have not dealt with is how to do consultations, but there are three papers on this topic, to which I refer the reader (Greaves, 1988; Kluft, 1988b; 1988c). This book is for clinicians, and its purpose is to teach them how to recognize and treat patients with MPD. If it serves that purpose, I will be satisfied. I recommend that anyone trying to put the principles and techniques I describe into practice with his first patient seek consultation and supervision, if possible, and attend conferences and workshops. It is difficult to learn any therapy solely from a book, and reading this one will not create a fully qualified MPD therapist. It will, however, provide a comprehensive understanding of people who have used dissociation in a complex, intricate way to cope with years of childhood physical, sexual, and emotional abuse. There are many such individuals in our culture.

History of Multiple Personality Disorder

*. . . gods, strange gods, come forth from the forest into
the clearing of my known self, and then go back.*

        D. H. Lawrence, Studies in Classic American Literature

    Multiple personality disorder (MPD) is a complicated clinical disorder. In order to treat it effectively, a number of different perspectives are required. One cannot take a narrow or "purist" point of view. For instance, MPD must be understood in a historical and cultural context. The treatment of MPD in North America in the 1980s and 1990s is culture-bound. It represents the attempts of therapists to relieve the suffering of a group of people whose disorder exists in a particular historical context. MPD was not diagnosed very often in North America only 10 years ago and it is rarely diagnosed in Great Britain and continental Europe today.

    Because the rate of diagnosis of MPD in North America is in a period of exponential increase, it is particularly important to be aware of the history of dissociation. The MPD patient in this culture has a dissociative disorder because of childhood sexual and physical abuse in the majority of cases; in other cultures or times the trauma giving rise to the dissociation might be war, famine, religious persecution, or natural disaster, and the symptoms and treatment would therefore be different.

It is important to understand that the cultural and historical aspects of MPD do not make it less serious, less worthy of treatment, or less a legitimate subject of scientific study than any other psychiatric disorder. MPD is not a disease in the sense that bacterial pneumonia is a disease, but it is a major public health problem in North America, and it is treatable. Untreated, MPD imposes great suffering on the patient and a great drain on societal resources.

The first step in understanding MPD is to review the history, placing the disorder in a broad context. By studying the past, one can learn a great deal about the range of dissociative phenomena and variations in symptomotology. One can pick up numerous clinical tips and ideas from the 19th-century specialists in dissociative disorders. One realizes by studying the history of dissociation that many recent findings were already known 100 years ago. Finally, the history provides researchers with ideas for research projects.

In this historical review of MPD I will be pursuing a number of interrelated ideas. In the first chapter I will begin with ancient history and will review developments up to and including Freud. The chapter will conclude with a discussion of Breuer and Freud's *Studies on Hysteria* (1895/1986) and the peak of interest in dissociation in the early 20th century. In the second chapter I will describe the decline and discrediting of MPD after about 1910, the gradual picking up of interest after World War II, and then the exponential increase in the diagnosis of MPD in the 1980s.

The interrelated ideas in this historical review are these:

1. Dissociative phenomena can be recognized throughout history. MPD is embedded in a universal historical context and is not a transient aberration.

2. Themes of the fragmentation of self and the transformation of identity are likewise universal.

3. The switching of executive control of the body from one psychic entity to another has occurred throughout history.

4. By reading case histories, one can chart a gradual evolution of demon possession into MPD in the Western world, with the final transition in the 19th century.

5. In the 19th century and up until 1910 or so, the study of dissociation was in the mainstream of Western psychology and psychiatry and received attention from many of the major figures such as Freud, Jung, Charcot, Janet, Binet, James, and Prince. The study of dissociation had clinical, experimental, and theoretical components.

6. MPD and dissociation fell into disrepute after 1910 because of Freud's

repudiation of the seduction theory and the new diagnosis of schizophrenia.

7. MPD also fell into disrepute because of major flaws in the leading
theories of dissociation.

8. The upsurge in the diagnosis of MPD since 1980 provides an opportunity for modern scientific study of dissociation. This could result in
dissociation being reestablished in the mainstream of psychiatry, on
equal footing with anxiety and depression. Alternatively, dissociation
could fall into disrepute again, repeating the events of the late 19th
and early 20th centuries.

To write a complete history of dissociation would require a large book in
itself. A number of books provide elements of the history. These include
Hysteria: The History of a Disease, by Ilza Veith (1965); *Multiple Man:
Explorations in Possession and Multiple Personality*, by Adam Crabtree
(1985); *The Passion of Ansel Bourne: Multiple Personality in American Culture*, by Michael G. Kenny (1986); *Split Minds Split Brains*, edited by Jacques
M. Quen (1986); and *Multiple Personality, Allied Disorders, and Hypnosis*,
by Eugene Bliss (1986). These are the books I have found the most valuable.
From them and from other sources I have drawn together the eight points
listed previously.

Towering above these books and demanding separate mention is *The
Discovery of the Unconscious*, by Henri F. Ellenberger (1970). This work
of amazing scholarship is very clear and persuasive; it should be read by all
students of dissociation.

The History Prior to and Including Freud

Multiple personality disorder (MPD) is not a transient aberration, peculiar to 20th-century North America. This can be shown by illustrations from ancient history: The fragmentation of self and the transformation of identity have been recognized by all races. Examples from different cultures give a sense of the universality of these themes. MPD has gradually evolved from its prehistoric origins, through intermediate phenomena, to its modern form.

THE FRAGMENTATION OF SELF IN ANCIENT EGYPT: THE OSIRIS COMPLEX

The history of ancient Egypt is organized into three kingdoms, each of which is subdivided into dynasties. The Old Kingdom, 3400–2445 B.C., included Dynasties I–VIII; the Middle Kingdom, 2445–1580 B.C., included Dynasties IX–XVII; and the New Kingdom, 1580–332 B.C., included Dynasties XVIII–XXX. Dynasties XXVII–XXX lasted from 525 to 332 B.C. and are called the Persian Dynasties because during this period Egypt was ruled by Persian kings. The Persian Dynasties came to an end in 332 B.C. when Alexander the Great occupied Egypt.

The Egyptian myth that best illustrates the fragmentation of self is that of Isis and Osiris. The cult of Isis reached its peak just after the end of the 30th dynasty, at which time it was centered on the island of Philae in the Nile River where a temple to Isis had been built.

After the 4th century B.C. the cult of Isis spread from Alexandria throughout the Hellenic world. It entered Greece in combination with the cults of Horus, who was the son of Isis, and Serapis, which was the Greek name for Osiris. Herodotus apparently identified Isis with Demeter, the Greek goddess of earth, agriculture, and fertility.

The myth, brought in by the consul Lucius Cornelius Sulla, entered the Roman world in 86 B.C. as a tripartite cult of Isis, Horus, and Serapis and became one of the most popular branches of Roman mythology. The last Egyptian temples to Isis were closed in the 6th century A.D. Thus the cult and its theme of fragmentation were widely influential throughout the civilized Western world for centuries, attesting to the compelling importance of fragmentation. MPD is the most extreme modern manifestation of the fragmentation of self.

In Egyptian mythology only the ocean existed at first. Then Ra, the sun, was born from an egg that appeared on the surface of the ocean. Ra in turn gave rise to two gods, Shu and Geb, and two goddesses, Tefnut and Nut. Geb and Nut had two sons, Set and Osiris, and two daughters, Isis and Nephthys. Osiris married his sister Isis and succeeded Ra as king of the earth. However, his brother Set hated him. Set killed Osiris, cut him into many pieces, and scattered the fragments over a wide area.

Isis gathered up the fragments, embalmed them, and resurrected Osiris as king of the nether world, king of the land of the dead. As king of the dead, Osiris, aided by 42 assistants, judged the dead and assigned them to thirst and hunger, or dismemberment, on the one hand, or to the fields of Yaru, which were paradise, on the other. According to Egyptian belief, it was the person's *ka* that survived death and was judged by Osiris. The *ka* could only survive if the dead physical body survived on earth, however. It was this belief that gave rise to embalming, mummification, and the pyramids. The dead person's corpse was embalmed according to the original ritual embalming of Osiris by Isis.

Isis and Osiris had a son, Horus, who defeated Set in battle and became king of the earth. Thus the myth illustrates the fragmentation, death, healing, and resurrection of the self in a new form. This is the cycle through which the successfully treated MPD patient must pass. Unfortunately, in our culture, the original agent of the fragmentation of self does not always receive divine retribution and is not always dethroned from a position of temporal power. As a result the myth is perpetuated in the form of continued child abuse and transmission of the abuse to future generations.

The MPD patient suffers from an Osiris complex, not an Oedipus complex. The cause of her disorder is not conflicted incestuous fantasies, as Freud theorized was true of his patients. The MPD patient has a fragmented self caused by real physical and sexual assault. Her fragmentation represents a creative strategy for coping with and surviving this assault. MPD requires treatment because, like all defenses gone wrong, it causes more suffering than it prevents, especially when the victim has become an adult and the original abuse is no longer occurring. To say that the MPD patient suffers from an Osiris complex, not an Oedipus complex, is not to propose a complete break with Freud. Osiris was murdered by his brother and healed by a woman who was both his wife and sister. His parents were brother and sister. There is no shortage of incestuous sexual drive in the Osirian family. The crucial difference is that the victim of the Osiris complex was actually sexually abused. Her resulting complex is the inevitable and normal consequence of this abuse in a highly dissociative individual and is not due to any intrinsic defect or abnormality in the victim.

There is no need to illustrate the theme of the fragmentation of self with further examples. Like any universal human theme, the Osiris myth is subject to variation and permutation from culture to culture. A myth is a stylized embodiment of living human themes, problems, and aspirations. In that sense MPD is a mythic disorder. It embodies, in a profound and dramatic way, the struggle of the self to maintain its integrity in the face of severe violation. That is a struggle in which we are all engaged to varying degrees.

The point of these remarks is to establish that MPD is not a curiosity or an incomprehensible aberration. It is a commonsense disorder, and its features are familiar from myth, legend, religion, and literature. Many secular representations of MPD aspects are found in our popular culture today, in comic books, movies, and elsewhere.

THE THEME OF TRANSFORMATION OF IDENTITY IN HAIDA MYTHOLOGY

Before the arrival of the white settlers, the North American Indians varied as much in physique, economy, and culture as the Europeans. In other words two North American Indians could be as different as a Sicilian and a Swede. One of the most intense focuses of native North American civilization is in the Pacific Northwest, and one of the tribes living in this area is the Haida.

The myth of the beginning of the Haida world (Clark, 1960) illustrates the theme of the transformation of identity, which is also one of the diagnostic criteria for MPD. In the beginning of the Haida world, when in fact there was no world, Sha-lana ruled in a kingdom in the clouds. Raven, who was his chief servant, fell into disfavor and was cast forth from the celestial realm. It was Raven who created our world through a series of transformations.

First, by beating his wings, Raven transformed part of the primordial ocean into rock, from which sand and then trees gradually appeared, thereby creating the Queen Charlotte Islands. Raven created the human race by piling up clam shells and transforming them into two human females. Because of complaints by the two women, he then transformed one of them into a male. Unfortunately for Raven, however, seeing the two humans together made him lonely, so he decided to make a visit to Cloudland.

In Cloudland Raven transformed himself into a bear and managed to be accepted by his chief as a playmate for the chief's son. Not only Raven but also the children of Cloudland would transform themselves into animals in order to play. One day Raven stole the chief's three children, who were in the form of bears, as well as the sun. Transforming himself into an eagle, Raven flew off with the three bear-children and the sun.

The people of Cloudland gave chase, but Raven dropped the three children, who were safely recovered. Sha-lana ordered the people not to pursue Raven to the earth because he was afraid that this might cause the ruler of the lower world to come to the celestial world. Sha-lana therefore created a new sun for Cloudland and allowed Raven to take the original sun to earth. Raven had stolen a fire-stick at the same time, and this is why there is sunlight and fire in our world.

There are countless myths and legends from around the world that make use of transformation of identity. Citing more examples would not strengthen the point. Children in our culture are familiar with transformation of identity from comics, movies, television, and books. Who has not watched a child zooming around on the sidewalk or in the backyard, pretending to be a superhero or some other figure? Who can doubt the child's intensity of imaginative involvement in this transformation? I think it is reasonable to say that the normal child partially believes in this transformation on a transient basis.

It is not necessary to wonder where the MPD child gets the idea of creating someone else inside to cope with the abuse. The strategy of transformation of identity to gain strength, coping power, and even invulnerability is readily available in the child's environment. Because this theme is universal, it would be surprising if MPD occurred commonly in North America but rarely elsewhere. The building blocks of MPD must be present in most if not all cultures.

DISSOCIATION AND TRANCE STATES
IN CIRCUMPOLAR SHAMANISM

Because circumpolar shamans are, geographically and historically, the closest representatives of cultivated dissociation, I have chosen them as illustrative of dissociative phenomena.

There is a controversy in the anthropological literature about whether shamans were mentally ill (Eliade, 1964). There is debate about whether they were hysterics or schizophrenics, for instance. This is an unproductive debate because it is not based on an adequate definition of schizophrenia or recognition of the complexity and heterogeneity of chronic psychoses. The same is true for allegations that shamans are hysterics. MPD patients are frequently misdiagnosed as schizophrenics or dismissed as hysterics, so it is not surprising that anthropologists make similar conceptual errors about shamans.

As far as I can tell, most shamans did not suffer from any mental disorder. With variations of emphasis, they functioned as weathermen, doctors, priests, hunting consultants, and conveyors of oral tradition. Their professional activities were adaptive, culturally integrated, and planned. They undertook a long period of training and mastered a large number of techniques as well as an esoteric technical vocabulary. They were masters of self-hypnosis and used their ability to enter trances and altered states of consciousness in their work. Except for Siberian use of the hallucinogenic mushroom *amanita muscaria* (Wasson, 1973), the circumpolar shamans did not make extensive use of drugs, unlike their more southerly counterparts (Harner, 1973).

Clements (1932, cited in Ellenberger, 1970) listed five types of psychic illness treated with psychotherapy in preindustrial culture. They were

1. Disease–object intrusion
2. Loss of soul
3. Spirit intrusion
4. Breach of taboo
5. Sorcery

Each of these types of illness, with its corresponding specific modality of treatment, was within the expertise of the circumpolar shaman. Contemporary therapists encounter modern equivalents of loss of soul, spirit intrusion, and breach of taboo in MPD patients. Many MPD patients feel that one or more of their alters are discarnate entities, intruders from the outside; and many feel that their original self is far away, lost, and unavailable for contact with the outside world. This is our equivalent of soul loss. I have been told by MPD patients about the effects of satanic cults, which are the modern form of black sorcery, and in a sense I have encountered disease–object intrusion. In shamanism, disease–object intrusion was concrete and was treated by the shaman sucking out the object through the patient's skin. In the MPD patient the intruding object is usually "bad feelings" that the patient "gets out," with help from the therapist, through verbal techniques and rituals. Most MPD patients are victims of violation of the incest taboo.

The shamans are interesting because they exhibit many of the dissociative features of the MPD patient. They differ from the MPD patient in that the shamans were healthy and used their dissociation in a culturally integrated way. The MPD patient tends to be dysfunctional and socially isolated. This difference between the circumpolar shaman and the MPD patient is one reason that MPD is a disorder. Dissociation is not intrinsically pathological. Any given dissociative phenomenon may be functional or dysfunctional, healthy or a sign of illness, depending on its context. As well as resembling the MPD patient, the shaman has much in common with the MPD therapist, a theme that must be left to a later work.

In his book, Eliade (1964) presents the equation "shamanism = technique of ecstasy" (p. 4). This could as easily read "shamanism = technique of dissociation." The following sections describe 11 dissociative features of the shaman's work that illustrate the presence of dissociation in other cultures.

Structured, Meaningful Hallucinations

Like the MPD patient, the shaman heard voices and saw visions. For the shaman these were not chaotic or meaningless symptoms of psychosis, as they are not for the MPD patient. The shaman deliberately induced special states of being in which he could communicate with the spirits, hear their voices, and visually enter their worlds. For instance, the shaman might travel to the underworld to negotiate with spirits that controlled the animals, asking the spirits to allow his people success in the hunt. Although it is a matter of philosophical principle whether the shaman's experiences were hallucinations or perceptions of actual reality, for the MPD patient similar experiences are clearly dissociative and psychologically meaningful.

Trance States

The shamans conducted public ceremonies in which, with the help of drumming, chanting, and ritualized movements, they entered trance states. While in trance they exhibited many of the phenomena of modern hypnosis, including talking as if they were another person or an animal spirit (Spanos, Weekes, Menary, & Bertrand, 1986). The trance state was an essential prerequisite for communication with the spirits and temporary incarnation of spirits in the shaman's body. MPD patients frequently enter trance.

Hypnotic Anesthesia

The shamans often demonstrated their power by public feats of hypnotic anesthesia such as holding hot objects, walking naked in the cold, or piercing themselves with sharp objects. According to tradition, prior to the decline of shamanism in recent centuries, the old shamans could perform feats that were beyond the limits of modern hypnotic trance, such as drying several wet sheets by wrapping them on their naked bodies during an arctic blizzard, or holding extremely hot objects for long periods of time without discomfort or injury. MPD patients often report anesthesia for the pain of abuse or self-inflicted pain.

Symbolic Dreams

The shamans were also specialists in spirit dreaming. They had dreams that resulted in the finding of game, foretold the future, helped the souls of dead people find their way in the afterworld, and performed other functions. Such dreams were sources of information about the real world, and in them the shamans carried out deliberate, conscious actions just as they would in the waking world. The MPD patient frequently has dreams in which information about past abuse, the organization of the personality system, or other knowledge is transmitted from alter personalities to the waking personality. The graduated recovery of abuse memories through dreams can be contracted for by the therapist.

Ritual Dismemberment

One way in which the shamans could be initiated into their profession was through a ritual dismemberment reminiscent of the death of Osiris. This involved specific ceremonies and the spiritual fragmentation of the self. The MPD patient, by definition, has undergone a dismemberment of the self for a specific purpose, in her case to survive childhood abuse.

Possession by the Souls of Ancestors

During ceremonial trances, the shamans would often deliberately become possessed by the souls of dead ancestors. The ancestors would speak through the body of the shaman for a variety of purposes, which might include practical advice or consolidation of social structure and tradition. Alter personalities claiming to be dead relatives of the patient occur in 20.6 percent of cases of MPD (Ross, Norton, & Wozney, 1989).

Possession by Helping Spirits

Another entity that frequently took possession of the shaman during rituals was the helping spirit. This might be an animal or a spirit entity. The shaman had a special relationship and was on familiar terms with his helpers. MPD patients almost always have helper personalities, some of whom claim to be from other dimensions or to be spirits. The helpers have usually been active prior to diagnosis and treatment and also cooperate with the therapist for the patient's benefit.

Exhaustion Following Strenuous Trance Work

Following a particularly rigorous ceremony, during which a shaman might dance a great deal and perform numerous athletic feats, there was often a period of exhaustion that could last several days. This can also happen following an intense MPD treatment session. The patient may feel drained and may lie down in bed for several hours, not fully recovering that day.

Stimulating Dissociation through Intoxication

The shamans by and large did not use hallucinogens in their work. Eliade (1964) feels that mushroom intoxication, when it was used, was "a mechanical and corrupt method of reproducing 'ecstasy,' being 'carried out of oneself'; it tries to imitate a model which is earlier and belongs to another plane of reference" (p. 223). The principal hallucinogen used was the mushroom *amanita muscaria,* also known as fly agaric, which is the red toadstool with white flakes on it depicted in fairy tales. The later shamans held *amanita* parties lacking structure or cultural purpose, which are an indicator of the deterioration of the shamans' dissociative skills (Harner, 1973). To achieve chemical dissociation, MPD patients frequently abuse substances and also switch to substance-abusing alters in order to be in a more permissive state before drug ingestion. They use drugs to escape from pain, but the technique is crude and self-destructive compared to psychological dissociation.

Out-of-Body Experiences

One of the skills of the shaman was astral projection, or out-of-body travel. The shamans would ascend to the sky world or descend to the underworld in order to carry out various tasks. They also sent spirit helpers out into the landscape searching for game. Many MPD patients have had out-of-body experiences, which originally occurred during childhood abuse. The little girl would float up to the ceiling and count the dots in the plaster or travel to another location to play with dolls or friends. Later in life such experiences can become more complex and can occur independently of traumatic events.

Transformation of Identity

During ceremonies the shamans would deliberately induce a state of possession. When the animal spirit entered the shaman's body, it could then use his voice and gestures to communicate directly with the audience. However, the shaman wasn't simply invaded by a foreign object. The possession state involved a reciprocal relationship between the two beings in which the shaman became the spirit and the spirit became the shaman. Thus there was a transformation of identity on the part of the shaman. This was controlled and transient. When the ceremony was completed, the shaman transformed back into his human self, and the spirit continued to exist as an independent entity outside him. This process is similar to the switching of alters in MPD patients, but not identical.

The purpose of describing these dissociative experiences of circumpolar shamans was to demonstrate that such experiences have occurred in many cultures throughout history. Any given dissociative experience may be part of a disorder, a culturally normal ceremony, or simply an individual experience. There is a group of experiences involving trance, auditory hallucinations, and transformation of identity that is universal and has different meanings in different cultures. The MPD patient has drawn on this region of human experience and ability to deal with trauma.

THE EVOLUTION OF DEMON POSSESSION INTO MULTIPLE PERSONALITY DISORDER

A full account of this history would require a book in itself. I am going to rely heavily on a book that has already done much of the work, *Possession Demoniacal and Other*, by T. K. Oesterreich (1921/1974). In Oesterreich's book one can trace the evolution of demon possession into modern MPD, although he doesn't make that an explicit theme.

Like MPD, demon possession is in many aspects an exaggeration of normal psychology. Oesterreich believes that there is a continuum from normality through obsessive states to possession, and that possession is a hypnotic phenomenon. With the possible exception of paranormal events associated with possession, all its phenomena can be reproduced in modern hypnotic trance.

Possession states share many of the properties of MPD. For instance, possession is subdivided into two categories depending on the presence or absence of one-way amnesia (see Chapter 4). In MPD one-way amnesia is said to occur if the presenting personality is amnesic for periods when alter personalities are in control of the body. In such cases the alters are fully aware of the main or presenting personality. There is debate about the status of amnesia as a diagnostic criterion for MPD (see Chapter 4), and there is likewise some controversy as to whether amnesia is required for true possession.

In fact the diagnostic criteria for possession do not differentiate it from MPD. In *Demon Possession* (Montgomery, 1976), Wilson (1976, p. 224) quotes the criteria of Nevius:

1. The chief differentiating mark of so-called demon possession is the automatic presentation and the persistent and consistent acting out of a new personality.
   a. The new personality says he is a demon.
   b. He/she uses personal pronouns; first person for the demon, third person for the possessed.
   c. The demon uses titles or names.
   d. The demon has sentiments, facial expressions and physical manifestations that harmonize with the above.

2. Another differentiating mark of demon possession is the evidence it gives of knowledge and intellectual power not possessed by the subject.

3. Another differentiating mark of demonomania intimately connected with the assumption of a new personality is that with the change of personality there is a complete change of moral character (aversion and hatred to God and especially to Christ).

I have integrated alter personalities that met all these criteria, using purely psychological methods, with no need for theological interpretations. In fact, personalities identified as demons occur in 28.6 percent of contemporary cases of MPD (Ross, Norton, & Wozney, 1989). These diagnostic criteria for demon possession are culture-bound, because in other cultures neither priest, patient, nor demon would have heard of Jesus, and the behavioral response to the name Jesus would not occur.

There is a close link between dissociative disorders and obsessive-compulsive disorder (Ross & Anderson, 1988), which is discussed in Chapter 7. This linkage is present in Oesterreich's (1921/1974) analysis of possession states as well. He believes that possession may occur by one of two pathways, the first of which involves the elaboration of an obsessive state. The two forms of classical possession are *lucid possession* and *somnambulistic possession*. Lucid possession is similar to MPD without amnesia, while somnambulistic possession is similar to MPD with amnesia between alters.

Lucid possession occurs when the possessed person does not experience amnesia. The victim of lucid possession remembers everything the demon said and did while in control of his body. The lucidly possessed person feels a separate being inside him controlling his speech and actions, and struggles to regain control of his body. In somnambulistic possession the possessed person is amnesic for everything the demon or spirit does during the periods of active possession. During treatment of MPD, as the amnesia barriers are dismantled, the patient passes in reverse order to a stage of lucid possession and then to a normal integrated state.

According to Oesterreich, possession may arise in two ways. The first pathway to possession begins with a state of clinical obsession. Through an undefined process that Oesterreich calls "crystallization" (1921/1974, p. 91), which is strongly influenced by cultural factors, the obsessed person progresses to a state in which he experiences an increasing sense of internal dividedness. This process may involve identification with someone in the environment or the past, hypnotic suggestion, or reinforcement by other people. The person then progresses to a state of lucid possession, in which he believes that his thoughts and impulses come not from himself but another being inside him.

As shown in Figure 1.1, from lucid possession the person may progress to somnambulistic possession, with amnesia, or to one of two other possibilities, namely successful fusion of the dissociated states or psychological deterioration.

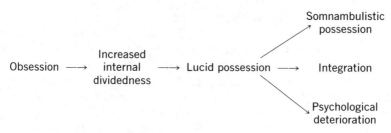

Figure 1.1. The First Pathway to Possession States

The other starting point for the development of possession, according to Oesterreich, is the existence of two incompatible emotional states that are not fully dual, such as are experienced by all people. In a culture in which one of the states is defined as morally bad, the drive to possession will be greater. Thus, as shown in Figure 1.2, the person, under the influence of his culture, progresses to possession, which may be either lucid or somnambulistic, depending on how hypnotizable the person is, and the expectations of the culture. Somnambulistic possession, according to Oesterreich, requires a deeper level of autohypnosis than the lucid form, an idea consistent with modern scales of hypnotizability, in which the capacity for posthypnotic amnesia defines the highly hypnotizable individual.

If the culture does not endorse the possibility of demon possession, then one would expect the process diagrammed in Figure 1.2 to lead to a secular version of demon possession, which in our world is MPD. Thus as our civilization evolved from the Middle Ages to the late 20th century, there was a decline in demon possession and a rise in MPD.

In medieval Europe there was a dissociation of certain elements of being based on theological disapproval of those elements. Oesterreich (1921/1974) remarks that there is no demon possession in Homer, a poet thought by Nietzsche (1872/1956) to be purely Apollonian. An Apollonian culture depends on dissociation of the Dionysian elements of being from public life, the Dionysian elements being sensuality, spontaneity, fertility, a pagan sense of religion, and physical ecstasy. These elements were punitively dissociated by the medieval church.

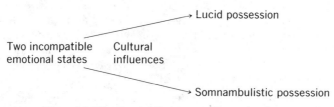

Figure 1.2. The Second Pathway to Possession States

Though dissociated, the Dionysian aspect was not absent. It was present as an incompatible set of impulses and knowledge in nuns, monks, peasants, and other medieval folk. When the dissociation broke down, the spontaneous sensual being regained control in a caricatured form as a demon. According to Oesterreich, exorcism reestablished the dissociation through hypnotic suggestion, although Oesterreich did not use the term *dissociation*.

The cases of classical demon possession were stereotyped and always conformed to cultural expectations. The exorcists engaged in theological debates and battles with the demons but made no attempt to understand the phenomena psychologically. Also, demon possession was highly contagious: epidemics could be prevented by physical isolation of the first case, a measure actually undertaken at times.

The transition from classical demon possession to MPD occurred in four overlapping stages, for each of which a case example is given below.

Classical Demon Possession

In classical demon possession the dissociated state identified itself as a Christian demon and uttered blasphemous statements. The exorcist engaged in theological debates with the demon, as well as using threats and commands prior to formal exorcism. The roles and attitudes of both demon and exorcist were highly structured and inflexible. In Christian culture demons might identify themselves as Leviathan or Beelzebub, but this, I assume, never happens in non-Christian cultures in which neither exorcist nor possessed person has heard of these particular demons.

There was invariably a strong contrast between the character of the possessed person and that of the demon, with the person being devout and polite, and the demon irreverent and insulting. This is similar to the dual personalities of 19th-century and modern popular entertainment; in these cases the alters are polar opposites, such as quiet depressed housewife and promiscuous partygoer.

Oesterreich (1921/1974) quotes a typical case of classical demon possession occurring in 1714:

At the unexpected rumour that two possessed women had been brought into the workhouse of that place, I followed the dictates of my pastor's conscience and went to the workhouse on the evening of the 14th of December, 1714. After . . . the paroxysm began in one of the possessed women, and Satan abruptly hurled this invective at me by her mouth: "Silly fool, what are you doing in this workhouse? You'll get lice here," etc. I made him this answer: "By the blood, the wounds and the martyrdom of Jesus Christ, thou shalt be vanquished and expelled!" Thereupon he foamed with rage and shouted: "If we had the devil's power we would turn the earth and heaven upside down, etc. . . . . What God doesn't want is ours!"

In the morning, towards 11 o'clock, this possessed woman came at my request, but not willingly, into the church of the place. There, in order that I might inform myself of her most wretched state, I began to sing the canticle: "May God the Father be with us," and after such preparation as I judged necessary I read from the pulpit the two remarkable passages concerning possession in the fifth and ninth chapters of St. Mark, so earnestly and for so long that Satan who was in the possessed cried to me from below the pulpit: "Won't you soon have done?" After I had replied: "When it is enough for God it will be enough for thee, demon!" Satan broke into complaints against me: "How dost thou oppress, how dost thou torment me! If only I had been wise enough not to enter thy church!" As he cried out impudently: "My creature must now suffer as an example!" I closed his mouth with these words: "Demon! the creature is not thine but God's! That which is thine is filth and unclean things, hell and damnation to all eternity." When at last I addressed to him the most violent exhortations in the name of Jesus, he cried out: "Oh, I burn, I burn! Oh, what torture! What torture!" or loaded me with furious invectives: "What ails thee to jabber in this fashion?"

During all these prayers, clamourings, and disputes, Satan tortured the poor creature horribly, howled through her mouth in a frightful manner and threw her to the ground so rigid, so insensible that she became as cold as ice and lay as dead, at which time we could not perceive the slightest breath until at last with God's help she came to herself. . . .

Although the possessed once more recovered her reason on this occasion without being able, be it noted, to remember what Satan had said by her mouth, he did not leave her long in peace after my departure; he tormented her as before. (p. 9)

In his book *Ecstatic Religion: An Anthropological Study of Spirit Possession and Shamanism,* I. M. Lewis (1971) argues very persuasively, with examples from many cultures, that spirit possession often serves a social function. For instance, women living in cultures in which they are politically powerless can acquire power, influence, autonomy, and partial satisfaction of thwarted needs through possession. In one culture there may be a special women's cult that exorcises the possessed: in another possession may confer relief from unpleasant duties. Demon possession in western Europe made possible the ritualized expression of Dionysian impulses and opinions that could not be stated directly, or even consciously acknowledged by the possessed person, because they were politically or theologically dangerous.

Demon possession was not always an effective strategy for the politically or theologically oppressed, being sometimes dealt with by witch-hunt and Inquisition.

Early Transitional Demon Possession

By 1830 possession states no longer invariably met the classical features. Instead of being possessed by demons, folk could be overtaken by dead neighbors or relatives, and the exorcists had shifted toward a psychological theory of possession. The social context of the possession had become more prominent in the narratives, but from reading them one could not form psychological hypotheses about identification, secondary gain, or other factors that might be operative.

The following case was observed in 1830 (Oesterreich, 1921/1974):

> The first woman possessed in the Biblical manner with whom I became acquainted, writes the Swabian poet and physician Justinus Kerner, I owe to the confidence of Doctor. . . . He had sent her to me for cure, informing me that all treatment by ordinary methods had been fruitless when applied to this woman.

> The patient was a peasant-woman of thirty-four years. . . . Her past life up to this time had been irreproachable. She kept her house and showed due regard for religion without being especially devout. Without any definite cause which could be discovered, she was seized, in August, 1830, by terrible fits of convulsions, during which a strange voice uttered by her mouth diabolic discourses. As soon as this voice began to speak (it professed to be that of an unhappy dead man), her individuality vanished, to give place to another. So long as this lasted she knew nothing of her individuality, which only reappeared (in all its integrity and reason) when she had retired to rest.

> This demon shouted, swore, and raged in a most terrible fashion. He broke out especially into curses against God and everything sacred.

> Bodily measures and medicines did not produce the slightest change in her state, nor did a pregnancy and the suckling which followed it. Only her continual prayer (to which moreover she was obliged to apply herself with the greatest perseverance, for the demon could not endure it) often frustrated the demon for a time.

> During five months all the resources of medicine were tried in vain. . . . On the contrary, two demons now spoke in her; who often, as it were, played the raging multitude within her, barked like dogs, mewed like cats, etc. Did she begin to pray, the demons at once flung her into the air, swore, and made a horrible din through her mouth.

> When the demons left her in peace she came to herself, and on hearing the accounts of those present, and seeing the injuries inflicted upon her by blows and falls, she burst into sobs and lamented her condition. By a magico-magnetic (that is to say, hypnotic) treatment . . . one of the demons had been expelled before she was brought to me; but the one who remained only made the more turmoil. (p. 10)

This passage by Oesterreich shows that a number of features of modern MPD and its treatment began to appear by 1830. First, the possessed person was classified as a *patient* and was treated by a physician. A number of traditional medical approaches were tried unsuccessfully, as often happens in MPD, and then treatment progress was made with hypnosis. There was a hint of a conception of possession as a form of hysteria, in that hysteria was thought to be treatable with marriage, sexual activity, and motherhood in at least some cases. Also, by remarking that the possession state began "without any definite cause," the narrator implies that some possession cases had discernible secular causes, which in turn implies that they were psychological not theological in nature.

The full transition to late 20th century MPD had not been made in this case, however, because the demon was treated by expulsion. This is a conception that lingered in muted psychological form into the 1980s, in the sense that undesirable (in the eyes of the therapist) alters were expelled, suppressed, or otherwise banished by some therapists, in order to ensure that the "real" self gained control.

Late Transitional Demon Possession

In late transitional demon possession, the conception of the therapist was purely psychological and so was the treatment. The patient complained of being demon possessed, but the demon was considered by the physician to be a dissociated psychic entity, and its purpose was psychological. The psychological theory and the therapeutic interventions are subtle and complex, and the case is related to a wide range of dissociative phenomena, other cases, multiple personality, and a theory of dissociation.

An excellent example of late transitional demon possession is the case of Achille, treated by Pierre Janet at the Saltpêtrière, where a great deal of work on hypnosis, hysteria, and dissociation was done. The case is quoted at length by Oesterreich (1921/1974), so I will summarize it.

Achille had no psychiatric problems until 1890 when, at the age of 33, he had a brief affair while away from his wife and child on a business trip. Upon his return he rapidly fell into a depression, which progressed to a state of demon possession, with the devil assuming executive control spontaneously. The devil made statements such as "Cursed the Trinity, cursed the Virgin!" and "Priests are a worthless lot!" (Oesterreich, 1974, p. 112). A priest was called who diagnosed Achille as mad and in need of medical treatment. The transition from classical possession to MPD was accompanied both by medicine taking over responsibility for these cases and by the church relinquishing responsibility.

Janet devised a treatment strategy derived from his knowledge of multiple personality and experimental work on automatic writing (Janet, 1901/1977, 1907/1965). He allowed the demon to "rave and rant as he pleased" (Oesterreich, 1974, p. 113), and while standing behind him quietly ordered him to make certain movements. This is an experimental technique for eliciting dissociated behavior that was used extensively in 19th-century French psychology. By automatic writing the demon entered into a conversation with Janet, during which he tricked the devil into cooperating with him. "To force the devil to obey me I attacked him through the sentiment which has always been the darling of devils—vanity" (Oesterreich, 1974, p. 113).

Janet tricked the devil into a demonstration of his power: The devil placed Achille in a hypnotic trance, which Janet himself had been unable to do. Once this was achieved, Janet was able to discover the extramarital affair, which had not been disclosed. He then began a systematic process of hypnotically transforming Achille's memories, thoughts, and feelings about the event, with the goal of relieving his guilt. Janet's summary of the treatment, which resulted in complete and lasting cure, is as follows (Oesterreich, 1974):

> If we wished to cure our unhappy Achille, it was completely useless to talk to him of hell, demons and death. Although he spoke of them incessantly, they were secondary things, psychologically accessory. Although the patient appeared possessed, his malady was not possession but the emotion of remorse. This was true of many possessed persons, the devil being for them merely the incarnation of their regrets, remorse, terrors and vices. It was Achille's remorse and the very memory of his wrong-doing which we had to make him forget. This was far from being an easy matter—forgetting is more difficult than is generally supposed.
>
> . . . The memory of his transgression was transformed in all sorts of ways thanks to suggested hallucinations. Finally Achille's wife, evoked by a hallucination at the proper moment, came to grant complete pardon to her spouse, who was deserving rather of pity than of blame. (p. 116)

I have called this a case of late transitional demon possession for several reasons, the first being, of course, that the dissociated state identified itself as a demon. More important, the treatment consisted of a refined psychological exorcism not of the demon but of the memory that resulted in creation of the demon. Few contemporary therapists would advocate such an approach except in exceptional cases, and most would strive for integration of the memory into the main body of consciousness, possibly with adjunctive marital therapy. The case is late transitional, also, because the demon made stereotypically demonic denunciations of Christian religion.

Since the final transition to modern MPD, demon possession has been viewed in purely psychological terms by most physicians and psychotherapists. For instance, a few days ago while covering for a colleague who was on holiday, I interviewed one of his inpatients. She was being treated for a psychotic depression and had stated that she was possessed by the devil, prior to responding to antidepressant and antipsychotic medication. Like her attending psychiatrist, I viewed the belief in demon possession as a depressive delusion. As a teaching exercise for the resident and medical students, I reviewed the differential diagnosis between possession states occurring as dissociative disorders and ideas of possession arising from cognitive errors made by the patient. A delusion is an extreme form of cognitive error.

In this case the patient concluded that she must be possessed as an explanation for her obsessive thoughts, which had started after the onset of her depression. Because the thoughts were uncharacteristic of her normal thinking and felt ego-alien, she concluded that they must not be coming from her. At no time did she have a sense of the palpable presence of an alien entity within her, she did not hear the voice of the devil, and she did not talk like a demon. She readily accepted both my explanation that obsessive thoughts can be a symptom of depression and my reassurance that they should go away with further resolution of her depression, which was in partial remission.

There was no hint of anyone on the ward considering exorcism. Demon possession, in such cases, in 1988, has been attenuated to the status of a delusional idea, with little or no behavioral manifestations. It really exists only as an ideational remnant of past culture. However, demon possession is still accepted as an actual possibility by some theologians and clinicians, giving rise to postdemonic possession.

Postdemonic Demon Possession

In the modern world, Christian religion no longer exists as the organizing principle or guiding core of most medical and therapeutic practice. Most psychotherapy is agnostic or atheistic. In professional journals and books there are no techniques, theories, or viewpoints it would make sense to call *spiritual*. Not surprisingly there is also no demon possession. In this cultural climate any alleged cases of demon possession can therefore be described as postdemonic, from the perspective of the mainstream.

Such cases are reported in a book called *Demon Possession* (Montgomery, 1976). This is a collection of papers arising from a conference on demon possession held by the Christian Medical Society at Notre Dame in 1975. Several cases of possible demon possession that are presented are indistinguishable from secular dissociative disorders and would be considered part of the regular caseload on any service specializing in dissociative disorders.

One of these is described by a physician (Wilson, 1976):

This 32-year-old twice-married female was brought in because of falling spells which had been treated with all kinds of anticonvulsant medication. She was examined on the neurological service and after all examinations including EEG, brain scan, and a pneumoencephalogram were negative, she was transferred to the psychiatric service. Her mental status examination was unremarkable and all of the staff commented that she seemed normal until she had her first "spell."

While standing at the door of the day room she was violently thrown to the floor bruising her arm severely. She was picked up and carried to her room all the while resisting violently. When the author arrived, eight persons were restraining her as she thrashed about on the bed. *Her facial expression was one of anger and hate.* Sedation resulted in sleep. During the ensuing weeks, the patient was treated psychotherapeutically and it was learned that there was considerable turmoil in her childhood home, but because she was "pretty" she was spoiled. She married the type of individual described by Jackson Smith as the first husband of a hysterical female. She was a "high liver" and after her separation and divorce, she was threatened with rejection by her parents. She remarried and her second husband was a "nice" but unexciting man. She continued to associate with her "high living" friends. When her husband demanded that she give up her friends and her parties, she started having the "spells." (p. 225)

My hypotheses about this woman are that the "turmoil" in her childhood was paternal incest; that the angry state was an alter who remembered the abuse; that there was at least partial amnesia for the "high living," which was carried out by a promiscuous alter; that there had been auditory hallucinations and amnesic periods prior to the recent "spells"; and that the patient was a "hysterical" female because she was a victim of childhood sexual abuse. Further, the acceptance of Christ this woman was said to have subsequently undergone (Wilson, 1976, p. 226) did not represent a real religious conversion of her whole being: It was a pseudoacceptance that reinforced the amnesia for the incest. If this is correct, then the patient would inevitably relapse.

My distrust of the theological hypothesis about this case is compounded by a statement that appears shortly after the case history: "Other examples of possible 'hysterical' demon possession meeting the criteria of Nevius may be found in *The Three Faces of Eve* by Cleckley, and in *Sybil* by Schreiber" (p. 226). One doesn't need to be a feminist to say that such clinico-theological treatment reinforces silence about the sexual abuse of girls and blames the adult survivor, who is said to be either hysterical or possessed, or both.

The hypothesis of demon possession in this case is an attempt to impose an out-of-date world view on secular phenomena that have superseded the old Christian culture. I say that as someone who is willing to believe that demon possession may actually occur and who sees the fragmentation and secularization of our society as cultural decay. Actually it is important for both clinical and religious reasons not to interpret dissociative disorders as possession, because such misinterpretation is both bad medicine and bad religion. It doesn't make sense to exorcise dissociative states, not because there are no demons, but because dissociative states are part of the whole person.

Perhaps it would make sense to leave the last word on demon possession to a patient of mine. This woman, who had been sexually abused by her father, wrote the following passage in her diary after I had seen her once in consultation, and several months before I started working with her psychotherapeutically:

Where do these feelings stem from the Religious beliefs that were so hypocritical and confusing that caused two different sides between the parts good/evil how from childhood they were taught to honour the mother and father no matter how abusive they are to you how that they must always be good and confess their sins or the devil will get them being that in the form of the father. what sins does a child have when growing up except for the ones that they were made to believe in. they were so instilled with miricales that they waited for miricals to happen to them because of all the suffering that they deserved one and when they didn't recieve them they became angry with God and possible created an evil part as a form of revenge not only on men but on God as well.

SCIENTIFIC STUDY OF DISSOCIATION IN THE NINETEENTH CENTURY

The authors mentioned earlier in this chapter, especially Ellenberger (1970), have detailed much of this history in books that are readily available, so I need only mention some of the main figures. When I speak of the 19th century, I really mean the period up until about 1910.

Especially in France and the United States a great deal of work was done on dissociation in the 19th century. This consisted of case studies of MPD and fugues, experimental studies of automatic writing and hypnosis, and theoretical treatises. Cases of MPD were reported from a number of centers. The main figures included Janet, Charcot, Bernheim, Liebault, Freud, Jung, Prince, and James.

In his *Principles of Psychology* (1890/1983), William James discussed multiple personality in a theoretical chapter on the consciousness of self. He spoke of a plurality of selves in the normal individual, which included the material, social, and spiritual selves, and the pure ego. These selves could undergo various derangements, some resulting in MPD. Thus the leading American psychological theoretician took MPD seriously, advocated further empirical study of the disorder, and believed that it had numerous theoretical implications for the field. There was no question of MPD being dismissed as unworthy of serious study.

Sidis and Goodhart published a case study of a patient called Hannah under the title *Multiple Personality* (1905) with a dedication to William James. Boris Sidis also coedited the *Journal of Abnormal Psychology* with Morton Prince, who wrote extensively on MPD. Prince's case study, *The Dissociation of a Personality* (1905/1978), is still widely referred to and has recently been reprinted. The leading figures of the day were interlinked both personally and professionally by their interest in dissociation.

Jung studied mediums and spiritism and presented case histories containing numerous dissociative phenomena in a treatise called "On the Psychology and Pathology of So-Called Occult Phenomena" (1902/1907). Jung's interest in parapsychology was one of the factors that led to his eventual split with Freud. If Jung's interest in the paranormal was intertwined with his study of dissociation, then to stay with Freud, he would have had to abandon his study of dissociation and related phenomena. It is well known that Freud repudiated the use of hypnosis, for instance.

Before discussing Freud, I want first to outline the major flaws in the two leading approaches to dissociation in 19th-century psychology, and second to discuss Alfred Binet, a neglected but major figure in the history of dissociative studies. The flaws in dissociative theory probably contributed to its being abandoned as a field of serious study after 1910.

Flaws in the Study of Dissociation

Janet is a chief representative of one approach. He believed that dissociation originates from real trauma. However, he also held that, like mental illness in general, dissociation is based on a biological predisposition. That is reasonable, except that the predisposition was called "mental degeneration" (Ellenberger, 1970, p. 539), a term derived from Morel. Patients were thought of as mental degenerates. They fell victim to dissociation, basically, because of weakness and an inability to *associate* psychic elements normally. Their disorders were based on incapacity. According to this view, one would develop MPD in response to childhood trauma because of an intrinsic biological defect. Such a theory is not able to account for the phenomena adequately, because integrated MPD patients do not display signs of degeneracy.

The idea that patients with posttraumatic dissociative disorders are tainted with "mental degeneracy" contributed to the discrediting of MPD. With the appearance of the diagnosis of schizophrenia, MPD patients were rediagnosed as schizophrenic, which really meant that they were viewed as suffering from an organic brain syndrome (see Chapter 2). If Janet had thought of the biological predisposition as a talent or ability, which I believe it is, it might not have been so easy for MPD to be swallowed up by organic mental disease.

Morton Prince (1905, p. 489) made the other major error in the field, one repeated by Thigpen and Cleckley in *The Three Faces of Eve* (1957). He decided that the best way to treat MPD is to force the disappearance of most alters, and to back the ascendancy of one. Such treatment consists of trying to get rid of the "bad" alters and keep the "good" or "real" ones. This does not work because the bad alters have a function, only appear to be bad when not understood, and are a necessary part of the whole. This kind of treatment is a secular version of exorcism that does not heal the pain, resolve the conflicts, or lead to integration, and that reinforces the dissociation.

These flaws in the theory of dissociation and its treatment made it easier for the field to fall into disrepute, because its foundations were not solid.

The theoretical, experimental, and clinical study of dissociation in the 19th century is exemplified by Alfred Binet, who, like other early figures, has been overlooked in the recent revival of interest in Janet (Haule, 1986; van der Hart & van der Velden, 1987).

The Work of Alfred Binet

Alfred Binet was born in Nice in 1857 and died in 1911. Besides his interest in intelligence, he wrote two major treatises on dissociation. *On Double Consciousness* was published in 1890, while *Alterations of Personality* appeared in 1896. Both have recently been reprinted (Binet, 1977a, 1977b). The two volumes contain a wealth of theory, clinical observation, and experimental evidence on multiple personality and dissociation.

For instance, Binet noted that experimental alters can be produced in normal highly hypnotizable subjects, thus anticipating work by Spanos et al. (1986) and others, who do not refer to Binet. He also observed that these alter personalities were transient and incomplete analogues of full MPD.

Binet viewed the doubling of consciousness as a common clinical mechanism that underlay a variety of psychiatric disorders, including somatization disorder, conversion disorder, and dissociative disorders, as classified in DSM-III (American Psychiatric Association, 1980), and DSM-III-R (American Psychiatric Association, 1987). He demonstrated that amnesia, muscle paralysis, auditory hallucinations, automatic writing, obsessive thoughts, and many other phenomena were associated with a doubling of consciousness. He also demonstrated that this doubling was the basic mechanism of the formation of these symptoms.

Binet performed experiments to demonstrate the leakage of information across amnesia barriers. These experiments have only been revived in the last decade or two, without acknowledgment of Binet. He also studied Hilgard's hidden observer (Hilgard, 1977, 1984) in a large series of experiments, acknowledging Richet as the first person to identify the hidden observer. The term "hidden observer" was not used in the 19th century, but it is the same experimental phenomenon. Binet (1890) said of Richet,

> He has brought out the fact, that in hysterical persons and in a great many individuals reputed normal, there exists a sort of permanent semi-somnambulism; in other words, there is, in these subjects, an unconscious ego, an unconscious activity, which is constantly on the watch, which contemplates, which gives attention, which reflects, which forms inferences, and lastly which performs acts—all unknown to the conscious ego. (p. 10)

The following is an example of one of Binet's experiments, a simple one: Binet took a person he called hysterical, hypnotized him or her, and induced an experimental anesthesia in one hand. He then had the person read an eye chart and adjusted the distance between the person and the eye chart so the person could just read the largest letters. The subject was then asked to read smaller letters on the chart but could not do so. The subject had not seen these smaller letters during the earlier phase of the experiment. In the next step, Binet placed a pen in the anesthetic hand, without changing the distance between the eye chart and the subject. The person was still unable to read the smaller letters, but the anesthetic hand was now able to write them down accurately. The subject denied any conscious awareness of the activity of the hand.

This was basically a hidden observer experiment. Binet used numerous experimental procedures and worked with pain, touch, hearing, memory, and other faculties. By the standards of modern experimental psychology his work was crude, but it was pioneering. His findings were entirely consistent with those of Hilgard. Binet also made a number of other interesting observations. He repeated Janet's observation that the naming of an alter personality crystallizes it, making it more formed and definite.

Binet stated that alters created experimentally can only be called out by the person who created them, whereas autohypnotic alters can be called out by anyone. This crucial observation has been lost for 100 years, but needs to be studied because it strikes to the heart of the field and bears directly on the controversy about iatrogenic influence in MPD.

This brief summary of Binet's work highlights the point that there was a great deal of clinical and experimental study of dissociation in the 19th century. Only in the last two decades have we started to repair a nearly complete discontinuity with that work.

Breuer and Freud's Studies on Hysteria

Freud and Breuer published *Studies on Hysteria* in 1895. The book consists of some case histories of Breuer and Freud's female patients and several theoretical chapters. All the women described in the case histories had dissociative disorders, and most had been sexually abused. Anna O., the subject of the most famous case history in the book, clearly had MPD. Up until 1895 Freud considered these patients to be suffering from the adult consequences of real childhood abuse. His treatment took the reality of the trauma into account both technically and theoretically.

Within a few years of publishing *Studies on Hysteria*, however, Freud repudiated the seduction theory. There are probably personal, social, and intellectual reasons behind this major shift in Freud's thinking. Several of them are apparent in Ernest Jones's biography of Freud (1953). For one thing, it would have been awkward for Freud to state publicly that his patients had been sexually abused as children. Many of the abusive fathers were part of his own social circle.

Anna O.'s family, for instance, lived one street away from Freud. In 1880 they moved to Vienna to a neighborhood called Liechtensteinerstrasse, which was one block away from a street called Bergasse, where Freud had both his home and office from 1891 until 1938. Anna O. was a friend of Freud's wife and visited in the Freud home more than once. Later Anna and Freud's wife, Martha, became related by marriage.

The sexual aspects of Anna O.'s symptomotology made Breuer very uncomfortable. The relationship between Breuer and Anna O. ended when she developed a hysterical pregnancy, for which Breuer was the father. The last time Breuer saw her was on a house call, during which she was in hysterical labor. Jones (1953) writes:

> Though profoundly shocked, he managed to calm her down by hypnotizing her, and then fled the house in a cold sweat. The next day he and his wife left for Venice to spend a second honeymoon, which resulted in the conception of a daughter; the girl born in these curious circumstances was nearly 60 years later to commit suicide in New York. (p. 247)

Breuer's wife had been jealous of her husband's preoccupation with Anna O. and the amount of time he spent with her. According to Jones, Martha Freud

> . . . identified herself with Breuer's wife, and hoped the same thing would not ever happen to her, whereupon Freud reproved her vanity in supposing that other women would fall in love with *her* husband: "For that to happen one has to be a Breuer." (p. 247)

Freud's repudiation of the seduction theory was a great misfortune for psychiatric patients. It resulted in a repudiation of the clinical realities of both abused children and adult survivors of childhood abuse. In order to explain the symptoms of his patients, in what he thought was the absence of any actual trauma, Freud felt compelled to invent a fantastic metapsychology, wasting intellectual energy on clinical and theoretical misconceptions. It is an aspect of his genius that, despite this false premise, he was then able to construct some valuable and lasting theory.

At the time of *Studies on Hysteria,* Freud was working with patients similar to those of Binet, Janet, and Prince. His ideas were consistent with their tradition and with a large body of experimental data. Following his repudiation of the seduction theory, however, Freud embarked on a metapsychological digression. This digression would have been idiosyncratic if it had not been influential. A second aspect of Freud's genius was his ability to create a socially acceptable theory that denied the reality of childhood sexual abuse.

The truth is that Anna O. had MPD. There is no evidence that she was sexually abused by her father. If she was, though, it would explain her conflict about nursing her father while he was dying. The diagnosis of MPD was made by Freud and Breuer, and also by Ernest Jones (1953), who said:

> More interesting, however, was the presence of two distinct states of consciousness: one a fairly normal one, the other that of a naughty and troublesome

child, rather like Morton Prince's famous case of Sally Beauchamp. It was thus a case of double personality. (p. 246)

It was actually a case of triple personality.

Anna O.'s MPD has been retrospectively diagnosed by a contemporary psychoanalyst, Walter Stewart (1984), who wrote:

> As a next line of defense she developed a double personality. In the normal state, she was oriented but depressed and anxious. In the *condition seconde,* she was abusive, rebellious, moody, and naughty. The split in personality was an attempt to isolate the angry aspect of her character. (p. 50).

The question is, what was Anna O. so angry about?

In order to establish beyond doubt that Anna O. had MPD, I will quote a number of passages from *Studies on Hysteria* (Breuer & Freud, 1895/1986).

Breuer noticed Anna O.'s MPD immediately:

> It was while the patient was in this condition that I undertook her treatment, and I at once recognized the seriousness of the psychical disturbance with which I had to deal. Two entirely distinct states of consciousness were present which alternated very frequently and without warning and which became more and more differentiated in the course of the illness. In one of these states she recognized her normal surroundings; she was melancholy and anxious, but relatively normal. In the other state she hallucinated and was "naughty"— that is to say, she was abusive, used to throw the cushions at people, so far as the contractures at various times allowed, tore buttons off her bedclothes and linen with those of her fingers which she could move, and so on. At this stage of her illness if something had been moved in the room or someone had entered or left it (during her other state of consciousness) she would complain of having "lost" some time and would remark upon the gap in her train of conscious thoughts. (p. 76)

These are classical signs and symptoms of MPD (see Chapter 5). Anna herself offered the diagnosis of MPD:

> At moments when her mind was quite clear she would complain of the profound darkness in her head, of not being able to think, of becoming blind and deaf, of having two selves, a real one and an evil one which forced her to behave badly, and so on. (p. 77)

The amnesia barrier between the two states is commented on repeatedly in the text, as is the switching from one state to another. There were several interesting features, including the two states speaking different languages, and the second state believing that the correct date was one year earlier than the actual date.

Breuer's account also contains an excellent description of the second state, or *condition seconde,* waking up disoriented. This kind of disorientation occurs commonly in MPD (p. 92). There is also a clear description of the phenomenon of copresence, which is similar to lucid possession (p. 100). Copresence occurs when an alter personality in the background takes joint control of the body without displacing the primary personality, or when it influences the primary personality's mental state from the background.

Later Breuer offers his own diagnosis of MPD: "It is hard to avoid expressing the situation by saying that the patient was split into two personalities of which one was mentally normal and the other insane" (p. 101). One can see here the same error that Morton Prince made: one personality is thought to be "bad," "insane," or "delirious," while the primary personality is viewed as desirable and normal. In psychoanalytic terms this is a major countertransference distortion of the reality of the patient.

Anna O. had a third state as well, which today would be called a hidden observer, internal self helper, or center. This was an entity described as follows: "A clear-sighted and calm observer sat, as she put it, in a corner of her brain and looked on at all the mad business" (p. 101). If Breuer had been able to enlist this state as a cotherapist, he might have uncovered earlier childhood trauma and provided a more effective treatment.

Anna O.'s real name was Bertha Pappenheim. Bertha Pappenheim became one of the first social workers in Europe. Her work was recognized in a commemorative German stamp issued in 1954. She was also an early feminist. Her work involved the establishing of homes for prostitutes and unwed mothers. It is possible that, in psychoanalytic terms, this career was an undoing of her own childhood sexual trauma and of the failure of any person in authority to validate its reality or offer comfort. This is a strange historical irony: Freud repudiated the seduction theory, thereby making effective treatment of such women unlikely, but based on that repudiation he went on to develop theory that accurately explains much of Bertha Pappenheim's career drive.

The other case histories in *Studies on Hysteria* are written by Freud. His patient Emmy Von N. had a dissociative disorder for sure, and almost certainly had MPD. She was an excellent hypnotic subject. In his first session with her Freud observed alternating states, one of which was probably a child alter personality that had been abused.

He writes:

What she told me was perfectly coherent and revealed an unusual degree of education and intelligence. This made it seem all the more strange when every two or three minutes she suddenly broke off, contorted her face into an expression of horror and disgust, stretched out her hand towards me, spreading and crooking her fingers, and exclaimed, in a changed voice, charged with anxiety: "Keep still—Don't say anything!—Don't touch me!" She was probably under the influence of some recurrent hallucination of a horrifying kind and was trying to keep the intruding material at bay with this formula. (p. 104).

We have here the embryonic beginnings of Freud's theory of obsession. I believe that the intruding material was actually an abuse memory. Put another way, I believe that the formula was communicating real trauma and that it was not an obsessive defense against conflict and fantasy.

Emmy Von N. had a history of past unsuccessful treatments, which is common in MPD. Freud understood her symptoms to be due to the "associative inaccessibility" of certain ideas and feelings. If psychic content is associatively inaccessible, that means it has been dissociated, of course. Freud was saying that this patient had a dissociative disorder. He spoke of the patient's "mnemonic symbols," which are equivalent to the "somatic memories" common in MPD (Kluft, 1987b). These physical symptoms symbolically express and communicate past trauma that is too painful to remember. Thus Freud was partly on track but was already forming theories that would lead away from the true etiology of his patients' disorders.

Freud notes that there was an amnesia barrier between Emmy Von N.'s two states (p. 157). On one occasion the *condition seconde* claimed to be a woman from the previous century, a claim sometimes made by contemporary alter personalities. Emmy Von N. displayed many of the primary and secondary features of late 20th-century MPD.

The case of Miss Lucy R. contains dissociative features as well, and in it Freud refers to "the splitting of consciousness in these cases" (p. 188). Katherina, another case, had dissociative features secondary to attempted paternal incest, but not MPD. Fräulein Elisabeth Von R. had a dissociative disorder that seemed to be based on adult conflict rather than childhood trauma. Freud said that her symptoms arose because "the incompatible idea had been forced out of her associations" (p. 227), which is to say, dissociated. Another case, Fräulein Rosalia H., is mentioned briefly: she had symptoms arising from attempted paternal incest.

One can see that the cases in *Studies on Hysteria* represent a range of dissociative disorders. There are some cases of full MPD. Not all patients had experienced childhood sexual abuse, but some had.

In the theoretical sections of the book both Freud and Breuer build a theory of trauma-driven dissociation. There are numerous references to splitting of consciousness, dissociated states, autohypnosis, and a spectrum of increasing severity and complexity of dissociation. Breuer and Freud write jointly, in italics:

The longer we have been occupied with these phenomena the more we have become convinced that *the splitting of consciousness which is so striking in the well-known classical cases under the form of* "double conscience" *is present to a rudimentary degree in every hysteria, and that a tendency to such dissociation, and with it the emergence of abnormal states of consciousness*

*(which we shall bring together under the term "hypnoid"), is the basic phe-
nomenon of this neurosis.* In these views we concur with Binet and the two
Janets, though we have no experience of the remarkable findings they have
made on anaesthetic patients. (p. 63)

Freud nearly decided that dissociative symptoms can arise from a rational,
intelligent sphere of consciousness. He spoke of his

. . . impression of there being a superior intelligence outside the patient's consciousness which keeps a large amount of psychical material arranged for
particular purposes and has fixed a planned order for its return to consciousness. I suspect, however, that this unconscious intelligence is no more than
an appearance. (p. 356)

He puts it another way:

The pathogenic material appears to be the property of an intelligence which is
not necessarily inferior to that of the normal ego. The appearance of a second
personality is often presented in the most deceptive manner. (p. 273)

If Freud had pursued this line of thinking, his topographical and structural
models of the mind would have been very different. With the repudiation
of the seduction theory, however, it became necessary for the unconscious
to have certain properties. One of these could not be rational memory of
actual abuse. We learn from MPD patients that the "unconscious" is not
unconscious. One can converse directly with the alter personalities who hold
the memories. The alters commonly control the rate of release of traumatic
memories to the primary personality, and in fact I contract with them for
this staged recovery of memory.

Concerning the "superior" intelligence of the dissociated ego in MPD
patients, some skilled therapists feel that the patient's center, or inner observer, embodies a superior spiritual knowledge (Comstock, 1987). It is my
experience that centers and inner self helpers can be excellent cotherapists,
but they do not have transcendental abilities. Nevertheless, Freud must have
had this intuition of superior intelligence for some reason. I will discuss the
extrasensory experiences and paranormal powers of MPD patients in Chapters 5 and 8.

In conclusion, I will repeat my contention that Freud's repudiation of the
seduction theory contributed to the discrediting of MPD. When he repudiated
the reality of his patients' childhood trauma, Freud, given his genius, felt
compelled to erect an elaborate theoretical explanation of their symptoms.
Although this theory contained much truth, it also contained much falsehood.
For many decades MPD patients were rarely diagnosed. They were not
understood as suffering from the adult consequences of real childhood trauma.
Instead their disorder was misclassified. Their symptoms were misunder-

stood in terms of incorrectly applied psychoanalytical theory. As a result they received either no treatment or the wrong treatment.

This historical error cannot be corrected by a repudiation of Freud because he contributed too much that is lasting. Corrected psychoanalytic theory can easily accommodate posttraumatic dissociation into its theory and therapy (Paley, 1988). Breuer was right when he said, "It is certain that we have only taken the first steps in this region of knowledge, and our present views will be substantially altered by further observations" (p. 316). The insight of *Studies on Hysteria* needs to be rescued from Freud's later distortions. Why? So that Anna O. can be correctly remembered as "the best known and clearest example of major hysteria with manifest '*double conscience*' " (1895/1986, p. 316). She was only partially treated. Correctly understood, Anna O., Breuer, and Freud have much to teach us.

CHAPTER TWO

Freud to the Present

Studies on Hysteria was published in 1895. The decline in diagnosis and study of multiple personality disorder (MPD) had set in by about 1910. As I proposed in the previous chapter, Freud's repudiation of the seduction theory was probably a major force in the discrediting of MPD. Patients with trauma-driven dissociative disorders were understood as suffering from unresolved incestuous fantasies. Their treatment did not take the true etiology of their symptoms into account and would be described as an elaborate form of blaming the victim in any feminist analysis (Rivera, 1987, 1988).

When Freud repudiated the seduction theory, he simultaneously repudiated hypnosis and Jung's interest in the paranormal. Because MPD, sexual abuse, autohypnosis, and extrasensory experiences are closely linked to each other (see Chapters 5 and 8), Freud effectively banned a large area of psychic reality from serious study. People who came to physicians and nonmedical therapists with dissociative posttraumatic stress disorders could not receive treatment that took the cause of their problems into account.

Along with the discrediting of hypnosis in the early 20th century, for which Freud was not solely responsible, there was an ascendancy of the view that MPD is an artifact. The artifact was thought to be the result of an interaction between a naive diagnostician and a gullible, hysterical patient. Hypnosis, it was held, amplified and entrenched the artifact. Both hypnosis and MPD were thrown out.

Another factor contributing to the decline of MPD and dissociation was the work of Pavlov. Professional energy and ideological commitment that did not flow into psychoanalysis were channeled into behaviorism. Hilgard (1987) has mentioned this aspect of the history, which I won't consider any further.

In this chapter I am going to discuss the history of MPD from 1910 to 1988. I will concentrate on events from 1980 onward, because this is when most of the important developments have occurred. During the period 1910–1980, MPD vanished from serious study, mentioned only in a few case reports and two review articles. Then in the 1970s a resurgence began. Starting in 1980 there was an exponential takeoff in the number of diagnoses of MPD made in North America.

The next major landmark is 1984. In this year the field began to become politically organized and, in publications, began a transition from a pres-cientific to a scientific literature. By 1990 this transition will be complete, and the field will be in the phase of early scientific development.

THE ROLE OF SCHIZOPHRENIA IN THE DECLINE OF MULTIPLE PERSONALITY DISORDER

Those MPD patients who were not classified as Oedipal hysterics after 1910 were likely to be called schizophrenic. In this instance it was not the patient's conflicts that were blamed for the symptoms, but her brain. Rosenbaum (1980) has documented the role of the term *schizophrenia* in the decline of diagnoses of MPD. His work is valuable but should be followed up with a detailed scholarly analysis of the relationship between MPD and schizophrenia in the 20th century.

Schizophrenia was called *dementia praecox* until the term schizophrenia was introduced by Bleuler. "Dementia praecox" is actually a better name than "schizophrenia" for this group of disorders; whereas "schizophrenia" is a better name for MPD than "multiple personality disorder." Schizophrenia means "split mind" from the Greek *schizo*, "split," and *phren*, "mind." It is actually MPD that is characterized by a split mind. This confused terminology has given rise to popular confusion about schizophrenia, which is often thought to be the same as split personality. The consensus view in modern psychiatry is that schizophrenia is not one illness but a group of related illnesses. Schizophrenia is widely assumed to be a physical disorder of the brain, although this hasn't been proven. There is no evidence that it responds to individual insight-oriented psychotherapy, but it does respond to medication. The medication suppresses the so-called positive symptoms of schizophrenia, which include delusions, hallucinations, and disturbed behavior. However the medications have no effect on the negative symptoms of emptiness, lack of drive, inner deadness, and deteriorating occupational and social function. The medications never cure the illness.

Today schizophrenia is viewed by many as a form of organic brain syndrome. It is not classified as an organic brain syndrome only because the specific physical causes of schizophrenia have not been identified. Schizophrenia is more closely related to Alzheimer's disease than to MPD. It makes some sense to call schizophrenia "dementia praecox," but no sense at all to call it "split-mind disorder," in Greek or English. Perhaps *dementia psychotica juvenalis* would appeal to some. Setting that neologism aside, the point is that schizophrenia is almost undoubtedly a disease of the brain requiring physical treatment. There is no evidence that there is anything structurally or physiologically wrong with the MPD brain. There is in fact no sound conceptual reason to suppose that there is a physical disturbance of the brain in the DSM-III-R dissociative disorders (American Psychiatric Association, 1987).

The effect of renaming dementia praecox *split mind disorder* was to absorb many MPD patients into the organic brain syndromes. There has been an ideological dichotomy in psychiatry over the last 80 years, which is not resolved. Initially, the Freudians were on one side, and the "biological" psychiatrists were on the other. The unitary Freudian camp has since been replaced by a welter of diverse schools. According to rumor, some biological psychiatrists have a very strong desire to be accepted as respectable medical scientists and never to be mistaken for psychoanalysts. The reciprocal morbid phobia is also in place. Where has this left the MPD patient?

With the same presenting features, she may be consigned to ineffective biological treatments, on the one hand, or ineffective psychological treatments on the other. In one case the diagnosis is schizophrenia, or, fancier, schizoaffective disorder, with an assumed organic etiology. In the other the diagnosis is borderline or hysterical personality disorder, with an assumed metapsychological etiology.

Rosenbaum (1980) has shown that from 1914 to 1926 there were more diagnoses of MPD than of schizophrenia made in North America. During that period 15 cases of MPD and 10 of schizophrenia were reported in the literature. Rosenbaum says that the diagnosis of schizophrenia "caught on" in the United States in the late 1920s and early 1930s. Following this catching on, there was a sharp increase in diagnoses of schizophrenia and a sharp decline in diagnoses of MPD. How is one to understand this?

It is commonly said today that MPD is an iatrogenic artifact and a transient diagnostic fad. What about schizophrenia? Could it be that many diagnoses of schizophrenia are incorrect and that they lead to negative iatrogenic complications? Could it be schizophrenia that is the fad, one driven by biological reductionism (Ross, 1986a)? Why should this not be the case? Why is MPD singled out for the criticism of iatrogenesis by mainstream psychiatry, but not schizophrenia? Because of data? No. Because of ideology.

Many dissociative posttraumatic stress disorders are misdiagnosed as schizophrenia in North America today (see Chapter 7). In a series of 236 cases of MPD reported to me by 203 clinicians throughout North America

(Ross, Norton, & Wozney, 1989), for instance, 40.8 percent had a previous diagnosis of schizophrenia. There is, I believe, a group of related organic brain syndromes that present with delusions, hallucinations, and deteriorating occupational and social function, as defined by the term *schizophrenia* in DSM-III-R. The problem in contemporary psychiatry is the inability of many psychiatrists to make an accurate diagnostic discrimination between two groups of illnesses (organic brain syndromes and posttraumatic dissociative disorders), which have different etiologies, treatments, and prognoses.

Another factor contributing to the decline of MPD after 1910 was probably the name of the disorder. The name leads to incredulity and arguments about whether the disorder is "real." Much of the argument is based on assumptions generated in the minds of adherents and skeptics by the term *multiple personality disorder*. The term suggests that it is necessary to debate whether one person can really have more than one personality, or, put more extremely, whether there can really be more than one person in a single body. Of course there can't. Nevertheless, MPD is a real disorder.

It may be, on the other hand, that the name of a disorder is irrelevant, as long as it is properly conceptualized, diagnosed, and treated. Misnaming a group of organic brain syndromes *split mind disorder* in the 20th century has not resulted in any systematic research attempting to show that schizophrenia is an expression of Oedipal conflict. The field is steadily moving toward an organic theory and treatment of schizophrenia, undistracted by the inappropriate name given to the illness. If it appears to be unnecessary to rename schizophrenia, why rename MPD?

I personally advocate retaining the terms *schizophrenia* and *multiple personality disorder,* classifying one as a presumed organic brain syndrome and the other as a posttraumatic dissociative disorder. There is much better evidence in favor of the posttraumatic nature of MPD than in favor of the organic etiology of schizophrenia. Anyway, what would the names be changed to? "Dissociated ego state disorder" (DESD) is too cacophonous for my ear.

What is needed is sound empirical research on the overlap and distinctions between trauma-driven dissociative symptoms and organic/psychotic symptoms. These points are discussed in more detail in Chapter 7. For now it is sufficient to note the role of the term *schizophrenia* in the decline of diagnoses of MPD.

REVIEW ARTICLES IN 1944 AND 1962

Two recent bibliographies of the MPD literature (Boor & Coons, 1983; Damgaard, Van Benschoten, & Fagan, 1985) provide a comprehensive list of publications on the subject. These span the period of this chapter up to and including 1984. I am going to highlight only a couple of landmarks between 1910 and 1980.

The first of these is a review article by Taylor and Martin (1944) that begins:

> Morton Prince, who founded this JOURNAL, made much of multiple personality. In articles, books, and lectures, he described cases and grouped them into types; he told how some of the cases were caused and how some were cured; he encouraged other authors to contribute like observations, particularly to this JOURNAL; and throughout his professional life he seemed to think of abnormal psychology, psychotherapy, and mental hygiene largely in terms of multiple personality. (p. 281)

One of the features of the article is a list of 76 cases of MPD taken from the entire literature available to the authors: of these, 57 percent were American, 18 percent French, 16 percent British, and the rest German and Swiss. Each case is listed by reporting professional, name of the patient, number of personalities, and references in which the case appears. As well, Taylor and Martin typed the cases according to a clearly defined classificatory scheme.

The classificatory system included such items as whether the case displayed mutual amnesia (two-way amnesia), one-way amnesia, coconsciousness, and other structural features. In addition certain qualities of the alters were tabulated: sex, differing ages, and general temperament. Many of these terms are consistent with or identical with Braun's (1986a) terminology.

A striking difference between this inventory of 76 cases and contemporary series (Putnam, Guroff, Silberman, Barban, & Post, 1986; Ross, Norton, & Wozney, 1989) is the much smaller number of personalities in the older cases. Of the 76 cases listed by Taylor and Martin (1944), 49 were dual personality, and only 6 had more than five alters. The average number of personalities was 2.9, while the median was 2.0. In contrast, in our series of 236 cases the mean number of alters was 15.7, and the median was 8.0. In Putnam's series of 100 cases the mean was 13.3 personalities, and the median was 9.0.

Just as demon possession evolved into MPD, MPD has continued to evolve over the last 100 years. The face of MPD may have been transformed again before current students of dissociation finish their careers; therefore, it is necessary to find historical constants in the phenomenology of dissociation. Another major feature of contemporary MPD, besides the larger number of alters, that does not appear in Taylor and Martin's review, is sexual abuse. The authors include no discussion of a traumatic etiology for MPD. The possible causes of MPD apparent in 1944 were "head injury, marked intoxication, extreme fatigue, lowered general energy, unbalanced urges, severe conflicts, and excessive learnings and forgettings" (p. 296).

Although less than 50 years old, that list is quaint for a contemporary clinician who has listened to MPD abuse histories. Several possible ways of accounting for the smaller number of alters and the absence of abuse histories in the older cases are apparent. First, it is likely that few of the clinicians seriously considered or inquired about sexual abuse. These older MPD patients may have had dual personality without an abusive etiology and therefore may not have needed to create a large number of alters to cope with severe, chronic trauma. Alternatively, the older cases may have had severe abuse histories that were remembered by undetected alters.

Advocates of iatrogenesis will say that MPD hysteria has escalated in recent years as clinicians feed into the charade. The most likely hypothesis, I believe, has three interrelated aspects: Since 1944 MPD has evolved into a syndrome with a posttraumatic etiology, whereas before it tended to have less severe external precipitants; our society has gotten sicker, and the abuse of children more bizarre; earlier clinicians missed the abuse history in many MPD patients, which was not as severe, on average, as that experienced by contemporary patients.

The incidence of MPD, then, is an indicator of the amount of child abuse occurring in Western society. Taylor and Martin made one concluding observation with which I agree, namely, "The mechanisms of multiple personality are those of normal personality working under abnormal conditions" (p. 297). I have listened to a child alter describe an incident in which her father came into her bedroom dressed in women's clothing. Before having intercourse with her, he stuffed live spiders into her vagina. I believed the story and considered the conditions abnormal. The key issue in the etiology of contemporary MPD is not iatrogenesis, it is whether the abuse histories are real.

If the abuse histories are real, then iatrogenesis becomes a minor influence for which one nevertheless has to be vigilant. If the abuse never happened, the disorder may be metapsychological or "characterological" in nature, but there is no more reason to think that it is primarily iatrogenic. In either alternative, iatrogenesis is a secondary issue.

The second review paper appeared in 1962 in the *International Journal of Clinical and Experimental Hypnosis,* a journal with a tradition of publishing papers on MPD. The authors, Sutcliffe and Jones, refer to Taylor and Martin's paper and present a bar graph of the number of cases reported from 1800 to 1940, based on the 1944 series of 76 cases. This graph shows very clearly a sudden increase in the number of cases reported between 1880 and 1900, then a decline from there. The decline in publications on MPD was accompanied by the disappearance of publications on all aspects of dissociation: Hilgard (1987) has pointed out that *Psychological Abstracts* shows 20 abstracts on dissociation from 1927 to 1936, 8 from 1937 to 1946, 2 from 1947 to 1956, and 3 from 1957 to 1966.

Sutcliffe and Jones divide the history of MPD into three periods:

Period 1 (until 1880). Hazy beginnings

Period 2 (1880–1900). Establishment and elaboration of MPD

Period 3 (1900–1962). Full maturity and a falling off of theoretical elaboration

There was some overlap between periods. They describe what they call "notable" cases from each of these periods: in Period 3 these include Miss Beauchamp (Prince, 1905/1978) and Eve White (Thigpen & Cleckley, 1957). I would say that Period 3 lasted from 1910 to 1980, followed by Period 4— resurgence of interest in MPD—and I would extend Period 2 until 1910.

It is difficult to set an end to Period 4, but I would place it in 1984. After this begins Period 5—modern scientific study of dissociation. Thus the revised chart of the history of MPD is as follows:

Period 1 (until 1880). Hazy beginnings

Period 2 (1880–1910). Establishment and elaboration of MPD

Period 3 (1910–1980). Full maturity and rapid decline

Period 4 (1980–1984). Resurgence of interest in MPD

Period 5 (1984–present). Modern scientific study of MPD

Sutcliffe and Jones conduct a lengthy and subtle discussion that deals with iatrogenesis, diagnostic habits, false positive diagnoses, philosophical climate, psychological theories, and a number of other factors affecting the reporting of cases of MPD.

They make criticisms suggesting that the number of true cases in Periods 1–3 may have been less than the number reported. They point out that diagnostic criteria were vague to nonexistent, and that some of the classical cases might be more accurately diagnosed as organic brain syndrome, epilepsy, or schizophrenia. Actually there were probably more false positive diagnoses in the opposite direction (see Chapter 7), that is, cases of MPD misdiagnosed as schizophrenia, brain damage, or epilepsy. Nevertheless, Sutcliffe and Jones are probably right that enthusiasm to report a case of MPD led to some incorrect diagnoses.

The most convincing example of a false positive diagnosis of MPD is the Sargeant of Bazeilles discussed by Binet (1896), who had damage to his left parietal lobe from a war injury. This man does not belong to the diagnostic category of contemporary MPD, because he did not have psychologically coherent alters, an abuse history, or a psychological rationale for the development of MPD.

In their discussion of iatrogenesis and the influence of hypnosis, Sutcliffe and Jones conclude that neither can account fully for the phenomena. However, they take the influence of suggestion, therapist expectations, subtle cuing by the therapist, and demand characteristics in general very seriously. This is a necessary scientific attitude today.

A major feature of Sutcliffe and Jones's review is the complete absence of trauma in the discussion. They discuss Janet's psychological theory of dissociation, and make several pointed criticisms of the circularity of much of Janet's reasoning, but they never focus on sexual or physical abuse. It is as if *Studies on Hysteria* had never been written.

After the repudiation of the seduction theory by Freud, an amnesia set in among psychologists and psychiatrists. Freud's evidence and argument about the traumatic origins of dissociation were lost. This occurred so suddenly that it cannot be attributed to passive scholarly forgetting. In fact the field developed a dissociative disorder, an active dismissal and forgetting of the role of sexual abuse and other childhood trauma in the formation of MPD. A feminist might comment that this was a convenient intellectual maneuver for the abusive patriarchy.

Overall in the period 1910–1980 there was little new work done on MPD. As Sutcliffe and Jones point out, any further cases accumulated did not add new theory or understanding to the field (Alexander, 1956; Brandsma & Ludwig, 1974; Congdon, Hain, & Stevenson, 1961; Copeland & Kitching, 1937; McKee & Wittkower, 1962; Winer, 1978). MPD had sunk so far into oblivion that Eve White was thought to be the only living case in the late 1950s. The book and the movie *The Three Faces of Eve* were both thought to be about an extravagantly rare curiosity. In Chapter 3, I will review experimental work on the production of features of MPD using hypnosis done in the 1940s.

The situation had begun to change in the late 1970s prior to the next major landmark in the history, which is the year 1980. A major event of the 1970s was Hilgard's publication of *Divided Consciousness* (Hilgard, 1977). This book inaugurates the serious modern study of dissociation. Valuable as it is, and despite its devoting over 20 pages to MPD, the book is not based on clinical experience with dissociative patients. Instead it is based on experimental psychology and therefore is not directly a part of the history I am outlining. Hilgard's neodissociation theory is discussed in the next chapter.

Three other factors at work in the 1970s contributed to the resurgence of interest in MPD. One was the revival of interest in hypnosis after World War II: the level of interest in hypnosis and MPD have always been intertwined and have covaried. The second factor was the Vietnam War, which brought with it an increased understanding and emphasis on the role of trauma in psychiatric disorders. The third was the Women's Movement, which helped to bring child abuse, and particularly incest, out of the closet. Each of these factors and their interrelationships need to be studied in more detail.

1980: A MAJOR LANDMARK IN THE HISTORY OF MULTIPLE PERSONALITY DISORDER

In the late 1970s a gradual increase in clinical experience with MPD began to be visible to a small number of specialists. Cornelia Wilbur treated a case described in the book *Sybil* (Schreiber, 1973), as well as a number of other cases. She and a group of clinicians including George Greaves, Richard Kluft, Bennett Braun, Ralph Allison, Eugene Bliss, David Caul, and others participated in an "oral tradition" that was transmitted partly through annual workshops at the American Psychiatric Association meetings, but this oral tradition was unknown to the psychiatric mainstream.

The year 1980 is a landmark in the history of MPD because in that year the disorder was given official diagnostic status in DSM-III. In addition, four important papers were published (Bliss, 1980; Coons, 1980; Greaves, 1980; Rosenbaum, 1980) in leading psychiatric journals. Bliss's work will be discussed in Chapter 7, and Rosenbaum's article has already been reviewed. The exponential takeoff in diagnosis of MPD in North America began in about 1980.

George Greaves (1980) wrote a paper that summarized the clinical experience with MPD of the previous 10 years. This paper is a landmark both because of its quality and because it is the last major review surveying an anecdotal MPD literature. Reviews after this take into account the results of large clinical series and preliminary scientific studies.

Greaves counted 33 cases of MPD reported from 1901 to 1944, and only 14 from 1944 to 1969. In his paper, however, he tabulates 50 cases either known to him personally or reported in the literature during the decade 1971–1980. This he regarded as a remarkable increase. Braun (1986a) estimated that 500 cases of MPD had been identified by 1979. According to Braun's estimates, this number had increased to 1000 by 1983, and 5000 by 1986. Coons (1986c) estimated that 6000 cases had been diagnosed in North America by 1986. These estimates, even though they are only educated guesses, indicate an exponential increase in the rate of diagnosis since 1980.

In his paper Greaves discusses the trauma-driven nature of dissociation, unlike the reviewers before him, which is a major advance. But he hasn't quite brought the severity or the frequency of the childhood abuse into focus. This is not a criticism of Greaves, rather it is an observation about the state of the field in 1980. In a 1972 paper entitled, "The Etiology of Multiple Personality," for instance, Horton and Miller note the occurrence of incest in their case but do not discuss trauma in a list of four MPD dynamics.

Greaves (1980) seems to imply in his paper that the abuse experienced by Sybil was unusually severe even for an MPD patient. Anyone working with MPD patients today, including George Greaves, has heard many patients tell equally horrific stories. Some patients have experienced trauma far beyond that inflicted on Sybil—these are the victims of ritual abuse by cult members. It is clear that in 1980 even leading experts in the field had not yet grasped the frequency or severity of the abuse experienced by MPD patients.

Coons (1980) made a clear statement of the role of trauma as a general cause of MPD. His discussion of the etiology of MPD focuses on childhood trauma, with a minimum of metapsychological speculation. Coons was an early exponent of empirical study of the role of trauma in MPD. He refers to two earlier cases (Schreiber, 1973; Stoller, 1973) that dramatically illustrate the role of childhood abuse in the formation of MPD and gives one of his own. Coons's paper is usually referred to because of his statement that amnesia is an essential diagnostic criterion for MPD. His early emphasis on trauma should not be overlooked.

In his discussion of the treatment of MPD, Greaves, for the first time in the history of the field, is able to draw on the extensive clinical experience of a group of contemporaries. He quotes principles of treatment enunciated by Bowers et al. (1971), Allison (1974), and Wilbur (Schreiber, 1973), which are discussed in Chapter 10, and is able to say that integration can be achieved in an average of 2 to 5 years by a skilled therapist. More rapid integration he holds to be possible only for a handful of particularly expert therapists.

The year 1980 thus marks the beginning of the resurgence of interest in MPD. At least half a decade of preparatory work by a small number of clinicians was required before the exponential increase in diagnosis could really take off. I am not able to give an inside account of the political work needed to get MPD into DSM-III, but this must have required a big effort against even bigger resistance. In the next period, 1980–1984, the field began to organize politically in preparation for transition from a prescientific to a scientific body of knowledge.

THE PERIOD 1980–1983

Much more took place in the study of MPD during this period than is evident from publications. During this period most residents in psychiatry did not receive a single lecture, handout, reference, or other didactic material on MPD. Most residents would not meet anyone who had diagnosed a case of MPD, would never hear MPD considered in the differential diagnosis of a patient, and would not hear anyone mention MPD in a lecture or seminar. MPD didn't come up any more often in professional conversation than it did outside work.

One important paper in this period was that by Myron Boor (1982), titled "The Multiple Personality Epidemic: Additional Cases and Inferences Regarding Diagnosis, Etiology, Dynamics, and Treatment." Boor went over the literature and found 29 more cases of MPD in 16 papers published between 1970 and early 1981, some of which had been missed by Greaves (1980). Boor added these 29 cases to the 76 described by Taylor and Martin (1944), and found that the overall female:male ratio was 8:1. He also noted the increased number of alters in recent cases, occurrence of headache in 17 of the 29 recent cases, suicide attempts in 22 of the 29, and high rates of childhood abuse.

Concerning etiology, Boor echoed Greaves's (1980) statement that trauma and environments that foster extreme ambivalence were the two main factors. He also speculated that the preponderance of females in MPD might be due to the fact that the males are in prison. This is an important but unresolved question in the literature. Boors's paper advanced the field by urging it toward analysis of large series of cases. This was a necessary step in the development from speculation based on single cases to scientific inquiry. Confer and Ables (1983) published a rarely cited book on MPD during this period, which does not appear to have had a major influence on the field.

Frank Putnam et al. (1986) made the next step when they presented a series of 100 cases of MPD at the American Psychiatric Association meeting in 1983. This was the first large series reported in a single study. Putnam's analysis of these 100 cases provided a great deal of detail on the clinical phenomenology of MPD, which is discussed in Chapter 5. The 100 cases were reported to Putnam by 92 clinicians responding to a questionnaire. Such studies have methodological limitations but are a necessary step in the evolution of any field. They provide a bridge between anecdote and valid, reliable diagnosis and clinical assessment.

The next event was the publication of a special issue of the *American Journal of Clinical Hypnosis* on MPD in October 1983. Although this was an important contribution to the field, the editors somewhat inconvenienced future historians by not holding the issue back till 1984. In 1984 three other psychiatric journals published special issues on MPD, in which the transition from a prescientific to a scientific literature occurred. The landmark year of 1984 starts in October 1983.

During this period much more was going on than is evident from publications. Work was being done to organize the first major conference on MPD, held in Chicago in 1984. Concurrently with that, leading figures in the field were preparing for formation of the International Society for the Study of Multiple Personality and Dissociation (ISSMP&D). The annual MPD meeting in Chicago and the growth of the ISSMP&D have been major factors in the development of the field. Some of the success of psychoanalysis early in the 20th century was due to its political organization, with formation of societies and meetings. Janet was politically unsuccessful, which is partly why he fell into obscurity. One cannot overemphasize the importance of the ISSMP&D and the annual Chicago meetings in reestablishing the study of MPD.

1984: THE TRANSITION TO A SCIENTIFIC LITERATURE

The other three journals that published special issues on MPD were *The International Journal of Clinical and Experimental Hypnosis, Psychiatric Annals*, and *Psychiatric Clinics of North America*. These four issues provided a large body of writing on MPD by a number of different people. Diverging and conflicting points of view were represented, in a healthy and alive intellectual atmosphere. For instance, the role of iatrogenesis in MPD was debated without polarization into warring factions, pro and con. The quality of the argument was high.

Virtually all of the main contributors to the MPD literature in the 1980s had one or more papers in these four special issues. But one observation needs to be made: Four men represented in these journals have not been involved in the ongoing development of the ISSMP&D or the annual Chicago meetings. These are Ralph Allison (1984, 1985), John Beahrs (1982), Eugene Bliss (1983, 1984a, 1984b, 1984c, 1985, 1986, 1988; Bliss & Jeppsen, 1985; Bliss & Larson, 1985), and Martin Orne (Orne, Dinges, & Orne, 1984). Why and how this occurred deserves more than a footnote in the history of psychiatry.

With the appearance of these four special issues Richard Kluft (1982, 1983, 1984a, 1984b, 1984c, 1985a, 1985b, 1985c, 1985d, 1985e, 1985f, 1985g, 1986a, 1986b, 1986c, 1986d, 1986e, 1987a, 1987b, 1987c, 1987d, 1988a, 1988b, 1988c, 1988d, 1988e; Kluft, Braun, & Sachs, 1984; Kluft, Steinberg, & Spitzer, 1988) and Bennett Braun (1983a, 1983b, 1984, 1985, 1986a, 1986b, 1988a, 1988b; Braun & Sachs, 1985) established themselves as the leaders in the field. This is a position they have maintained throughout the rest of the 1980s by writing, editing, treating patients, consulting, organizing conferences, doing political work, and encouraging the development of young clinicians and researchers. Bennett Braun has established the world's leading Dissociative Disorders Unit at Rush-Presbyterian-St. Luke's Medical Center in Chicago. In 1988 the first issue of the first journal devoted exclusively to dissociative disorders appeared, with Richard Kluft as Editor-in-Chief (*Dissociation*, Vol. 1, No. 1, January 1988).

In these four special issues something new appears in the modern clinical study of MPD: *data*. Many of the papers are summaries of clinical experience, but several kinds of scientific data are presented. Prior to 1984 only a few scattered studies had contained any scientific information, such as a physiological study by Ludwig, Brandsma, Wilbur, Benfeldt, & Jameson (1972), but none of these were based on large series. Now in 1984 there are reports about the characteristics of series of 30 or more patients, with data about clinical features and treatment response. More elaborate descriptive models of the etiology and maintenance of MPD are formulated as well.

I won't review all of the papers in these journals because I will be referring to many of them throughout the rest of this book. One noteworthy paper by Bliss (1983) is an outline of a book he published 3 years later (Bliss, 1986). By 1984 the relationship of MPD to childhood abuse had been clearly recognized, as had the severity and chronicity of the abuse (Stern, 1984; Wilbur, 1984). The posttraumatic nature of MPD was a given in the field, and discussion of the relationship between MPD and other posttraumatic stress disorders had begun (Spiegel, 1984).

A second important relationship, that between MPD and borderline personality disorder, is the subject of two papers. One of these, by Clary, Burstin, and Carpenter (1984) is highly metapsychological in nature, but the other contains a detailed analysis of borderline features in 33 cases of MPD based on DSM-III criteria (Horevitz & Braun, 1984). This paper also provides a discussion of the relevant literature, and thereby stands as the first comprehensive review of a particular subproblem in the MPD field. Previous reviews have dealt with the field in a general way.

It is evident from the preceding papers that the relationship of MPD to other psychiatric disorders was under serious study by 1984. This was a new development. Another important advance was the recognition and description of childhood MPD (Kluft, 1984b). In his paper Kluft states that a review of the literature yielded one childhood case of MPD, that of an 11-year-old girl named Estelle, who was treated by Despine Pere from 1836 to 1837 (Ellenberger, 1970; Fine, 1988). Kluft goes on to describe four cases of his own and to give a list of predictors of childhood MPD. This is the first sign of the field moving toward its most important objective: the recognition and treatment of childhood MPD. Based on clinical experience to date, rapid treatment of childhood MPD appears to be possible, with lasting stable integration in the absence of further abuse. This in effect means that primary prevention of adult MPD is possible.

Another important set of papers dealt with the Hillside Strangler case (Allison, 1984; Orne, Dinges, & Orne, 1984; Watkins, 1984). In these papers Ralph Allison, Martin Orne, and John Watkins, all of whom had been expert witnesses in the trial of Kenneth Bianchi, argued their positions in detail. Bianchi was found by the judge to be faking MPD and therefore to be ineligible for a defense of "not guilty by reason of insanity." It is of interest that Watkins concluded Bianchi had genuine MPD, Allison that he had atypical dissociative disorder caused by the forensic psychiatric examinations, and Orne that he was faking MPD. Watkins teaches a course every year at the MPD meetings in Chicago, and Allison and Orne do not attend.

In the four special issues there are a number of papers on the use of hypnosis in diagnosis and treatment of MPD. There are also several papers on physiological aspects of dissociation, all of which acknowledge the tiny amount of hard data available. Frank Putnam (1984a, 1984b) contributed two papers on research and methodological issues and stated, "The scientific study of multiple personality disorder is just beginning" (1984b, p. 61). These papers are characteristic of later workshops, seminars, and conference presentations: they were much expanded and developed 2 years later (Putnam, 1986a, 1986b).

In these four journals the leading contemporary writers in the field had begun to make their characteristic contributions. The organizational and editorial skills of Bennett Braun were evident, as was his gift for clinical work; Richard Kluft (1982) had expanded his careful observation of a large series of cases and was leading the field in study of childhood MPD; Frank Putnam was defining more rigorous scientific studies; Philip Coons was writing scholarly, clear papers on diagnosis and phenomenology, characteristic of his large body of work (1980, 1984, 1986a, 1986b, 1986c, 1986d, 1988a, 1988b; Coons, Bowman, & Milstein, 1988; Coons and Bradley, 1984; Coons and Milstein, 1984; Coons & Milstein, 1986; Coons, Milstein, & Marley,

1982; Coons and Sterne, 1986; and Eugene Bliss (1984a) was exploring the hypnotic nature of MPD and related disorders. These five men have published the most work and have generated the bulk of the data on MPD in the 1980s. Their contributions are not limited to this highlight of their published work.

Although they have not written as much or contributed as many original observations to the literature, Cornelia Wilbur (1984), who treated Sybil (Schreiber, 1973), and David Caul (1984), who treated Billy Milligan (Keyes, 1981), were present in these journals. They have been major contributors to the development of the ISSMP&D and to the nourishment of young clinicians, as has George Greaves. Finally, as mentioned earlier, David Spiegel (1984) had begun to write on posttraumatic stress disorder and MPD, a theme he has pursued since (Spiegel, 1986a, 1986b, 1988; Spiegel, Hunt, & Dondershine, 1988). Spiegel is a contributor to MPD studies who has moved into the area with a preestablished reputation (Spiegel & Rosenfeld, 1984; Spiegel & Spiegel, 1978). I hope that this will occur more often in the 1990s because the movement of established investigators into the field will raise standards, guard against insularity and stagnation, and provide credibility for dissociative studies.

The other major events in 1984 were the formation of the ISSMP&D and the First Annual International Conference on Multiple Personality/Dissociative States in Chicago. The ISSMP&D has grown steadily to a membership of over 1000 at the time of the 1988 meeting. Among its many functions, the ISSMP&D publishes a newsletter that contains a variety of features and announcements. A future historian will have to record in detail the formation and evolution of this organization and its impact on psychiatry. If dissociative disorders enter the mainstream of psychiatry in the 1990s, this will in large part be due to individual and organizational efforts of ISSMP&D members. The ISSMP&D and the annual Chicago meetings, organized by Bennett Braun, are closely interlinked.

In the 1970s authors submitting papers on MPD to journals did not have an easy time. In the 1990s members of ISSMP&D will be acting as reviewers of many papers on MPD submitted to North American journals. This means that a major ideological barrier to publication of MPD papers will have been removed. As in any new area of endeavor, the establishment of dissociative disorders as a legitimate field of scientific inquiry has depended on this personal service and behind-the-scenes political work. In the late 1980s, however, the field of psychiatry as a whole remained highly skeptical about MPD.

The annual MPD meetings in Chicago have provided a forum for in-person contacts, presentation of papers with many different foci, workshops, political organization, and research collaboration. ISSMP&D committee meetings are held concurrently. By the end of 1984 the field had moved from a prescientific stage to an early scientific level of development, with some data, an annual meeting, and a professional organization. Each of these components is essential if MPD is to be more than a passing fad, destined to fall into disrepute and obscurity after a decade or two, in repetition of events that occurred 100 years ago.

DEVELOPMENTS FROM 1985 TO 1988

I am not going to review all the developments during this period because most of them will be taken up elsewhere. Over the 3-year period from 1985 to 1988 important work was being done in a number of centers throughout North America, with the formation of inpatient units, structured programs, study groups, and research collaborations. The exponential increase in the rate of diagnosis of MPD is not an isolated phenomenon: it is a correlate of a great deal of organizational and education effort.

During this period Richard Kluft (1985d, 1985f, 1987a) wrote the three major review papers in the field. These are radically different from the reviews published in 1944, 1962, and 1980. The 1987 paper, for instance, entitled "An Update on Multiple Personality Disorder," contains 95 references, all but 10 of them from the 1980s and all but 7 of them directly on MPD. Greaves's (1980) review, in comparison, contains 85 references, of which 26 are not directly related to MPD and 33 antedate 1970. The volume of literature that a reviewer had to assimilate expanded greatly in 7 years. General reviews by a variety of authors appeared in a variety of journals, attesting to the growing interest in MPD (Krasad, 1985; O'Brien, 1985; Ross & Fraser, 1987; Ross & Norton, 1987).

Kluft's three review papers contain data on or refer to several large series of cases. He has outcome data to present, can define the general principles of a treatment protocol, references and discusses a variety of treatment techniques, gives a detailed list of primary and secondary diagnostic features, reviews the clinical phenomenology and natural history, and can base his discussion of etiology on data. He is able to make preliminary remarks about the epidemiology. Very little of this was possible for a reviewer less than 10 years earlier. The evolution of review papers on MPD give another measure of the exponential growth of the field.

Two important books on MPD were published by the American Psychiatric Press (Kluft, 1985a; Braun 1986b) during this period. These continue the rapid development of the field. But now a potential problem begins to appear, one commented on by Margolis (1988), who thought it was apparent in the 1984 special issue on MPD of *Psychiatric Clinics of North America*. Contributors to Braun's book are Barkin, Braun, Caul, Kluft, Putnam, Sachs, Spiegel, and Wilbur. Contributors to Kluft's book are Braun, Coons, Frischholz, Goodwin, Hicks, Kluft, Putnam, Sachs, and Wilbur. The contributors cross-reference each other extensively.

On the one hand, this is entirely appropriate and commendable, because the list includes the major contributors to the field. On the other hand there is a potential danger of an in-club forming, with little tolerance for dissenting opinion. The remedy to this problem is not to recruit a second generation of ISSMP&D contributors, but to make a deliberate effort to engage outsiders in serious dialogue. This is a remedy already in place in the form of a debate at the 1988 American Psychiatric Association Annual Meeting. Richard Kluft and David Spiegel supported, and Martin Orne and Fred Frankel opposed, the resolution "Multiple Personality is a True Disease Entity."

The APA debate was incorrectly titled because MPD is not a true *disease* entity in the biomedical sense. It is a true psychiatric entity and a true disorder, but not a biomedical disease. The debate was nevertheless an important event and should be ongoing.

To return to the two American Psychiatric Press books, they feature the diagnosis and treatment of childhood MPD, discussion of the familial incidence of MPD, and overall a systemic life-cycle approach to the disorder. This is an important development in dissociative studies; MPD must be placed in a social context, taking the life histories of families into account. Still, though, there is virtually no anthropological or cross-cultural perspective evident in the two volumes, although such can be found elsewhere in the field (Krippner, 1986; Stevenson & Pasricha, 1979; Varma, Bouri, & Wig, 1981; Villoldo & Krippner, 1986). A cultural analysis is another antidote for insularity. To achieve scientific rigor in our understanding of late 20th-century North American MPD, we should be more actively pursuing an anthropological viewpoint.

Despite those concerns about the breadth of the two books, they are major contributions. Jean Goodwin's (1985) chapter on "Credibility Problems in Multiple Personality Disorder Patients and Abused Children," is a particularly well-written contribution. Another chapter worth noting is one on the use of medication in MPD by Barkin, Braun, and Kluft (1986). This chapter is important because it highlights the need to conduct controlled, well-designed studies of the use of medication in MPD (see Chapter 11). To date, one can use medication only on an empirical-trial basis, with little assurance as to the indications or likely response.

Setting aside their content, these two books are an important event in the field for several reasons. They show that mainstream psychiatry is willing to take MPD seriously, because the publisher is the American Psychiatric Press. The books demonstrate as well that a critical mass of contemporary scholars is in communication and able to collaborate on projects. A third consideration, which gives a measure of the growth of the field, is that there is enough material to fill 450 pages in two volumes. Two such books would not have been possible 10 years earlier, because there wasn't enough content in the field to support them. Another important book published in this period is *Multiple Personality, Allied Disorders, and Hypnosis* (1986) by Eugene Bliss. This book is thoroughly reviewed by Gruenewald (1988). I will discuss Bliss's book further in Chapters 3 and 7. *Split Minds Split Brains* (Quen, 1986) provides a broader cultural and historical perspective on the field and is cross-linked with the American Psychiatric Press volumes because it contains a chapter by Frank Putnam. The problem with this book, in terms of linking clinical studies with historical and anthropological work, is that it is not clinical enough. That is in a sense an irrelevant criticism, because the editor wasn't setting out to bridge contemporary clinical practice and other scholarly studies. However, the problem remains in the field.

The same applies to *The Passion of Ansel Bourne* (Kenny, 1986). A book published in this period, though, that embodies a historical and cultural perspective on clinical dissociation is *Multiple Man: Explorations in Possession and Multiple Personality* by Adam Crabtree (1985). Although this book has been out for 4 years, there is little evidence of its influence on the field as a whole. Crabtree provides a historical review of MPD and then moves into the most interesting, clinical sections of the book. These contain numerous examples of dissociative disorders he has encountered in practice. Crabtree is able to bring a great deal of scholarship to bear on his clinical work, which is in itself a rare attribute. His thinking challenges preconceptions and stimulates alternate perspectives in a way that is potentially fruitful both for research and other clinicians (Crabtree, 1986).

In the years 1985 and 1986, then, six scholarly books on MPD were published in North America. This is a great deal of work and further evidence of the maturing of the field. Before closing this chapter I want to highlight one other development in this period. That is the publication and/or presentation at conferences of the first scientific instruments for the measurement of dissociation and the making of dissociative diagnoses. Prior to this period, research was hampered by the absence of self-report instruments and structured diagnostic interviews. Both of these are absolute prerequisites for modern scientific study of any psychiatric disorder. Other psychiatric disorders such as schizophrenia, affective disorders, and anxiety disorders have been studied with standardized instruments for some time. The specifics of these instruments are discussed in Chapter 6.

During this 3-year period the transition from a prescientific to a scientific body of knowledge was consolidated. The field is now in the stage of early scientific development. This does not mean that there is no further place for case reports, however. An example of a case report that makes an important contribution is a paper by Coons (1988a), which describes the misuse of forensic hypnosis and a false positive diagnosis of MPD. Such reports are required to define problems in the field for further inquiry. They also provide useful clinical instruction. The field is evolving, though, to a point at which the need for case reports will be much less than it was in the 1970s.

During this period early signs of preparation for multicenter treatment outcome studies started to become visible. General principles of treatment were defined (Braun, 1986a), an effort to standardize terminology was made (Braun, 1986a), and techniques of treatment were presented by a variety of clinicians (Ross & Gahan, 1988b). Methodological difficulties facing the field were described by Putnam (1986b). The possibility of beginning to prepare for such multicenter studies was a topic of conversation among specialists in MPD: A few years earlier such talk would have been idle dreaming.

These developments in the last half decade make it unlikely that MPD will once again fall into oblivion after a short period of enthusiasm. The field is creating a data base that should bring it into the psychiatric mainstream. One of the most important events in this regard was the launching of the journal *Dissociation* in 1988. With a professional society, a journal, a major specialty meeting, a number of scholarly books, and papers in a variety of journals, the dissociative disorders have begun to establish themselves in psychiatry, as the anxiety disorders did only a short while ago. There are many patients with treatable dissociative disorders in North America who could benefit from greater awareness, prompter diagnosis, and more skilled treatment than is often available to them.

PART TWO

Diagnosis and Clinical Features of Multiple Personality Disorder

This section reviews the clinical phenomenology, diagnostic criteria, epidemiology and associated symptoms and diagnoses of multiple personality disorder (MPD). In Chapter 8, a discussion of nonclinical dissociation is provided to embed clinical dissociation in a broader context. Chapter 8 looks back to the first two chapters in this regard.

MPD can be diagnosed with a high degree of validity and reliability. However, it will not be recognized without making a specific inquiry for its signs and symptoms. This inquiry is not part of a standard psychiatric assessment, which is why so many cases are missed. By the end of this section, the reader, with the assistance of the Dissociative Disorders Interview Schedule (see Appendix A), will know how to make the diagnosis.

What is MPD? MPD is a little girl imagining that the abuse is happening to someone else. This is the core of the disorder, to which all other features are secondary. The imagining is so intense, subjectively compelling, and adaptive, that the abused child experiences dissociated aspects of herself as other people. It is this core characteristic of MPD that makes it a treatable disorder, because the imagining can be unlearned, and the past confronted and mastered.

MPD patients are among the most disturbed individuals who seek the services of mental health professionals, yet they are often among the most treatable. The treatment must be guided by an understanding of the nature of MPD and its historical antecedents. The complex details of the personality system can overwhelm the therapist who doesn't have a broad framework within which to conduct therapy.

The process of diagnosing an MPD patient leads naturally into the treatment, because the vast majority of patients have been severely traumatized in childhood. The trauma makes itself known in an array of symptoms and disturbed behaviors that fall into a pattern if the diagnostician knows what pattern to look for. Once the pattern is recognized, specific intensive psychotherapy follows naturally. The symptoms are severe and disabling and do not appear to remit with nonspecific interventions, although definitive data on this point are not available.

MPD patients, when they are studied carefully, reveal many inadequacies in the current diagnostic system in psychiatry, as described in DSM-III-R. Therefore I discuss a number of different psychiatric disorders from the point of view of dissociation in this section and propose a revised diagnostic system for disorders linked to psychological trauma. The study of MPD can potentially yield valuable insight into a variety of issues in both biological and psychosocial psychiatry.

CHAPTER THREE

Etiology

Multiple personality disorder (MPD) is a controversial diagnosis. The controversy centers on disagreement about its etiology, from which follow disagreement about its treatment, status as a psychiatric diagnosis, and relationship to other disorders (Atwood, 1978; French & Chodoff, 1987; Kluft, 1986d; Ludolph, 1985). There is more opinion on the etiology of MPD than data, a situation that hasn't prevented the expression of extreme views. My view is that MPD is a legitimate diagnosis, that it responds to treatment, and that it is directly linked to severe childhood trauma. Many professionals, however, feel that MPD is an iatrogenic artifact.

A qualification is necessary. My clinical experience and research, except for one case, do not involve forensic psychiatry. This book is about MPD as encountered in a clinical setting. In forensic assessments the potential benefits for malingering are much greater, therefore the odds of encountering faked MPD are greater. The benefits to the "patient" of being defined as a patient rather than as a criminal are potentially large. This may result in outright faking of MPD or a more unconscious simulation of MPD in the context of a forensic assessment.

This chapter sets forth the main models of MPD that have been proposed in the literature. These include a variety of different approaches to understanding MPD that can quite readily be tied together into a single comprehensive model of the etiology and maintenance of the disorder. The main framework I will use is the descriptive clinical model proposed by Richard Kluft (1984c), with some modifications. I will conclude with a discussion of MPD in the forensic context.

ᴛʜᴇ IATROGENESIS OF MULTIPLE
PERSONALITY DISORDER

There is a theory that MPD is an artifact of the doctor–patient relationship. This "theory" is not really a theory and has never been stated in print in a complete and clearly argued way. The iatrogenic theory, or model, is really an attitude or ideological stance, but it is nevertheless very influential in modern psychiatry.

Serious students of dissociation have thought about the artifactual aspects of MPD since the 19th century (Binet, 1896/1977). There is irrefutable evidence that features of MPD can be created in experimental subjects (Harriman, 1942a, 1942b, 1943; Kampman, 1976; Leavitt, 1947; Spanos, Weekes, & Bertrand, 1985; Spanos et al., 1986). This fact is established beyond doubt and is an important facet of the understanding of MPD. The question is, what is the significance of these experiments?

First, one must understand that none of these experiments result in the creation of MPD. MPD is not a transient phenomenon existing only in cross-section. Nor does it exist in isolation from a wide range of signs and symptoms that accompany it. There is no doubt that one can get college students to act as if they have alter personalities quite easily. But these students do not have a history of childhood abuse, numerous psychiatric symptoms, extensive involvement with the mental health system with limited benefit, and specific primary and secondary features of MPD stretching back for decades (see Chapter 5). None of the experiments with normal college students have resulted in the creation of anything even remotely approaching full MPD.

Imagine that there was a controversy about the iatrogenesis of osteoarthritis. Imagine that Spanos took a group of normal college students and, in an experimental setting, got them to limp and complain of hip pain. Would that prove, or even suggest, that osteoarthritis is an artifact of the doctor–patient relationship? Obviously not. But Spanos is arguing, by analogy, that because he can get college students to limp, patients who are diagnosed by doctors as having osteoarthritis are manifesting an artifact created by the doctor's questions, expectations, and rewards of prescribed medications, physiotherapy with attractive young women, home support, disability pension, and further appointments.

There is a catch. Osteoarthritis can be demonstrated on X ray. The equivalent of an X ray does not exist for any psychiatric disorder, other than a few specific intoxication states or organic brain syndromes. Lack of an MPD "X ray" does not, however, explain why MPD is singled out among all psychiatric disorders for the charge of iatrogenic artifact. Why not borderline personality disorder or panic disorder? Because of ideology and bias, not because of data or science.

Compare MPD to panic disorder, for instance. Panic disorder was rarely diagnosed by psychiatrists 20 years ago, but now it is recognized to be common, has specific effective treatments, and is the subject of a great deal of research (Walker, Norton, & Ross, in press). Few if any North American psychiatrists worry that panic disorder is artifactual. It is a clinical commonplace that coming to the doctor's office for appointments often causes the patient to panic. Some patients are so housebound that home visits are necessary.

Does anyone argue that because panic patients get anxious coming for their appointments, the disorder is artifactual? The treatment for panic involves exposure, a procedure deliberately designed to evoke symptoms. In the initial stages of treatment, the patient may have more anxiety due to the exposure exercises than she had while avoiding the supermarket before treatment. This increase in symptoms is an unavoidable consequence of exposure treatments for panic. The increase in panic symptoms that can occur as a byproduct of treatment has never been used to argue against the validity of either the diagnosis or treatment.

The same logic should apply to MPD. In treatment, as the patient is exposed to her traumatic memories, which had been hidden behind amnesia barriers, dissociative symptoms transiently increase. Because MPD is a more complex and severe disorder than panic disorder, the duration and complexity of these increased symptoms is greater. The MPD patient has been using dissociation to avoid an internal phobic stimulus, namely the abuse memories, whereas the panic patient has been using restriction of her physical movement to avoid an external stimulus. Any increase in symptoms during the initial stages of treatment is a perfectly comprehensible consequence of the nature of the disorder, for both panic disorder and MPD.

It is also possible to compare MPD to paranoid schizophrenia. A paranoid schizophrenic comes to the emergency department complaining that the CIA and his mother have been conspiring since his birth to control his thoughts. His mother, the patient says, signed a consent to have a device implanted in his brain at age 2 days. The CIA uses this device to control his thoughts and actions because agents know that he has state secrets for the KGB, and they want to prevent him from completing his education. The CIA is afraid that if he completes his education, he may be able to move to Russia.

The patient is admitted. Two weeks later he has incorporated the psychiatric staff into his delusional system. The patient now states that all the rooms on the ward are bugged by the CIA, the nurse is actually his mother who has undergone plastic surgery, the doctor is a CIA agent, and the medication is a substance given to reprogram the device in his brain. Does it make sense to blame the doctor for the schizophrenia or for the inclusion of the staff in the patient's delusional system? No. It is the nature of the patient's disorder that anyone in contact with him becomes incorporated into his delusional system. The same logic should apply to MPD.

When paranoid schizophrenics see psychiatrists, they may create delusions about the psychiatrist. Panic patients may get anxious coming to see their doctors. Patients with MPD may display more dissociative symptoms.

In each case this is a comprehensible consequence of the nature of the patient's disorder. There is no sound reason to classify MPD as more iatrogenic than other psychiatric disorders based on experiments with college students or on an increase in dissociative symptoms in the early phases of treatment. As discussed in Chapter 5, much of the increase in dissociative symptoms during the early and middle phases of treatment is probably due to the uncovering of preexisting alters, rather than to the creation of new ones in treatment. In this case the analogy is with exploratory surgery that identifies unsuspected metastases in a cancer patient.

Of course, it would be bad medicine for the paranoid schizophrenic's psychiatrist to introduce himself as a CIA agent. It would be bad practice to prescribe exposure for agoraphobia if there was no benefit to the patient. Likewise in MPD, one must be careful not to amplify the patient's symptoms unnecessarily, and one must be aware of potential secondary gains the patient may get from displaying symptoms. The treatment needs to be structured to control and minimize artifactual amplification of the illness. However, this does not imply that MPD is inherently artifactual, anymore than sciatica is invalidated as a diagnosis by fraudulent compensation cases.

The experiments on creation of analogues of isolated features of MPD are valuable for a number of reasons. Rather than undermining the status of MPD as a legitimate psychiatric disorder, these experiments help us to understand its true nature. MPD is often thought to be an extravagant deviation from normal experience, a rare curiosity with little connection to everyday psychology or reality. Probably the main reason it has been considered to be rare is the perception of MPD as fantastic and improbable. Experiments by Spanos and others cited previously help to correct this misperception and lead to a different guess as to how common the disorder is in North America.

The ability to create analogues of alter personalities is a capacity of the normal mind. Many college students can easily create such analogues when the right demands are made of them by a psychology professor. It is important to recognize that these experiments involved intensive signaling and shaping by the experimenters. Besides the possibility of course credit, approval for providing data the experimenter can publish, the enjoyment of play-acting MPD, and self-approval for participating in science, there were numerous instructions to behave in an unusual way. The environment of the experiments was highly structured to elicit certain behaviors, and these behaviors were reinforced in many ways.

What does that say about MPD? It reveals that normal individuals can easily create alter personalities in the right environment. The ability to create alters, as I see it, is a specialized development of the normal ability to become intensely involved in childhood play, books, or movies. Creating imaginary identities is a normal aspect of child development, as any parent knows. MPD patients have drawn on this ability demonstrated in normal childhood play, and in Spanos' experiments, to cope with trauma. What better way to survive incestuous abuse than to imagine that it is happening to someone else?

The normal highly hypnotizable mind has the ability to erect amnesia barriers. The MPD patient has used this ability to create amnesia barriers between her imaginary "people." As the abuse goes on year after year, the amnesia and the illusion that the alters are really different people are reinforced and entrenched. What is surprising or difficult to understand about this process? In my view, MPD is a commonsense disorder that draws on capacities of the normal mind. The evidence used by iatrogenesis theorists to invalidate MPD actually points to its essential nature and helps us to understand why MPD is treatable.

MPD is not a fantastic curiosity in which there is more than one person in the same body. There is only one person, an abuse victim who has imagined that there are other people inside her in order to survive. This is an adaptive use of the human imagination that, at least in its rudiments, appears to be available to a large segment of the population. Because childhood sexual and physical abuse are common and the ability to create alters is common, MPD should be far from rare, both in its full classical form and in partial forms.

I think that MPD is singled out for the accusation of iatrogenic artifact primarily because of the link between MPD and childhood physical and sexual abuse. Not long ago, incest was thought to be as rare in North America as one in a million families (Weinberg, 1955). That estimate, it is now known, was out by four orders of magnitude. Memories of childhood incest are still assumed to be fantasies by many North American psychiatrists, however. In this social and ideological context, it is not surprising that MPD is singled out for dismissal as an iatrogenic artifact. The charge of artifact is a second line of defense against dealing with the reality of childhood abuse in North America.

A popular superstition in North America is that children are the most valued resource and that the intact nuclear family is a good place to grow up. For many children this is a lie. The intact family, for many North American children, has been a war zone of physical and sexual abuse, a private Vietnam. It is not acceptable to dismiss the psychic scars and amputations resulting from this childhood trauma as artifact.

Properly understood and used, the experiments about creation of analogues of MPD are important and valuable. They point to social factors in the creation and maintenance of MPD that tend to be underemphasized by the therapist with an intrapsychic bent. They provide a reminder of the need for careful diagnostic assessment and monitoring of the effects of treatment interventions. There is no doubt that treatments can go wrong and that patient and therapist can get stuck because of harmful amplification of dissociative symptoms. The same applies to bad surgical technique, which can make cancer spread more rapidly or an aneurysm rupture prematurely.

We have gathered data that argue against the theory that MPD is an iatrogenic artifact. In a series of 236 cases (Ross, Norton, & Fraser, 1989), we identified 44 cases reported by 40 Canadian psychiatrists and 48 cases reported by 44 American psychiatrists. The Canadian psychiatrists were generalists who had seen an average of 2.2 cases of MPD, whereas the Americans were subspecialist members of the ISSMP&D who had seen an average of 16 cases of MPD.

We reasoned that if MPD is an iatrogenic artifact, the more experienced therapists ought to be influencing their patients to exhibit features they would not otherwise display. There should be important differences between cases seen by specialists in MPD and those seen by general psychiatrists, if the specialists' cases are artifactual. The data did not support such iatrogenisis.

The two groups did not differ in age, sex, marital status, or number of children. There were no differences between the two groups in the percentages that met each of the five NIMH diagnostic criteria for MPD, the number of personalities at the time of diagnosis, or the number of personalities at the time of reporting. It was the Canadian psychiatrists who diagnosed MPD in first-degree relatives most frequently, and this difference was statistically significant.

Although these data provided strong evidence against the iatrogenesis of MPD, we wanted to examine the effects of hypnosis on the clinical features of cases in the overall series of 236 cases. We found that information on the use of hypnosis was provided by the respondents for 214 cases. Of these, 176 (82.2 percent) had been hypnotized. This meant that 17.8 percent had never been hypnotized. A further 85 (48.3 percent) had been hypnotized only after diagnosis, and 56 (31.8 percent) had been hypnotized both before and after diagnosis. If hypnosis has an effect on the clinical features of MPD, comparison of these three groups (never hypnotized, hypnotized only after diagnosis, hypnotized both before and after diagnosis) would demonstrate it. The statistical power of the analysis was sufficient for quite small differences between groups to be significant at $p = .05$.

The results showed no differences among the three groups on frequencies with which cases met each of the five NIMH diagnostic criteria for MPD, the number of personalities identified at diagnosis, or the number of personalities identified at the time of reporting (Ross & Norton, in press). MPD patients who are hypnotized before and/or after diagnosis are no different from those who have never been hypnotized, at least not in the specific features of MPD. The three groups did not differ in age, sex, marital status, or number of children.

Taken together, these two studies provide evidence that MPD is not an iatrogenic artifact. Although there are methodological limitations to the research, as for any questionnaire study, the questionnaire method is as likely to amplify observer bias, making it easier to detect, as to conceal it. Therefore reservations about the unreliability of the diagnoses actually make the data stronger, because such unreliability would be expected to result in greater variation between cases than actually exists, or to magnify idiosyncracies of the respondents.

These two studies provide the only empirical evidence on the iatrogenesis of MPD available to date. Anyone who wishes to establish the correctness of the iatrogenic theory is going to have to provide very strong data on clinical MPD in order to overcome our evidence against iatrogenesis. The burden of proof that MPD is artifactual now lies on the shoulders of the skeptics, because the available data are against that hypothesis. The main problem with the iatrogenic theory, of course, is that it is founded on the classical cognitive error of dichotomization, or all-or-nothing thinking. In reality MPD is far too complex a phenomenon to be entirely noniatrogenic or purely artifactual.

Discussion and research should focus on the influence of demand characteristics, secondary gain, and the ideology of the diagnostician on the presentation and treatment of MPD, without making dichotomous assumptions or overgeneralizing the results of studies of normal college students. Otherwise, an unproductive and polarized confrontation ensues, accompanied by behind-the-scenes political machinations to have the "enemy" discredited or at least not published.

PSYCHOANALYTIC MODELS OF MULTIPLE PERSONALITY DISORDER

I am not going to discuss purely psychoanalytic models of MPD. There are several reasons for this:

1. Such models cannot be tested, or even modified by data.
2. They are too closely linked to Freud's repudiation of the seduction theory.
3. They overemphasize the Oedipus complex and underemphasize the Osiris complex.
4. They reify a semantic distinction between splitting and dissociation.
5. Only a tiny proportion of MPD patients could make use of classical analysis.
6. MPD occurs in a systemic context and cannot be adequately understood by an exclusively intrapsychic school of thought.
7. The vocabulary of psychoanalytic theory is obscurantist.
8. Psychoanalytic theory has too many autistic and tautological qualities, which make it difficult to integrate with other schools of thought.

Instead of discussing classical psychoanalytic theories of MPD, I will do what I do in practice, which is to blend certain Freudian ideas into my thinking throughout. For instance, one needs to be aware of transference and countertransference in a commonsense way, in the treatment of MPD. This does not mean that a classical analysis of transference is required. What I say to residents, who in my medical school receive training in psychoanalytic psychotherapy, is that the treatment of MPD involves long short-term dynamic psychotherapy. By this I mean that the treatment resembles more the style of active short-term dynamic psychotherapies than of classical analysis, but it takes a few years.

Analytic papers on MPD, for the interested reader, include ones by Clary, Burstin and Carpenter (1984), Gruenewald (1977, 1984), Lasky (1978), Marmer (1980), and Wilbur (1986). This is an incomplete list. Because Richard Kluft and Cornelia Wilbur both advocate the psychoanalysis of selected cases of MPD and the use of psychoanalytic principles in all cases, and because I respect these two MPD specialists, there is probably more apparent than real difference between the approach defined in this book and psychoanalytic treatment of MPD. Probably the differences are more important in the written theory and would be less visible in videotapes of therapy sessions. Why bother with all the complicated theory and jargon of psychoanalysis then?

MULTIPLE PERSONALITY DISORDER AS AUTOHYPNOSIS

There is a strong connection between MPD and hypnosis, in etiology, phenomenology, and treatment. Clinical experience and research evidence to date support the belief that MPD patients are highly hypnotizable. They frequently enter trance states, and Bliss has shown that they have high scores on standard scales of hypnotizability. Bliss's work appears in a series of papers: These papers are further developed in his book (Bliss, 1986). Because Eugene Bliss has done most of the work on the autohypnotic etiology of MPD, I will refer to him.

The special issue of the *American Journal of Clinical Hypnosis* on MPD in October 1983 contained a number of articles on hypnosis. Other papers by Braun (1984), Kline (1984), and Miller (1984) in the special issue of *The International Journal of Clinical and Experimental Hypnosis* on MPD address the relationship between MPD and hypnosis as well. Hypnosis is generally referred to throughout the MPD literature and is discussed at length by Ellenberger (1970) and Hilgard (1977). These references will lead any interested reader into the literature.

Autohypnotic models of MPD basically state that MPD is created by self-hypnosis. The data in support of the model are the high hypnotizability scores of MPD patients; the numerous phenomena of hypnosis displayed by MPD patients; the usefulness of hypnosis in treatment; the ease with which transient analogues of MPD can be created in normal subjects using hypnosis; the historical link between interest in hypnosis and interest in MPD, which suggests the two are related; and the close relationship between MPD and other disorders that seem to be autohypnotic in nature.

A major problem with the autohypnotic model of MPD is that it is basically tautological. As enunciated by Bliss, it takes the following logical form:

1. MPD patients are good hypnotic subjects.
2. MPD patients display phenomena of hypnosis.
3. All MPD phenomena must be autohypnotic.
4. The etiology of MPD must be autohypnotic.

This is equivalent to stating that pneumonia is caused by fever. Just because fever is one of the phenomena of pneumonia does not mean it is the cause. Also, Bliss arbitrarily describes MPD patients as entering trance when they switch from the presenting personality to any other personality. This is arbitrary, because it could just as easily be the presenting personality who is in trance and other alters with more complete memories who are not.

Empirically, it will be difficult, if not impossible, to demonstrate whether MPD is autohypnotic when it arises in childhood. If one discovers a child in whom MPD is forming, it immediately becomes necessary to stop the abuse, which interrupts the natural experiment. Conceptually, as Kluft (1987a) has pointed out, it is possible that MPD patients are born highly hypnotizable and that only people with high dissociative capacity can form MPD in the face of severe trauma. On the other hand, MPD patients may be born with an average dissociative ability, which is environmentally reinforced, whereas that of nonabused children is not. This seems possible because it is known that hypnotizability scores decline through childhood and adolescence in the overall population. As is usual in nature versus nurture arguments, reality probably combines the two possibilities in ratios that vary from case to case.

In either event it is tautological to label MPD phenomena as autohypnotic and then to classify MPD as an autohypnotic disorder. Such a classification is an artifact of the initial labeling. The autohypnotic model is based on inferring etiology from phenomenology, a common error in psychiatry. A similar error is made by biological psychiatrists who assume that a positive dexamethasone suppression test implies that the patient's depression is a biomedical illness (Ross, 1986a).

The autohypnotic model of MPD isn't really a model. It is more a comment that MPD patients display many phenomena of hypnosis. In fact the field lacks an adequate theory or model. Nevertheless, Bliss has done a great deal of original work. There is no doubt that dissociation and hypnosis are closely related. Perhaps hypnosis is a special form of dissociation, others being meditation, absorption in a movie or book, and hearing voices. From a medical school teaching point of view, MPD patients are superb subjects for teaching medical students about hypnosis. Many hypnotic interventions can be used in the treatment of MPD (see Chapter 11). A comprehensive model of MPD needs to take into account much more than autohypnosis, however. The autohypnotic model suffers from the same limitation as the psychoanalytic one: It is too focused on intrapsychic events within the individual patient.

ROLE PLAYING AND SOCIAL LEARNING MODELS

The idea that MPD is an artifact of the doctor–patient relationship, based on role demands, cues by the doctor, mutual reinforcement of role performance by doctor and patient, and similar mechanisms, is most developed in the work of Spanos (Spanos, et al., 1985; Spanos et al., 1986). I have discussed this model at length in the section of this chapter on the iatrogenesis of MPD.

Role theory provides insight from a blind man examining a small portion of the total elephant. Such theories, models, and schools make valuable contributions, except that they tend to be grossly overextended by their advocates. This is especially the case for armchair-quarterback explanations of MPD based on experiments with normal college students, conducted by professors who have never met a patient with MPD. The findings from such studies should be generalized to MPD patients with caution. As data relevant to the understanding of clinical MPD, Spanos's work is equivalent to a small number of experiments with rats in a single laboratory. No matter how interesting, such rat data could never explain a complex, heterogeneous phenomenon like human cancer or MPD.

The real value of social role theory will be its contribution to our understanding of the interactions in abusive families, during the time that MPD is forming in the children. The social cues, reinforcements, and role demands coming from the sexually abusive father and the mother who does nothing are important etiological factors. Spiegel (1986b) has written about the role of double binds in the creation of MPD; his analysis points to a line of empirical research. Social psychologists should make detailed maps of the interactions in families of children with MPD. Combined with a mapping of the cognitions that accompany these interactions (Ross & Gahan, 1988a), a data-based cognitive-social psychological treatment package could be developed.

In the meantime, in the absence of such studies, social role theorists have made a minor contribution to the understanding of clinical MPD.

NEUROLOGICAL CAUSES OF MULTIPLE PERSONALITY DISORDER

Since the time of Charcot in the 19th century there has been a suspicion that MPD might, at least in some cases, be a neurological disorder. It was thought that MPD might be the psychological and behavioral manifestation of epileptic discharges in the temporal lobes. Since 1980 a number of reports have appeared in the literature describing small series of patients with concurrent MPD and temporal lobe epilepsy (Benson, Miller, & Signer, 1986; Mesulam, 1981; Schenk & Bear, 1981). These cases were interpreted by the authors as suggesting that MPD might be a form of seizure disorder. Another issue is whether MPD might be an interictal disorder secondary to epilepsy (Benson, 1986).

In Chapter 7 I will discuss the relationship between MPD and temporal lobe epilepsy at length and will present data demonstrating that MPD and temporal lobe epilepsy are separate disorders with little phenomenological overlap.

A second possible neurological cause of MPD that has been proposed is a disconnection of the left and right hemispheres (Benner & Evans, 1984). Sidtis (1986) has provided the definitive analysis of this possibility and has discounted it. The main problem with hemispheric disconnection theories is that they were devised to explain dual personality but cannot possibly account for complex MPD. In any case, it is hard to see how a neurologically caused disorder could be cured by psychotherapy. Dual personality, which is the form of MPD that most lends itself to explanation by disconnection theories, is probably the easiest form of MPD to treat with psychotherapy. This does not make sense if dual personality is the form of MPD most likely to have a cause in the hardware of the brain.

There is no evidence that MPD is a neurological disease. Conversely, there is substantial evidence that it is a psychosocial disorder. In a computer analogy, MPD is a disorder of software, occurring in patients whose brain hardware is intact. Because structure and function are interwoven in a complex way in the human mind and brain, however, the computer analogy is a gross oversimplification. The physiological study of brain function in MPD may yield important insights into mind–body interaction (Larmore, Ludwig, & Cain, 1977; Mathew, Jack, & West, 1985), and physiological techniques may prove to be useful in the study of MPD (Loewenstein, Hamilton, Alagna, Reid, & deVries, 1987). None of these will imply that the etiology of MPD is biological, though. That is all there is to say about neurological models of MPD.

THE FEMINIST ANALYSIS OF MULTIPLE PERSONALITY DISORDER

When I speak of the feminist analysis of MPD, I am referring to the writing of Margo Rivera (1987, 1988), who has done extensive work on this aspect of the disorder. As pointed out by Rivera, MPD occurs in a broad social context. This context includes the division of power between the sexes, sex role socialization of men and women in North America, and institutionalized sexual exploitation of women and children in our society. It is an error to view the sexual abuse of children as an isolated phenomenon.

Such abuse, according to the feminist analysis (Rush, 1980), is an extreme expression of the patriarchal power structure that dominates our society.

Women are sexually exploited in advertising, films, locker room jokes, the workplace, the home, and the massage parlor (a short list) in North America. Sexual abuse of girls by men is the earliest and most extreme aspect of the socialization of women into subservient roles. The patriarchal role for women, at least in our society, is a combination of sex object, property, doormat, and punching bag. MPD, then, is caused primarily by a sick social structure. The sexually abusive father is an embodiment of patriarchal corruption. Although officially abhorred, his behavior is consistent with societal norms. That is why incest and child pornography are so widespread: They are inevitable consequences of the power structure.

There is a lot of truth in this analysis. There are also some problems. The main one is that the feminist thesis blames men for the sickness of modern society and almost completely absolves women. This is itself sexist. The feminist analysis is based on linear or nonsystemic thinking. Although girls are abused more often than boys in our society, boys too are victims of a billion-dollar pornography industry, homosexual prostitution, physical abuse by their fathers, and pathological socialization. Their development is warped and scarred by perverted sexuality in North America.

The female:male ratio in clinical series of MPD is 9:1 (Ross, Norton, & Wozney, 1989). However many males with MPD are probably in prison or do not go to see doctors, so the ratio in the overall population is probably lower. As discussed in Chapter 5, there is no difference between MPD in males and females (Ross & Norton, 1989a). Males with MPD have as much abuse, as many personalities, as many suicide attempts, and many other features in common with females. The feminist analysis of the causes of MPD founders on these data. The actual reality is a complicated web of victim-perpetrator-victim-perpetrator within and between generations; it is much more complex than simple cause-in-men and effect-in-girls.

A second problem with the feminist thesis is that many of the incestuous fathers probably have MPD themselves. They are themselves victims of abuse by MPD parents, both fathers and mothers. Over the next 10 years we may gain insight into an extremely intricate multigenerational transmission of incest, involving amnesia, abusive paternal alters having intercourse with alters in their children, and MPD mothers amnesic for their own direct contributions to the cycle. Once the linear flaws are corrected in the feminist analysis, it provides an essential component of the full understanding of MPD.

There is no doubt that orthodox psychiatry is mistaken if it resists the corrected feminist analysis. In the future, the task for the feminists is to translate their theory into the gathering of scientific data. In the absence of such data, social and political action is still imperative, as the feminists insist (Rush, 1980).

HILGARD'S NEODISSOCIATION THEORY
OF DIVIDED CONSCIOUSNESS

Hilgard (1977) has provided an extensive discussion of dissociation that places it in a broad and general context. He reviews the history, experimental data of his own and others, clinical cases, related literature, and theory. His book single-handedly revives the serious study of dissociation. Hilgard reconnects us with the 19th century while taking modern discoveries about information processing (Andorfer, 1985), divided attention, and brain processing into account.

His focus is not on MPD, however, and he does not appear to have seen a case himself. Hilgard does not provide a synthesized understanding of MPD itself, rather he organizes a great deal of background information and allows us to see the disorder in the context of modern experimental psychology. His theory is called neodissociation theory partly because it takes 19th-century understanding into account without making an ideological commitment to any one of the 19th-century schools.

One of the most helpful ideas in the book for a clinician treating MPD is Hilgard's distinction between vertical and horizontal splitting. Vertical splitting results in dissociation, whereas horizontal splitting results in repression, as shown in Figure 3.1. In my view, splitting and dissociation are synonyms. I believe that repression is a form of dissociation (Jorn, 1982), dissociation being a general term. Which terms are used in which way is not essential, but it is necessary to arrive at consistent use of terms in the field.

Following a vertical split, psychic material is pushed to the side or to the back of the mind. The dissociated material is not unconscious, however, it is merely dissociated. It is available for direct transaction with the external world. This is very different from supposedly unconscious, repressed material, which can only be recovered using "deep" techniques. MPD teaches us that dissociated material, in the form of alter personalities, can be rational,

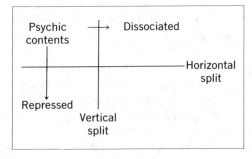

Figure 3.1. Vertical and Horizontal Splitting

organized, and coherent. Contacting the material hidden behind a vertical split is usually fairly easy from a technical point of view.

The "depth" psychologies and psychotherapies are based on an assumption that horizontal splitting is the more important defense. This is repression in Freud's sense. MPD teaches us that much of what was thought to be repressed id material, governed by primary process and available only using free association, or dream analysis, is in fact not far away and is easy to get at. Much of what was thought to be the unconscious is actually dissociated ego. In this sense MPD teaches us that the unconscious is not unconscious. Hilgard's model helps us to understand this.

An example will clarify what I mean. A patient presents with a conversion paralysis of the left arm. If this is due to an unconscious conflict hidden behind a horizontal split, understanding why the patient's arm can't move will require deep exploration of the unconscious. Considerable time and a great deal of complicated, untestable theory will be required to analyze and treat the problem. If the cause of the paralysis is hidden behind a vertical split, however, one simply calls out the alter personality who is causing the paralysis. One asks the alter why she is doing that, an explanation is given, a different solution to the problem is negotiated, and cure of the symptom is contracted for. This may take a while if the alter is hostile, but the process is one of rational negotiation and discussion. There is nothing deep or hidden. There is no need for obscure theory and jargon.

It is important in treating MPD to try to be as shallow as possible. Hilgard's (1977) book is important because it sets the treatment of MPD in a modern scientific context. I will discuss what I mean by the treatment of MPD being "shallow" at greater length in Chapters 10 and 11.

STATE-DEPENDENT AND STATE-OF-CONSCIOUSNESS MODELS OF MULTIPLE PERSONALITY DISORDER

About the time this book goes to press, Frank Putnam's (1989) book on MPD should be published. Although I haven't read his manuscript, from attendance at his workshops and from conversation, I am confident that he has written extensively on these two sets of models. I refer the reader to his book.

This line of thinking about MPD has a number of important features. For one, it leads directly to experimental work on dissociation (Silberman, Putnam, Weingartner, Braun, & Post, 1985). It is linked to a large empirical literature on mood and state-dependent learning. It has immediate implications for many other psychiatric disorders. For instance, Putnam is interested in what the switching process in MPD might teach us about the onset of panic attacks, switches from depression to mania in bipolar affective disorder, rapid changes of state in borderline personality disorder, and a

host of other phenomena (Putnam, 1988). These models w
view that MPD is an isolated curiosity.

An intriguing aspect of Putnam's thinking is the observa
switch rapidly from one state to another and that their st
discontinuous. There is apparently a large literature on this aspect of this
development. It is possible that the switching of alters in MPD draws on
this normal ability. MPD may represent an adaptive developmental delay in
the maturation of the ability to integrate experience. If this is so, MPD may
offer insights about normal child development.

It is possible to study MPD using metaphors and principles from physics,
within the framework of these models. Physicists have studied boundary
phenomena extensively, as well as the transmission of signals across boundaries. Their discoveries might shed light on the boundaries between alters.
It is conceivable that physicists might in turn learn something from MPD.
These models have no specific limitations, because they are abstract and
systemic in nature. The danger with them is that the individual human patient
could be overlooked by investigators preoccupied with abstractions. The
field is more prone to error in the opposite direction, however. Personally,
I have made many errors in the treatment of MPD, but none of them have
been based on data; all of them have been based on my own necessarily
anecdotal thinking. Therefore we should welcome these models and investigations that stem from them into the field.

Like MPD patients, the field is greater than the sum of its parts. State-
dependent theories and models are one part of many in the field of dissociative studies, but a potentially important part.

DESCRIPTIVE CLINICAL MODELS OF MULTIPLE PERSONALITY DISORDER

It is important that the clinical treatment of MPD be guided by science,
data, and rigorous thought. But it is the treatment of patients that provides
meaning and purpose for the science. Without patients who can benefit from
treatment, the science becomes a hobby for academics who have no serious
work to do in the world.

The most important clinical understanding of the etiology of MPD comes
from Richard Kluft (1984c) and Bennett Braun (1986a, 1986b; Braun & Sachs,
1985). These two men have not worked in isolation and have borrowed a
great deal from others, but they have written and edited the most important
work. Braun and Sachs propose a 3-P model of MPD derived from the
standard predisposing, perpetuating, and precipitating factors used in clinical
psychiatry. Kluft has proposed a four-factor theory of MPD.

Both these clinical accounts of the etiology of MPD emphasize two points:

1. Patients with MPD are extremely good at dissociation.

2. Patients with MPD have used dissociation to cope with severe childhood trauma.

In a nutshell, that is all that needs to be said about the etiology of MPD. Because this is a book, not a nutshell, I will say a bit more.

As a model, Kluft's four-factor theory encompasses Braun and Sachs's 3-P model. Therefore I will refer only to it. Although Kluft lists a number of examples illustrating each of the four factors in his theory, these are really only lists and have not been woven together into what could properly be called a theory. The first two factors are the two items already given: dissociative ability and trauma.

The third factor in the etiology of MPD is "shaping influences and substrates that determine the form taken by the dissociative defense" (Kluft, 1984c, p. 15). This is too analytical. Kluft lists, among other things, multiple systems of cognition and memory, libidinal developmental lines, and imaginary companionship as relevant to this factor. Actually integrating all of these into a theory, rather than simply listing them, would be a major intellectual feat (the contents of the list should be modified because there is an unintended pun on "multiple"). Kluft's fourth factor is "inadequate provision of stimulus barriers and restorative experiences by significant others, for example, insufficient 'soothing' " (p. 15).

Restated in plain language, these are the third and fourth factors in the etiology of MPD:

3. The form and structure of MPD vary depending on the person's temperament and nonabuse experience.
4. The abuse didn't stop, and the victim did not receive enough consistent love and care to heal her wounds.

The third factor encompasses social and cultural factors that contribute to the creation of MPD. The fourth factor points to the power of the reinforcers for dissociation, and the huge number of times they were applied throughout childhood and adolescence, in complex cases of MPD.

The clinical descriptive model of MPD is the best one. It was arrived at by therapists who had spent thousands of hours working directly with MPD patients. The model is simple, and that is one of its best properties. As a general outline it accounts for all the major features of MPD, provides a rationale for treatment, and is consistent with the response to treatment. Confirmation of the model is given by alter personalities in response to open-ended questions: The alters state the four factors directly to the therapist, in response to questions such as, "Why were you created?"

What is MPD? MPD is a little girl imagining that the abuse is happening to someone else. Because the human mind and human culture are complicated, the disorder is not a simple one. We should not lose sight of the basic simplicity of this "etiological model" of MPD, nor should we cloak it in too much jargon or fancy language.

There is a great deal of data to support the descriptive clinical model of MPD. Rather than reviewing it here as evidence in support of the model, I will discuss the abuse histories and other features of MPD patients in detail in Chapter 5. A comprehensive account of the etiology of MPD must take into account all the schools and viewpoints I have outlined in this chapter. It isn't necessary to produce a complicated diagram with arrows and boxes, showing supposed relationships between all of these: as more data accumulate, everything will fall into place. For now all that is required is an acknowledgment that MPD is a complex biopsychosocial disorder with numerous determinants. MPD is a strategy for surviving a traumatic childhood.

MULTIPLE PERSONALITY DISORDER IN FORENSIC PSYCHIATRY

In this section I am going to review selected aspects of forensic MPD. I am not a forensic psychiatrist and can't make detailed recommendations about how to do assessments of criminals with MPD. My focus will be on what we can learn about nonforensic MPD by considering criminal cases.

Coons (1988a) has published a case that illustrates the harmful effects of the abuse of forensic hypnosis. In his case a woman lost her job and children because of incorrect interviewing, misused hypnosis, and a false positive diagnosis of MPD. The patient appeared to be innocent and to have no interest in simulating MPD. The supposed MPD was never used as a defense because she was not brought to trial. Nor was she detained on psychiatric grounds. The negative consequences ensued because of events set in motion by the false diagnosis and included losing her children in custody disputes.

Those concerned that criminals might fake MPD for secondary gain should be aware that a false positive diagnosis of MPD may create more loss than gain. The difficulties of establishing whether a criminal has real MPD are illustrated by the debate about the Hillside Strangler (Allison, 1984; Orne et al., 1984; Watkins, 1984). I was persuaded by Martin Orne's argument that Kenneth Bianchi was faking, but it was a complicated case. Perhaps both malingering and genuine MPD were coexistent in Bianchi.

Whatever the truth is about that one case, there is no test or battery of tests that can establish scientifically, beyond doubt, whether a given criminal has genuine MPD. This means that expert testimony is based on clinical judgment and is inexact and imperfect. It is therefore necessary to be cautious about the relevance of MPD in criminal proceedings.

Many professionals think that MPD is an artifact of the doctor–patient relationship. What does forensic MPD teach us about the possibility that clinical MPD is an artifact? Faked MPD in the forensic context is an artifact, not of the doctor–patient relationship, but of the legal system. It makes sense to fake MPD, when charged with crimes, only if that is a good legal strategy. If the legal system were structured such that criminals with MPD received jail sentences twice as long as the ones given to criminals without MPD, malingered MPD would not be seen in forensic psychiatry. In fact malingered false negative diagnoses of MPD would likely occur. In this scenario criminals would not manifest artifactual MPD no matter how many leading or suggestive questions the psychiatrist asked.

In forensic psychiatry faked or unconsciously simulated MPD is not caused by the doctor or by the relationship between doctor and criminal. The causality is systemic in nature, and both doctor and criminal are players in a systemic game. The cause of the MPD is the rules of the system, which make it "smart" to have MPD. Both criminal and doctor are playing according to rules that reward criminals for displaying mental illness.

The problem, in forensic assessment of MPD, is a systemic rule saying criminals can be found not guilty by reason of insanity (Ross, 1986b). Not guilty by reason of insanity is a legal sleight of hand that makes a mockery of both psychiatry and the law. Not guilty by reason of insanity is also bad therapy for MPD patients. It is unfortunate that psychiatry has sanctioned expert testimony involving metapsychological fictions such as irresistible impulses, lack of conscious intent to commit a murder, and the possibility of not being guilty because of one's mental state.

Today we have a legal system in which a defendant who killed a child while driving drunk can claim that it was the bartender's fault for serving him too much alcohol. This can actually result in a lighter sentence and the possibility of a suit against the bar owner. Even without that added twist, criminals may get lighter sentences for murder if they were drunk at the time. Rapists get lighter sentences if they express remorse, seek counseling, or go to church. There are currently court challenges in the United States based on the claim that some murderers on death row are not mentally competent to be executed. In my view, using MPD as a tactic on this perverse playing field, which we call the legal system, may be good legal strategy, but it does not teach patients how to take ownership of their lives or responsibility for their actions. Therapists are misguided if they try to "help" their MPD patients by telling the judge that the patient wasn't responsible, on the grounds that an alter personality committed the crime.

I am not saying that forensic psychiatry is a waste of time. Quite the opposite: It is an extremely important branch of medicine. What I am talking about is shutting down the rewards for artifactual MPD. Psychiatrists should not participate in a system of game playing, psychopathic legal strategies, and manipulation of juries, because that is bad for patients, psychiatry, the law, and society. A case in which MPD was used as a defense illustrates the perversity of "not guilty by reason of insanity": In the case of Billy Milligan (Keyes, 1981), the patient might have spent less time locked in institutions and received less harassment after discharge if he had been found guilty and served his time as a regular criminal. A psychiatric defense is not always in the defendant's best interest, even as a strategy for getting a lighter sentence.

The simple solution to the artifactual creation of MPD in criminal cases is that mental state and psychiatric history should be irrelevant to a determination of guilt. If you did it, you are guilty. If you didn't do it, you are innocent. And, you are innocent till proven guilty. Those basic principles would immediately eliminate all secondary gain for having a psychiatric diagnosis. But should mentally ill criminals be treated the same as other criminals? No, of course not. They need psychiatric treatment if they have treatable psychiatric disorders. Such treatment is in the best interests of both the criminal and society.

Criminal trials should be held in two stages. In the first stage no testimony about mental state or psychiatric history would be allowed. If the person was found innocent, proceedings would stop. If he was found guilty, then the defending lawyer would have the option of asking for psychiatric testimony to be heard in determination of sentencing. This would only delay courtroom manipulation and secondary gain, however, if a psychiatric diagnosis could result in a lighter sentence. Therefore the length of sentence should be set at the end of the first stage, and the defending lawyer should only be able to request psychiatric testimony after that.

Why bother with psychiatric testimony, then? To determine whether the prisoner should serve his time in regular prison, the psychiatric wing of a prison, or the forensic ward of a psychiatric hospital. A sentence not involving a jail term would not require psychiatric testimony. I'm sure many people will find this proposal highly objectionable. Whatever flaws it might have, such a system would eliminate motivation for persons on trial to fake or unconsciously simulate MPD, and for genuine MPD patients charged with crimes to augment, exacerbate, or perpetuate their disorder for secondary gain.

The first point I am making, in a book about clinical MPD, is that it is possible to shut down secondary gain, to minimize faked or artifactual dissociation, and to keep a focus on recovery and improved function. The second point is this: If artifactual clinical MPD does occur, it is not caused by the doctor in a simple linear manner. Like forensic MPD, clinical MPD must be analyzed in a systemic context. For instance, in a health care system in which psychotherapy for depression was paid for but psychotherapy for MPD was not, there would be a strong drive toward false positive diagnoses of depression, and false negative diagnoses of MPD. Reverse the billing procedure, and the "incidence" of MPD would increase. In either case, both patient and doctor are players in a systemic game, and the features of MPD are influenced by systemic rules.

If artifactual MPD occurs, it is the product of a wide social context, not of the doctor–patient relationship as an isolated entity. Analyzing the causes of MPD involves a much wider focus than the doctor–patient relationship. Blaming the doctor for MPD is like blaming him for the sore back of a carpenter on compensation. The doctor doesn't *cause* the sore back. He is a participant in a social ritual that has defined rules, structure, and outcomes. The doctor assesses some genuine sore backs and some fake ones, and has trouble differentiating the two.

The same logic applies to the causation of genuine MPD during childhood. The abuser doesn't cause the child to develop MPD in a linear or Newtonian cause-and-effect manner. The development of MPD is a complex response to a wide range of social realities, reinforcements, rules, and adaptive options.

The defense of not guilty by reason of insanity is bad therapy for MPD patients, as well as bad law. Two of the foundations of MPD treatment are defining the patient as not crazy, and expecting the patient to be and/or to become responsible for her life and actions. These are essential principles of therapy. The treatment of MPD involves defining the disorder as a good survival strategy, one based on talent and ability, not on defect or incapacity. The patient did not develop MPD because there was something wrong with her brain, her ego, or any other aspect of her. The MPD was a creative and adaptive strategy for surviving a traumatic childhood. Treatment is required in adulthood because the strategy has become self-defeating.

If treatment is based on this essential principle, how can the MPD patient who commits a crime be not guilty by reason of insanity? You can't have it both ways at once, except in an inconsistent, contradictory, and double-binding world, such as the one MPD patients grow up in. It is also essential, especially in working with severely disturbed multiples, who are prone to theatrical, manipulative, and double-binding behavior, to insist that the patient is responsible for the behavior of all alters. To let her off because it was an alter who broke a window, molested a child, or broke the treatment contract is to reinforce secondary gains for dissociation.

Many MPD patients have been molested by parents who themselves have MPD (Braun, 1985). The fact that the parent had an abusive alter, hidden behind an amnesia barrier, does not excuse the abuse. It does not make the abuse less wrong, less criminal, or less destructive. Nor does the fact that the parent had MPD mean that the child's dissociated anger is less legitimate. If the abusive MPD parent is not let off, in an emotional sense, within the therapy of his child, why should the child be let off for criminal behavior of her own? Why should the child be let off for abusive, manipulative, or destructive behavior directed at the therapist, office furniture, or other staff?

As I see it, sane therapy requires clear, consistent rules. Therefore I am opposed to the defense of not guilty by reason of insanity for MPD and other dissociative disorders.

CHAPTER FOUR

Diagnostic Criteria

Until 1980 multiple personality disorder (MPD) did not have well-de-fined and accepted diagnostic criteria. With the publication of DSM-III (American Psychiatric Association, 1980) the disorder first attained official recognition as a legitimate psychiatric entity. This was an important political event and undoubtedly contributed to the exponential increase in the diagnosis of MPD in North America in the 1980s. Outside North America, where DSM-III and DSM-III-R are used much less, MPD is still rarely diagnosed. My sense of the situation is that MPD is still vastly underdiagnosed even in North America.

At the present time a great deal of skepticism remains about MPD. This situation will probably change within the next 5 years. Certainly before the end of the century, there is likely to have been an about-face by those who are currently hostile. By the year 2000, most mental health professionals will probably have diagnosed at least one case of MPD. Not only that, people will be making a point of mentioning their MPD case, in order to let colleagues know that they are competent diagnosticians and don't miss cases.

By the year 2000 the psychiatrist who has never diagnosed a case of MPD may be looked on with suspicion. Within a span of 10 years, we may evolve from extreme underdiagnosis of MPD to a situation in which the major problem is false positive diagnoses. This may necessitate a tightening up of the diagnostic criteria, which isn't required now. Given the state of the profession today, there are more false negative diagnoses than false positive, therefore overinclusive diagnostic criteria are in the best interest of patients.

I have not yet encountered a false positive diagnosis of MPD made by another mental health professional.

This chapter will include a review of the DSM-III and DSM-III-R (American Psychiatric Association, 1980, 1987) criteria for MPD. The bridge between these two was DSM-III-R Draft (American Psychiatric Association, 1985). The chapter will also provide data on the National Institute of Mental Health (NIMH) criteria (Putnam, personal communication, 1986), which are five in number. In addition I will discuss MPD in the context of a spectrum of dissociative disorders, a concept not adequately elaborated in DSM-III-R (Ross, 1985). In Chapter 7, I will set the dissociative disorders in a broader context of what I call trauma disorders and propose a revised classification. First, though, a brief discussion of the function of diagnostic criteria is required.

THE FUNCTION OF DIAGNOSTIC CRITERIA AND THE ORGANIZATION OF DSM-III-R

The function of diagnostic criteria is to define illnesses in a valid and reliable way, in order to guide treatment and provide a prognosis. The first problem is that many disorders in DSM-III-R are not biomedical illnesses. Some have no known effective treatment, and for many the natural history and prognosis are uncertain. For instance, very little is known about the lifetime course and outcome of panic disorder. The disorders in DSM-III-R vary widely in presumed etiology and treatment. Alcohol withdrawal has a single specific cause, whereas bulimia probably has numerous contributing causes that vary widely from patient to patient. The management of alcohol withdrawal probably does not vary much throughout North America, but bulimia might be treated with antidepressants, short-term cognitive therapy, psychoanalysis, self-help groups, or any one of numerous different approaches. The natural history of alcohol withdrawal is short-term resolution or death, whereas bulimia lasts for years in most cases.

According to DSM-III-R, mental retardation, premature ejaculation, schizophrenia, narcissistic personality disorder, and stuttering are all "mental disorders." No category can meaningfully encompass so many disparate phenomena, and no organizational rules can adequately account for all of them. In fact DSM-III-R has many different principles of organization within its different sections. To understand the diagnostic status of MPD, it is necessary to have some idea of how DSM-III-R is organized. It is also important to realize that DSM-III-R is a resting point en route to DSM-IV and later editions of the manual.

DSM-III-R is organized into a number of major sections that bear no stated logical relation to each other. These include organic mental disorders, schizophrenic disorders, affective disorders, anxiety disorders, and personality disorders. The dissociative disorders have a section of their own. Within each of these sections there are a number of diagnoses that may or may not have a specified relationship to each other.

The principles of organization of the different sections of DSM-III-R, and even different diagnoses within one section, vary widely. The concept of a continuum is a frequently used organizing principle, but the continuum may take many forms. Examples of different principles of organization within sections of DSM-III are available in a paper of mine (Ross, 1985). The point is that there are many possible organizational principles that could bring conceptual unity to the dissociative disorders.

How are the dissociative disorders organized? The answer is that they aren't. The dissociative disorders are simply listed in DSM-III-R, without a statement as to how they are related to each other. Bennett Braun (1986a, 1988a) and I (Ross, 1985) have proposed independently that the dissociative disorders be organized on a continuum from normal to MPD. I have not heard a specialist in dissociative disorders object to this scheme and have concluded since 1985, based on research data and clinical experience, that MPD should be reclassified in the context of trauma disorders (see Chapter 7). Within the trauma disorders, however, the relationship of the different dissociative disorders remains the same as that proposed by Braun and me. This chapter discusses only the dissociative disorders, without setting them in the larger context.

DISSOCIATIVE DISORDERS ON A CONTINUUM OF INCREASINGLY LARGE AMOUNTS OF DISSOCIATED PSYCHIC MATERIAL

The dissociative disorders should be classified on a continuum of increasingly large amounts of dissociated psychic material. This is a simple organizational principle that fits with clinical experience. There is insufficient research evidence to date to support or refute this or any other organizational principle for the dissociative disorders. We have to go with what seems to make sense.

The simplest dissociative phenomenon is a normal dissociative state such as absorption in a movie. The simplest dissociative *disorder* is psychogenic amnesia. Psychogenic amnesia is defined in DSM-III-R as ''Sudden inability to recall important personal information that is too extensive to be explained by ordinary forgetfulness'' (p. 275). The disorder cannot be due to a known organic cause, such as blackouts during alcohol intoxication (I will propose that alcohol blackouts are often actually psychogenic dissociative phenomena, and not necessarily organic in nature, in Chapter 7). MPD is an exclusion criterion for the diagnosis of psychogenic amnesia. In other words, if one has MPD, one cannot also have psychogenic amnesia, because such amnesia is a facet of the more complex dissociative disorder.

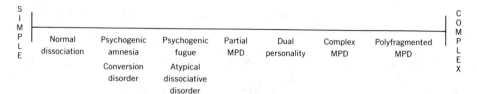

Figure 4.1. The Spectrum of Dissociative Disorders

There is a problem with the definition of psychogenic amnesia in DSM-III-R. I have met quite a few patients who have extensive amnesia for childhood events but no recent amnesia and no more complex dissociative disorder. In my experience, these patients usually suffer from chronic trauma disorder and are amnesic for childhood abuse. They do not meet criteria for psychogenic amnesia because of the word "sudden" in the criteria. This word should be dropped from DSM-IV, so that posttraumatic amnesias of long duration can be properly diagnosed. As it stands, psychogenic amnesia is incorrectly defined as an acute disorder, in effect an adjustment disorder with amnesia. The prototypical DSM-III-R psychogenic amnesia occurs in a woman who is amnesic for a period of 2 days during which a rape occurred.

Moving further along the spectrum, as illustrated in Figure 4.1, one encounters psychogenic fugue and atypical dissociative disorder (which is called *dissociative disorder not otherwise specified* in DSM-III-R). Atypical dissociative disorder currently encompasses partial forms of MPD that in fact are not at all atypical, and are probably common. The term *atypical dissociative disorder* should be reserved for disorders that cannot be placed on the continuum. Therefore I have put psychogenic amnesia and partial MPD in Figure 4.1, although the latter is not DSM-III-R nomenclature. Fugue and partial MPD are more complex dissociative disorders than simple amnesia.

I have left out depersonalization disorder on purpose. This is the only diagnosis in our structured interview with a low interrater reliability ($r = .56$). It is the only dissociative disorder that does not occur more frequently in MPD than in panic disorder or eating disorders (Ross, Heber, Norton, & Anderson, 1989a). Further, it is the only dissociative disorder that occurs more commonly in partial complex seizures than in controls (Ross, Heber, Anderson, et al., 1989). Depersonalization, in my opinion, is a symptom not a disorder. It may occur as a feature of MPD, in partial complex seizures, as a limited symptom panic attack, or as a feature of other psychiatric disorders. The data suggest that it should be dropped from DSM-IV. I won't discuss depersonalization disorder further.

DSM-III-R describes

> . . . cases in which there is more than one personality state capable of assuming executive control of the individual, but not more than one personality state is sufficiently distinct to meet the full criteria for Multiple Personality Disorder,

or cases in which a second personality never assumes complete executive control. (p. 277)

These are examples of dissociative disorder not otherwise specified, in DSM-III-R terms. These are partial forms of MPD. They are not atypical or difficult to place on the continuum.

At the extreme end of the continuum is MPD. MPD is not subtyped in DSM-III-R, but clinical experience indicates that it could be divided into at least three forms of increasing complexity: (1) dual personality, and cases with less than 5 alters; (2) cases with 5 to 20 alters; (3) complex and poly-fragmented MPD. We do not have enough empirical data to say whether the cutoff for complex MPD should be 20, 25 or more personalities, and personality fragments. It appears that the simpler forms of MPD are probably associated with less severe trauma and are easier to treat, but data are lacking.

The subtyping of MPD requires standard terminology for different types of personality states. Braun (1986a) has proposed that alter personalities be differentiated from fragments, and most clinicians appear to agree with him. Personalities are relatively full-bodied, complete states capable of a range of emotions and behaviors. Alters usually have been in executive control some substantial amount of time over the person's life. Fragments, on the other hand, are relatively limited psychic states that express only one feeling, hold one memory, or carry out a limited task in the person's life. A fragment might be a frightened child who holds the memory of one particular abuse incident. I personally use the terms alter, alter personality, and personality as synonyms. I call more limited states fragments, fragment alters, or fragment personalities. That is all the nomenclature I use.

In complex MPD usually not more than seven or eight major personalities have handled the bulk of the life experience and do most of the work in therapy. Then there tend to be a number of fragments with each of which the therapist may spend minutes or a few hours throughout the therapy. Braun (1986a) proposes that fragments be subtyped as special purpose fragments and memory trace fragments, but I don't see the clinical utility of these differentiations. In complex MPD the therapist will usually contact most or all of the named alters and fragments at least once, even if only for a brief conversation prior to an integration ritual.

In polyfragmented MPD there may be hundreds of states with separate names and ages. There is no empirical basis for deciding the cutoff for the transition from complex to polyfragmented MPD. It is logistically impossible and therapeutically unnecessary to contact all these states directly, although the patient may have them all recorded in a chart. Patients with polyfragmented MPD have taken the process of dissociation to its extreme. Hundreds of experiences are split into separate pieces and given names and ages. When there are hundreds of fragments, the process may not be the same as the formation of alters; the person may name memories in a "labeling" manner, without dissociation as such occurring. It is important not to fall victim to the illusion that there are hundreds of personalities inside one person in such cases. Such claims discredit MPD as a serious disorder and stretch the meaning of the word *personality* far beyond any meaningful limit.

What are the DSM-III criteria for MPD? There are three of them. Instead of listing the DSM-III criteria separately, I will list the five NIMH research criteria for MPD, of which the first three are the DSM-III criteria (Putnam, personal communication, 1986; Ross, Norton, & Wozney, 1989):

A. The existence within the individual of two or more distinct personalities, each of which is dominant at a particular time.

B. The personality that is dominant at any particular time determines the individual's behavior.

C. Each individual personality is complex and integrated with its own unique behavior patterns and social relationships.

D. Two or more alter personalities must exhibit individually distinct and consistent alter personality-specific behavior on at least three occasions.

E. There is evidence of some type of amnesia or combinations of types of amnesia among alter personalities (e.g., one-way amnesia, mutual amnesia, etc.). The amnesia does not have to include all of the alters.

These criteria had not been published prior to our paper reporting the findings on 236 cases of MPD (Ross, Norton, & Wozney, 1989). They are tentative criteria for research purposes. In my experience all complex cases of MPD have met all of these criteria, and all have had severe abuse histories. The question is whether there is any benefit in using five criteria instead of two or three.

One argument in favor of more elaborate diagnostic criteria is that MPD is insufficiently operationalized and that the DSM-III-R criteria will result in too many false positive diagnoses. This is an argument I have advanced myself (Ross & Fraser, 1987). The only empirical data bearing on this issue indicate that there is little utility in having more elaborate criteria.

In our series of 236 cases we excluded any cases reported to us that did not meet the first two criteria, so by definition all 236 cases met NIMH Criteria A and B. For the remaining criteria, 94.4 percent met Criterion C, 95.7 percent met D, and 94.9 percent met E. What does that reveal? It means that, consistent with my own experience, most cases of MPD meet all five NIMH research criteria. There would be little point then in using all five criteria. Using more rigorous criteria would exclude only a small number of cases as false positives. These are true cases of MPD, however, and should be excluded only from the more complex subtypes of MPD, not from the overall category of MPD.

Because there are too few cases for statistical analysis, our data do not tell us whether cases that do not meet Criteria C, D, and E are dual or simple cases, have experienced less trauma, are easier to treat, or differ in any other meaningful way. It appears, though, that complicated diagnostic criteria are of potential use only for subtyping MPD.

The other side of the diagnostic dilemma is false positive diagnoses of MPD. Do the NIMH criteria result in fewer cases that are not MPD being falsely diagnosed as having MPD, compared to DSM-III-R criteria? There are no data on this question. However, as mentioned earlier, I have never encountered a false positive diagnosis of MPD made by another clinician, so a requirement for more rigorous criteria has never arisen. The upshot of these considerations is that the simplified DSM-III-R criteria are sufficient for the present time.

There is a nit-picky problem concerning the relationship between DSM-III and DSM-III-R criteria for MPD. This problem is of interest to researchers who are trying to develop diagnostic instruments for MPD but is of little practical clinical importance. In changing from DSM-III to DSM-III-R criteria, the committee on dissociative disorders made several changes at once. The committee compressed the three DSM-III criteria into two while changing the wording and dropping part of Criterion C. At the same time they expanded Criterion B. These are the DSM-III-R (1987, p. 272) diagnostic criteria for MPD:

A. The existence within the person of two or more distinct personalities or personality states (each with its own relatively enduring pattern of perceiving, relating to, and thinking about the environment and self).

B. At least two of these personalities or personality states recurrently take full control of the person's behavior.

The first half of DSM-III-R Criterion A is equivalent to DSM-III Criterion A. The second half of DSM-III-R Criterion A (in parentheses) is a slightly softened version of DSM-III Criterion C. DSM-III-R Criterion B is a combination of DSM-III Criterion B and a softened version of DSM-III Criterion C. As well, DSM-III Criterion B has been softened while being incorporated in DSM-III-R Criterion B. This was done to take account of copresence and coconsciousness (these terms are discussed in Chapter 5), which are common features of MPD, as explained by Kluft, Steinberg, and Spitzer (1988).

These changes are a bit confusing. The clinical meaning of the changed criteria is clear: Not all cases of MPD involve alters with separate social relationships, nor is there always a clear differentiation of which alter is in control at any given time. The DSM-III-R criteria acknowledge the clinical reality of MPD more effectively than the DSM-III criteria (see Chapter 5). However there is a problem determining whether all DSM-III MPD cases would also meet DSM-III-R criteria, and vice versa. It appears that all cases that meet DSM-III criteria would also meet DSM-III-R criteria. This is important because it means that no DSM-III cases reported in the literature since 1980 will be lost as false positives.

The problem I have encountered in thinking about our series of 236 cases, and about the structured interview data, is that both inquire about the NIMH criteria. In all studies to date I have included cases that meet the first two DSM-III criteria and have referred to them as meeting the DSM-III-R criteria. Some may question this assumption. I think it is warranted because the first two DSM-III criteria are more inclusive than the DSM-III-R criteria. Any MPD case that has had fully distinct alters determining the individual's behavior will have alters that meet DSM-III-R Criterion B, even though the wording is different.

In the end, this reduces to a problem of legalistic arguing about wording and the letter of the law, which is irrelevant to clinical reality. The committee has created a problem for developers of structured interviews, however. It is a general problem of DSM-III-R that the relationship between DSM-III criteria and DSM-III-R criteria is insufficiently discussed throughout the manual. Problems of transition from one manual to another will occur for obsessive-compulsive personality disorder, brief reactive psychosis, and other diagnoses. Likely only those with obsessive personalities will worry much about this, but they will be at risk for brief reactive psychoses.

To repeat the conclusion: DSM-III-R diagnostic criteria are adequate for current clinical and research purposes.

SECONDARY FEATURES OF MULTIPLE PERSONALITY DISORDER

The primary diagnostic criteria for MPD, which are the DSM-III-R criteria, are straightforward, as they should be. Anyone can look them up. It is the secondary features of MPD that are most valuable to the clinician. Usually MPD does not present in an obvious overt fashion. Patients will not walk into the office announcing that they have MPD and spontaneously exhibiting named alters, in most cases. Kluft (1985e) found that in a research series of his, 5 percent of cases presented as self-diagnosed but were generally disbelieved by their psychiatrists, 15 percent openly dissociated during assessment or treatment, 40 percent presented with signs that could alert a clinician with a high index of suspicion for MPD, and 40 percent of cases were highly disguised and were discovered while he was testing a special diagnostic protocol.

MPD often presents in a highly covert fashion even when the patient is being assessed by Richard Kluft, who has made a more detailed analysis of more patients than anyone in the world. The longest I have personally worked with a patient before contacting an alter personality is 2 years; this was a case of atypical dissociative disorder, not MPD, and the entity was not a

DSM-III-R alter personality (Ross & Anderson, 1988), but the case illustrates the hidden nature of such major dissociation.

Clinicians who say that they have been in practice 10 or 20 years and have never seen a case of MPD are really saying that they have never seen a case that falls into Kluft's 5 percent, the self-diagnosed group. In my experience, clinicians who do not seriously consider MPD in their differential diagnoses can observe florid dissociation without seeing it as a diagnostic clue for MPD. They therefore do not pursue the diagnosis with detailed, specific inquiry and never "see" cases.

During a period of 1 year, from July 1, 1985, to June 30, 1986, I diagnosed MPD in 3 of 68 (4.4 percent) general adult inpatients assigned to me (Ross, 1987). These were cases that had come to emergency and were assigned to me on the ward. There was no strong selection bias, and my overall caseload was similar to that of any general inpatient psychiatrist in North America. Yet no other inpatient psychiatrists at my hospital made a diagnosis of MPD during this period, out of a total of nearly 500 admissions. The three patients I diagnosed had 1 to 13 previous admissions for borderline personality disorder under other psychiatrists.

All three had exhibited numerous secondary features of MPD for years. Of the three, two have since been treated to integration, and one was followed at another hospital for 3 years with unknown outcome, before being referred to me for treatment: She still had active MPD. Does this mean that I am the only competent inpatient psychiatrist at my hospital? No. It means that I am the only psychiatrist who seriously considers MPD in his differential diagnoses and makes a specific inquiry for its signs and symptoms. If the other psychiatrists did the same, they too would diagnose cases on a regular basis. I estimate that any teaching hospital in North America with 500 inpatient psychiatric admissions per year is admitting a minimum of 10 cases of undiagnosed MPD per year, and probably in the range of 20–30 cases.

I believe that most university departments of psychiatry in North America are currently treating enough undiagnosed cases of MPD to provide one treatment case for every resident in the department. If that is correct, it is important for clinicians to become familiar with the primary and secondary features of MPD, to realize that MPD usually presents with only secondary features, and to include the necessary questions in clinical assessments.

Our Dissociative Disorders Clinic has developed a structured clinical interview to assist in making the diagnosis of MPD, as well as the other dissociative disorders, which is described in Chapter 6 and in Appendix A. The clinical features of MPD as it presents before diagnosis and during treatment are described in the next chapter. I will conclude this chapter by reemphasizing that the clinician should be aware of both the primary and secondary features of MPD and should inquire about them systematically as part of regular clinical practice. The day has passed when MPD can be considered a curiosity, of interest only to subspecialists. This is even more true of the dissociative spectrum as a whole; pathological dissociation is frequently a component of many psychiatric disorders.

Clinical Features

The clinical features of multiple personality disorder (MPD) consist of two main subsets: generic or nonspecific symptoms, and symptoms specific for MPD. The clinician must be familiar with both. There are in turn two main reasons why the clinician needs to be aware of the features described in this chapter: to aid in diagnosis, and to guide treatment. With this in mind, I am first going to describe a general scheme for thinking about dissociation, which will be expanded on in Chapter 7. Next I will briefly review what is known about the epidemiology of MPD. Then I will discuss the diagnostically nonspecific features of MPD and will conclude with those aspects of the disorder that do not occur in other psychiatric illnesses. The specific aspects of MPD are subdivided into phenomena most important in diagnosis and those most relevant in treatment.

A GENERAL SCHEME OF DISSOCIATION

MPD is a dissociative disorder and is by definition based on the defense mechanism of dissociation. Unfortunately, however, there is not a good definition of dissociation. Dissociation is defined in DSM-III-R (1987) as "a disturbance or alteration in the normally integrative functions of identity, memory, or consciousness" (p. 269). This is a rough-and-ready clinical definition of dissociation that does not have a lot of empirical support. It arbitrarily limits dissociation to those areas of the brain concerned with identity, memory, and consciousness. There is an overlap between a number of related concepts including fantasy proneness, hypnotizability, absorption, and dissociation (Lynn & Rhue, 1988). Trying to sort these out into meaningfully distinct terms is a difficult research problem.

As well, there is a problem about the difference between splitting and dissociation (Clary, Burstin, & Carpenter, 1984; Gruenewald, 1977; Horevitz & Braun, 1984; Ross, 1985; Young, 1988). I consider splitting and dissociation to be synonyms, and I consider borderline personality disorder, which is based on splitting, to be an Axis I dissociative disorder. Because there is a great deal of ideological investment in the term *splitting,* it is difficult to enter into an empirically grounded dialogue with colleagues who hold that multiples are really just borderlines. The relationship between MPD and borderline personality disorder will be discussed in detail in Chapter 7.

I favor a simple definition of dissociation. Dissociation is the opposite of association. It is not a coincidence that, in the 19th century, academic psychologists were preoccupied with theories of mental association and studied clinical dissociation. For definitional purposes the psyche may be reduced to a collection of elements in complex relationships with each other. Psychic elements include thoughts, memories, feelings, motor commands, impulses, sensations, and all the other constituents of psychic life. Any two psychic elements may be in a dynamic relationship with each other, in which case they are associated, or relatively isolated and separate, in which case they are dissociated.

The normal mind carries out an infinite number of associations and dissociations as part of its everyday function. On one day, for instance, the smell of a perfume, a memory of a romantic dinner, and a calculation about next year's foreign travel budget may be closely linked together in conscious awareness. The next day these three elements will have been dissociated, to be recombined later with the same or other elements. Dissociation is an ongoing dynamic process in the normal psyche, subject to modulation and control by numerous other psychic contents.

Because dissociation is a pervasive aspect of normal mental function, one would expect disordered dissociation to be a feature of many, if not all, psychiatric illnesses. Logically, pathological dissociation may arise in two ways: as a failure of normal association, or as abnormal dissociation. A person with a psychogenic anesthesia of the right hand, for instance, cannot learn to associate the visual image of a hot object with a sensation of pain (unless this association has been learned prior to the onset of the anesthesia). This may be viewed as a failure of normal association or as a dissociative disorder in the sensory sphere. Association and dissociation are opposite sides of the same coin.

Dissociation can occur in several forms. Two elements that are normally linked together may be split apart and separated. A common example of this in MPD is the patient's feelings about her father and her memory of incest. The host personality may enter treatment with unconflicted positive feelings for her father and complete amnesia for the incest. Dissociation can occur when normally dissociated elements are held in rigid separation from each other. This would be a failure in the fluidity and reversibility of normal dissociation. Or there may be a dysregulation of dissociation/association such that two psychic elements are abruptly reassociated and then equally as abruptly redissociated. It is possible to imagine and classify numerous permutations of dissociation along such lines.

Psychodynamically, dissociation is the basic defense mechanism that precedes and underlies the other defense mechanisms. For instance, before conflicted psychic material can be projected onto the environment or displaced from one location in the environment to another, it must first be dissociated from its normal psychic connections. If this did not occur, projection would either not work or result in complete emptying of the mind. Likewise, before two psychic elements can be abnormally associated, as in symbolic and paralogical thinking, they must be dissociated from their normal connections. Any psychiatric disorder characterized by abnormal defense mechanisms therefore exhibits abnormal dissociation.

Dissociation can be subdivided into four main quadrants, as illustrated in Figure 5.1. Dissociation can be normal or abnormal, and it can be biologically or psychosocially driven. These distinctions are in practice often impossible to make; this is simply a general scheme for organizing one's thinking. There is an arbitrary tendency in psychiatry to assume that dissociation is by definition a psychologically driven process. This is not true. For example,

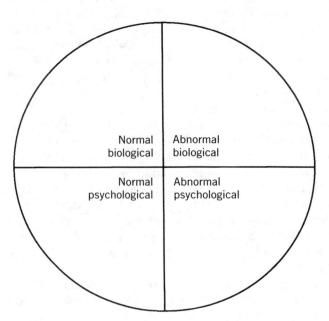

Figure 5.1. The Four Dissociative Quadrants

an alcoholic may have to get drunk to remember where he hid a bottle the last time he was drinking. Sober, he can't remember. In such state-dependent learning, a memory is organically dissociated from the sober consciousness. Organically driven dissociation may be reversible by hypnosis, and psychologically driven dissociation may be reversible by sodium amytal.

There is no sound reason to assume two separate spheres, one of biologically caused and treated dissociation, another of psychological etiology and treatment. However the assumption of two separate spheres is implicit in much clinical thinking about dissociation and is one reason dissociation is limited to identity, memory, and consciousness in DSM-III-R (biological dissociation is not recognized by DSM-III-R). I will suggest an example in each of the four quadrants:

1. *Normal Psychosocial Dissociation.* Daydreaming during a boring lecture

2. *Normal Biological Dissociation.* Forgetting that you got up in the night to go to the bathroom

3. *Abnormal Psychosocial Dissociation.* Amnesia for incest

4. *Abnormal Biological Dissociation.* Amnesia following a concussion

These examples illustrate that dissociation may involve the trivial or the traumatic. Some forms of dissociation would be hard to classify as biological or psychological. For instance, anesthesia for battleground wounds must be based on an ancient evolutionary skill, one built into the central nervous system. On the other hand, the same degree of injury in a civilian car accident is likely to require more morphine because of the different meaning, social context, and consequences of the tissue damage. Psychological and biological causation may coexist. This is probably true in MPD, which draws upon primitive skills and properties of the brain, but in a highly complex social context.

Dissociative disorders are arbitrarily limited to disorders of memory and identity in DSM-III-R. Dissociation can presumably occur throughout the brain, including all regions of the limbic system, cortex, and reticular activating system. MPD is a complex dissociative disorder, in which dissociation occurs in virtually all psychic functions, including sensation, memory, motor function, feeling, and cognition. It makes sense that there should be simpler examples of dissociative disorders limited to one or two psychic functions. DSM-III-R allows only one of these: psychogenic amnesia, which is a simple dissociation of memory.

What about a simple dissociation of motor function? This is a conversion disorder. Or a simple dissociation of enraged behavior? This is an impulse control disorder. A simple dissociation of the ability to have an orgasm? This is a psychosexual dysfunction. Dissociative disorders are scattered throughout DSM-III-R and are grouped with other disorders in an inconsistent fashion (see Chapter 7).

The purpose of this general scheme of dissociation is to lay the ground-work for a comprehensive clinical description of MPD, which includes its relationship with other psychiatric disorders. MPD almost always coexists with other DSM-III-R psychiatric disorders, some of which could be thought of as independent concurrent entities, but many of which are actually further examples of pathological dissociation.

EPIDEMIOLOGY OF MULTIPLE PERSONALITY DISORDER

Very little data exist on the epidemiology of any of the dissociative disorders. Dissociative disorders were not inquired about in any of the major psychiatric epidemiology studies, and no one has done even a small pilot study in the general population. Everything that can be said about the prevalence of dissociative disorders in North America in the 1980s and early 1990s is therefore guesswork. Up until 1980 MPD was thought to be extremely rare, so rare in fact that at the time of publication of *The Three Faces of Eve* (Thigpen & Cleckley, 1957), Eve White was thought to be the only living case. By 1986 Coons (1986c) estimated that 6000 cases had been diagnosed in North America, but many clinicians believe that this is a gross overestimate.

Generally speaking, MPD is still thought to be rare by most clinicians, but it is now acknowledged to be a little more common. My estimate is that MPD has a point prevalence of somewhere between 1 in 50 and 1 in 10,000 persons in urban North America. Where did I get this from?

I live in a city of about 600,000 people. In the last 3 years I have seen about 40 cases of MPD among residents of Winnipeg, plus additional cases from outside the city and outside the province. For round figures, I will use 40 cases seen in 3 years in a catchment area of 600,000 people. If there are no undiagnosed cases of MPD left in Winnipeg, then the prevalence is one in 15,000 people (only a few of these people are integrated, and all 40 would have had active MPD at the same time). If I have seen half the existing cases, the prevalence is one in 7,500. I personally doubt that I have seen even 10 percent of the cases. If I have seen 5 percent or less, the prevalence is greater than 1 in 1,000. From this reasoning I conclude that active classical MPD must be more common than one in 10,000 people in North America.

What about the 1 in 50? This is a figure that I find very hard to believe, but that is what our preliminary data tell us. Lynne Ryan (1988) has completed a Ph.D. thesis under my supervision in which we screened students at the University of Manitoba for dissociative experiences and dissociative disorders. We had students from a variety of faculties and undergraduate years complete the Dissociative Experiences Scale (DES) (Bernstein & Putnam, 1986). The DES is a 28-item self-report instrument that can be used as a screening instrument for dissociative disorders (see Chapter 6). This resulted in 345 completed DES forms. We then interviewed 20 high scorers and 22 low scorers with the Dissociative Disorders Interview Schedule (DDIS) (see Appendix A). These 42 subjects also completed the Million Clinical Multiaxial Inventory (MCMI) (Millon, 1977), and the SCL-90 (Derogatis, Lipman, Rickels, Uhenhuth, & Covi, 1973). The person administering the DDIS was blind to whether subjects were in the high or low DES group. The study is described in more detail in Chapter 7.

The DDIS yielded no dissociative disorder diagnoses in the low group. Among the 20 high subjects, however, 25 different dissociative diagnoses were made. There were 14 subjects who had one or more dissociative disorders and 6 who had no dissociative disorder. There were 8 cases of MPD. It is reasonable and also consistent with DSM-III-R rules, to regard the existence of MPD as an exclusion criterion for other dissociative disorders. On that basis, our data indicate that there were 8 cases of MPD and 6 other dissociative disorders, of which 5 were psychogenic amnesia and 1 was a depersonalization disorder. I should emphasize that in over 150 interviews with nondissociative clinical subjects we have never had a false positive diagnosis of MPD, therefore all 8 cases of MPD in the college students could well be true cases.

The finding, then, is that there is a minimum of 8 cases of MPD per 345 college students. This works out to 2.3 per 100 students. However, the 20 high scorers were drawn from a pool of 40 people who scored above 22.6 on the DES; we had to contact this many people to find 20 who would consent to interview. This means that, if the 20 we interviewed were a representative sample of the 40 who scored above 22.6 on the DES, we would have found 16 cases of MPD if we interviewed all 40. This would make a point prevalence of 4.6 cases per 100 college students. If one adds to that a few cases that score under 22.7 on the DES, the estimate is that about 5 percent of university students have MPD.

This is not necessarily preposterous. A similar percentage of college students might reasonably be expected to suffer from an anxiety disorder at any given time. A similar percentage would meet criteria for alcohol or drug abuse, and 5 percent would be a reasonable percentage of college students to have a major depressive episode, dysthmic disorder, or adjustment disorder with depressed mood at any given time. If our study had focused on anxiety, depression, or substance abuse, no one would be astounded at the findings. At most, critics might complain that 5 percent was too high and that 2 percent was more realistic. Why should MPD be rare? Why shouldn't it be relatively common, roughly as common as panic disorder or substance abuse?

In the 1980 edition of the leading textbook in psychiatry, John Nemiah (1980) estimated the prevalence of obsessive-compulsive disorder to be 0.05 percent, or one person in 2000 in the general population. Subsequent epidemiological study has yielded an actual figure of 2–3 percent (Robins et al., 1984), meaning that obsessive-compulsive disorder is 40 to 60 times as common as thought to be the case 8 years ago. This 40-fold increase in the estimated rate of obsessive-compulsive disorder occurred over 4 years. As far as I am aware, no one attributes the increase to iatrogenesis or false-positive obsessive-compulsive diagnoses.

If only 200 cases of obsessive-compulsive disorder had been reported in the literature, one might conclude that it is an intrinsically rare disorder because of its exotic symptoms. In fact it is common. The same epidemiological error and the same error in reasoning have not yet been corrected for MPD. MPD is no more strange than obsessive-compulsive disorder, and it is about as common.

Clearly, these are very preliminary findings. I personally believe that they will stand up with further research. Dissociative disorders are as common as anxiety disorders and affective disorders. They can be reliably diagnosed and effectively treated, with response rates similar to those of anxiety and affective disorders. But what does it mean to say that MPD is common, whether its prevalence be 1 in 50, or 1 in 500? Many would say that such a prevalence makes the diagnosis meaningless, a mere variant of normal, or little more than a metaphor for ambivalence. Why? No one says that schizophrenia and manic-depressive illness are unreal just because they both affect one person in 100. Why should a similar prevalence invalidate MPD?

No matter how one interprets, refutes, or criticizes the Ryan (1988) study, it is remarkable that so many college students feel as if there is another person inside them who sometimes takes control of their bodies. Even if these people don't have clinical MPD, they clearly have a dissociated experience of self. It is even more remarkable that the DES can perfectly predict which students will not endorse MPD on structured interview and which ones may. Something real, dissociative, and common has been detected in this study, even if it is not MPD.

MPD is not rare in clinical populations, although it is rarely diagnosed. In the course of a year I had 73 inpatient admissions under my care (Ross, 1987). Five of these admissions were for patients of mine already diagnosed as having MPD. When these 5 admissions are excluded, I had 68 admissions in a year, most of whom I had no previous contact with. The patients came to emergency, were admitted by the on-call staff, and were assigned to me depending on the caseloads of the inpatient psychiatrists. In other words this was an unselected group of psychiatric inpatients. Overall my inpatient caseload consisted of 40 percent schizophrenia and affective disorders, was 48 percent male, had an average age of 34.8 years, and had an average length of stay of 20.5 days. It is not unreasonable to assume that this sample of 68 admissions is roughly similar to general adult psychiatric inpatients throughout North America.

Out of the 68 admissions I diagnosed MPD in 3 (4.4 percent). These 3 patients were female and had previous admissions for borderline personality disorder under other psychiatrists, ranging in number from 1 to 13 admissions. All had manifested numerous primary and secondary symptoms of MPD prior to these hospitalizations under other psychiatrists. In terms of treatment response, 1 of these 3 patients was followed at another hospital with unknown outcome for 3 years and has recently been referred back to me with active MPD. The second patient is integrated.

The third patient had 13 previous admissions at another hospital, some of which included use of wrist and ankle restraints for extended periods. She had been abusing drugs and alcohol and had not worked for 6 years prior to admission under me. Two years after admission under me she is integrated, has been out of the hospital for a year, has completed a 3-month nonacademic course, is enrolling in school full-time in several months, does not abuse substances, is on no medication, has no dissociative symptoms, has not been to an emergency department since discharge a year ago, and is an important source of support to nonintegrated MPD patients. This patient was polyfragmented with over 300 named personalities and fragments.

It is because of outcomes like this that it is worth diagnosing MPD and establishing the true epidemiology. Several other reports have suggested that MPD may be common among psychiatric inpatients and outpatients (Bliss & Jeppsen, 1985; Putnam, Loewenstein, Silberman, & Post, 1984), but properly designed multicenter studies are required before these early findings will be accepted.

Concerning the other dissociative disorders, my clinical experience is that psychogenic amnesia is common, and this is supported by the study of college students (Ryan, 1988). Psychogenic fugue appears to be rare, occurring at the rate of frequency previously thought to be true for MPD. I have seen only one case of classical fugue. There are few modern papers on fugue, and it is not discussed much by MPD specialists. Advocates of the iatrogenesis theory of MPD should account for why MPD is being created iatrogenically, while fugue is not, because fugue is equally as dramatic. I do not consider depersonalization disorder to be a true diagnosis, so I don't have an opinion on its epidemiology. If it does occur as a freestanding disorder on occasion, I suspect that it is much less common than MPD and psychogenic amnesia.

In summary, MPD and psychogenic amnesia are common, valid, reliable, and treatable disorders. More research is required before these facts will be generally accepted, however. Thigpen and Cleckley (1984), for instance, have not diagnosed MPD frequently since treating Christine Sizemore (Eve White), despite numerous referrals, and they are highly skeptical about the diagnostic acumen of people like me who do diagnose the disorder on a regular basis.

GENERIC OR NONSPECIFIC ASPECTS OF MULTIPLE PERSONALITY DISORDER

MPD patients rarely come for treatment with obvious or overt multiplicity. It is curious that in the 19th century syphilis was regarded as "the great imitator'' in medicine. It could present with the signs and symptoms of almost any other medical illness. The task of the clinician was to perceive the underlying unity in the phenomenology, in order to make the diagnosis and provide treatment (which became specific and effective in the 20th century). Syphilis is directly linked to sexuality, often to disordered or deviant sexuality.

In the 20th century MPD is the great imitator in psychiatry, and it too is directly linked to sexuality: In our series of 236 cases, 79.2 percent had been sexually abused as children (Ross, Norton, & Wozney, 1989). In adult MPD sexual dysfunction is usually present (Coons & Milstein, 1986), and conflicts about gender identity and sexual orientation are frequent as well. Like syphilis, MPD is often highly treatable and could be prevented by a modification of sexual behavior in society at large, although this is unlikely to happen.

In our 236 cases, 19.1 percent had worked as prostitutes. This means that there is a concrete connection between MPD and syphilis. More importantly, there is probably a large number of acquired immune deficiency syndrome (AIDS)-positive male and female prostitutes with MPD in North America. Many of these people would potentially stop prostituting if they were diagnosed and treated for their MPD. The connection between MPD, childhood sexual abuse, prostitution, sexual promiscuity, and venereal diseases including AIDS, makes MPD a major unrecognized public health problem in North America. If the rate of diagnosis of MPD continues to increase exponentially through the 1990s, these patients will strain the mental health system and compound the effect of AIDS on our health care budget.

The amount of money spent on MPD research in North America is a tiny fraction of 1 percent of the amount spent on AIDS research. This makes sense only if MPD is rare. If it is common, social interventions for control of AIDS must take dissociation into account to be effective. Otherwise, AIDS-positive dissociative individuals will not be in a position to make responsible decisions about their sexual behavior, because they are unaware of much of it. These concerns will seem far-fetched to those who think that MPD is rare.

An additional thought: Education is often proposed as an intervention for teenage pregnancy, drunken driving, smoking, failure of homosexuals to use condoms, and myriad other targets of social change. But education is often surprisingly ineffective. Perhaps this is because the targets of the education are unable to transfer educational information from the state that receives it, to the state that carries out the behavior. This does not mean that everyone who fails to respond to public health education has MPD, but dissociation might play a role in the failure of public health programs.

There are two large published series of MPD cases, ours of 236 and Putnam et al.'s (1986) series of 100. These series were gathered independently, and I had not seen Putnam's questionnaire or data before mailing out my own questionnaire. Putnam's series was first presented in 1983 at the American

Psychiatric Association meeting, and mine was presented at the Fourth Annual International Conference on Multiple Personality/Dissociative States in 1987, so the series are separated in time by 4 years.

Despite the limitations of questionnaire methodology, the two series are consistent in their findings, suggesting that MPD has a stable set of core symptoms throughout North America. Interest has been expressed in translating my questionnaire and replicating the study in Europe, which I would very much like to see done. I would expect some differences in the features of MPD in Europe, but I don't have an intuitive sense of what they might be. In any case, this chapter deals only with contemporary North American MPD.

There are many striking findings in the two series: One of these is the long period of time MPD patients spend in the mental health system from first presentation for symptoms of MPD to diagnosis. In Putnam's series the average length of time was 6.8 years, and in ours 6.7 years. Because our figure was actually 6.74 years, I quote the average for the two series as being 6.8 years. These and other findings from the two series are presented in Table 5.1.

Most MPD patients will come for treatment with a long history of involvement in the mental health system. They will have had a number of previous therapists and an average of 2.7–3.6 previous psychiatric diagnoses. The picture in old charts, discharge summaries, consultation notes, and agency reports will likely be inconsistent and confusing. Table 5.2 shows the percentage of our 236 cases who had received various psychiatric diagnoses prior to diagnosis of their MPD.

Table 5.1. Two Large Series of Multiple Personality Patients

Item	Ross (N = 236)	Putnam (N = 100)
Mean age in years	30.8	35.8
Years in mental health system prior to diagnosis	6.7	6.8
Other psychiatric diagnoses	2.7	3.6
Mean number of personalities	15.7	13.3
Percentage of:		
Males	12.3	8.0
Childhood sexual abuse	79.2	83.0
Childhood physical abuse	74.9	75.0
Suicide attempts	72.0	71.0
Child personality	86.0	85.0
Personality of opposite sex	62.6	53.0
Amnesia between personalities	94.9	98.0

*Note.*From Ross, Norton, and Wozney (1989), *Canadian Journal of Psychiatry, 34*(5), pp. 413–418. Copyright 1989 by the *Canadian Journal of Psychiatry.* Used with permission.

Table 5.2. *Other Diagnoses Given to Multiple Personality Patients*[a]

Diagnosis	Percent
Affective disorder	63.7
Personality disorder	57.4
Anxiety disorder	44.3
Schizophrenia	40.8
Substance abuse	31.4
Adjustment disorder	26.1
Multiple personality disorder	19.7
Somatization disorder	18.8
Eating disorder	16.3
Organic mental disorder	12.8

Note. From Ross, Norton, and Wozney (1989), *Canadian Journal of Psychiatry, 34*(5), pp. 413–418. Copyright 1989 by the *Canadian Journal of Psychiatry*. Used with permission.
[a] $N = 236$.

During my psychiatry training I observed, and was told, that histories like this usually mean undiagnosed borderline personality disorder. I wasn't told that many of these borderlines also have MPD, which is the case. I remember being on call at night as a resident and being asked to see a middle-aged woman with a thick hospital chart. She was accompanied by her very concerned and involved social worker. Previous diagnoses included substance abuse, histrionic personality disorder, adjustment disorder, bipolar affective disorder, schizoaffective disorder, and several other psychiatric ailments.

Previous presenting problems included requests for medication, suicidal ideation, and mood swings, among others. During the interview she displayed classical idealization/devaluation or splitting. She idealized me and devalued other physicians who would not give her diazepam, until she discovered that I wouldn't either, at which point she switched to being hostile and verbally abusive of me. She was not admitted, and I diagnosed borderline personality disorder. I missed the MPD, which was probably there. Even if that particular woman didn't have MPD, she gave the kind of history and had the kind of chart typical of MPD patients. She left the emergency department in her initial positive state, having switched back from hostility and aggression to pleasantness.

As well as long histories of involvement in the mental health system, MPD patients have often been extensively involved with legal, welfare, and other social systems. They may have complicated nonpsychiatric medical histories, even to the extent of having Munchausen's syndrome (Goodwin, 1988). MPD patients experience many symptoms of somatization disorder. In our series, 11.9 percent of patients had been convicted of a crime, and 12.3 percent had been in jail.

Most patients are female and in their 20s or 30s. When Putnam's and our series are added together the female:male ratio is almost exactly 9:1, and the mean age is in the early 30s. This means that the clinician's index of suspicion should be raised whenever he is assessing a young woman with a long inconsistent psychiatric history.

At this point a caution is in order. The two clinical series I have been describing almost certainly represent a highly biased sample of MPD patients. There may be in the general population a large number of people with MPD who are high-functioning, relatively free of overt psychopathology, and no more in need of treatment than most of their peers. They may not have abuse histories and may have evolved a creative and adaptive multiplicity. If these people exist, virtually nothing is known about them. The sample of 336 cases also probably fails to describe the most severely disturbed multiples, who are dead, in jail, or living on skid row.

I think it's safe to say that the 336 cases are reasonably representative of cases currently in treatment in North America, however. In our series we had 28 males, which allowed for statistical comparisons of males and females with MPD. We found no difference in the specific features of MPD and little difference in their general psychopathology (Ross & Norton, 1989a). The differences we did find were those we expected to observe: males were convicted of crimes and had been in jail more often; females received a diagnosis of depression more often, were prescribed antidepressants, benzodiazepines, and hypnotic-sedatives more often, and overdosed more often. These are differences between males and females one would expect to see in the general population. The net conclusion is that the diagnostic clues and features of MPD are basically the same in men and women.

The female:male ratio of MPD in the general population is probably closer to 1:1 than to the 9:1 figure seen in the two large clinical series. The clinical ratio will probably drop over the next decade as MPD is diagnosed in prisons and other settings. Given that women and men are equally hypnotizable and do not appear to differ in dissociative experiences in the general population, the sex ratio of MPD ought to be about the same as the ratio for abuse (somewhere between 1:1 and 9:1). For the moment, though, female sex is a clinical risk factor for MPD.

There is a problem concerning the other psychiatric diagnoses given to these patients before their MPD is diagnosed: Are the other diagnoses errors or correct concurrent diagnoses? The answer: They may be either. Many MPD patients experience classical panic attacks (Fraser & Lapierre, 1986) and clinical depressions, for instance. In 20 MPD subjects we interviewed with the DDIS (Ross, Norton, & Wozney, 1989), 17 (85 percent) had met the DSM-III criteria for major depressive episode at some time in their life. We found that 7 (35 percent) met the criteria for somatization disorder. This compares to 18.8 percent who were reported as having received a past diagnosis of somatization disorder in our series of 236 cases.

Our structured interview findings and clinical experience suggest that the rates of other psychiatric disorders in the series of 236 cases are conservative estimates of the actual rates. This is true for affective disorder, personality disorder, anxiety disorder, substance abuse, somatization disorder, and eating disorder. MPD patients can often meet the DSM-III or DSM-III-R criteria for 10 or more diagnoses simultaneously. Clinicians who have made these diagnoses in the past are therefore not mistaken. Their error is not to have diagnosed the MPD.

Self-destructive behavior is very common in MPD. Of the 236 cases, 72 percent had attempted suicide and 2.1 percent had killed themselves. The most common forms of self-destructive behavior were drug overdose (68 percent), self-inflicted burns or other injuries (56.6 percent), and wrist slashing (49.3 percent). The patients may be amnesic for their suicide attempts or may report that they felt depersonalized while harming themselves: This is because of the copresence of another alter who was responsible for the behavior (copresence can be confirmed in conversation with the alter at some point in treatment). The self-destructive behavior is not usually primarily a "cry for help" or "attention-seeking" and is most often a sign of internal dispute and hostility in the personality system.

We divided our series of 236 cases into those who had attempted suicide ($n = 167$) and those who had not ($n = 48$), in an attempt to identify risk factors for self-destruction (Ross & Norton, 1989b). We found that the parasuicidal group had more physical abuse, sexual abuse, and rape. They also had more severe psychopathology. This was evidenced by higher rates of affective disorder diagnoses, which would be expected. However the parasuicidal group also had a higher frequency of past diagnoses of schizophrenia, substance abuse, adjustment disorder, somatization disorder, and organic mental disorder. They had more frequently been treated with antidepressants, nonbenzodiazepine sedatives, benzodiazepines, antipsychotics, and lithium. They more frequently experienced seven of the Schneiderian first-rank symptoms of schizophrenia as well, including voices arguing, voices commenting, made-impulses, audible thoughts, delusions, made feelings, and thought withdrawal.

We took these findings to be evidence both of the more severe general psychopathology of the parasuicidal group, and of greater diagnostic and therapeutic confusion on the part of clinicians when faced with these patients. The findings strike one optimistic note. Because the self-destructive behavior occurred partly during a 7-year period in which the MPD was not diagnosed, it is possible that earlier diagnosis might reduce the suicide attempts. The parasuicidal group had spent twice as long in the mental health system prior to diagnosis as those who had not harmed themselves. I plan to redistribute the same questionnaire in 10 years to see if this and other characteristics of MPD have changed with greater awareness of the disorder.

An interesting finding (Ross & Norton, 1989b) was a clinical triad of Schneiderian made-impulses, voices in the head, and suicide attempts. This triad should alert the clinician to the possibility of MPD, especially if the made impulse is self-destructive, and the voice is commanding suicide or is hostile and critical. The triad is indicative of the activity of a dangerous persecutor personality and has a differential diagnosis that includes schizophrenia.

The self-destructive MPD patients also differed in the specific features of MPD. They had manifested twice as many personalities by the time of reporting (an average of 18 personalities, compared to an average of 7.4 for nonsuicidal patients). They had more of four out of nine types of alter personality inquired about on the questionnaire. These were protector personality, personality of opposite sex, demon personality, and personality identified as a dead relative. The self-destructive MPD patient tends to have a more complex personality system and a more severe abuse history. The inner logic and meaning of the different personality types will be discussed later in this chapter.

A diagnostic clue for MPD mentioned by Kluft (1985d) is the failure of the patient to respond to adequate trials of conventional treatment. A good place to look for undiagnosed MPD is among treatment nonresponders in drug trials. If these people could be screened out, the active medication response rate might improve while the placebo response rate declined. As well, exclusion of previously unrecognized MPD cases from biological studies in psychiatry would increase the sensitivity of biological markers for mental illness (Ross & Anderson, 1988).

Among our 236 cases (Ross, Norton, & Wozney, 1989), 89.7 percent had received psychotherapy, and 74.6 percent had been admitted to a psychiatry ward at some time. Medications had been extensively prescribed: 60.3 percent had received a benzodiazepine, 59.9 percent a nonbenzodiazepine sedative, 68.9 percent antidepressants, 54.5 percent antipsychotics, 21.9 percent lithium, and 12.1 percent electroconvulsive therapy (ECT). This figure of 12.1 percent of MPD patients having received ECT is disturbing to me. It may also be politically costly to psychiatry, because misdiagnosed and mistreated MPD patients are likely to be among the most vocal members of the antipsychiatry movement. The first test case I am aware of concerning failure to diagnose and treat MPD was reported in the *Psychiatric News* (O'Connor, 1988). The case has not been decided.

In our series of 236 cases (Ross, Norton, & Wozney, 1989), 40.8 percent had a previous diagnosis of schizophrenia. I believe these to be almost all false positive diagnoses of schizophrenia. I have never seen, heard of, or read about a confirmed false positive diagnosis of MPD in a patient who later turned out to have schizophrenia. But I have met an MPD patient who has received between 8 and 10 courses of electroconvulsive therapy for schizophrenia "when the voices get bad." Anyone with a diagnosis of schizophrenia who does not seem to have blunted affect, a thought disorder, or the empty, deteriorated air of chronic schizophrenia should be suspected of having MPD. The differential diagnosis can be complicated when the MPD patient reports that the injections she has been getting every 2 weeks for 10 years "calm my nerves."

I participated in an interrater reliability training session for use of the Brief Psychiatric Rating Scale in a multicenter study of a new medication for schizophrenia. There were three videotaped vignettes of schizophrenics being interviewed by research psychiatrists. One of the patients was a suicidal middle-aged man who heard voices in his head and thought he was going crazy, but who displayed no illogical thinking. He reported blank spells lasting half a day in which he had a vague intimation that he did things very out of character. He was a drinker. Although a possible diagnosis was alcohol hallucinosis, this man probably has MPD. The diagnosis could probably be established in less than half an hour if the right questions were asked.

I mention this vignette to illustrate that well-trained, research-oriented psychiatrists miss cases of MPD on a regular basis. This is not because they are stupid or incompetent. It is because they have been trained to think that MPD is rare and not trained to ask the necessary questions to establish the diagnosis. Of all the diagnostic errors in psychiatry, a false positive diagnosis of schizophrenia is probably the most dangerous and the most difficult to reverse. It can lead to a self-fulfilling prophecy of lifetime medication and deteriorating function in the absence of correct treatment.

I used to think that it is the MPD patient's voices that lead to a false positive diagnosis of schizophrenia, and I stated this in print (Ross & Fraser, 1987). I was wrong, at least according to the available data. In our series of 236 cases we compared cases with and without a past diagnosis of schizophrenia (Ross & Norton, 1988). The cases did not differ in the frequency with which they experienced auditory hallucinations or thought out loud. It is the other Schneiderian first-rank symptoms of schizophrenia that are leading clinicians astray. Schneiderian symptoms are very common in MPD and are another diagnostic clue (see Chapter 7).

In the 236 cases, the average number of Schneiderian symptoms per patient was 4.5. This is similar to an average of 3.4 in a series of 30 MPD patients reported by Kluft (1987b). In our 20 cases assessed by structured interview the average number of Schneiderian symptoms per MPD patient was 6.6. This was not significantly different from the average of 4.4 Schneiderian symptoms endorsed by 20 schizophrenics interviewed in the same study (Ross, Heber, Norton, & Anderson, 1989a). I will discuss Schneiderian symptoms and the relationship between MPD and schizophrenia further in Chapter 7.

The quality of the MPD patient's auditory hallucinations should be touched on here, though. It is a general rule of thumb that MPD voices tend to come from inside the head, whereas schizophrenics experience their voices as coming from outside. The MPD patient's voices may be commanding and persecutory and may order the patient to harm herself or others. Alternatively, they may be soothing and reassuring. The two types of voices may discuss the patient, referring to her in the third person. Usually the MPD patient does not have a thought disorder and describes the voices in a lucid manner. The content of the voices' statements is usually not bizarre and "crazy," though it may be.

It is often possible to engage MPD voices in an indirect conversation. To do this one explains to the patient that one wants to try to talk to the voice. One then asks the voice a question, the voice answers, and the patient reports what the voice said. It may be necessary to identify the voice being addressed in the following way: "I want to ask the voice that Mary says sounds like a little girl a couple of questions. I want the voice to answer, and Mary will tell me what the voice said. First I want to know if the voice that sounds like a little girl can hear me." If the patient answers that the voice said, "Yes," one then proceeds with further questions.

The next major but diagnostically nonspecific feature of MPD is childhood abuse. I say that abuse is diagnostically nonspecific, but the association between MPD and childhood trauma is stronger than for any other psychiatric disorder. As the disorder is conceptualized in Chapter 3, MPD is a form of posttraumatic stress disorder with dissociative features. In my experience, complex MPD with over 15 alter personalities and complicated amnesia barriers is associated with a 100 percent frequency of childhood physical, sexual, and emotional abuse—I have never met or heard about a complex multiple who had not experienced all three. Therefore to say that abuse is diagnostically nonspecific is true only for the whole spectrum of MPD, which may include atraumatic nonclinical cases and cases with mild trauma and simple personality systems.

In our series of 236 cases, 79 percent had a history of childhood sexual abuse, and 74.9 percent a history of childhood physical abuse. Altogether, 88.5 percent had either or both physical and sexual abuse. When we took the missing data and "unknown" responses into account, it was possible that the *absence* of physical or sexual abuse in childhood occurred in as few as 3.6 percent of the male and 4.3 percent of the female cases. This is similar to the 97 percent of Putnam's cases who had experienced physical or sexual abuse, neglect, abandonment, or other major trauma in childhood.

Concerning the possibility that some of these abuse histories are based on fantasy, I am willing to allow an error of a few percentage points for this possibility, but that, in my opinion, is overcompensated for by the patients with real abuse histories who are still amnesic. In other words I consider these to be conservative estimates of the true abuse rates in MPD. This is not to deny that everyone's memory involves distortion, selectivity, and confabulation. There is a difference between distortion and elaboration, and making up years of abuse out of the blue, however.

The final nonspecific diagnostic clue is blank spells. Like childhood abuse, blank spells occur in virtually all cases of complex MPD, but not in all cases across the full spectrum of MPD. Some patients do not remember having had blank spells and are "amnesic for their amnesia," Kluft (1985d, p. 4).

Others may fill the blank spells with confabulation or be so afraid to acknowledge them that they will deny amnesia. Besides voices in the head, the blank spells are often the symptom that most frightens patients. The blank spells and the voices make patients think they are going crazy. I always begin my inquiry about blank spells with open-ended, general questions about "trouble with your memory," and then make my questions more and more detailed and specific.

Classical MPD blank spells have a discrete onset and ending. They may vary from seconds or minutes to hours or days. Some patients have amnesic episodes of years, periods when other alters were continuously in control. Because the blank spells are really specific features of MPD, once the differential diagnosis has been pursued, I will discuss them in more detail. A final common feature of MPD is headache, occuring in 78.7 percent of cases. The headache is often associated with switching, so that headache followed by a blank spell is a strong clue for MPD.

MPD headaches are complicated, like much else about the disorder. They may be migraine, tension, or mixed (Packard & Brown, 1986). I have seen MPD migraine respond to prophylactic ergotamine, and tension headache unaffected by huge amounts of aspirin or acetaminophen. The switching headache may be distinct from the migraine, and the headache may dramatically resolve on integration. Alternatively, one kind of headache may resolve at integration, whereas another persists.

There are a number of nonspecific diagnostic clues for MPD, then, that, when they occur together, make MPD by far the most likely diagnosis. In fact, I would speculate that nearly 100 percent of the patients who present with these features have classical MPD:

1. History of childhood sexual and/or physical abuse
2. Female sex
3. Age 20–40
4. Blank spells
5. Voices in the head or other Schneiderian symptoms
6. DSM-III-R criteria for borderline personality are met or nearly met
7. Previous unsuccessful treatment
8. Self-destructive behavior
9. No thought disorder
10. Headache

This list summarizes the main features of MPD that are not specific for the disorder. Most complex multiples exhibit most of these features, whether male or female. The list, like MPD patients, touches on most of the content of a general textbook of psychiatry.

FEATURES SPECIFIC FOR MULTIPLE PERSONALITY DISORDER

MPD is an unusual disorder in that it can almost be diagnosed from a constellation of nonspecific signs and symptoms. The important word is *almost*. You don't have a case of MPD until you have talked to the alters. There is an exception to this rule when clear, reliable collateral observation of alter personalities is available. Certainly, from a research point of view, no subjects should be included in studies as having MPD if alters have not been observed directly by a reliable professional.

Strictly speaking, the only specific features of MPD are the DSM-III-R criteria. Once these are met, MPD is the only possibility, other than malingering. A group of secondary features that are specific for the disorder, though, need to be inquired about. These are the secondary features of MPD listed in the DDIS (see Appendix A). These features are evidence of the existence, activity, and influence of the alters. They all follow logically from the existence of alter personalities that take control of the body and for which the presenting personality is amnesic.

The patient will describe blank spells, as mentioned earlier. These may have a pattern or may appear to be random. For instance, a patient may state that she always seems to blank out whenever a male approaches her sexually. Later, one can learn about the life history and motivation of the sexually promiscuous personality responsible for these spells. Alternatively, the responsible personality may be assaultive and hostile to men. The triggers for blank spells are the triggers for switching.

Examples of triggers for switching include a color, touch, sexual arousal, the need to perform a specific function, the company of certain people, a specific emotion such as fear or anger, looking in the mirror, hearing a baby cry, a phone call from a past abuser, physical pain, having a bath, and a psychotherapy appointment. Alters hostile to therapy may take control shortly before an appointment and relinquish it after the hour is up. This may result in confused phone calls from the patient inquiring about whether she was at her appointment.

As one can see from the list, the triggers for blank spells are infinite in number and often are related to specific details of the childhood trauma. In behavioral terms, the treatment can be thought of as a desensitization to these triggers, combined with exposure to the avoided internal stimuli, which are memories and feelings. Whether the therapist identifies himself as a behaviorist, a thorough analysis of the triggers for switching is part of the treatment.

When sustained and organized behavior in an alert state is reported by observers during a period for which the patient is amnesic, MPD is really the only possibility. Only those desperate for an organic explanation for everything will cling to epilepsy as a possible diagnosis. A related misdiagnosis is the fiction of murder committed by a somnambulist. In a recent case in Ontario (Sneiderman, 1988), a man got out of bed in the night, drove 23 kilometers (about 14 miles), crossing nine traffic lights, and killed his mother-in-law. He was examined by five psychiatrists and let off on the grounds that he was sleepwalking. This seems to me a more serious clinical and legal error than any defense related to MPD.

The five psychiatric witnesses were reported to have ruled out fabrication because of the consistency of the man's reports of amnesia. One psychiatrist was quoted as saying that the sleepwalker's brain is "effectively in a coma," and another that the killing was "unconscious activity, uncontrolled and unpremeditated" (Sneiderman, 1988, p. 7). Because I have access only to a newspaper editorial by a law professor describing the case, I cannot challenge these five expert witnesses. I will tell a story, though.

I was referred a patient who had been treated for epilepsy with medication for 20 years. She was referred to me for an opinion as to whether her seizures might be panic attacks. The "seizures" consisted of her waking up in the night terrified and disoriented. She spoke only French, did not recognize her family, and tried to run away. She was amnesic for these spells. She also had short memory blanks during the day and would sometimes come to with bruises, lying on the floor or in another room. Epilepsy? Sleepwalking? If she killed someone in this state, would that mean her behavior was unconscious, uncontrolled, and unpremeditated? It would be impossible to know without examining the altered state.

 In this case the "seizure" state was a child alter personality who could easily be called out. She was unaware of the passage of time since the sexual abuse in her childhood, was frightened that the abuse was about to begin again, and spoke rationally with us. The child alter remembered us immediately when called out in a second session. She spoke only French because the woman had not learned English until chronologically older than the age of the alter. The amnesia barrier between the child personality and the adult was easily lowered, and an explanation was given that this was a special kind of dreaming. A more complete explanation would have been given, but the patient declined psychotherapy.

I find it very doubtful that anyone could drive 14 miles and murder his mother-in-law while asleep, in a coma, or sleepwalking. The amnesia barrier should be breached in this case. The most likely diagnosis is MPD. The behavior may recur if the man is not treated, or, alternatively, this may not be the first murder. These are the possible consequences of mental health professionals not learning about MPD. Apparently sleepwalking has been used as a successful defense against homicide in 50 cases in legal history. Subjects diagnosed as suffering from somnambulism (or sleepwalking disorder, as it is called in DSM-III-R) should be carefully screened for dissociative disorders (Kales et al., 1980).

The blank spells may not be complete. Instead they may consist of "fuzzy" periods of partial recall. This represents the memory component of the presence of an alter, just as depersonalization may represent the identity component, and made-impulses the behavior. Such fuzzy periods should not be dismissed as due to drugs or alcohol, even when a patient abuses both. MPD blank spells may be mistaken for alcohol blackouts (see Chapter 7) and may occur *prior* to alcohol ingestion in a carefully taken history. This was the case for the man whose interview by a research psychiatrist I watched on videotape.

In my experience another variation of the blank spell usually occurs on a contracted basis during treatment and rarely on a spontaneous basis prior to diagnosis. This is the "playback" of a memory. During treatment, one may contract with an alter to allow the amnesic host personality to remember the conversation, or a specific memory, or all memories held by the alter. One switches back to the host and waits while she gets the memory back as an internal videotape. Patients may report various ways of recovering memories at later times.

The blank spells have usually occurred over an extended period of time, but there may be periods of years in the past when the alters were quiescent. A variation on this is the patient who reports a period of years during which she experienced frequent depersonalization but no amnesia. During this time the alters were copresent without amnesia. Or the MPD may simply have gone into remission (Kluft, 1985e). A general rule in MPD phenomenology is that all possibilities have happened to some patient somewhere.

The discrete blank spells are often accompanied by a massive, general amnesia for childhood that cannot be attributed to the presence of any one personality. This is a form of amnesia similar to the amnesia for childhood in patients who do not have complex dissociative disorders, but who were abused as children. An individual personality can have amnesia for her own experience as well. I had to hypnotize an alter to recover her adolescent memories of having, in a trance, repeatedly entered her parents' bedroom carrying a knife, in the middle of the night. The sexual abuse by these parents continued into the patient's 20s and, as far as we can determine, included being raped by a man her father hired for the purpose. If this girl had killed her father, would that have been sleepwalking, insanity, or justifiable homicide? Murder or self-defense? This alter had blank spells which coconscious alters also experienced. Sometimes an alter may simply repress a memory in the usual psychodynamic fashion.

One consequence of these complex distortions of memory is that the integrated multiple has trouble understanding what normal forgetting should be like. She may ask whether it is normal not to remember minute details from early childhood or all of last week's daily activities. Other distortions of memory besides amnesia also occur. One of these is hypermnesia, which is unusually complete memory. The MPD patient has an incredible volume of detailed childhood memories stored in her alter personalities. The quantity of memory presents a problem: How much is accurate recall, and how much is elaboration? This is the sort of problem that should be answerable with the techniques of cognitive psychology. Often the details of abreacted abuse are confirmed by sisters who witnessed or were victims of the same abuse (to witness is to be abused). MPD patients provide a rich field for investigation by the cognitive psychologist interested in normal and/or abnormal mental function.

When the patient is fully amnesic for times when other personalities are in control, several associated phenomena occur. These are probably highly culture-bound. For example, I fly to a native community in the north on a regular basis to do consultations. I have seen quite a few native people with classical panic attacks, and these are indistinguishable from those that affect urban whites. But I don't see the same kind of agoraphobia. There are no buses, elevators, traffic lights, huge crowds, or other agoraphobic stimuli that urban dwellers learn to avoid. There is a parallel with MPD.

MPD patients often report that they come out of a blank spell in another location, often a bar, in the company of strangers. They report that strangers claim to know them, or call them by a different name. This couldn't happen to people in an isolated native community in which there are no strangers. Friends tell them about things they have done, which they don't remember. All of this is evidence of the activity of alter personalities in a complex urban society.

The patient may state that objects are frequently missing, including money. Alternatively, objects may be present in her environment that she can't account for. Again, these symptoms could not occur in a culture without bank accounts, stores, and the acquisition of consumer goods. Kluft (1985b) has pointed out that these features are likely to be muted or absent in urban childhood MPD, because children do not have the independence and mobility of adults. Similarly, an MPD patient in a wheelchair in a nursing home would have fewer secondary features than in earlier years.

A diagnostic cue for MPD that is mentioned in the literature is speaking of oneself as "we" or "us." In my experience few patients speak this way about themselves before entering therapy, at least not on a habitual basis. Speaking about oneself in this way can't happen if the presenting personality is unaware of the existence of the other personalities, which is often the case at diagnosis. As in any therapy, patients pick up the jargon of the school of therapy. Patients in a behavioral group for agoraphobia talk about "exposure" and "avoidance." Similarly, MPD patients well into treatment talk about "switching" and "integration," and refer to themselves as "we" or "us." I suspect that talking in the first person plural might be a better cue for malingering than for genuine MPD. At any rate, it is a minor secondary criterion.

Although I am skeptical about sleepwalking as an explanation for the murder in Ontario, MPD patients report histories of sleepwalking more frequently than patients with schizophrenia, panic disorder, or eating disorders (Ross, Heber, Norton, & Anderson, 1989a). This argues for the classification of sleepwalking as a dissociative disorder, one which may occur as a physiologically based developmental lag in otherwise healthy individuals or as a feature of a complex dissociative disorders in traumatized children. The author of *Macbeth* considered sleepwalking to be a symptom of profound psychological disturbance.

MPD patients also enter trance states spontaneously more often than patients from other diagnostic groups. Going into trances may be a good predictor of MPD in children (Goodwin, 1985; Kluft, 1985b). Such persons may look "spaced-out" or as if they are daydreaming. While in this state, the person may be nonspecifically blanked out, or an intense, detailed inner interaction between the alters may be going on.

A third related characteristic of MPD patients is imaginary companions in childhood (Schultz, Braun, & Kluft, 1985). MPD patients have had imaginary playmates in childhood more often than schizophrenics or patients with panic, depression, or eating disorders. Childhood companions are developmentally normal, but in the MPD patient they often persist into late adolescence or even adulthood. Some companions may evolve into alter personalities, some disappear with time, and some persist.

Imaginary companions may be human or nonhuman and exist on a spectrum from conscious fantasy to dissociative hallucination. I recently assessed an 8-year-old boy who has a "creature" inside him and who has been mildly sexually abused. At times he is aware that "the creature" is "just a story, Dr. Ross," but at times it almost seems real to him. The creature never takes executive control but can be engaged in conversation indirectly by my asking it questions, with the boy telling me what the creature has answered. When I ask for the creature to talk directly, the boy talks in a squeaky voice and is obviously "putting it on."

When I asked some particularly disturbing questions of the creature, the boy reported that the creature had immediately taken off in a spaceship and was out of contact. I understand this creature to be a precursor of an alter personality, but at present it is an internal imaginary companion. Some imaginary companions seem to be able to shift back and forth from inside to outside, whereas some are always only one or the other. Monsters under the bed or in the closet are related normal childhood phenomena but may be linked to severe disturbance in the traumatized child.

Changes in handwriting frequently occur in MPD, especially in diaries and journals. The changes may be subtle or obvious. Some child personalities write in large printed letters with childish spelling errors, letter omissions, and letter inversions; sometimes these seem "a bit much" or "put on." Angry alters may leave furious scratchings or angry statements in a script that embodies their rage. Slant may switch from left to right, and occasionally personalities write in reverse script, which has to be read in a mirror. To a naive person, the different scripts look like the handwriting of distinctly different people.

A related diagnostic clue occurs when the alters sign different names or different forms of the presenting personality's name. Some clinicians deliberately ask their patients to keep a diary and scan it for changes in hand-writing. Often the changes in script will be accompanied by references to the author of previous paragraphs as "she." This is even more suggestive of MPD. If the patient is amnesic for part of what is in her diary, and there are passages in the first and third persons, the likelihood of MPD must be close to 100 percent.

Sometimes the changes in handwriting, recognition by strangers, objects missing and present, and other secondary features can result in a degree of paranoid thinking. Not aware that she has MPD, the patient may think that an elaborate trick is being played on her. Less extreme explanations include the patient's hypothesis that she must have a "familiar face" or that there must be a lot of people who look like her. Another aspect of MPD that differentiates the disorder from other diagnostic groups is the experiencing of extrasensory perception (ESP). MPD patients experienced an average of 5.5 different ESP phenomena in the group of 20 subjects we interviewed with the DDIS (Ross, Heber, Norton, & Anderson, 1989a). These phenomena included mental telepathy, telekinesis, clairvoyance, seeing ghosts, poltergeist contacts, and other classical paranormal experiences. I will discuss this in more detail in Chapter 8. In our study of college students (Ryan & Ross, 1988) we found that ESP experiences cluster with diagnostic criteria for MPD, secondary features of MPD, Schneiderian symptoms, trances, borderline personality, and sexual abuse as a dissociative factor.

Extrasensory perception is not "respectable" in mainstream psychiatry, but the experiences will be reported by MPD patients if inquired about, have differential diagnostic utility, and are interesting in their own right. Whether they are hallucinations of a dissociative nature or experiences of reality is not relevant phenomenologically. The first step is to describe and classify the reported experiences, the second to link them to related phenomena, the third to study their etiology, and the fourth to consider the need for treatment. They should not be enshrined as first-rank symptoms of MPD, but are worthy of serious study by mainstream psychiatry.

These are the main clinical features of MPD that are relevant for diagnosis. The rest of the chapter describes the features of the personality system in MPD, which are highly variable. This is the phenomenology that is most important to understand in planning treatment.

FEATURES OF THE PERSONALITY SYSTEM IN MULTIPLE PERSONALITY DISORDER

The specific features of MPD are the DSM-III-R diagnostic criteria and the details of the personality system. Once the diagnosis is made and treatment started, both the general psychopathology of the patient and the features specific for MPD must be taken into account. Both facets of treatment are indispensable for recovery.

The first problem in treating MPD is how to think about the personality system. Some of the resistance to the diagnosis is due to nomenclature. What are we saying when we say that a patient has a number of different personalities inside her? What do we mean by multiple personality disorder? Probably a lot of the resistance would melt away if MPD were renamed dissociated ego state disorder or borderline personality disorder with fragmented personality states (not all MPD patients are borderline).

Part of the problem, I suspect, is that clinicians are not comfortable with the term multiple personality disorder. To them it implies something exotic, rare, and not-quite-respectable. To diagnose MPD is a bit like admitting you believe in UFOs: It calls your professional reputation into question. What, you diagnose MPD? Or, he used to be a transcendental toe massage therapist, now he treats MPD.

The most important thing to understand is that alter personalities are not people. That might seem obvious, but it is a truth one can lose sight of during therapy. Alter personalities are highly stylized enactments of inner conflicts, drives, memories, and feelings. At the same time they are dissociated packets of behavior developed for transaction with the outside world. They are fragmented parts of one person: There is only one person. The patient's conviction that there is more than one person in her is a dissociative delusion and should not be compounded by a *folie à deux* on the part of the therapist.

There is a lot of drama in MPD. This does not invalidate the diagnosis. It is a fact about a serious and treatable form of human suffering. The second thing to remember about the personality system is that it is driven by pain. Despite the color, complexity, and fascinating theater of the personalities, their wars, love affairs, and internal friendships, they are not people, and they exist to help the patient cope with pain. There is no need to be wistful or regretful about the disappearance of an alter on integration, because that is a step towards healing the pain. The patient may mourn the loss of the alter, but the therapist shouldn't.

MPD is an elaborate pretending. The patient *pretends* that she is more than one person, in a very convincing manner. She actually believes it herself. Some MPD patients enter therapy aware that the different parts are all parts of one person, but most don't. Someone asked me at a workshop once if integration results in a loss of richness and creativity for the patient. Isn't the patient more interesting as a multiple than as a unified person with problems? My answer was to say that the personality system is driven by pain. MPD isn't pleasant entertainment. Part of the problem with the iatrogenesis and social-role explanations (which are really dismissals) of MPD is that they imply that patient and therapist are having an interesting tea party together, making up mutually satisfying illusions. Therapy is hard work for both parties.

The alters, put another way, are *devices*. Like any theater, the personality system is based on certain conventions and structural rules. Part of the therapy is mapping and dismantling these, replacing them with normal, happier, and more functional rules and structure. The patient is acting *as if* she is more than one person, but she isn't. This is different from Hollywood acting because the patient is so absorbed in the different roles that she believes in their reality. When I discussed this point with a drama professor, he said that acting students who become too absorbed in their roles, become poorer actors. MPD is not acting in the sense that Hollywood actors perform a role.

It only takes a moment's reflection on the film industry to realize this. An actor has to do many takes, jump from scene to scene numerous times in a day, start and stop acting instantaneously, make minute adjustments in posture, tone, and facial expression, and carry out numerous other highly controlled actions. If the actor really felt like a cowboy or science fiction hero, he wouldn't be motivated to act and would probably be perplexed as to where he was and what was going on. The actor who became too absorbed in his role would be disoriented and dysfunctional, like the MPD personality who comes out of a blank spell in a bar, surrounded by strangers.

The personality system can be organized in any one of an infinite number of ways, or it can lack structure and definition. Some MPD patients have highly structured systems with rigid amnesia barriers, defined switching sequences, sharply demarcated switches, and clear-cut identities for the main alters. Others present more of a shifting sea of partial presences and uncertain identities. It is important for the beginning diagnostician or therapist to realize this. Otherwise the lack of clarity in the system may be attributed to inexperience on the part of the therapist.

What are the most common types of personality in MPD? In our series of MPD cases (Ross, Norton, & Wozney, 1989) we inquired about nine types of alter personality, which were reported to be present in the frequencies shown in Table 5.3.

As one can see from the table, four personality types occur in about 85 percent of cases. The child personality usually holds the abuse memories and carries out the most intense abreactions. The personality of different age may be adolescent, adult, or older than the chronological age of the patient. The protector usually forms a treatment alliance quite readily, whereas the persecutor personality is hostile and uncooperative. Most persecutor personalities are in fact helpers who are using self-destructive strategies. Details concerning alliance formation, contracting with the different personality types, and understanding their function will be discussed in Chapter 11.

In the series of 236 cases, the average number of personalities identified at the time of reporting was 15.7, compared to 13.3 in Putnam's series of 100 cases. This means that the basic personality types often have more than one representative: There may be a large group of children, for instance, several helpers and persecutors, and personalities with ages spanning three or more decades. The more exotic personality types occur less often but are not rare.

Table 5.3. Frequency of Different Types of Alter Personalities[a]

	Mean (S.D.)	Median
Personalities identified at diagnosis	3.5 (6.2)	2.00
Personalities manifested by time of reporting	15.7 (22.1)	8.00

Kind of personality	Cases in Which Alter Occurs (%)
Child	86.0
Different age	84.5
Protector	84.0
Persecutor	84.0
Opposite sex	62.6
Demon	28.6
Another living person	28.1
Different race	21.1
Dead relative	20.6

Note. From Ross, Norton, and Wozney (1989), *Canadian Journal of Psychiatry.* Copyright 1989 by the *Canadian Journal of Psychiatry, 34*(5), pp. 413–418. Used with permission.
[a]N = 236.

Child Personalities

Child personalities are often frightened and untrusting. This characteristic is compounded when the child fears abuse by the therapist. Spontaneous abreactions by "hysterical," terrified child alters are a diagnostic clue for MPD, and can be difficult to manage. The child may cower in the corner, curl up in a fetal position, suck her thumb, call for Mommy, or simply ask, "Who are you?" Some child alters, on the other hand, are poised, confident, and friendly young adults, despite a claimed age of 7 or 8 years. Others are spontaneous, childish, and delightful. Like alter personalities in general, the children can display the full range of human traits and characteristics. Some children may be relatively full-bodied and capable of a number of different emotions, attitudes, and behaviors. Others may represent a single memory and mood and never express anything else.

Another characteristic of child alters that applies to MPD personalities in general is that they may evolve during therapy. Initially hostile and abusive, a child alter may later become a good friend of the therapist, and an ally in treatment.

Each child personality may be an independent entity, or there may be a suborganization of the children. There may be two or three leaders among the children who control the release of memories, abreactions, and amnesia barriers between different children, and between the children and the presenting personality. These leaders may be cooperative or hostile to each other. Because there are innumerable permutations on all these themes, there is no need to attempt an exhaustive list of examples.

The children, again like alter personalities in general, may exhibit differential aging. One child personality may have been 10 years old when created at chronological age 6 and still be 10 years old at chronological age 33. Another may have been a child alter when created at chronological age 6 but may have grown up at the same rate as the presenting personality (who, as far as I am aware, always ages at the normal, real-world rate). Most of the time, personalities do not age, or age at the chronological rate. In my experience it is unusual for an alter to age faster or slower than chronological time, except during hypnotic rituals.

Other possibilities are an alter who ages at the chronological rate for a while, goes into inner hibernation without aging, then reemerges to begin aging again. Sometimes personalities may stop aging at a certain point, whereas others do not have a specified age or are unsure of their age. Some personalities, usually not children, claim to be ageless, from another dimension, or thousands of years old. Usually, personalities created in childhood that were older than the chronological age of the patient are protectors or carry out a specific function, such as prostitution, physical fighting, schoolwork, or housecleaning. By the time the patient is 35, these alters may still be 10 or 12, but usually seem mature for their age.

It is clear that many child alters do not actually function at their alleged age level cognitively. They often understand long words, abstract concepts, and moral dilemmas in a way that would be rare for a normal child of that age. Others do seem to have a childish way of thinking. The cognitive function of alter personalities of different ages cries out for systematic study by developmental psychologists. I expect that there will be mixed findings along the lines I have just described.

A scientific demonstration that child alters do not function cognitively at their alleged age would not invalidate MPD. It would only prove that they are not real children. However such evidence would challenge the overliteral psychoanalytic view, according to which alters represent a concrete fixation of libido, accompanied by a fixation in cognitive development. In my view child alters are not packets of *childness* retained in a surrounding sea of adult psyche. They are stylized packets of adult psyche. That may seem like a hairsplitting differentiation, but it has implications for therapy and for legal accountability and responsibility.

Freud wrote about alters as being in delirium. This was an error. Child alters may appear delirious because of their frightened behavior and belief that the present and the past are the same thing. The vast majority of child alters have a clear sensorium, are alert, and are cognitively intact. Treating the undiagnosed MPD patient with antipsychotic medication to control the spontaneous emergence of child alters is a serious clinical mistake.

The emergence of a child alter is usually easy to recognize. There is often a change in posture. The toes may be pointed in, head may be bowed, sideways glances may occur, and the hand movements may become tense, fidgety, or childish in some other way. The facial expression can vary widely, depending on the affective state of the personality, but usually has a childish quality. The speech may be lisping, quiet, monosyllabic, whining, or lilting, or it may display any of countless qualities. Childish vocabulary, immature handwriting, and grammatical errors or primitive grammar may be used. The topic of conversation as well as the content will often be immature.

One of the most intense aspects of MPD treatment is helping the children through their abreactions. During an abreaction the child alter may beg the parent to stop, scream, cry, express intense sadness, or clutch her lower abdomen. There may be hand movements to push the father out of her vagina or motor movements accompanying the abreaction of an oral rape. The genuineness and intensity of the abreactions is one of the most convincing features of MPD. For the therapist it is almost like having to watch a real rape, then talk with the victim afterward.

Occasionally one will meet alters alleged to be less than 1 year old. These alters are usually claimed to hold specific abuse memories. For me this is stretching things too far and emphasizes the fact that alters are enactments rather than literal realities. I have been told about intrauterine alters created because of the trauma of a parental argument; these alters are alleged to have understood who the parents were and that fighting is a bad thing, and even to have worried about what life was going to be like after delivery. Patients may be able to find therapists willing to treat such intrauterine dissociation, but not in our clinic.

One shouldn't believe that child alters are really children, anymore than one believes that demon alters are really demons or that the patient is really possessed by her dead mother when an alter claims to be the mother. On the other hand, one works within the patient's beliefs and world view to a varying extent.

Protector Personalities

Protectors come in many forms and protect in many ways. They are usually older than 10 and often are the same age or a bit older than the chronological age. Protectors tend to overlap with another major class of personalities, which is the observers. This makes sense because in order to protect one must be aware. However some observers make very few or no interventions, or they communicate their fuller awareness to protectors who carry out the action.

The protectors that form prior to age 10 are often adolescents; these alters may age at the chronological rate or not age at all. Many adolescent protectors fall into one of two types: relatively calm and mature, or else volatile and aggressive. The calmer ones tend to help by providing a broader range of more mature coping strategies, by controlling switching, by avoiding situations, and by taking steps to stay out of trouble.

The aggressive adolescent protectors can cause serious trouble during the early phases of therapy. They may be responsible for behavior that meets the adolescent criteria for antisocial personality disorder in DSM-III (to have this diagnosis one must have exhibited a number of behaviors from a checklist prior to age 15). These alters may destroy property in the office or assault the therapist. Often their aggression is turned inward as well as outward, so that they are simultaneously protectors and persecutors. They may attempt to kill the host personality in a form of misguided euthanasia, reasoning that she has suffered too much in life. They often abuse substances.

Another group of protectors is the avoiders, who have a narrow range of skills. Sometimes these alters are children. For instance I have met a child personality who was skilled at hiding from her sexually abusive father. This was all she did. When she hid on the ward once, it took quite a while to find her. Other personalities may be skilled at out-of-body experience, trance states, inner reverie, or other techniques for surviving trauma. Some protectors have no feelings, are physically numb or anaesthetic, or come out to block physical abuse by agitated, rocking behavior. These alters embody one or a few skills from the huge repertoire that any abused child has potentially available.

Adult protectors tend to be more cognitive and rational in their strategies. They may be excellent consultants to the therapist. Sometimes they control switching and are in charge of who is out at any given time. They in effect match the alter to the task or situation. Adult protectors tend to be less amnesic than child personalities, but this is only a general rule. I have had a patient whose protector had the ability to pull all the personalities in, leaving the patient in a catatonic stupor. Such stupor is not uncommon in MPD, must represent a primitive survival mechanism, and is not usually as exquisitely well controlled as in this particular patient.

The observer function of the protector can be split off into a pure observer personality, often called the observer. Observers tend to be rarified, abstract, bloodless entities with little or no feeling. This may be a cultural artifact of popular concepts of artificial intelligence. Perhaps in other cultures the observers act more like mystical entities charged with spirit power. In North American clinical MPD the observers often have no direct stake in the outcome of treatment. They simply record and retain memories.

Some North American observers do have mystical pretensions. These entities are called inner self-helpers or centers (Comstock, 1987). Some therapists feel that centers have transcendental abilities including healing and psychic powers. Inner self-helpers are both observers and protectors, although some only help by knowing, not by doing. The observers seem to represent a dissociation of memory, but they usually have only a part of the full phenomenon of memory available to them. They have only the information component, not the feeling, the physiological arousal, or the sensory intensity of the memory. These aspects are parceled out to the children and others.

There is probably a connection between inner self-helpers and the hidden observer (Hilgard, 1984). The hidden observer is an experimental artifact of hypnosis experiments rediscovered by Hilgard and rigorously studied by him (see Chapter 1). In Hilgard's opinion, which is scientifically cautious, it is a mistake to extrapolate too quickly from his experiments to the phenomonology of MPD. However common sense dictates that there must be a connection.

Persecutor Personalities

The persecutors are often responsible for suicide attempts, "accidents," self-destructive and self-defeating behavior, and outwardly directed aggression. They may be antisocial in other ways, including theft, prostitution, and substance abuse. They are often adolescent but may claim to be demons, dead relatives, or other figures. They often present as tough, uncaring, and scornful, but this is usually just a front for an unhappy, lonely, rejected self-identity. One persecutor I worked with was abusing the other personalities because she felt rejected, because she felt they did not appreciate the hard work she did holding all the anger, and because they were always blaming her for everything that went wrong.

Persecutors carry out their hostile attacks on the other personalities by psychic and physical means. They may burn the host personality with cigarettes, cut her wrists, force her to take pills, or jump in front of a truck, then go back inside just before impact, leaving the host to experience the pain. Their motives can vary widely as discussed below in the cognitive analysis of MPD. It is quite common for persecutors to have a delusion of separateness and to believe that they can harm another personality's body without their own body being affected.

Persecutors also cause internal trouble in a variety of ways. They can make another personality hallucinate, feel frightened or anxious, or be disoriented. They may torture the children by tricking them into believing that the boyfriend is really the abusive father or by locking them up in a room or closet in the patient's inner world. They can cause muscle twitches, pains, and any other symptom imaginable. They may bully or threaten the alters verbally and may chase them through internal landscapes. One patient had a persecutor alter who was her dead, sexually abusive father. Fortunately there was a tree the children could go to when he was attempting to abuse them. The dead father alter could not come near the tree, so the child personalities were safe there.

Often the persecutor's motivation is actually positive. As mentioned above, euthanasia is a common rationale for suicide attempts. Persecutors are probably responsible for more positive borderline criteria and more Schneiderian symptoms than any other personality type. That does not make them easy to work with.

Personalities of Opposite Sex

These are common. In our series of 236 cases, 62.6 percent had a personality of opposite sex. Because most patients are female, most opposite-sex alters are male; however, males and females do not differ in the frequencies of any of the nine types of personalities we inquired about (Ross & Norton, 1989a). This means that roughly two thirds of MPD patients, regardless of sex, have a personality of the opposite gender. There can be more than one per patient.

In my experience male alters in female MPD patients usually serve one of two main functions: They act as tough protectors, or embody the homosexual drive of the patient. The latter occurs when a female patient has a heterosexual male alter who is sexually attracted to women. Biologically this alter's sexual activity is lesbian, but psychologically it is heterosexual. The inverse can occur when a male alter in a female patient is homosexual: This alter is sexually attracted to males, and his behavior is biologically heterosexual. In this case the alter functions as a denial of the patient's heterosexual drive; the homosexual male alter in a female body may allow good heterosexual function and pleasure to occur in dissociation from the patient's morbid fear of intimacy with men. This is an example of the paradoxical cost–benefit of MPD, because the person gets but yet never gets satisfying sexual relations with men.

Female MPD patients often have alters who exhibit a form of secondary lesbianism. They can't have normal sexual relations with men because of the past sexual abuse by father, uncle, brother, husband, and father's friends. This is perfectly understandable. The alters are therefore sexually attracted to women, but primarily as a way of getting physical intimacy, affection, and warmth. For these alters, sex is a secondary issue in their sexual activity. This is analogous to male heterosexual rape, in which the real issues are power, anger, and revenge, not sex. If the patient has a problem with a self-identity of homosexual, she may create a male alter to carry out the sexual relations with women, while remaining heterosexual herself. A same-sex homosexual alter is an alternate solution to the same problem (pun intended).

These solutions to problems of sexuality raise a central puzzle about MPD. The creation of a heterosexual opposite-gender alter or a homosexual same-gender alter solves the problem of how to have sex with persons of the same gender, while maintaining a heterosexual self-identity. Why is an amnesia barrier required, then? The amnesia seems to be a second level of security in the system. But once the amnesia is in place, why have an alter personality? Why not have pure amnesia for heterosexual activity, without MPD? The alter could be a second backup system in case the amnesia barrier fails, I suppose. The unsolved problem is why it is necessary to create separate identities, rather than to have a single self with complex amnesia?

The same combination of possibilities exists in males, but I have only spoken with a small number of female alters in males. One of them wanted a sex change operation, which was the reason I was consulted on the case (I recommended strongly against surgical reassignment). In female patients the tough protector is based on a cultural stereotype of the macho male. These alters present as two-dimensional caricatures of the tough male. The model for the caricature is itself a caricature: the television male cop, trucker, or cowboy. Opposite-sex alters in women tend to come from Marlboro country. I wouldn't be surprised if opposite-sex alters in females smoke more than opposite-sex alters in males. When the tough protector gets a bit too tough, the patient can end up getting convicted for assault, or worse.

The repertoire of alter personalities is highly culture-bound, as is the repertoire of therapeutic techniques. In our culture therapists are at particular risk for one form of bad therapy: relating to alters as if they are real people. This may be more likely to occur in North America than in some other cultures because North Americans are accustomed to two-dimensional caricatures on television, in movies, and in popular books. North Americans, such as movie critics, often do not seem to be able to tell the difference between an implausible Hollywood caricature of a human being and a fully created dramatic character.

Therapists will have trouble telling the difference between alter personalities and people if they respond to a television caricature with intense personal feeling. A person who can't differentiate television characters from real people, is more likely to grant MPD personalities independent legal and therapeutic status. This doesn't mean that therapists need to be highbrows: They just need to be able to tell the difference between narrow caricature and full humanity. Another way of making the same point is to remark that the characters on leading television programs are actually fragment personalities, not real people. They have the restricted range, simplicity, and shallowness of MPD fragments.

All of this is a matter of degree, not of dichotomous absolutes, of the "real" versus "Hollywood." These days, there can be more Hollywood in reality than in Hollywood. It is an everyday occurrence in urban North America, for instance, to observe gestures and facial expressions and to hear phrases learned from television. The influence of advertising, television, and movies on the phenomenology of MPD is a subject unto itself, one worthy of serious study. The control sample in such a study would represent the phenomenology of everyday life.

The tough male alter in a female patient will often exhibit posture, facial expressions, and tone of voice that are less than convincing portrayals of maleness. This is partly because the women have had such disturbed models of maleness in their lives. Some will accept the existence of male alters without a fuss; others will think it deviant, perverted, or "weird" to have men inside them. On the other hand, it can be comforting to have a personal internal bodyguard around in case of emergency.

Other male alters can be playful children. One female patient had a boy personality who had not taken executive control since childhood, until I called him out. He was created in childhood when the patient lived on a farm. Each summer itinerant farm laborers were hired on her parents' farm and on neighboring farms. Each spring the patient and her sister had their hair cut short, were dressed in overalls, and were called by boys' names for the summer. This was a deliberate strategy on the part of the nonabusive parents to prevent the girls from being sexually assaulted by farmhands. It worked quite well, in the sense that the patient was only assaulted once. However she was a highly dissociative child and created an alter with the name the parents used in the summers. The patient did not require further active MPD treatment at the time of consultation, and the boy was content to rest quietly inside indefinitely. There was a girl alter who was the victim of the assault.

Opposite-sex alters are easily sensationalized but are actually just dramatic embodiments of drives, conflicts, and transactional strategies. The patient has one gender, although conflict about sexuality and sexual orientation is universal in complex MPD. Opposite-sex alters can be integrated with no disturbing effect on primary gender identity.

Less Common Types of Alter Personality

It is my sense, though there are no data, that the more exotic types of alter personality are more culture-bound. I would expect child, protector, and persecutor alters to occur in most cultures. If opposite-sex alters are linked to childhood sexual abuse, their prevalence in other cultures would depend on whether sexual abuse is an etiological factor for MPD in a given society. There is no shortage of demon alters in our culture, because these occur in 28.6 percent of cases. One might have thought that the demon alter would be a transcultural phenomenon from our point of view.

The demon alter, I believe, occurs in our culture because of a fundamental dissociation at the root of Christian religion, a dissociation of religious consciousness from the physical body (see Chapter 8). In Christian culture the spontaneous, pagan sources of physical vitality, including but not limited to sexuality, are dissociated and disavowed. They are then identified as evil and undesirable, needing to be fought and contained. It is culturally normal for MPD patients to create demon alters to embody irreverent, hostile, and "bad" aspects of themselves, and for the "badness" to be linked to sexuality.

This hypothesis is supported by the evolution of demon alters into unhappy secular persecutors, then therapeutic allies, prior to integration. However, one should be clear that it is scientifically impossible to prove demon alters are or are not demons. There is no diagnostic test or trick to determine whether a patient is possessed by a demon or has an alter personality identified as a demon.

If a demon writhes and contorts in response to holy water or oil, this does not prove it is a demon, because a psychological entity will play its role correctly and exhibit the same writhings. ESP powers do not prove possession, because there is no proof that ESP is demonic. Likewise, if an entity disappears permanently following exorcism, this does not prove that it was a discarnate entity: The exorcism may simply have functioned as a culturally sanctioned integration ritual for a purely psychological entity. The inverse is true: Successful secular integration does not prove that a true demon was not present, because an integration ritual may work as an exorcism. This is the same logic that limits diagnostic inferences in psychiatry based on response to medication (Ross, 1986a).

There is an important corollary of the above logic: A belief in demons is neither more nor less scientific than a belief that they don't exist. Treating entities as demons and exorcising them is not less scientific or respectable than MPD psychotherapy or than prescribing medication for schizophrenia. Scientifically, the main concern is empirical: Which approach works better for which patients in which cultures? Until there is a scientific way of identifying demons, a pragmatic treatment–outcome approach is the only correct one. If demons don't exist, no other approach will ever be possible, because one can't prove that something doesn't exist by failing to detect it.

The Bible describes a test for demons, which is to expel them into a nonhuman experimental animal, one assumed not to be prone to suggestion. So far no one has received a grant for such studies.

The evolution of demonic alters over time, as described in Chapter 1, implies that they are culturally determined psychological entities. Demons I have met are secular in nature, except that they claim to be demons. They are angry and irreverent, but in a chip-on-the-shoulder kind of way. Sometimes the therapist will be infected with a demonic chill transmitted by the patient, but I have integrated such chilling entities and found them to be frightened children who are putting on a tough act. So far I have not observed any phenomena that require a theological explanation, although I am ideologically prepared to make such an explanation if it appears to be the best one in a given case.

I believe that the frequency of demon alters varies with geographical area in North America, with more demons in the "Bible belts." MPD patients as individuals are probably more likely to have demon alters if they belong to a fundamentalist church, irrespective of geographical location.

Related to demons are numerous types of discarnate entities. These may be beings from other universes, spirit guides, dead people from long ago, astral entities, psychic intrusions, or relatively undifferentiated beings of uncertain origin. It is important not to react to these with naive enthusiasm. Also, it is not necessary to devise a complex classificatory scheme for alters, because this won't guide treatment decisions in any meaningful way and would simply be a catalog of the types of mythical being known in folklore and mythology.

In all cases, one must try to understand the function of the alter and its overall role in the personality system, then negotiate toward integration.

Personalities of different race are similarly culture-bound. I suspect we have far fewer black alters in white bodies in Canada than in the United States.

Personalities identified as another living person or as a dead relative are slightly different from the other less common personality types. They usually represent a clear-cut identification with a person close to the patient. If the identification is with an abuser, the alter will be a persecutor. If it is with a nurturing grandmother, it will be a protector. One patient had an alter that was a seagull named Jonathan. Not surprisingly, this alter soared in freedom above the patient's troubles, much like Jonathan Livingston Seagull.

Our team has exorcised one dead grandmother from a patient. She had been an abuser. Prior to exorcism, we did extensive "couple therapy" with the patient and her dead grandmother, resolving longstanding issues between them. The grandmother was formally helped to leave the body and ascend to heaven, and she reported while departing that she was going into a bright light and could see people waiting for her there. She also reported a great sense of peace while departing. The exorcism was conducted jointly by a member of our clinic and a chaplain. In this case the dead grandmother knew only things about her life that the patient knew and couldn't remember anything about her life the patient didn't know, despite intact cognitive function.

In another case I judged the commotion caused by a dead mother at home, which consisted of throwing her daughter off the couch and making hostile statements through her mouth, to be yet another histrionic attempt to stay in therapy indefinitely. I declined to do anything about the problem, which resolved spontaneously and has remained so for 3 years of once-a-year follow-up. I mention these cases here, rather than in the chapters on treatment, because of their bearing on conceptualization of paranormal alters in MPD. Papers by Allison (1985), Bowman, Coons, Jones, and Oldstrom, (1987), Kenny (1981), and Krippner (1986), provide further commentary on this aspect of MPD. Adam Crabtree's (1985) book is the major source.

Structure of the Personality System

The personality system is often highly complex and detailed in structure. At other times, as mentioned previously, it may be fluid and amorphous. It is necessary to know the structure of the system in order to proceed in therapy. Some therapists like to diagram the system on paper, others make a few notes, still others rely more on memory. In one way or another, all therapists make a map of the system.

The simplest system is dual personality, represented by two circles with a name, age, and sex for each circle. Dual personality is uncommon in modern clinical series. Simple MPD systems with less than 10 alters are usually relatively easy to map. I am only going to describe a few of the principles of organization of MPD systems, because general principles are not clarified by exhaustive examples.

One type of system is a simple linear one. In such a patient the alters, usually not too many in number, can be represented as integers on a line. In one patient with this kind of system, the primary personality was on the left, and the other alters were arranged in chronological order by date of creation, from left to right. In order to switch from one personality to another, the patient had to switch internally from alter to alter, then stop at the one she wanted to be in executive control. It was not possible to skip alters, and there was a built-in stop instruction at each end of the register, which the patient didn't have to think about. This kind of system is analogous to the way enzymes read up and down DNA.

In another patient, the system was represented by a large number of circles of varying size. This patient drew diagrams on a regular basis to chart her progress in therapy. The sizes of the circles represented the power of the alters. The relative positions represented coalitions and hostilities in the system, with friendly alters close to each other. Both size and position were constantly shifting. Sometimes circles would go inside other circles, representing temporary protection. Circles disappeared on integration of alters. Sometimes the patient put alters into internal hibernation, which she called "putting them in darkness" or "covering them with darkness": Alters in this condition were darkened circles, rather than empty white ones. One personality was represented as a triangle because its name was The Black Triangle. In this personality system there were no defined switching sequences.

The system of another polyfragmented woman consisted of over 300 entities with names and ages, the vast majority of whom we never met. Her personality system was organized into "teams," with a leader for each team. The leaders were adolescent or adult alters, whereas team members tended to be children and fragments. Each team loosely represented a certain affective theme or conflict. As well, this patient had two centers who did not belong to any team: The centers dictated the membership of each team to the patient, who recorded them on a large chart. This may be similar to the experience of William Blake, who said that he was only the secretary, while the real authors of his works were independent beings in eternity.

Another case exhibited two interesting phenomena: layering, and rigid switching sequences. In the initial layer of alters encountered, there was the host, a child, and two adolescents. Actually this set of alters existed in two sublayers, as shown in Figure 5.2. The presenting personality (who was also the host) was amnesic for periods when the other personalities were in executive control, whereas the other three alters were continuously conscious no matter who was out and could talk with each other. Technically, there was one-way amnesia between the presenting and alter personalities.

If our team members wanted to talk to the second adolescent alter, Donna, we had to first talk to Janice, the child alter. One could only gain direct access to Donna by switching from Janice to Donna. If Susan, the other adolescent, was out, and one tried to call out Donna, nothing would happen.

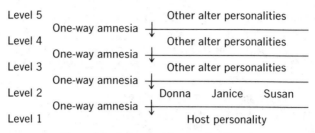

Figure 5.2. A Layered Personality System

Likewise, if we were finished talking to Donna, the only personality we could call out next was Janice. If we tried to call out Susan or the host personality, nothing would happen. Switches between the other three personalities could be done in any sequence. We had trouble remembering this patient's switching rules, but the patient always corrected us when we tried to do a switch that was not permitted by the rules of the system.

Later in therapy, we discovered that Donna had not disclosed her complete function and knowledge in the complex personality system that unfolded. She was the only alter on her level who was coconscious with alters on higher levels. She communicated with these other alters in secret, without Susan and Janice suspecting anything. The complete personality system in this patient was organized in successive levels, with a one-way amnesia barrier between each level and the one immediately below it. This meant that, with the exception of Donna, who functioned as a kind of back door in the system, in computer terminology, all personalities were coconscious with alters on their own and lower levels and amnesic for alters on higher levels. We worked through a number of such levels before the patient was integrated.

Layering is a complex strategy for hiding memories and behavior, and its function is usually not difficult to understand. Kluft (1986b, 1988e) has written most of the published work about layering. The switching rules that some patients exhibit are puzzling. In the patient just described, there was no obvious reason why Donna had to be isolated as she was, in terms of switching, although this seemed to be related to her being coconscious with higher levels. Alters one level above Donna were not coconscious of her awareness of alters two levels up and higher but could listen in on her conversations with Susan and Janice. The switching rules, in my experience, have the impersonal, apsychological quality of laws of physics. They are just structural rules of that universe.

When there is a change in the structure of the system, either through integration of alters, or removal of amnesia barriers, the system exhibits a discontinuous change. Old rules are gone and new ones appear. As long as the system is stable in any given configuration, though, the rules are immutable, and errors in switching sequences do not occur. These phenomena occur only in highly structured systems. The apsychodynamic quality of the switching rules, to my mind, is strong evidence in favor of the reality of MPD. The rules cannot be explained by Freudian psychology, suggestion, or role theory. Someone building a model of MPD *de novo,* with no prior knowledge of the disorder, would be highly unlikely to construct such switching rules. Where do they come from, then? Where do alter personalities come from, and who or what creates them?

This is the fundamental aspect of MPD that prompts transcendental hypotheses. There seems to be a higher organizing principle or intelligence responsible for the rules and structure of the system. In philosophy this line of reasoning is known as the argument from design. Ancient philosophers argued for the existence of God by saying that a complex creation like the universe must have a Creator, because so much structure, detail, and aesthetic unity could not arise blindly. The argument from design is regarded as a weak one. Despite that, these patients evoke a sense of higher intelligence in the therapist (as they did in Freud, see Chapter 1). This is no less so when the patient has an average IQ.

The sense of a higher intelligence at work, evoked by the complexity of the system and the vast quantity of information it organizes, stores, and accesses, provides the MPD therapist common ground with molecular biology. Working with the MPD patient, one has a sense of being on the ground floor of the mind, looking directly at its basic structure, much as one must when studying DNA. In the case of DNA, one studies the basic driving force of soma rather than psyche, the two being complementary realities. Studying the apsychological laws and structure of the mind is the route by which psychiatry could become a science like physics. Modern psychological psychiatry is too personal. Concurrently, modern physics is handicapped by its inability to bring mind into its equations. The basic laws of mind are part of the fundamental equations of the universe. A complete mathematical model of the universe must take mind into account, because mind is one of the basic psychophysical properties of matter.

Such thoughts do not occur in the mind of every MPD therapist. They occur in mine but are not stimulated in me by patients with panic disorder and would be incongruous in a book on panic disorder (Walker, Norton, & Ross, in press). Whether one agrees with the thoughts, there is something about the reality of MPD that stimulates them (a potential diagnostic test for MPD). This quality of MPD, I think, is directly connected to the paranormal experiences multiples report more frequently than patients with other disorders (see Chapter 8).

Another patient had a personality system that was organized into two "communities." There were four families in each community, with an amnesia barrier between communities. Each family had six personalities. In each family, the six personalities were organized in pairs called "sisters." In addition, there was an overseer, or Observer personality, for each system. The chart of the system prepared by the patient had a horizontal line in the middle of the page: There were four vertical columns above and below the line, with the paired sisters in them. The Observers were positioned above the families in each community. Each family also had a "head," who was an adult responsible for management of that family.

In this system, all the antisocial, acting-out personalities were in one community, whereas the other community prided itself on "never causing any trouble." Although there were no switching rules in this system, the sequence of integrations was highly structured. Sisters were integrated first; the products of the integration of sisters were then fused so that an entire family was integrated; families were then integrated until there was only one personality plus the Observer in each community; the Observers were then integrated with their respective personalities; finally the two personalities representing each community were integrated. The patient would not allow fusions to be attempted out of sequence and said they would not work.

This system exhibited a common feature, which is protector alters assigned to care for specific children. This took the form of adults paired with sister children or adults caring for a pair of child sisters. The major personalities in the system had clearly defined functions and, although there were no defined switching sequences we had to follow, there was a specific set of "escalations" the alters could go through. One personality was very critical, verbally hostile, and litigious. When she became too angry or threatened, she would switch to a personality called the Destroyer (a common name for persecutor alters). The Destroyer was self-abusive and assaultive. If the situation was particularly serious, the patient would then switch to Flash, who was extremely assaultive.

There was an interesting derivation for Flash's name. Names often make sense: alters can be named by function (the Observer, the Friend, the Evil One); named after a specific person such as the patient's mother; be given a descriptive name that matches one of their qualities (Universe, Spirit, Dream); have the same name as the host; have variants of the host's name (Beth, Bessie, Liz); have no name; be given temporary names in therapy in order to keep track of everyone (I called one hostile alter Number Six, because she had no name and was the sixth alter identified); be called by the host's name with a prefix (Little Susan, Angry Susan); have the legal middle name as their only Christian name; or other variants. Names may have been deliberately chosen by the alter herself or other alters or may just be "there," with no personality seeming to be responsible for choosing the name. Alters can also have more than one name.

Flash was so-called because in early childhood the patient was forced by her father to act in child pornography films. A child alter did the acting. A woman watching the filming used to say, "Is a baby, is a baby," repeatedly, in reference to the patient. This became slurred into Isabella, which became the child alter's name. Flash would come out when Isabella was too disturbed by the events being filmed to tolerate any further executive control. This usually occurred when flashbulbs were going off or when the bright overhead lights were on, hence the name Flash. During the early and mid phases of preintegration treatment, the other personalities would see a blinding flash of internal white light and feel a surge of rage before Flash came out and were amnesic for Flash's activities. The patient also had a pleasant adult alter with the same name as the woman who said "Is a baby."

Mapping the system is a way of keeping track of the conflicts and issues that must be dealt with in therapy. It is not an end in itself, although it is very interesting. Other attributes of the personalities can be recorded on the map as well, such as height, hair color, and hobbies. Personalities can identify themselves as being prettier than other alters, as being older, younger, of different race, or as varying in any imaginable way. Another form of mapping is to record the cognitive errors made by each of the personalities, and in the system generally. This is what I will focus on in the next section.

THE COGNITIVE MAP OF MULTIPLE PERSONALITY DISORDER

The cognitive aspects of MPD have not been written about as much as the psychodynamic, although Kluft (1988e) acknowledges their importance and says that he focuses on them during treatment. Only one paper to date (Caddy, 1985) has presented a case example of a treatment claimed to be specifically cognitive-behavioral in conceptualization. I believe that most or all therapists deal with MPD cognitive errors, however. Consequently Pam Gahan and I decided to define what we thought was the generic cognitive map of MPD (Ross & Gahan, 1988a). Like the map of the system's structure, the cognitive map provides information for treatment planning.

In research on cognitive therapy (Beck, Rush, Shaw, & Emery, 1979; Beck & Emery, 1985; Emery, Hollon, & Bedrosian, 1981; Freeman, 1983), there are several problems that have been tackled with preliminary success. One is to show that certain cognitive errors are specific for certain diagnoses. This is important because a lack of specificity would undermine the rationale for cognitive therapy. The efficacy of cognitive therapy for nonpsychotic unipolar depression has been conclusively demonstrated. The efficacy of cognitive interventions in MPD has never been studied beyond the anecdotal clinical level, however. This needs to be done.

Another problem in cognitive therapy research is to demonstrate that specific cognitive errors are present when the disorder is active and absent when it is in remission. If this cannot be shown, the rationale for the therapy is called into question, even if its efficacy has been demonstrated. Cognitive therapists also hope that correcting the cognitive errors specific for the active phase of an illness improves prognosis by reducing relapse.

MPD offers an excellent opportunity to demonstrate all of these properties of pathological cognitive errors. In MPD, as in depression, there is a set of assumptions or guiding beliefs that appear to underlie and drive the disorder, cognitively speaking. These core beliefs arise from the patient's abusive childhood: Usually the person has been brainwashed into believing them by the abusive parents. The core beliefs, like much about MPD, are often paradoxical in nature and related to childhood double binds (MPD patients frequently put their therapists into double binds, a phenomenon one could call double-binding transference).

Illustrative examples of two of these paradoxes are

1. I am responsible for the abuse.
   I am not responsible for my own behavior.
2. I deserve punishment.
   Why is this happening to me?

MPD patients make these statements directly to their therapists. The cognitions are not something one infers about the patient, they are observed verbal behaviors, to use jargon. Often there is a child alter created to be the victim of the abuse who feels responsible for it. The two examples just given are generic cognitive errors made by MPD and non-MPD abuse victims.

The core beliefs of the MPD patient may be stated as erroneous syllogisms or logical propositions. The propositions, as in depression and like double binds, often begin with a moral injunction that illustrates one of the classical cognitive errors such as all-or-nothing thinking, personalization, or over-generalization. An example is

1. Good children should love their parents.
2. I don't love my parents.
3. I am bad.
4. I deserve to be punished.

This syllogism is not specific for MPD and would be encountered in nondissociative traumatized children, adult children of alcoholics, and other groups.

We (Ross & Gahan, 1988a) have identified eight core assumptions in MPD, from which a number of cognitive errors are derived. Some of these are specific for MPD. The core beliefs are

1. Different parts of the self are separate selves.
2. The victim is responsible for the abuse.
3. It is wrong to show anger (or frustration, defiance, a critical attitude . . .).
4. The past is present.
5. The primary personality can't handle the memories.
6. I love my parents but she hates them.

7. The primary personality must be punished.
8. I can't trust myself or others.

Particular cognitive errors are derived from these core assumptions. This is the general structure of cognitive maps: There is a set of hierarchically superior assumptions and below them, in a diagram, a set of derivative cognitions. This is a bit like the axioms and corollaries in Euclidean geometry.

I will now review each of the core assumptions, and the cognitions derived from them in detail.

1. *Different parts of the self are separate selves.*
   a. We have different bodies.
   b. I could kill (or slash, burn, force to overdose) her and be unaffected myself.
   c. Her behavior is not my responsibility.
   d. The abuse never happened to me.
   e. They're not my parents.

These cognitions are statements made by patients and are evident concretely in their behavior. It is common for persecutor alters to have an entrenched delusion of separateness, without which their self-destructive behavior does not make sense. This feature of MPD differentiates it from psychosis, despite the presence of delusions: In MPD the delusions are rationally derived from erroneous assumptions and are treatable with psychotherapy. The patient can be argued out of her delusions, although this takes substantial effort. The incorrect assumptions made by the patient are comprehensible in the context of her abuse history and strike the therapist as mistaken rather than crazy.

I will fill in the map in more detail in Chapter 11. Here I am presenting the map's abstract outlines, so to speak.

2. *The victim is responsible for the abuse.*
   a. I must be bad otherwise it wouldn't have happened.
   b. If I had been perfect, it wouldn't have happened.
   c. I deserve to be punished for being angry.
   d. If I were perfect, I would not get angry.
   e. I never feel angry—she is the angry one.
   f. She deserves to be punished for allowing the abuse to happen.
   g. She deserves to be punished for showing anger.

This set of cognitions is linked to both self-destructive and obsessive-compulsive behavior. One alter tries to be perfect, while a persecutor attempts suicide. The phenomenology of MPD can be understood as a dissociative strategy for simultaneously maintaining incompatible cognitions. The crazy-making double binds of childhood are manifested isomorphically in the adult MPD patient's cognitions and in the structure and function of her personality system (Spiegel, 1986b). Creating other people inside is an excellent short-term solution to the abused child's problems.

3. *It is wrong to show anger (or frustration, defiance, a critical attitude . . .).*
   a. When I showed anger, I was abused.
   b. If I never show anger, I will not be abused.
   c. I deserve to be punished for being angry.
   d. If I were perfect, I would not get angry.
   e. I never feel angry—she is the angry one.
   f. She deserves to be punished for allowing the abuse to happen.
   g. She deserves to be punished for showing anger.

Many of the cognitive errors in MPD, such as Statement 3(a) are accurate observations about the realities of an abusive childhood. They become pathological cognitive errors when they are overgeneralized and extended into adulthood, in linkage with the other cognitive errors I am describing. The third core assumption, from a cognitive perspective, results in the presenting personality entering treatment as a nervous, depleted, depressive person, with a restricted range of affect. This is frequently the case. The intense and conflicting welter of conscious feelings in the patient are stored in the children and the persecutors and can be readily accessed.

4. *The past is present.*
   a. I am 8 years old.
   b. The abuse is still happening.
   c. I am scared.
   d. The doctor is going to abuse me now.
   e. No one will protect me.

These thoughts are linked directly with abreaction, in which one observes the direct behavioral and affective consequences of the core assumption. Rather than viewing spontaneous abreaction by child alters as ridiculous, hysterical, or attention-seeking behavior, one should attempt to map the associated intrapsychic structure. Suppression of the abreactions by behavioral and pharmacological means is not good medicine, if that is all that is done.

5. *The primary personality can't handle the memories.*
   a. We have to keep the memories.
   b. You can't tell her about us.
   c. If she has to remember, we will make her crazy.

   d. If she remembers, she won't like us.
   e. The abuse never happened.
   f. They must be sick to think those things happened.
   g. My parents are not like that.
   h. She is weak—I am strong.

This set of cognitions drives the amnesia barriers. Often the patient will enter therapy with an idealized picture of the parents and amnesia for the abuse. The amnesia is maladaptive in adulthood because, like other aspects of the disorder, it makes balanced, intimate adult relationships difficult: only a part of the person is available to become engaged in any relationship. Besides that, negotiating one's way through the day with missing chunks of time is logistically complicated and difficult to orchestrate smoothly. The alters in the background will often go to great lengths to maintain the amnesia and to resist the removal of amnesia during treatment. This is why a treatment alliance must be formed with as many alters as possible.

6. *I love my parents but she hates them.*
   a. She is the bad one.
   b. You have to get rid of her.
   c. Nobody could ever be friends with her (or like her).
   d. She wants to hurt me.

One can see by this point that the core assumptions and their cognitions are interlinked and overlap in a complex network. Sometimes the core assumptions appear to be derived from each other or from their cognitions. For instance the sixth core assumption cannot be made prior to the first, which is the assumption that leads directly to the diagnostc criteria for MPD. It is not necessary to make endless decisions about which assumptions and cognitions are primary, and which secondary, because one is dealing with a field, a complex region of positive and negative feedback loops and other regulatory mechanisms.

The different cognitions will be stated sequentially by different alters, with accompanying affect, facial expression, and gesture. The linkages between the different thoughts, their ownership by different alters, and their function in the system, can only be mapped over a series of sessions. Like everything else about the treatment of MPD, cognitive mapping takes time.

7. *The primary personality must be punished.*
   a. It's her fault the abuse happened.
   b. She deserves all the bad things that happen to her.
   c. Everything bad that happens to her happens because she is bad.
   d. She has suffered enough—she would be better off if I killed her.
   e. I can punish her and be unaffected myself.
   f. I (the punishing alter) was never abused.

g. Nobody would ever want to be close to me (persecutor alter).

h. I am unlovable.

These cognitions are usually and mostly held by persecutor personalities. They provide good examples of attributional error. An attributional error occurs when one attributes the cause of an event to the wrong thing. Misattributions are influenced by culture, social situation, the individual's cognitive set, and life experience (a short list). The most pervasive misattribution in MPD, which is not diagnostically specific, is blaming oneself, or another part of oneself, for the abuse. These attributional errors are associated with entrenchment in an ongoing role as martyr/abuse victim. They probably occur more frequently among residents of shelters for battered wives, for instance, than in the general population.

8. *I can't trust myself or others.*
   a. People have always abused me.
   b. I always end up choosing abusive relationships.
   c. I want to be abused.
   d. My parents were never consistent with me.
   e. Previous doctors wouldn't believe me (concerning abuse history and diagnosis).
   f. Whenever people get close to me, they leave.
   g. She trusted before and she got hurt.
   h. We won't let anyone get close to her.
   i. I can't trust her—she gets herself in situations she can't handle.

The eighth set of cognitions is more likely to be stated by protectors than persecutors. It also tends to be more pervasively endorsed, in its various permutations, by the entire personality system, which is highly defended against adult intimacy. The issue of trust is a major one throughout therapy: The trustworthiness of the therapist may be tested beyond its breaking point.

This description of MPD cognition is an outline of the rich, human detail encountered in therapy. The basic outline of the phenomenology of MPD, which has a cognitive aspect, is a necessary, but not a sufficient tool for MPD therapy to be successful. Generous amounts of Rodgerian and other principles are also required.

An important thing for diagnosticians to remember is that MPD patients display great variability in their lives, symptoms, cognitions, and personality systems. There are always exceptions, and there is no way that "it has to be." The phenomenology of MPD attests to the ingenuity and creativity of the human imagination. Another truth is also important to bear in mind: There are patterns and consistency in the phenomenology that make valid and reliable diagnosis possible. MPD has a stable set of core symptoms throughout North America. The instruments for making the diagnosis detect this consistent pattern and are the subject of the next chapter.

CHAPTER SIX

Structured Interview and Self-Report Measures of Dissociation

A number of instruments have been developed for the measurement of dissociation, of which three have been published (Bernstein & Putnam, 1986; Ross, Heber, Norton, & Anderson, 1989a; Sanders, 1986) and two have been presented at conferences (Dyck & Gillette, 1987; Steinberg, 1987; Steinberg, Howland, & Cicchetti, 1986). Compared to the instruments for assessing depression or anxiety, this is a very modest list, one which provides a measure of the level of maturity of the field.

I am going to focus on two of these instruments, the Dissociative Experiences Scale (DES) (Bernstein & Putnam, 1986; Ross, Norton, & Anderson, 1988) and the Dissociative Disorders Interview Schedule (DDIS) (Ross, Heber, Norton, & Anderson, 1989a). Although more replication studies using these instruments are required, together they provide an effective, easy-to-use, practical standardized assessment battery for the clinician.

There are a number of reasons why good self-report and structured interview questionnaires are required in psychiatry. First, it is essential to establish the reliability of a given psychiatric diagnosis: One must show that different people in different places are talking about the same disorder when they present findings on multiple personality disorder (MPD). More important, the diagnosis must have validity, which can be subdivided into a number of different types: Making the diagnosis must mean something in terms of differentiating the condition from other disorders. There should be a difference in prognosis, treatment, function, or some other meaningful aspect of the patient's life, otherwise the reliable diagnosis is clinically useless.

The DDIS and the DES can be used in a number of ways. In a forensic case, they would strengthen the assessment of an MPD patient. They can be used in screening clinical and nonclinical populations for MPD. They can be an aid to diagnosis, and they provide detailed systematic information for clinical use. In our clinic we give the DES and the DDIS to every person referred to us in consultation in Step 1 of the assessment, then make a general clinical assessment in Step 2.

DISSOCIATIVE INSTRUMENTS BESIDES THE DDIS AND DES

The Perceptual Alteration Scale (PAS) developed by Sanders (1986) is not yet ready for widespread clinical use. It has a number of weaknesses that make it of less use than the DES. The PAS is a self-report scale derived from the Minnesota Multiphasic Personality Inventory (MMPI). It has good initial reliability but has not been tested in a clinical population, thus its utility in screening for MPD or documenting the symptoms of patients with dissociative disorders has not been demonstrated.

Many of the MMPI questions in the PAS do not seem to have much to do with dissociation and the questions in the different factors do not always seem to be related to the name of the factor. For instance, "I feel that my mind is divided" (Sanders, 1986, p. 98) is an item in the factor called Modification of Affect but doesn't refer to affect as such. "Even when I have missed several meals I find that I am not hungry" (p. 99) is an item in a factor called Modification of Cognition but doesn't seem to have anything in particular to do with dissociation, unless it represents a dissociation of hunger, which would be an example of dissociation of sensation, not cognition.

Hopefully more work on the PAS will demonstrate that it has some clinical utility. Because many of the questions are not examples of clinical dissociation, as usually described, the PAS may yield surprising or unexpected insights into dissociative psychopathology, by showing a relationship between classical dissociative symptoms and other phenomena.

Some work has been done with the Rorschach (Lovitt & Lefkof, 1985), but it does not yet have the status of a specific diagnostic tool. Coons and Fine (1988) have demonstrated that the MMPI can be used effectively for screening for MPD. Their study involved diagnostically blind raters of the MMPI and showed that the MMPI hit rate for MPD is as good or better than for many other disorders. Further work may yield a more specific MPD profile, but differentiation of MPD from borderline personality disorder is problematic.

The Dyck-Gillette Dissociative Symptom Inventory (DSI) (Dyck & Gillette, 1987) looks very promising and may prove to be as useful as the DES. It is a self-report instrument with five subscales that is clinically derived and that has been tested in clinical populations. It has excellent reliability and validity and can discriminate individuals with dissociative disorders from those without. Because the DSI is a 70-item instrument, it gathers more data than the DES, so it may provide more information for use in treatment. It may also prove to be a more useful treatment outcome measure than the DES. Probably the two scales will prove to be complementary. I am not dealing with the DSI further only because it has not been published and no replication studies have been conducted.

The Structured Clinical Interview for DSM-III-R-Dissociative Disorders (SCID-D) (Steinberg, 1987) is a structured interview for making dissociative disorder diagnoses. It is specifically designed to fill a gap in the SCID, the Structured Clinical Interview for DSM-III, which is used to make many DSM-III diagnoses, but does not inquire about dissociative disorders. None of the standard psychiatric structured interviews make dissociative diagnoses. The SCID-D has not been published, so complete assessment of it is not yet possible. It makes a very detailed and comprehensive assessment of dissociation and has good initial reliability and validity.

The SCID-D could be incorporated into the SCID if accepted, which would give it a great advantage in the comprehensive assessment of psychopathology. The drawback of this is that the administration of most standardized structured psychiatric interviews is time consuming, tiring, and not straightforward to learn. Consequently they are not used in clinical practice. This will be the limitation of the SCID-D, which requires considerable training to administer and clinical judgments on the part of the interviewer. The SCID-D and the DDIS should be administered to a large group of MPD patients to establish that the two instruments are consistent in their diagnoses, despite their different structure. Time will tell what the relative uses of the two instruments in the field turn out to be. Like the DES and DSI, the two instruments will probably prove to be complementary rather than competitive.

THE DISSOCIATIVE EXPERIENCES SCALE

The DES is a 28-item self-report instrument that can be completed in 10 minutes or so. It is easy to understand, and the questions are framed in a normative way that does not stigmatize the respondent for positive responses. A typical DES question is "Some people have the experience of finding new things among their belongings that they do not remember buying. Mark the line to show what percentage of the time this happens to you."

(Bernstein & Putnam, 1986, p. 733). The respondent then slashes the line, which is anchored at 0 percent on the left and 100 percent on the right, to show how often he or she has this experience. The DES contains a variety of dissociative experiences, many of which are normal experiences.

The DES has very good validity and reliability. The scale is derived from extensive clinical experience with and understanding of MPD. In the initial studies during its development the DES discriminated MPD from other diagnostic groups and controls at high levels of significance (Bernstein & Putnam, 1986).

It is important to emphasize that the DES is not a diagnostic instrument. It is a screening instrument. High scores on the DES do not prove that a person has a dissociative disorder, they only suggest that clinical assessment for dissociation is warranted. This is how we report DES scores in our consults, as within or not within the range for MPD, and as consistent or not consistent with the clinical and DDIS diagnosis of MPD. Sometimes MPD subjects can have low scores, so a low score does not rule out MPD.

The DES is the only dissociative instrument that has been subjected to a replication study (Ross, Norton, & Anderson, 1988). We found that it discriminates MPD from other groups very well, with scores similar to those Putnam found. Although more work is needed to confirm the findings to date, most adults with DES scores over 30 have MPD or posttraumatic stress disorder.

In another study (Ryan, 1988; Ryan & Ross, 1988), we administered the DES to 345 college students with a median age of 24 years and 168 adolescents aged 12 through 14 years. We found that DES scores decline with age on a curve similar to the decline in hypnotizability scores with age (Berg & Melin, 1975; Gordon, 1972; Morgan & Hilgard, 1973; Spiegel & Spiegel, 1978). The 12-year-olds had a median score of 20.2, the 14-year-olds a median score of 14.8, and the college students a median of 7.9. The difference between 12- and 14-year-olds was significant at $p = .00001$.

Hypnotizability and dissociation are closely linked, so it is a confirmation of the DES that it appears to yield scores that vary with age the way hypnotizability does. The DES may be a good screening instrument in subjects as young as 12.

In the same study, we wanted to find out if the DES is a useful screening instrument in a nonclinical population. We therefore administered the DDIS, the SCL-90 (Derogatis, Lipman, Rickels, Vhenhuth, & Covi, 1973), and the Millon Clinical Multiaxial Inventory (MCMI) (Millon, 1977) to 20 high scorers and 22 low scorers on the DES, among the college students.

The high and low DES scorers differed on each subitem and the overall score of the SCL-90. They differed on 15 of 20 scales on the MCMI, and they differed drastically on the DDIS. There were 25 different dissociative disorder diagnoses made in the high group, for instance, and none in the low. This means that the DES can predict who will not and who may have a dissociative disorder with very high accuracy. In addition, the DES taps into the dissociative component of general psychopathology, as evidenced by the SCL-90 and MCMI findings. This is consistent with everything in the clinical literature about dissociative disorders (see Chapter 5). The DES is not just picking out a dissociative anomaly which is unconnected to anything else.

Because of these properties of the DES, it is the best self-report instrument for measuring dissociation available to date. The complete scale is available in the original paper (Bernstein & Putnam, 1986), except that Question 25 is inadvertently missing. Question 25 reads, "Some people find evidence that they have done things that they do not remember doing. Mark the line to show what percentage of the time this happens to you."

THE DISSOCIATIVE DISORDERS INTERVIEW SCHEDULE

The DDIS (Ross, Heber, Norton, & Anderson, 1989a) is reproduced in Appendix A along with its consent form and scoring key. The DDIS was developed because every area of psychiatry requires a valid and reliable structured interview, both for research and clinical purposes. Also, findings from structured interviews are essential for publication and for establishment of the dissociative disorders as a legitimate area of study. Although more replication work is required, the DDIS has shown that MPD is a valid and reliable diagnosis, that it has a consistent set of features, and that it is worthy of serious attention. We have also gathered preliminary evidence on the epidemiology showing that both dissociative experiences and dissociative disorders are common.

The DDIS can be administered to a normal subject without an abuse history in less than half an hour. Interviews with complex multiples can usually be completed in 30 to 45 minutes. The overall interrater reliability of the DDIS is 0.76, which is as good as the standard psychiatric structured interviews. The interrater reliability for the diagnosis of MPD is 0.78. The DDIS has been used in a number of published studies (Ross & Anderson, 1988; Ross, Heber, Anderson, et al., 1989; Ross, Heber, Norton, & Anderson, 1989a, 1989b); which means that it has passed peer-review in a number of different journals.

The DDIS has good clinical validity. It has a sensitivity of 90 percent and a specificity of 100 percent for the diagnosis of MPD. In over 150 clinical interviews conducted to date, we have not yet had a false positive diagnosis of MPD on the DDIS. The criterion for assessing for false positives is the clinical diagnosis of the patient. In other words, no one has been diagnosed as MPD by the DDIS who we did not feel actually had MPD.

I have studies in the planning stage in which a large number of high-DES scorers will be interviewed with the DDIS. Subjects will have two interviews, given by untrained interviewers. These studies will demonstrate that the DDIS can be used reliabily by untrained interviewers. I also plan to do blind clinical validation interviews on subjects positive for dissociative disorders to further demonstrate the validity of the instrument. I will use age and sex-matched high-DES scorers without dissociative disorders as controls.

Finally, I am in the process of gathering multicenter data on over 100 cases of MPD using the DDIS. These data are predicted to demonstrate that the phenomenology of MPD is consistent at different centers. The DDIS is easily used in clinical practice and has been shown to be useful in a variety of published studies. Further work will confirm this, we hope.

CONSISTENCY IN THE FEATURES OF MULTIPLE PERSONALITY DISORDER USING THE DES AND DDIS

We have done several studies that, cross-linked together, indicate the validity, reliability, and consistency of MPD and its associated features. First there is the study of 236 cases reported to us by 203 different clinicians throughout North America (Ross, Norton, & Wozney, 1989). The findings in this study are remarkably consistent with those of Putnam et al. (1986). Putnam's study was done 4 years earlier using a different instrument, which we had not seen. The findings in these two studies are consistent with other unpublished studies and the clinical literature. For instance, Gray and Braun (1986) reported that 126 MPD patients averaged 6.9 years in the mental health system prior to diagnosis, whereas ours averaged 6.7 years and Putnam's 6.8 years.

Second there is the ability of the DES to discriminate MPD from other disorders in two independent studies. Our multiples in Winnipeg resemble those in Putnam's study on self-report. In our replication of the DES, we reported DES scores for 17 of our MPD patients (Ross, Norton, & Anderson, 1988). All of these 17 patients participated in the development of the DDIS, in which we interviewed a total of 20 multiples. We therefore know that their diagnoses are valid and reliable.

The 17 MPD subjects who did the DES are also part of a group of 22 MPD cases to be reported in a third study. This group of 22 MPD subjects included the 20 subjects in the original DDIS study (we have been adding subjects to our data base as we go along). In the third study we compared three groups of MPD subjects using the same questionnaire. The first two groups came from the series of 236 cases. These were 48 cases reported by 44 American psychiatrists specializing in MPD, and 44 cases reported by 40 Canadian general psychiatrists. The third group was our 22 subjects.

We found no differences between our MPD cases and those of the American and Canadian psychiatrists, in the diagnositic criteria for MPD or number of personalities. There was, as well, little variation in general psychopathology between the three groups. This told us that our MPD cases were similar to those being seen by Canadian general psychiatrists and American specialists in MPD.

Our MPD cases are similar to those elsewhere in North America by self-report (DES scores) and on a questionnaire filled in by the clinician. When our multicenter DDIS data have been analyzed, we will then have a set of cross-linked studies demonstrating consistency in the features of MPD throughout North America. Once all these data have been published, there will be little scientific basis for saying that MPD is not a legitimate diagnosis. It is important that this be established because of the vast improvement in prognosis that results from correct diagnosis and specific treatment for many MPD patients, who number in the tens if not hundreds of thousands in North America.

In summary, we now have instruments available that are practical, easy-to-use, clinical tools for the diagnosis of MPD. They are useful in research, for screening purposes, in confirming clinical diagnoses, in forensic work, and as data for third-party insurers. What we lack in the field is good treatment outcome measures as well as measures to demonstrate that a specific MPD therapy is being delivered. In order to demonstrate the efficacy of a treatment, it is necessary to show that a reliable and valid disorder is being treated; that a specific treatment is being delivered; that the treatment is cost-effective and can be taught to others; and that both a general and a specific beneficial response occur. These are challenges that will face the field in the 1990s.

CHAPTER SEVEN

Multiple Personality Disorder and Other Psychiatric Disorders

The main purpose of this book is to describe the clinical features and treatment of multiple personality disorder (MPD) in detail. The second is to place MPD in the context of general psychiatry. MPD would be interesting if it were a rare curiosity, but it is much more than that. Freud's early patients were dissociative and included cases of classical MPD (see Chapter 1). When Freud repudiated the seduction theory, he abandoned dissociation and led psychiatry astray for much of the 20th century.

For instance, it is mainly dissociative patients who exhibit symbolic conversions, sexually driven somatization, and other defenses Freud overgeneralized to all forms of psychiatric illness. Freud discovered the mechanisms, repudiated the etiology—which, simplified, is trauma plus autohypnosis, as stated by Breuer (Breuer & Freud, 1895/1986, p. 329)—then devised a set of secondary metapsychological "explanations" for his patients' problems. Because the dissociative disorders were held to be atraumatic in later Freudian theory, other atraumatic disorders could be "explained" by the same theory. Eventually everything from jokes to religion was "explained" by the theory.

Freud's massive overgeneralization concealed the true nature of the disorders from which his theory originally developed. His therapeutics were also overgeneralized, until psychoanalysis became the treatment for everything from schizophrenia to panic disorder to stuttering.

The dissociative disorders became an obscure corner of psychiatry, rare and irrelevant to the mainstream. The decline of Freudian psychoanalysis, in power and political influence, is occurring at the same time as the rediscovery of dissociation. This is not a historical accident. There is a mutually exclusive relationship between the repudiation of the seduction theory and the understanding of trauma-driven dissociation. As psychoanalysis wanes in North American psychiatry, the dissociative disorders wax. That is one reason why there is so much resistance to the diagnosis of MPD: MPD will make much of Freudian theory irrelevant, just as mainstream psychiatry made MPD irrelevant for many decades. Put another way, modified, corrected psychoanalysis is what I and others in the field practice.

For much of the 20th century, Freudian and biological psychiatry maintained a mutually advantageous homeostasis, despite their mutual disdain. In classical psychiatry, the biologists, who were virtually all reductionists, claimed certain phenomena as their own. One example of this is Schneiderian first-rank symptoms of schizophrenia (Kluft, 1987b; Ross & Norton, 1988), which are widely held to be symptoms of biologically driven major mental illness, though not unique to schizophrenia. MPD patients have numerous Schneiderian symptoms that can be cured with psychotherapy. MPD patients demonstrate that much supposedly hardcore biological symptomatology is trauma-driven and treatable with psychotherapy. At the same time, MPD necessitates major revisions in Freudian theory and therapy.

This is why MPD is an important diagnosis. Study of dissociative disorders will lead to changes in the official diagnostic scheme, in our understanding of phenomenology, and in therapeutics. Many of these changes will probably not occur until DSM-V and DSM-VI. The challenge to specialists in dissociation is to generate data, tools, and therapies that have a solid scientific basis. If this doesn't happen, dissociation may again fall into obscurity: This time it would probably be discredited by biological psychiatry, which dominates the field today.

In this chapter I am first going to propose a reclassification of MPD as a subtype of chronic trauma disorder. The reclassification is consistent with the available data and integrates MPD into the mainstream. I will then discuss borderline personality disorder and malingering, which are the leading items in the DSM-III-R differential diagnosis of MPD. Then I will review a number of other psychiatric diagnoses: Some should be reclassified as dissociative disorders, others have prominent dissociative features insufficient to justify reclassification.

CHRONIC TRAUMA DISORDER AND ITS SUBTYPES

As described in Chapter 5, MPD patients also meet diagnostic criteria for other psychiatric disorders, including depression, borderline personality disorder, somatization disorder, substance abuse, bulimia and anorexia nervosa, panic disorder, and others (Atlas, 1988; Markowitz & Viederman, 1986). It is not unusual for an MPD patient to meet DSM-III-R criteria for 10 different disorders at the same time. This doesn't make any sense. It violates a principle of science called *Occam's Razor,* according to which, "Entities are not to be multiplied without necessity" (Russell, 1945). Occam's Razor means that the simplest explanation consistent with the facts is the best explanation and that entities are not to be postulated if they are not required to explain a phenomenon.

In 19th-century physics there was a great deal of theorizing about a substance called *ether,* which was thought to fill the universe. Experimental attempts were made to measure the ether wind, which was thought to result from the drift of ether through the universe. If there was an ether wind, it would be blowing in opposite directions relative to an observer on the surface of the earth, at intervals 6 months apart, because the earth would be on opposite sides of the sun. No such effect was detectable. The main reason ether was dropped from physics, though, was that it became an unnecessary postulate and fell before Occam's Razor.

MPD will have the same effect on the Oedipal conflict as an explanation for dissociation: Oedipal theory becomes an unnecessary postulate. Another analogy can be made: In Ptolemaic astronomy a vast machinery of cycles and epicycles was invented to explain the motion of the stars and planets. The cycles and epicycles were circular mechanical pathways that exerted force on the heavenly bodies and interacted like gearwheels to coordinate their motions. After Kepler the entire machinery was simply dropped. There are no epicycles in nature.

Although Ptolemy was a genius, his astronomical theory is best described as antiquated. His genius lay both in his ability to observe and in his theory, but the theory was wrong. This is the situation with Freud. His vast and elaborate theoretical machinery is currently in peril and is endangered by Occam's Razor. As an observer of psychopathology, Freud will always be one of the greatest psychiatrists.

Concerning the ideological response of some psychiatrists to the transition from classical to modern psychiatry (the transition out of the classical biological-Freudian homeostasis), the history of gross anatomy is instructive. The anatomy of Galen dominated medicine for over 1500 years, until new discoveries pushed it into decline. For hundreds of years, however, professors of anatomy taught that dissection was unnecessary because one could refer to Galen. To dissect was in fact heretical, because it implied that there was a need to check on Galen. This was the ultimate appeal to authority. Those who wanted to make dissection of cadavers part of medical training often suffered political consequences.

When dissection was introduced in a few medical schools, some professors contended that when the anatomy of a cadaver differed from that of Galen, it was the cadaver that was wrong. One example of such a difference involved details of the blood supply to the uterus, which Galen described based on incorrect theory about the cause of menstruation. The idea, popular in 19th-century medicine, that hysteria is caused by a wandering uterus, is derived from the same theory. The terms *hysterectomy* and *hysteria* come from the Greek word for "uterus." Indeed, hysterectomy was recommended as a treatment for certain female psychological disorders as late as the 19th century (Veith, 1965), as were marriage and sexual intercourse (marriage was the necessary social structure for intercourse to occur, intercourse being the curative agent). Theoretical errors in medicine may have far-reaching practical consequences, many of which do not go over well with feminists.

Freudian theory is supported by a similar appeal to authority—to question it may be heretical—and it is based on incorrect ideas about sexuality. Biases can be so strong that a woman's account of childhood sexual abuse is dismissed as fantasy or as a symptom of disordered brain function, in classical Freudian-biological psychiatry. In contemporary medical schools derisive dismissals of MPD are common. These may originate from either of the two main camps. Hopefully, however, empirical reality will prevail, as it has in the study of human anatomy, and posttraumatic dissociative disorders will enter the mainstream.

Returning to Occam's Razor, a problem with MPD is that it doesn't fit into DSM-III and DSM-III-R properly. This is because of the numerous concurrent diagnoses MPD patients have and the need for a more parsimonious single diagnosis that encompasses all of the symptomatology. MPD doesn't do this, because it accounts for only a small part of the specific dissociative symptoms of these patients. Part of the problem is with the conceptual bases of DSM-III and DSM-III-R.

DSM-III and DSM-III-R can be described as Newtonian documents. They are based on classical Cartesian psychiatry. In them psychiatric disorders, or at least groups of disorders, are related like the billiard balls in 19th-century physics metaphors. This tendency is more pronounced in DSM-III-R than in DSM-III. According to DSM-III-R rules, one can have an affective disorder, anxiety disorder, dissociative disorder, eating disorder, and personality disorder (probably borderline) all at the same time. There is no necessary or conceptually compelling relationship between all these independent entities.

The Newtonian logic leads to futile but common debates about whether bulimia is an epiphenomenon of affective disorder, or whether MPD is an epiphenomenon of borderline personality disorder, among a long list of such debates. Bulimia and depression are viewed as independent billiard balls in such thinking, with a causal, linear relationship between the two. The depression billiard ball has specified position and momentum and *causes* secondary movement in a billiard ball we call bulimia. Treat the depression billiard ball, to correct its disordered momentum, and the disordered movement in the bulimia billiard ball will not occur. Many studies are designed to elucidate the relative positions and momenta of psychiatric disorders on this single plane.

Single plane? DSM-III-R has five Axes, someone will reply. That doesn't matter. Axis II is a vestigial remnant of the classical biological-Freudian homeostasis. The personality disorders are separated out on Axis II because Freudian and biological theory have not been integrated. Axes III through V are not *diagnostic* axes. MPD patients demonstrate that the diagnostic system doesn't make sense. MPD patients are an anomaly that cannot be incorporated into the classical psychiatric paradigm. Hence the resistance to MPD, which is a resistance to paradigm shift.

The first step in rewriting DSM-III-R requires a new, encompassing diagnosis that will take all the features of MPD into account. The diagnostic term should be politically acceptable, conceptually sound, and result in MPD being integrated into the mainstream. What is MPD? It is a polydiagnostic disorder of childhood onset, arising from childhood trauma. The first term I thought of was childhood onset polydiagnostic posttraumatic stress disorder. The main problem with that term is trying to remember it. As well, it suggests that MPD is an anxiety disorder, because posttraumatic stress disorder is misclassified as an anxiety disorder in DSM-III-R (as operationalized in DSM-III-R, posttraumatic stress disorder has more dissociative than anxiety features).

I therefore decided to call MPD chronic trauma disorder. This wasn't satisfactory, though, because some people with chronic childhood trauma don't develop MPD. The next step was to make MPD a subtype of chronic trauma disorder, similar to the subtyping of panic disorder in DSM-III-R according to the degree of agoraphobia. This would take the spectrum of increasing severity of dissociation into account. Chronic trauma disorder can be divided into three subtypes: chronic trauma disorder without MPD; chronic trauma disorder with partial MPD; and chronic trauma disorder with full MPD.

What is the relationship between different diagnoses such as depression, panic disorder, bulimia, and borderline personality disorder within chronic trauma disorder? Chronic trauma disorder is an *exclusion* criterion for any of these other disorders. If chronic trauma disorder is present, none of these other diagnoses can be made as a freestanding entity. They must be listed as subdiagnoses of the inclusive disorder. This doesn't mean that the bulimic behavior doesn't exist, but the patient has only one disorder. That is the formal relationship between the MPD patient's many different concurrent diagnoses. What about the conceptual relationship? I would call this the dynamic relationship, if readers could guarantee that no Freudian connotations of that term would occur in their minds.

MPD stands in a hierarchically inclusive relationship to depression, substance abuse, and the other diagnoses. The other disorders occur lower in a hierarchy depicted in Figure 7.1. One passes vertically up the hierarchy as a function of two variables: increasing severity and chronicity of trauma (one variable with two subcomponents), and dissociative ability. The most severely abused and dissociative patients develop MPD. Others who are less severely traumatized, or who are less gifted at dissociation, develop

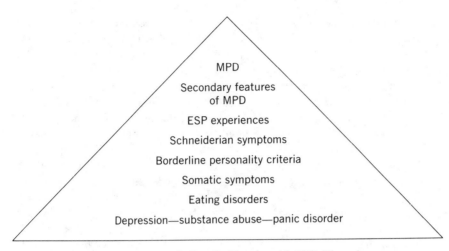

Figure 7.1.   Chronic Trauma Disorder with MPD Hierarchy

drug habits, personality disorders, and depression. There is no necessary or invariable relationship between the disorders lower in the hierarchy, which can occur in different combinations in different patients.

The relationship between the subdiagnoses of chronic trauma disorder is best understood using a metaphor from quantum mechanics. Chronic trauma disorder is a single field, with distinct regions. These different regions are called affective disorder, eating disorder, and so on. MPD teaches us that numerous regions of the field can be activated simultaneously in a given patient. Phenomenologically, movement from one region of the field to another takes the form of transitions through a continuum of changing density, rather than discrete jumps from one billiard ball to the next. The subregions of the field (MPD, bulimia, drug abuse) do not interact according to Newtonian principles, rather they are interrelated by complex postclassical mechanisms.

What difference does this make clinically? Inconclusive, anecdotal, but extensive experience to date indicates that MPD is a hierarchically inclusive diagnosis within chronic trauma disorder (Kluft, 1987a). If one attempts to treat, say, the depression in a chronic trauma patient, without diagnosing the MPD, the patient's response is idiosyncratic or nonexistent. If one makes the diagnosis of MPD, however, and treats the MPD, the hierarchically lower diagnosis of depression goes into remission. This is why the diagnosis makes a difference. Chronic trauma disorder, with its subtypes, brings conceptual order to the data available in the literature.

I couldn't use chronic trauma disorder in the title of this book, because no one has ever heard of it. There is a small scientific problem as well. The hypothesis that treating hierarchically lower disorders is ineffective and has no effect on the hierarchically superior MPD is based on treatment failures subsequently diagnosed as MPD and successfully treated with special MPD techniques. What about the treatment successes? I mean the patients with MPD whose MPD was never diagnosed, but who went into remission when they were given antidepressants, group therapy for substance abuse, cognitive-behavioral therapy for bulimia, or some other hierarchically lower treatment. If such patients exist, MPD specialists never see them. The therapeutic utility of chronic trauma disorder as a diagnosis depends on such patients not existing or being a small minority in the overall universe of MPD.

All possible combinations of treatment response and failure could be tested in properly designed trials, although this would be logistically and ethically difficult. For instance, chronic trauma patients could be entered into a randomized, double-blind, placebo-controlled trial of a tricyclic antidepressant, and response of all the subdiagnoses and symptoms could be monitored. The hypotheses generated by the diagnosis of chronic trauma disorder are all testable, scientific hypotheses, unlike those of classical analytical theory. Are there any data to support the idea of chronic trauma disorder? In fact it was data that impelled me to coin the term.

Geri Anderson, Sharon Heber, and I (Ross, Anderson, Heber & Norton, in press) administered the DES and DDIS to 20 subjects with MPD, 20 prostitutes, and 20 strippers. We did this because we knew that 19.1 percent of MPD patients in our series of 236 had worked as prostitutes. We also knew that at least 50 percent of prostitutes have been sexually abused as children (Silbert & Pines, 1981, 1982, 1983, 1984). We therefore expected to find abuse histories and dissociative disorders in prostitutes. Strippers were included for several reasons. First, women shift back and forth between stripping and hooking or do both at once, so strippers should also be dissociative.

I also wanted to include the prostitutes and strippers in a larger study, which I haven't done yet. This would involve interviewing actresses and ballet or jazz dancers. These groups, MPD subjects, prostitutes, strippers, actresses, and dancers, would provide varying combinations of performance, prostitution, and dissociation. For instance, the dancers should have less dissociation and sexual abuse than strippers, but they are specialists in physical performance. The actresses are performers, but not so physical. Both dance and acting can be highly erotic, but neither are pornographic (pornographic film actresses are a separate group, virtually certain to have chronic trauma disorder).

Prostitutes perform, usually but not always in private, and are highly sexualized. MPD patients perform for their therapists, according to the iatrogenesis theory, often in a highly sexualized manner, and tell many pornographic stories. And so on. These groups should help separate out the *acting* component of MPD and show that it is not linked to dissociation.

In our study of MPD patients, prostitutes, and strippers, the degree of dissociation was clearly linked to the severity and chronicity of abuse. The MPD patients had an average duration of physical abuse of 15.0 years, compared to 4.2 years for the prostitutes and 4.3 years for the strippers. The MPD subjects had an average of 2.5 different physical abusers, compared to 0.7 for the prostitutes and 0.6 for the strippers.

In terms of sexual abuse, the MPD patients had an average duration of sexual abuse of 12.7 years, compared to 2.7 years for the prostitutes and 2.1 years for the strippers. They had an average of 1.7 different sexual abusers, compared to 0.8 for the prostitutes and 0.7 for the strippers. Finally, the MPD patients had experienced an average of 3.6 different forms of sexual abuse, compared to 1.4 for the prostitutes and 1.5 for the strippers. The MPD subjects differed from the prostitutes and strippers on all these measures of trauma at $p = .02$, or greater.

The MPD patients were also more dissociative. They had more dissociative diagnoses and scored much higher on the DES. They had many more secondary features of MPD and Schneiderian symptoms. However, there were no differences between groups in the frequencies of depression, substance abuse, or borderline personality disorder. The hypotheses underlying chronic trauma disorder were supported. All three groups had trauma histories, but the group with the most severe trauma had the most dissociation. Hierarchically lower phenomena did not differ between groups.

I expect these findings to stand up across studies and centers with a variety of subject groups. Dissociative features and diagnoses are hierarchically superior elements of chronic trauma disorder. Dissociative symptoms include secondary features of MPD, Schneiderian symptoms, ESP experiences, and borderline diagnostic criteria. In the study of prostitutes and strippers, ESP experiences and borderline personality did not differentiate groups. This suggests that there may be hierarchical structure even within the dissociative cluster, but further studies are required to examine this possibility.

Another diagnosis is required: MPD without chronic trauma disorder. Whether this should be an Axis I diagnosis or a V code awaits further study as well. The V codes in DSM-III-R are a set of problems such as academic difficulties and uncomplicated bereavement, which are deliberately defined as life problems. They are not psychiatric disorders. Atraumatic MPD may, at least in some individuals, not even be a problem, but simply be a mode of organization for a high-functioning self. I have never met a clinical case of complex MPD that did not have chronic trauma disorder, however. MPD without chronic trauma disorder would be like agoraphobia without panic attacks, which is rarely if ever encountered by clinicians.

THE RELATIONSHIP BETWEEN CHRONIC TRAUMA DISORDER AND OTHER TRAUMA DISORDERS

It wouldn't make sense to create a new diagnosis called chronic trauma disorder and not define its relationship to other trauma disorders, of which the only official one is posttraumatic stress disorder (PTSD). PTSD is currently defined in DSM-III-R as an anxiety disorder, although it has more dissociative features than anxiety symptoms (Brende & Benedict, 1980; Spiegel, 1984; Spiegel, 1986a; Spiegel, 1986b; Spiegel, Hunt, & Dondershine, 1988; Young, 1987). DSM-III-R PTSD is much more dissociative, both in its criteria and in the discussion section, than DSM-III PTSD. Spiegel, Hunt, and Dondershine have done work on the dissociative aspects of PTSD, as has Spiegel alone (1986). These and other studies will probably result in PTSD being shifted out of anxiety disorders. It would be an error to shift it into dissociative disorders, however.

Concerning the anxiety disorders, both PTSD and obsessive-compulsive disorder are classified as anxiety disorders because of the residual influence of Freudian theory. Neither has anxiety as a cardinal feature, any more than do MPD or schizophrenia. For both, anxiety is a secondary epiphenomenon. Both should be taken out of the anxiety disorders, leaving generalized anxiety, panic, and the phobias as a truly related group of disorders. Some cases of obsessive-compulsive disorder are dissociative in nature (Ross & Anderson, 1988) and are presenting features of chronic trauma disorder. Others could be assigned to affective, delusional, or other diagnostic groups. At any rate, obsessive-compulsive disorder is not primarily an anxiety disorder, and neither is PTSD.

A new group of disorders called the trauma disorders should be created. These should be subdivided into acute and chronic trauma, childhood and adult onset, and dissociative or nondissociative, bearing in mind that dissociation occurs on a continuum. The organization of the trauma disorders is shown in Figure 7.2. Adult onset acute trauma disorder of the nondissociative type would correspond to the DSM-III-R diagnosis of adjustment disorder. Adult onset trauma disorder of dissociative type would correspond to PTSD. This means that a highly dissociative adult could develop simple MPD in response to a single trauma. This is a testable hypothesis. The trauma disorders would result in the elimination of the adjustment disorders. It is likely that mild trauma, such as that which usually precedes adjustment disorders, can be handled without the mobilization of dissociative defenses, except in individuals who have chronic trauma disorder. They use dissociation all the time.

It is possible that dissociation is the strategy par excellence for coping with severe trauma and that even otherwise nondissociative individuals will mobilize their evolutionary ability to dissociate if the trauma is extreme enough. This would result in more dissociative symptoms occurring in a population exposed to extreme trauma than in one exposed to intermediate trauma, assuming that pretraumatic DES scores were the same in both groups. These hypotheses could be tested by measuring hypnotizability and dissociation in all military inductees and following those persons who did and did not enter combat. Such a study might eventually lead to selection of combat soldiers at lower risk for adult onset acute trauma disorder and better pre-

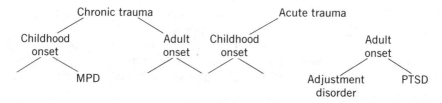

Each subdiagnosis occurs on a spectrum from low to high dissociation.

Figure 7.2.   The Trauma Disorders

ventive interventions for those high-dissociators who do have to enter combat. Maybe nobody with a DES score over 30 should become a marine. On the other hand, healthy high-dissociators might make the best marines, because they could dissociate terror, cold, and fatigue, and maintain their function. The issue might be separating healthy from pathological dissociators.

I mention these possibilities to indicate the potential utility of the reorganization of trauma disorders. Obviously, one study of 20 MPD patients, 20 prostitutes, and 20 strippers cannot provide sufficient data to make the case.

BORDERLINE PERSONALITY DISORDER

Borderline personality disorder is one of the most controversial diagnoses in psychiatry, although it is much more accepted, studied, funded, and diagnosed than MPD (Kernberg, 1975; Masterson, 1976). In a symposium of nine papers on borderline personality in the *Canadian Journal of Psychiatry* (Links, 1988), MPD is not mentioned once. This demonstrates that MPD has had virtually no effect on the clinical thinking of mainstream psychiatrists. However, unrecognized concurrent MPD is present in many borderlines. To understand borderline personality disorder, one must review the history of the diagnosis and the origins of the term itself.

As described in Chapter 2, MPD fell into disrepute following Freud's rejection of dissociation, the seduction theory, and hypnosis; other contributing factors were the ascendancy of Bleuler's schizophrenia and the transfer of academic energy into behavioral studies. *Schizophrenia* means "split-mind disorder," which is actually the correct term for MPD, not for schizophrenia. Many MPD patients were misdiagnosed as schizophrenic and mistreated within biological psychiatry because of the mistaken term.

Alternatively, MPD patients were treated psychoanalytically for their disordered Oedipal fantasies and hysterical symptoms. Shortly after World War II, however, Hoch and Polatin (1949) noticed that many patients were atypical and did not fit in with dementia praecox or psychoneurosis. Hoch and

Polatin described these patients as suffering from "pseudoneurotic schizophrenia" (p. 276), a term similar to "hysterical psychosis," "hysterical schizophrenia," and other related terms. The term pseudoneurotic schizophrenia was an odd one because it could have been neurotic pseudoschizophrenia. In any case the term did not stick. Hoch and Polatin conclude their paper by saying that, "A few of these 'borderline' cases are described and their symptomatology analyzed. It is suggested that these patients be classified 'pseudoneurotic form of schizophrenia' " (p. 276). The term pseudoneurotic schizophrenia did not stick, but "borderline" did.

Hoch and Polatin present five cases of pseudoneurotic schizophrenia. Their patients had undiagnosed MPD and suffered from posttraumatic dissociative disorders, as did the patients in *Studies on Hysteria* described 54 years earlier by Breuer and Freud (1895/1986). Hoch and Polatin note that their patients suffered from all the symptoms of neurosis, had no thought disorders, had "incestuous ideas" (p. 253), exhibited complex sexual conflicts, and often had extensive amnesia for childhood. In addition they had "brief psychoses" (p. 253), which is why they were called schizophrenic.

Hoch and Polatin's Case 2 is quoted as saying of herself, "I'm divided. Part of me is here and part of me is floating away" (p. 264). Case 3 was quoted as saying:

My subconscious mind plays tricks on me. I was in a trance. I seemed to be separated from my body. My conscious mind has to pass on everything my subconscious mind does. My subconscious mind tries to do and say things that other people have in their minds. I feel what they think. The words I cannot understand are "positive" and "negative." It means that I'm trying to be certain about things. I feel like I'm hypnotized. Did you hypnotize me? At times I have the feeling as if a voice was telling me to go to sleep and act like a child and be babied (p. 267).

In another passage about Case 3, Hoch and Polatin write, "I have a male mind and a female body and I don't like women" (p. 268). Asked how long she had been hearing the voice, she said, "On and off for about 2 years" (p. 268). Sometimes it was a real voice, sometimes she thought it was her own ideas "which became loud" (p. 269). Of Case 3, Hoch and Polatin note that "early memories were blocked" (p. 268). Case 4 was a male with MPD. Case 5 presented with

. . . marked self-recriminatory ideas, a feeling that she is two persons, a desire to kill members of her family and a fear that her husband might kill her. . . . She also complained about hearing motors roaring in her ears; began to think of herself at times very objectively; and she would smile at her own activities and reactions. She also could hear herself talk to herself as if there were two persons. At times she would laugh at her own feelings. She had a sensation of voices inside her head repeating things she had previously thought of, or reminding her of what she had done. She realized that these voices were products of her own thinking, nevertheless she could not control them; she felt obsessed by them (pp. 272, 274).

In Chapter 1 we saw that demon possession, obsession, dissociation, and MPD are the same phenomena, in different cultural-historical contexts.

Hoch and Polatin's patients often gave them the diagnosis of MPD directly and explained the dissociative nature of their symptoms. Hoch and Polatin couldn't hear because they were trying to fit the patients into a preconceived conceptual system that couldn't accommodate them. The history of psychoanalysis and the history of borderline personality disorder both start with small series of MPD patients.

Within the Freudian-biological classical homeostasis, the undiagnosed MPD patients, partially recognized by Hoch and Polatin, presented a problem. They appeared to have more than a personality disorder but less than a major chronic psychosis. They did not fit into either subparadigm very well. They were on the borderline between personality disorder (the Freudian camp) and psychosis (the biological camp). The attempts to account for these patients involved extensive metapsychological theorizing, on the one hand, and efforts to classify them as *formes frustes* of biological psychosis on the other. In the end they were called borderlines.

Today many clinicians regard borderline personality disorder as a legitimate diagnosis. Looking at MPD patients from the borderline vantage point, they hold that MPD is an epiphenomenon of borderline personality. Basically, the argument is that MPD specialists create an MPD artifact in borderlines. Such clinicians rarely diagnose MPD because they deal with the "real" disorder, borderline personality, without introducing an additional hysterical illusion. In this context "hysterical" has theoretical pretensions but really means hysterical in the sense of a hysterical woman screaming about a mouse in the closet. The woman needs a slap on the face and settling down, while a man takes care of the mouse.

One doesn't have to look far in the contemporary borderline literature to find cases of undiagnosed MPD. In a paper called "Prolonged Psychotic States in Borderline Personality Disorder," Lotterman (1985) describes eight borderline patients with "hysterical psychoses" (p. 36). He addresses the problem of how to account for the fact that borderline patients have personality disorders and psychotic features at the same time. This is an unreal problem because borderlines don't have either personality disorders or psychoses: They have chronic trauma disorder.

In the longest case history Lotterman describes a 27-year-old female inpatient with auditory hallucinations, depression, depersonalization, derealization, fugue states, sleepwalking, pseudoseizures, self-abusive behavior, suicide attempts (including ingestion of 4 grams of amitriptyline in one overdose), "autohypnotic trance-like states" (p. 38) alternating with lucid states, absence of a thought disorder, alternating homosexual and heterosexual states, and a fantasy of chopping up her parents. Lotterman does not comment on whether she did or did not have an abuse history. The patient failed to respond to large doses of chlorpromazine and haloperidol, or to a course of 20 ECT treatments. Lotterman comments that

> A factor which appeared to exacerbate her symptoms was the fact that in her first two months of treatment, she had four separate psychotherapists, due to the rotation of psychiatric residents on her unit. For this adopted woman, this was probably a particularly potent stressor (p. 38).

The patient's diagnoses were changed prior to successive trials of different treatments and included depression, hysterical personality (on psychological testing), borderline personality, hysterical schizophrenia, and schizophrenia. Lotterman is to be thanked for his detailed account of the failure to diagnose MPD in this patient and the numerous errors of omission and commission in her treatment.

The other seven patients in Lotterman's report also had auditory hallucinations, courses of 20 or more ECT treatments with transient response, sexual delusions and hallucinations, and other features common in the histories of undiagnosed MPD patients. Not all of the patients described in the series sound strongly dissociative, but one had been cutting and scratching herself since the age of 8: "One important feature of this patient's history, was incestuous relations with her father. This fact emerged only after several years of treatment" (p. 41). It is important to emphasize that I am not singling Lotterman out for fault. In fact the reverse is true: He is to be commended for his scholarship, his efforts to diagnose and treat his difficult patients, and his frank discussion of what, for classical psychiatry, is their "inexplicable" symptomatology. Lotterman writes of his patient: "Throughout this time, something still seemed inexplicable" (p. 37).

The classification of borderline personality disorder in DSM-III-R is an artifact of the Freudian-biological homeostasis. In DSM-III and DSM-III-R most adult psychiatric disorders, including MPD, are diagnosed on Axis I. The personality disorders are separated out on Axis II and are widely regarded as being psychodynamic in nature. Axis I is the territory of the biologists, Axis II that of the psychoanalysts, although each camp tries to claim the other's territory, in an insoluble struggle over disputed desert. So-called neurotic disorders also occur on Axis I, but the reductionist view is that they are either mild biological illnesses or not psychiatric disorders and better left to social workers. In their efforts to explain the inexplicable, analysts try to move MPD onto Axis II, and biologists try to reduce it to chemicals on Axis I.

Perhaps Axis I should be renamed Chemical Axis, and Axis II, Freudian Axis. The neurotic Axis I disorders could be reclassified as social work disorders rather than psychiatric disorders.

There is a precedent for moving a disorder from Axis II to Axis I. In DSM-II, dysthymic disorder was classified as "dysthymic personality disorder," along with the other personality disorders. In DSM-III it is a poorly operationalized affective disorder on Axis I. In DSM-III-R it is a well operationalized affective disorder on Axis I. The percentage of dysthymic patients treated with antidepressants has gone up, and the percentage treated with psychoanalysis gone down, in conjunction with this nosologic shift. There is a precedent, then, for moving an analytic disorder off of Axis II onto Axis I, despite a metapsychological investment in "characterological depressions." Borderline personality should be moved off of Axis II onto Axis I in DSM-IV, or at least in DSM-IV-R.

In the sparse literature on borderline personality and MPD (Benner & Joscelyne, 1984; Buck, 1983; Clary et al., 1984; Fast, 1974; Gruenewald, 1977; Gruenewald, 1984; Horevitz & Braun, 1984; Ross, 1985; Young, 1988), a distinction is made between splitting and dissociation. Splitting is held to be the foundation of borderline personality, and dissociation the basis of MPD. This means that the distinction between the two disorders is real only if the distinction between splitting and dissociation is real, which it isn't. Young (1988) unintentionally points this out in reviewing the relevant literature. He refers to Kernberg's (1975) definition of splitting as "alternative activation of contradictory ego states" (p. 33), and defines dissociation as a defense that "maintains conflict-laden material and painful affects in dissociated states" (p. 33).

In Young's reading of the literature, the distinction between splitting and dissociation hinges on two points: Splitting is based on *contradictory* ego states, whereas dissociated states are incompatible but not necessarily contradictory; splitting is based on splitting of introjects, whereas dissociated states need not be linked to introjects. Young therefore concludes that MPD and borderline personality are distinct entities. The first problem is that these distinctions are very difficult if not impossible to demonstrate empirically with any interrater reliability.

Young makes three arguments in favor of the distinction between MPD and borderline personality: Not all MPD patients are borderline; not all alters are based on introjects; and in many patients there are too many alters for them all to be based on *contradictory* states.

There is an error of reasoning here. Contradictory states are a *subset* of incompatible states. That is why some alters are based on contradiction, but not all. In addition, incompatible states are not necessarily linked to introjects. That is why some alters identify themselves as specific other living or dead people, but many don't. Splitting is a subset of dissociation. This being the case, it is not surprising that MPD and borderline criteria exist in the same dissociative cluster.

The same holds true phenomenologically. The borderline patient switches states. In fact this is the metapsychological hallmark of her disorder. In one state, she disavows her affect and behavior while in other states. It is as if she has an amnesia at the level of affect and behavior, but not at a cognitive or informational level. The borderline patient has a severely impaired continuity of identity across states. If the amnesia barrier was made complete, and the sense of separate identity of the split states elaborated a little, one would be dealing with an alter personality. Phenomenologically, alter personalities are elaborations of borderline splitting.

This dissociative model of borderline personality is consistent with Braun's (1988a, 1988b) BASK model of dissociation. In the BASK model, dissociation can occur in four continua: behavior, affect, sensation, and knowledge. The borderline patient dissociates in all but knowledge, although there is impairment even in that continuum. The MPD patient has completed the dissociation of knowledge, or informational awareness. The BASK model of borderline personality is in turn consistent with Gunderson's (Gunderson & Kolb, 1978; Gunderson, Carpenter, & Strauss, 1975; Gunderson, Kolb, & Austin, 1981; Gunderson & Singer, 1975) phenomenological observations about the frequency of dissociative features in borderlines. The problem with Gunderson's analysis is that he makes dissociation a subfeature rather than the core of borderline personality.

Gunderson also writes about the brief psychotic episodes experienced by borderlines. These are probably dissociative. This is partly a matter of definition: In my vocabulary, psychotic symptoms are features of a chronic major mental illness of presumed biological etiology, or of delirium; dissociative symptoms belong to a cluster including hypnosis, absorption, imaginative involvement, and fantasy, and are usually posttraumatic in origin. Dissociative and psychotic symptoms may be indistinguishable phenomenologically. This is accepted to be the case for symptoms of mania and schizophrenia—a given symptom may occur in identical fashion in either disorder. Diagnostically this means that one cannot reliably distinguish mania and schizophrenia on cross-sectional mental status examination alone. One must consider course, family history, treatment response, associated features, premorbid personality, and other factors in making a diagnosis.

The same is true for distinguishing dissociation and psychosis. In this regard I will discuss the interview techniques relevant to the differential diagnosis of auditory hallucinations later in this chapter under schizophrenia.

The point I am making about MPD and borderlines is that MPD is not a rare, obscure diagnosis of little relevance to mainstream psychiatry. It is common, especially in patients classically diagnosed as borderline, and has numerous implications for psychiatric nosology, theory, and therapeutics. Are there any data supporting the idea that borderline criteria are part of a dissociative cluster? Yes.

In the only empirical study of the relationship between MPD and borderline personality, Horevitz and Braun (1984) found that 70 percent of 33 cases of MPD also met criteria for the Axis II disorder. Their feeling was that borderline personality is a measure of the overall function of the patient, but not necessarily related to the MPD. I have directed three studies of the relationship between the two disorders that provide consistent evidence in favor of a dissociative model of borderline personality.

In the first study (Ross, Heber, Norton, & Anderson, 1989a), we interviewed 20 MPD, 20 schizophrenic, 20 eating disorder, and 20 panic disorder patients with the DDIS. The only difference between groups in frequency of borderline personality was that the MPD group met the criteria more often than the panic patients, $p = .01$. This showed that borderline personality was no more characteristic of MPD than of schizophrenia or eating disorders, in our sample. Based on our data, it is inconsistent to dismiss MPD as an artifact of borderline personality, unless one makes a similar dismissal of schizophrenia, which no one would do. Gunderson, Carpenter, and Strauss (1975) and others (Sheehy, Goldsmith, & Charles, 1980) have shown that borderline personality and schizophrenia can be reliably differentiated, just as we have shown is the case for MPD and schizophrenia. Although it is always good to have more data, there is really no doubt that MPD is not an artifact of borderline personality disorder.

In our study, of the eight DSM-III borderline criteria, only one, instability of affect, differentiated MPD from all three other groups. Two items, identity disturbance and unstable relationships, did not differentiate MPD from any other group. To have borderline personality disorder, according to DSM-III rules, one must be positive for five or more of the eight criteria.

A very different picture emerged when we compared the groups on number of positive borderline criteria. The MPD subjects had a mean of 5.3 positive borderline symptoms, eating disorder 3.4, panic disorder 2.4, and schizophrenia 3.0. In this comparison MPD differed from each of the three other groups at $p = .003$ or greater, while none of the other groups differed from each other. These data show that "borderline personality" as a discrete entity does not differentiate MPD from other disorders very well. However, "borderlineness," as one form of dissociation, does. Psychiatric patients who are more dissociative are more borderline. This supports the idea of borderline criteria being items on a spectrum of increasingly severe dissociation, rather than criteria for a freestanding entity.

In a second study (Ross, Anderson, Heber, et al., in press) we increased the number of MPD patients interviewed with the DDIS to 40. Of these, 27 (67.5 percent) met criteria for borderline personality and 13 did not. This is close to Horevitz and Braun's 70 percent. The percentage of MPD patients who meet criteria for borderline personality disorder is probably lowest in a private practice in which clients pay fees themselves and highest in tertiary care hospital-based practices like mine and Braun's. In our experience, borderlineness is a measure of the behavioral difficulty, intensity and complexity of double binds, acting out, and involvement with social agencies we can expect during treatment.

In the second study we compared MPD patients with and without borderline personality. The borderline multiples were more dissociative. They had more Schneiderian symptoms, more secondary features of MPD, more ESP experiences, and more trance states. All these are items in the dissociative cluster. The borderline multiple were positive for a mean of 7.1

borderline symptoms, the nonborderlines for a mean of 3.1, $p = .0001$. The borderlines were more borderline, which makes sense if they are also more dissociative and if borderline criteria are dissociative symptoms.

There was no difference between the two groups in frequency or duration of childhood physical or sexual abuse or in number of perpetrators of each form of abuse. Nor was there a difference in the number of types of sexual abuse. This is a crucial finding consistent with the hierarchical nature of chronic trauma disorder with MPD. Borderline symptoms occur lower in the hierarchy than MPD symptoms.

Conversely, if subjects in a research borderline clinic were interviewed with the DDIS and DES, it is likely that a highly dissociative subgroup could be readily identified. This subgroup would have more MPD, secondary features of MPD, Schneiderian symptoms, positive borderline criteria, and ESP experiences. They would probably have more somatic symptoms as well. They would have more severe abuse histories. These findings would clinch my model of chronic trauma disorder, once sufficient replication was done. I would anticipate that such findings would be the outcome of screening borderlines for dissociation.

Overall, 85 percent of our 40 multiples had been sexually abused as children, and 77.5 percent had been physically abused. These figures are close to those in our series of 236 cases seen by 203 clinicians throughout North America: Of the 236 cases, 79.2 percent had been sexually abused, and 74.9 percent had been physically abused. Our 40 MPD patients are probably a representative sample of MPD as it presents throughout North America, as shown in other studies (Ross, Norton & Anderson, 1988; Ross, Norton, & Fraser, 1989).

The third study on the relationship between MPD and borderline personality was the study of 345 college students (Ryan, 1988) described in an earlier chapter. Three hundred forty-five university students completed the DES. From these, 20 students scoring above 22.6 and 22 scoring below 5.0 completed the SCL-90, Million Clinical Multiaxial Inventory (MCMI) and the DDIS. In this study we were comparing nonclinical high dissociators and low dissociators. Items occurring more frequently in the high group might therefore be part of a dissociative cluster.

The same pattern of dissociative cluster items was found in this study. The high group had more somatic symptoms, Schneiderian symptoms, secondary features of MPD, ESP experiences, and positive borderline criteria than the low group. They also had higher rates of sexual abuse. It appears that somatic symptoms are clearly dissociative in nature although they are less consistent discriminators of dissociative and nondissociative subjects than the other items in the cluster.

We (Ryan, 1988; Ryan & Ross, 1988) did two other analyses of the college student data that were consistent with all our other findings. We did Spearman correlations of items on the DDIS with DES scores and found that four items on the DDIS correlated at $p = .0001$. These were secondary features of MPD ($r = 0.78$), Schneiderian symptoms ($r = 0.67$), borderline criteria ($r = 0.67$), and ESP experiences ($r = 0.59$).

When we did a regression analysis of the data, we found that the item on the DDIS that best predicted DES score was secondary features of MPD ($R^2 = 0.71$, beta weight 0.60). This finding validates the DDIS against the DES, because the secondary features section contains dissociative experiences inquired about by the DES but in different wording. There were seven factors in the regression model. In the order they entered the model, these were secondary features of MPD, trance states, psychogenic amnesia, MPD, borderline personality disorder, childhood sexual abuse, and Schneiderian symptoms.

There is a strong and clear pattern in these data. The reason the different sections of the DDIS are in the DDIS is that clinicians have been observing the dissociative cluster in their MPD patients for the last 10 years. When replication studies are conducted at other centers, the dissociative cluster will likely be verified.

One final piece of data on the college students: The high and low groups did not differ on the narcissistic, histrionic, and antisocial subscales of the MCMI, but they differed at $p = .0001$ on the borderline subscale. This suggests that MPD and dissociation are not linked to histrionic personality style and that borderline criteria belong to a dissociative cluster rather than to the group of personality disorders on Axis II referred to as Cluster B. Cluster B includes borderline, histrionic, narcissistic, and antisocial personality disorders.

The removal of borderline personality criteria from Axis II might be the first step in dissolving Axis II altogether. Cluster A should probably go onto Axis I in the region of schizophrenia. The remaining personality disorders in Cluster C would then be no more, nosologically, than a collection of descriptions of different types of people. Taking a patient's character into account can be important in medicine, but that does not justify the creation of a group of psychiatric illnesses called personality disorders on a separate diagnostic Axis.

In my experience, the diagnosis of borderline personality disorder doesn't usually have much to do with the DSM-III or DSM-III-R criteria in any case. It is very rare to see documentation on a chart of which criteria the patient meets and which she doesn't. Probably if one asked a random sample of residents and psychiatrists to list the DSM-III-R criteria for borderline personality, very few could list all eight, and many could list only two or three. In practice, I think that many clinicians diagnose a patient, usually female, as borderline, when they can't even say what the criteria for diagnosis are or which ones the patient meets. This is very different from the clinical diagnosis of depression, which is usually based on detailed inquiry about specific diagnostic criteria, with good interrater reliability.

What is the clinical diagnosis of borderline personality disorder based on, then? Gut feeling, I think. What is the gut feeling based on? For one thing, it is often based on not liking the patient. When a patient is called borderline, in my experience, it usually means that the diagnostician finds her difficult and stressful to deal with. It also means that the clinician is stuck in one or more double binds. A typical double bind is the following: If you send me home I will kill myself; if you admit me I will deteriorate. The patient states only the first half of the bind.

The clinician on call in emergency, usually a resident, is then put in a second double bind by the system: If you send her home and she kills herself, that shows poor judgment on your part; if you admit her, it shows you can't handle borderlines in emergency. Next the patient is put in a counter-double bind: We don't admit borderlines because they deteriorate and disturb the milieu; if you act out enough we will certify you. The resolution of the double-bind usually involves a compromise, which can be an overnight stay in emergency, referral to the outpatient department, a short-term prescription for medication, or contact with the therapist by the resident, all of which demonstrate the benevolence of the resident.

The patient diagnosed as borderline is usually the victim of negative characterological attributions by mental health professionals. For instance, instead of attributing the borderline's refusal to attend group therapy to untreated panic disorder with agoraphobia, the patient is described as manipulative and acting out. The agoraphobia does not get treated, and the staff decides to "set limits" on the patient. The patient responds by threatening suicide. It is impossible to work with intensely borderline patients without getting endlessly caught up in such power struggles.

Often, if the dissociative, anxiety, and depressive symptoms of the borderline patient are successfully treated, the borderline personality will melt away. I have had the experience of watching apparent borderline personality disorder with concurrent major depressive episode vanish after several weeks of therapeutic doses of antidepressant, concurrently with remission of the depression. And I have seen a nonborderline bipolar man become severely narcissistic-borderline while hypomanic, then transform back into a well-adjusted person on lithium, with concurrent remission of his hypomania. This could be called the epiphenomenology of borderline personality disorder.

Borderline, in actual clinical reality, doesn't refer directly to DSM-III-R criteria. Borderline is a term describing a general way in which the patient–mental health professional system is organized. The core of this organization is the double bind. In fact "borderline" has nothing in particular to do with "personality," a widely used but nebulously defined term in psychiatry. Borderlines do not have something wrong with their *personalities*. Neither do MPD patients. Both have dissociative disorders involving numerous psychic functions, including affect, behavior, memory, cognition, and perception.

In fact "borderline" organization is characteristic of many different systems. Consider the legal system. The legal system has borderline personality disorder. At least in my jurisdiction, the legal system is perverse, destructive, and prone to aggressive acting out. The core of the Unified Family Court in Winnipeg, for instance, is the double bind. The legal system is a system of justice designed to protect honest citizens and punish criminals, supposedly. In practice, in family law, one is actively rewarded for fraudulent affidavits, unethical behavior, self-interested abuse of family members, and psychopathic opportunism. One is punished for honest and decent behavior, which is not "smart" according to the rules of the system. To be "smart" and to "win" in the justice system, one must be a moral criminal.

Clinicians who dismiss MPD patients as "just borderlines" are in error. Neither diagnosis has anything in particular to do with "personality," neither is a psychosis or a personality disorder, and both are aspects of chronic trauma disorder in the majority of patients treated by mental health professionals. Borderline personality should not be in the differential diagnosis of MPD in DSM-IV. All the available data reviewed in this section support that contention: There are no disconfirming data.

MALINGERING

According to DSM-III-R, malingering of MPD "can present a difficult diagnostic dilemma, which often can be resolved only by obtaining additional data from ancillary sources, such as hospital and police records and family members, employers, and friends" (p. 272). The Kenneth Bianchi case (Allison, 1984; Orne et al., 1984; Watkins, 1984) provides ample evidence in support of that caution by the Advisory Committee on Dissociative Disorders. As I said earlier, though, I am writing about clinical MPD, not forensic MPD. In the forensic context, malingering is always in the differential diagnosis, no matter what the symptoms are.

There's something curious about malingering getting boldface emphasis in the differential diagnosis of MPD, when it isn't even mentioned in many other sections of DSM-III-R. Why is that? One of the major reasons for the decline of MPD early in the 20th century was the mistaken conviction that diagnosticians were being duped by their patients. There was a reaction against the diagnosis because no one wanted to be regarded as an easy con. Is malingering emphasized in DSM-III-R, in the differential diagnosis of MPD, partly to send out a signal that specialists in dissociation are nobody's fools? If so, perhaps the necessity of the boldface will lessen as the diagnosis is accepted, and we could give malingering quieter press in DSM-IV.

More importantly, it occurred to me that there must be some dynamic reason, in a non-Freudian sense, why borderline personality and malingering are so strongly emphasized in the DSM-III-R differential diagnosis of MPD. The reasons for borderline personality are reviewed in the preceding section. What about malingering? What does lying have to do with MPD? Wondering about this, it occurred to me that lying is a form of dissociation. To lie, one must dissociate.

What is a lie? A lie is a deliberate untrue statement. One consciously intends to lie and when caught is morally responsible. Liars get punished, or at least admonished. Lying is not "okay," in conventional morality. Lying about one's innocence is not a defense in a court of law: There is no defense called "not guilty by reason of lying." Lying is not insanity or a sign of illness. It is more like a sin. Most people would agree with this view of lying.

Is Santa Claus a lie? When a parent tells his young child that Santa is coming, that is a deliberate untrue statement. But it is not a lie. No one calls the parent a liar.

What about Munchausen's Syndrome, which can be a presenting feature of MPD (Goodwin, 1988)? The Baron von Munchausen was a delightful liar (lying can be lots of fun for both liar and audience), but patients with his syndrome are not delightful. Munchausen's patients fake illnesses, change their names, and trick doctors into unnecessary surgery, investigations, prescriptions, and hospitalizations. But are they lying? Munchausen's patients seem to be at least partially victims of that well-known malady, "believing your own bullshit." Where is the dividing line between lying and delusion? What about lying to yourself? Where is the transition point between lying and self-deception?

I am no expert in the philosophy of lying, which is probably the subject of a large literature. I know that deciding what is a lie, what is a delusion, and what is misinformation can be a very difficult clinical problem. There is not even a set of well-defined clinical categories that provide a differential diagnosis of lying. If a patient makes a statement that *might* be a lie, what else could it be, clinically? A delusion, an overvalued idea, an obsession, a misattribution, what else? This isn't something one gets taught about in psychiatric training.

I said that to lie one must dissociate. To dissociate is to split apart and separate psychic states and contents. To lie, one must do this. In a lie one *disavows* reality and knowingly substitutes a falsehood. The liar places reality, and his knowledge of it, to one side. This is a mild, minor, consciously controlled form of dissociation. Like other dissociative phenomena, it occurs on a spectrum from normal lying through to pathological dissociation.

An alter may state that her biological father is not her father, while acknowledging that he is the biological father of the body and of the presenting personality. Is this a lie? Should one tell the alter to "Smarten up, and stop lying"? No. This is a dissociative symptom of a treatable mental illness. It is not surprising, then, that malingering, which is the clinical term for lying, occurs in the differential diagnosis of MPD. The creation of alter personalities is an extreme extension of the normal psychic mechanism of everyday malingering.

Item 10 on the Dissociative Experiences Scale reads, "Some people have the experience of being accused of lying when they do not think they have

lied. Mark the line to show what percentage of the time this happens to you''
(Bernstein & Putnam, 1986, p. 733) This item is in the DES because MPD
patients disavow behavior for which they are amnesic. People accuse them
of lying because they don't realize that there is amnesia involved. Like all
other items in the DES, this item has a Spearman correlation of $p = .0001$
with overall DES scores in both adolescents and college students, which
suggests strongly that it is a dissociative symptom.

Item 10 is one of the most elevated items on the DES among normal
adolescents (Ross & Ryan, unpublished data). Why? I'm not exactly sure.
But there seems to be a developmentally normal form of dissociation that
occurs in young adolescents and makes them appear to others to be lying.
This is different from getting caught lying. There is a potential field of study
that involves the normal developmental relationship between dissociation
and lying, and the pathology of lying at various ages. Confabulation in Kor-
sakoff's patients, for instance, is an organically driven symptom that might
be related to the high scores of normal adolescents on DES Item 10. Both
involve the substitution of falsehood for reality, but neither are lying.

These are speculations, but I think there is some inner necessity or logic
to the fact that malingering is in boldface in the differential diagnosis of MPD
in DSM-III-R. There is more to it than historical artifact and forensic caution.
This is what I mean by a *dynamic* relationship between lying and dissociation.

SCHIZOPHRENIA

MPD is often mistaken for schizophrenia (Ross & Norton, 1988). In this
section, though, I am going to discuss the relationship between correctly
diagnosed schizophrenia and correctly diagnosed MPD. My ideology is that
schizophrenia is an organic disease of the brain and that its primary treatment
is physical. It is a medical illness in the strictest biomedical sense of the
term. The comprehensive treatment of schizophrenia involves intensive psychosocial interventions, however (the same is true for rheumatoid arthritis).
The ultimate goal of schizophrenia research is to find biological methods for
preventing it. MPD, on the other hand, could be prevented by stopping
childhood trauma. This means that primary prevention of schizophrenia is
more likely than the eradication of MPD.

MPD may be roughly as common as schizophrenia. It causes as much
morbidity for the individual, economic cost for society, and emotional cost
for friends and relatives of the patient. At the present time MPD is more
treatable than schizophrenia. Obviously these are very rough, ballpark gen-
eralizations.

I think that when MPD and severe schizophrenia coexist in the same
patient, the MPD often gets lost in the fragmentation and disorganization of
the patient's psyche. Psychotherapy for the MPD is probably of limited or
no use in such cases, of which I have encountered one. The patient should

probably be treated as a schizophrenic, even in an ideal world of unlimited resources. In a finite world of severely limited resources, such patients should not get psychotherapy when there are better prognosis candidates on the waiting list.

There may be a dissociative subtype of schizophrenia, however. This subtype may have a different prognosis or treatment response. One of my just-initiated research projects is to attempt to identify such a subtype. If it exists, it should be incorporated into future DSMs, along with catatonic, paranoid, and other subtypes.

Dissociative schizophrenia is probably characterized by Schneiderian symptoms, ESP experiences, bizarre somatic delusions, borderline criteria, and childhood trauma. The patients may have a borderline premorbid character, rather than schizoid-schizotypal. Or the "mystical" adolescent interested in demonology, who retires into his bedroom for months before his first psychotic break, may be highly dissociative. I don't know.

My main prediction is that the Schneiderian symptoms occurring in schizophrenics are dissociative in nature. This may be true of positive symptoms in general. The main features that differentiate MPD and schizophrenia are the negative symptoms of schizophrenia and the posttraumatic dissociative feature of MPD. The negative symptoms of schizophrenia are occupational and social deterioration, emptiness, loss of drive, and the other "burnout"-type features. The negative symptoms appear to be irreversible deficits in brain function caused by a progressive biological illness. Antipsychotic medications have no effect on the negative symptoms of schizophrenia.

In a very simple model, which is no simpler than the dopamine theory of schizophrenia, the deterioration of the schizophrenic brain causes positive symptoms during acute flare-ups and in the initial years of the illness. These are due to the irritation of the brain by the etiological agents of the illness, which might be a virus and dysregulated immune cells in one patient, endogenous toxins in another. The brain of the schizophrenic gets "feverish" during acute phases. In this model the neuroleptics are nonspecific firehoses that cool the brain off temporarily, until the "fever" subsides. Their clinical site of action could be in the walls of cerebral capillaries as easily as in the synapses.

Patients who develop the biological illness of schizophrenia should be more likely to display dissociative features if they have abuse histories. One would want to compare four diagnostic groups on the DES and DDIS: dissociative schizophrenia, paranoid schizophrenia, MPD without chronic trauma disorder, and chronic trauma disorder with MPD. This study would yield four clusters: abuse-dissociation–schizophrenia; no abuse-no dissociation–schizophrenia; no abuse-dissociation–no schizophrenia; and abuse-dissociation–no schizophrenia. I when I say no abuse, I mean no more abuse than in controls without psychiatric disorders.

A question would arise concerning the group with dissociative schizophrenia. Do they have two diagnoses or one? Do they have dissociative schizophrenia only, or do they have schizophrenia and chronic trauma disorder concurrently? Unlike the question about whether borderlines have a psychosis or a personality disorder, that would be a real question. I'm not sure how to go about sorting it out. One consideration would be treatment response.

Generally, one cannot infer etiology from treatment response in psychiatry (Ross, 1986a). Pragmatically, the question is whether patients with dissociative schizophrenia benefit from psychotherapeutic interventions derived from the MPD literature. Historically, the psychotherapy of schizophrenia has been more or less abandoned, although Meichenbaum (1977) has shown that cognitive-behavioral interventions can reduce delusional statements made by schizophrenics. It may be that the positive features of dissociative schizophrenia can be treated at least partially with psychotherapy, though. Because schizophrenia carries such severe morbidity, this is a possibility worth investigating. The first step, clearly, is to determine whether a dissociative subtype of schizophrenia exists and to show that it can be reliably differentiated from other subtypes.

Globally in psychiatry, I think, we have become sloppy clinicians in our study of schizophrenia because of the biological model of the illness. I am not personally exempt from this sloppiness. The tendency now is away from spending any amount of time talking with the schizophrenic patient in an attempt to understand his or her *mind*. Once we check off a few symptoms, make the diagnosis, and start medication, detailed study of the psychosis becomes clinically irrelevant, in much of daily practice. One monitors the patient only carefully enough to track treatment response, which is usually not very carefully. There is no reason to try to understand the patient's mind in detail, as there is in a long-term psychotherapy case, because the symptoms are just biologically driven craziness that needs to be suppressed with medication.

These remarks are directed at the general tendency of most clinical practice in North America. The medical treatment of schizophrenia isn't really psychiatric these days, although the physicians who provide it are called psychiatrists. It is really neurological, and the physicians are psychiatric internists. Within the biomedical camp this is viewed as highly desirable. But I think we have become third-rate phenomenologists of schizophrenia. We should consider putting the psychiatry back into schizophrenia treatment, not just with educational groups, social support, and similar interventions, but with *mind* interventions that are specific for the illness and effective. This would have to involve something very different from psychoanalytic psychotherapy.

MPD taught me something about the clinical examination of auditory hallucinations. Contemporary psychiatry is like a cardiology in which one examines the radial pulse but never listens to the heart with a stethoscope. In the clinical examination of auditory hallucinations, a major feature is simply left out of all the standard textbooks. In the routine clinical assessment of auditory hallucinations one should determine whether it is possible to talk to the voices. This exercise is an important method for subtyping dissociative schizophrenia, or at least I think it will become that. As things stand now, the only people who talk to patients' voices are MPD therapists. In mainstream psychiatry this doesn't even occur to the examiner as a possible intervention.

Although one must avoid tautological definitions, it is possible that one cannot talk to psychotic voices, but only to dissociative voices. If one can hold conversations with the voices of a patient who has correctly diagnosed schizophrenia, this would be evidence in favor of a dissociative subtype. There are two main ways to talk to voices.

The first steps in the clinical examination of auditory hallucinations are those of classical psychiatry. One must find out if there are voices, the number of different voices, what they say, the tone or mood of their speech, their association with other symptoms, and the patient's understanding of them and response to them. The voices may talk directly to the patient; if they order her to do things, that is called a command hallucination. Or the voices may talk to each other, in a cooperative, argumentative, or other fashion. The voices may comment on the patient and her thoughts, feelings, and actions in the third person.

Voices can do other things. They can repeat the patient's thoughts out loud or say them just before the patient was going to think them. They can perform thought insertion and thought withdrawal. It is important for the examiner to think about the voices *as if* they are actual people and try to find out what they are like, what they are doing, and what their motivation seems to be. In other words, one should examine *all* auditory hallucinations as if they come from alter personalities, in order to positively rule dissociation in or out. This applies no matter what the clinical diagnosis.

In severe acute schizophrenia the voices are often bizarre and irrational. The patient may describe CIA agents talking in his testicles, or Martians talking through a microphone implanted in his brain. The content of the voices' speech may be incoherent, irrational, or bizarre. Such voices tend to be psychotic, rather than dissociative. One cannot engage them in conversation, nor can the patient. Often they do not come from inside the patient's head, whereas dissociative voices tend to. All these distinctions are based on clinical experience, not on designed studies.

Psychotic voices tend to be associated with thought disorder and acute phases of a psychotic illness, whereas dissociative voices tend to be chronically present even when the patient is functioning well. All of these distinctions are only general rules of thumb. The distinction between psychotic and dissociative voices may be semantic. Psychotic, in this regard, may be a subset of dissociative, because dissociation must occur in some form for a mind to hear part of itself talking and to experience that as nonself talking. If that is the case, psychotic voices are a form of dissociation with certain characteristics, one of which is that they occur in a chronic major mental illness of presumed biological etiology. But there are other differences.

I examined a young native man with schizophrenia. He had numerous severe negative symptoms, inappropriate affect, poverty of speech and movement, a psychotic sister, and a supportive, warm, nonabusive family. But I could talk to his voices. He had two main voices with whom he held conversations. Both spoke in English and were white, although other minor voices spoke in Cree. He described one as good and one as bad. The bad one wanted him to assault people and generally act in an unpleasant manner. The good one tried to soothe him and advised more socially acceptable behavior. The bad one sometimes claimed to be the Devil.

Previous to my examination a social worker had talked directly with the Devil briefly, when he had taken executive control spontaneously. I was unable to induce a switch, but I had a long rational conversation with the two voices. They both gave their points of view on the patient and each other, spoke politely, and would be described as "cooperative to examination" in a classical mental status examination report. The voices in this patient were more than chaotic symptoms of insanity. They were in fact sane. Schizophrenic voices tend to be crazy.

In this patient, his dissociative features have not led to any novel interventions or any change in the standard biomedical therapy, or in the broader biopsychosocial management of the case, which includes periodic family meetings with the parents, the patient, and the psychotic sister. The parents reported transient positive improvement after a series of traditional native medicine interventions.

To engage the patient in such a conversation with the voices, one explains in a straightforward fashion that sometimes it is possible for the doctor to ask the voices questions. One then explains simultaneously to the patient and the voices how the procedure works:

> I am going to ask the voices some questions now. What I want the voices to do is listen, then answer to John. John will tell me what the voice said, then I will ask another question. If any of the voices want to ask me a question, they should feel free to: John will tell me what was asked, and I'll try my best to answer. First I want to talk to the voice John calls the white voice. The first question I have is, white voice, can you hear me and understand what I'm saying?

If the patient reports that the voice answered, "Yes," one proceeds with whatever line of questioning seems required. If the voice said, "No," I might reply:

> Because the voice said, "No," I know that means he can hear me and understand me. I can't force you to talk, white voice, in fact I don't even want to try to force you to do anything. I would like to talk to you a bit, though,

because what you have to say might help me understand John better and figure out how to help him. What do you think of that, white voice?

I use various strategies to try to engage the voice. If none work, I leave open the possibility of talking to me or another doctor later. All this is done with no formal induction of hypnosis, in a straightforward fashion and in a normal tone of voice. If there is no response from the voices of any kind, one can fish a bit in various ways, just as one might with a hostile adolescent who won't talk.

When trying to talk to the voices, with or without success, it is always important to monitor the patient's affective and physiological state. There may be no answer, but the patient may feel a wave of anger coming from somewhere, or may get tense or frightened. These are signals that dissociated affect is linked to the psychic region from which the voices emanate. This is suggestive evidence that a substantial amount of psyche has been dissociated and that it has internal structure. Simple psychotic voices often don't appear to have any psychic structure linked to them.

Psychotic voices probably come from very small fragments of psyche, too small even to be "fragments" in the sense of fragment personalities. I lean toward a continuum of increasingly small amounts of psyche dissociated (Ross, 1985) as one passes downward from personalities, to fragments, to psychotic voices.

Hierarchically, the next step after engagement of the voices in conversation, with the patient as intermediary, is inducing a switch of executive control and talking directly with the voices while they have executive control. Techniques for doing this are described in Chapter 11.

Here is another example of a patient whose voices I talked with indirectly. This man is amnesic for a rape–murder and two rapes with attempted murder committed 8 years prior to examination. He has been in a mental hospital since the crimes and has been unfit to stand trial. In the past he has had numerous conversion and dissociative symptoms. He has two female voices, one friendly and one extremely hostile. They are difficult to engage in conversation because of the hostility of the bad voice.

Whenever the patient gets too close to a woman, including female staff, the bad voice starts instructing him to perpetrate a violent sex crime on her. The voices are not affected by his antidepressant and antipsychotic medication. I could not talk with the voices very long because of the hostility of the bad voice and therefore could not rule MPD in or out. For a man like this, and for society, there are two options, if one excludes capital punishment: (1) He can stay in hospital or prison until he dies; (2) regular intensive psychotherapy can be conducted for years. From Option 2, there are two possibilities: He can be cured and set free eventually, or he is untreatable and can never be safely released. In practice he could eventually be released neither treated nor safe.

The bad voice is the portal of entry into that region of the man's psyche that holds the memory and motivation for the crimes. Even if classical MPD isn't present, the only possibility for cure lies on the other side of the amnesia barrier, with the voice. The cost of the psychotherapy would be a minute fraction of the total cost of housing this man in hospital or prison. In addition, knowledge of other unsolved crimes and the fate of unlocated missing persons may be locked away behind the amnesia barrier. To me these are possibilities that warrant aggressive investigation.

In conclusion, MPD potentially can teach us much about schizophrenia and psychotic features that occur in schizophrenia, mania, delirium, and other organic brain syndromes. The examination of auditory hallucinations is incomplete if one does not try to talk with the voices. For these reasons MPD should not be ignored by biological psychiatry.

OBSESSIVE-COMPULSIVE DISORDER

As suggested earlier, obsessive-compulsive disorder is not an anxiety disorder, contrary to its classification in DSM-III and DSM-III-R. Anxiety is a minor secondary feature of the disorder. Often, obsessive-compulsive disorder is just one of the subdiagnoses of chronic trauma disorder. In other cases it is probably a variant or feature of depression, Tourette's syndrome, schizophrenia, or another primary diagnosis. A minority of obsessive-compulsive patients appear to have a freestanding disorder limited to the specific obsessions and compulsions. Historically, obsession was related to demon possession, which is a dissociative phenomenon.

We have done one small study that demonstrates the existence of a dissociative subtype of obsessive-compulsive disorder, occurring in patients with chronic trauma disorder with partial MPD (Ross & Anderson, 1988). During the course of our clinical work we did sodium amytal interviews on two obsessive-compulsive patients refractory to treatment. Under sodium amytal, both manifested alter personalitylike entities who claimed responsibility for the patients' obsessions and compulsions. Neither of these entities ever took executive control outside the sodium amytal interview, but both used copresence to inflict symptoms on the patients. Neither are full alter personalities.

We were able to differentiate these two patients from a third obsessive-compulsive patient on a variety of measures. The third patient did not have chronic trauma disorder and did not manifest an alter personalitylike entity on sodium amytal interview. We also compared the three obsessive patients to three MPD patients on the measures used. The two dissociative obsessive patients resembled the MPD patients more than the nondissociative patient.

The measures used in this study were the DDIS, DES, the Anxiety Disorders Interview Schedule, the SCL-90, and the Lynfield Inventory for obsessive-compulsive disorder. The nondissociative patient had lower scores on all measures and met criteria for far fewer diagnoses. Although this was only a small pilot study, it provides the measures and ideas for definitive identification of a dissociative subtype of obsessive-compulsive disorder.

One would give these measures to, say, 100 consecutively seen obsessive-compulsive patients, with enrollment at several Anxiety Disorders Clinics. Next, an MPD specialist blind to the results of the interviews and self-report questionnaires, would attempt to contact an alter personalitylike entity using sodium amytal. The measures would predict which patients would clinically dissociate under sodium amytal. The patients could then be triaged into controlled behavioral and pharmacological treatment outcome studies, in a blind, randomized fashion. Clinicians assessing the treatment response of the obsessive-compulsive disorder would be blind to the measures of dissociation and the results of sodium amytal interview.

I expect that such a study would identify a dissociative subtype of obsessive-compulsive disorder that is harder to treat with chlomipramine or behavioral techniques. Conversely, screening out patients with the dissociative subtype would yield a better differentiation of placebo and active treatment response rates in nondissociative obsessive-compulsive disorder.

The presence of highly dissociative individuals in a wide variety of diagnostic groups is probably confounding studies of many kinds in psychiatry, including nosologic, treatment outcome, and biological marker studies. They are increasing the variability, narrowing the gap between placebo and active treatment, and increasing the percentage of nonresponders. Screening out these people should be of great interest to the pharmaceutical industry, if no one else.

Clinically, obsessions and compulsions are much like the Schneiderian symptoms in MPD. They arise from a large, structured, dissociated portion of psyche. Until I worked intensively with MPD patients, it never occurred to me to ask where obsessions and compulsions come from. I was taught that they are "ego alien" and heard some implausible analytic discussion of their site of origin. But by and large, where the symptoms come from was never asked. It didn't seem to be an important question: The obsessions just came from "out there," somewhere. Out there was perfunctorily assumed to be "the unconscious," and there wasn't much else to say about it.

To me, having worked with MPD patients, where the obsessions come from is a crucial clinical question. The dissociative view of general psychopathology flows inevitably from intensive work with MPD, if one listens to the patients. If you work with multiples a lot, all patients start to sound dissociative. This is similar to the specialist in depression, for whom everyone seems to be depressed. I expect the reader and the field to take my bias into account and to weigh my data and argument accordingly. Having said that, I will not refrain from occasional dogmatism.

Like much else in general psychopathology, obsessions and compulsions seem to arise from dissociated aspects of the psyche. They *must*, otherwise they wouldn't be experienced as obsessions and compulsions. The therapeutic question is whether it is necessary, or helpful, to work directly with the dissociated psyche in order to alleviate the symptoms. This is the case in MPD. Why not in obsessive-compulsive disorder? In practice, the expedient approach might be to do a sodium amytal interview in all patients who fail to respond to adequate trials of chlomipramine and/or behavioral treatment. Depending on the findings on sodium amytal interview, dissociative interventions could be attempted next.

If the patient has chronic trauma disorder with MPD, however, the hierarchically superior treatment should be instituted first.

CONVERSION DISORDER

Once one begins to think dissociatively, conversion disorders appear to be dissociative in nature. In fact conversion disorders are classified as dissociative disorders in the International Classification of Diseases (ICD-10; Sartorius, personal communication to Coons, 1988). I'm not sure why North Americans have a problem seeing the correctness of this. In my clinical experience conversion disorders occur in two forms: as isolated conversions in the absence of overt severe general psychopathology, or as features of chronic trauma disorder.

According to the model of dissociation outlined in Chapter 5, dissociation can occur in any area of the brain, with the function corresponding to that brain region being dissociated. A pure, simple dissociation of memory is psychogenic amnesia; a dissociation of motor or sensory function, a conversion disorder. To me this is self-evident. I am trying to make it other-evident.

In DSM-III and DSM-III-R conversion is classified as a type of somatoform disorder. This is the case for two reasons: first, because the body is involved; second, because of the vestigial influence of Freudian theory. Freud attempted to make distinctions between repression, conversion, and somatization that are untestable and not clearly thought out.

Conversion disorder is called conversion disorder because Freud said it was based on conversion. If it was based on somatization, it would be called somatization disorder; if on repression, repression disorder with physical symptoms, I suppose. Conversion disorder couldn't be called somatization disorder in DSM-III because that name is used for Briquet's hysteria (Mai & Merskey, 1980). The symptoms of Briquet's hysteria are part of the dissociative cluster, however. Chasing phantom metapsychological distinctions between the items of the dissociative cluster is confusing and pointless. The somatoform disorders need extensive reorganization. As they stand, they are a group of heterogeneous disorders thrown together as a group of illnesses because they have physical symptoms.

There should be two major categories in DSM-IV: the trauma disorders and the dissociative disorders. The existence of a trauma disorder is an exclusion criterion for the diagnosis of a dissociative disorder. Conversion disorder is a dissociative disorder without chronic trauma disorder, conversion subtype. It can be called conversion disorder and be listed among the dissociative disorders, because the longer name is too unwieldy and is implied by the inclusion/exclusion rules. Psychogenic amnesia would be dissociative disorder without chronic trauma disorder, amnesic subtype, but would just be called psychogenic amnesia. The term conversion should be retained because everyone knows what it means. Similarly, chronic trauma disorder should be an exclusion criterion for a freestanding diagnosis of somatization disorder. There should be a dissociative disorder without chronic trauma disorder, somatization subtype, named simply somatization disorder. Psychogenic fugue should be similarly classified.

This reorganization would bring greater conceptual consistency to the field and would group things as they are grouped in nature. In nature, similar treatments are effective for similar disorders. The etiology, natural history, and treatment of conversion disorder and psychogenic amnesia are very similar. For conversion disorder and hypochondriasis they are very different. Yet conversion is classified in a group of somatoform disorders that includes hypochondriasis. This makes sense only as the outcome of a set of unresolved historical forces, not as a scientific classification.

Some cases of psychogenic pain may represent positive dissociative symptoms. Dissociation can result in something being present that is usually absent or something being absent that is usually present. Dissociative headache is a good example of dissociative psychogenic pain. Psychogenic pain is probably a heterogenous group of disorders, with some cases actually being organic pain of unrecognized etiology. There may be a dissociative subtype, but the diagnosis should not be moved to the dissociative disorders.

INTERMITTENT EXPLOSIVE DISORDER

I have never seen a case of intermittent explosive disorder, but I have met quite a few intermittently explosive alter personalities. This diagnosis is a dissociative disorder by definition, regardless of etiology. It is defined as intermittent switching to explosive states. DSM-III notes that there can be partial or complete amnesia for the explosive state, a fact highly suggestive of undiagnosed MPD.

If a series of patients with alleged intermittent explosive disorder were reviewed by an MPD expert, I believe that at least half would have partial or full MPD. Of the other half, in most a switch of state could be induced quite easily by hypnosis, sodium amytal, or experimental oral alcohol.

The Cartesian mind–body dichotomy in psychiatry is evident in opinions that intermittent explosive disorder is a form of epilepsy or other organic brain illness (implying that the patient is not legally responsible for the explosive behavior). This results in acting-out adolescents being treated with antiepileptic medication to control their "seizures." That is fine if the medication works, but the dissociative phenomenology of the "illness" has not been explored, consequently neither have curative psychotherapeutic possibilities derived from the MPD literature.

TEMPORAL LOBE EPILEPSY

Related to the issue of whether intermittent explosive disorder is a form of epilepsy is the idea that temporal lobe epilepsy should be seriously considered in the differential diagnosis of MPD. It shouldn't. I am discussing it in this chapter because there is no chapter on MPD and neurological disorders. Temporal lobe epilepsy is classified as complex partial seizures in the official nomenclature. I will refer to it as temporal lobe epilepsy because readers are likely more familiar with that name.

The inclusion of temporal lobe epilepsy in the differential diagnosis of MPD, in the MPD literature, is based on a few reports of small series of patients with concurrent MPD and temporal lobe epilepsy (Benson, Miller, & Signer, 1986; Cocores, Bender, & McBride, 1984; Mesulam, 1981; Schenk & Bear, 1981). For me personally, inclusion of temporal lobe seizures in the differential diagnosis of MPD was based on a desire not to be "caught napping" by general or biological psychiatrists. I felt I had to include the epilepsy to show that I was a real doctor and not treating brain tumors, epilepsy, and other neurological illnesses with psychotherapy. If I left it out of my differential, I felt, critics would say I was being a poor physician. I found out that the critics were being poor scientists.

The first trouble with the alleged cases of MPD/temporal lobe epilepsy in the literature is that many of them don't have MPD. These are in fact the only false-positive cases of MPD I know of in the psychiatric literature prior to 1988 (Coons, 1988a). That is curious, because these papers are sometimes thought to discredit MPD as a legitimate psychiatric diagnosis. In Benson, Miller, and Signer's (1986) paper, for instance, the "MPD" consists of intermittent psychotic states with Capgras's syndrome. These probably represent *status epilepticus*. The states have none of the structure, rationale for existence, or function of alter personalities. There is no evidence of childhood abuse. In other papers, some of the cases don't have full MPD.

There isn't a single case in the literature of classical MPD responding to antiepileptic medication. Collective clinical experience in North America, if it were assembled in a single report, would document hundreds of MPD patients with blood level-controlled trials of epilepsy medication with no effect on the MPD. In fact not a single case of an adequate trial of epilepsy medication in a well-described case of MPD, with adequate observation of symptom-response, is documented in the literature.

In the only study comparing MPD patients with and without temporal lobe epilepsy, Putnam (1986a) found no difference between the two groups in abuse histories or features of their MPD. In the only study comparing groups of MPD ($N = 20$) and temporal lobe epileptic patients ($N = 20$) with reliable instruments, we found that the two disorders differed on all dissociative sections of the DDIS, and on the DES, at high levels of significance (Ross, Neber, & Anderson, et al., 1989). The 20 temporal lobe epileptics did not differ from 28 controls with other neurological disorders, except that they more often met criteria for depersonalization disorder. We interpreted the finding on depersonalization as evidence that it is not a freestanding disorder, but a symptom of other disorders, in this case of epilepsy.

The data show that MPD and temporal lobe epilepsy can be clearly differentiated on a large number of clinical features at high levels of significance. A recent study by Loewenstein and Putnam (1988) confirms this. As well, temporal lobe epilepsy has no effect on the features of MPD in patients who have both disorders. Basically, this shows that the relationship between MPD and temporal lobe epilepsy is a research dead end. Clinically, there are no positive reasons to consider temporal lobe epilepsy in the differential diagnosis of MPD any more than any other neurological disorder. Perhaps this piece of reductionist-driven clinical lore can be laid to rest.

ALCOHOL IDIOSYNCRATIC INTOXICATION

Alcohol idiosyncratic intoxication is also called pathological intoxication. It is defined as abrupt "maladaptive" changes of behavior markedly atypical for the person when not drinking. The changed behavior is usually aggressive or assaultive and occurs "within minutes of ingesting an amount of alcohol insufficient to cause intoxication in most people" (DSM-III-R, p. 129). The differential diagnosis includes temporal lobe epilepsy and malingering. The disorder is classified as an organic mental disorder (Goodwin, Crane, & Guze, 1969).

Alcohol idiosyncratic intoxication is basically intermittent explosive disorder triggered by pharmacologically insignificant doses of alcohol. Yet the two appear in unrelated sections of DSM-III-R and neither is mentioned in the differential diagnosis of the other. This doesn't make sense. It shows that DSM-III-R has MPD: Its sections are produced by dissociated fragment committees, many with two-way amnesia barriers between them.

The authors of the discussion section of alcohol idiosyncratic intoxication in DSM-III-R try to account for the observed fact that a pharmacologically meaningless dose of alcohol is involved by postulating a lowered biological threshold of sensitivity to alcohol. They suggest several mechanisms for this including subclinical temporal lobe epilepsy, encephalitis, brain injury, debilitating physical illness, and old age. This is pushing biological explanations a long way. Interestingly, Goodwin, Crane, and Guze (1969) note one individual in their series of 100 cases who "believed he could produce a blackout at will, as a kind of 'self-hypnosis' '' (p. 1036). This suggests that careful screening might have yielded more cases of psychogenic dissociation.

What doesn't get consideration is psychological dissociation triggered by the psychosocial context and meaning of alcohol ingestion. Pathological intoxication is basically a state-switching disorder triggered by the social act of drinking alcohol. Placebo alcohol in the same social setting would probably work just as well. Like intermittent explosive disorder, many people with idiosyncratic alcohol intoxication probably have partial or full MPD: All have angry states dissociated from their host states. Accessing and interviewing these dissociated states would probably be technically straightforward.

The exclusively biological account of alcohol idiosyncratic intoxication in DSM-III-R is an extreme example of reductionist ideology creating a dissociated diagnostic system. It is also symbolic of a general bias in the field of substance abuse. People with different forms of substance abuse experience altered states and amnesia on a regular basis. Much of this is no doubt biologically driven. But much is probably psychological and dissociative in nature. Everything tends to get written off as a result of drugs, however. If I am correct, the phenomenology of substance abuse disorders needs major revision.

Some alcohol blackouts start before alcohol ingestion—is this retrograde organic amnesia or a switch to a substance-abusing alter? Does anyone ever ask the question? Similarly, at least some chemically dependent patients refractory to the usual treatments probably have MPD: In such cases the addicted alter never gets treatment and sits scornfully coconscious in the background while the host personality dutifully attends treatment. The patient never gets better because the wrong "person" is in treatment. The therapist might as well be treating the patient's brother, uncle, or neighbor.

Alcohol idiosyncratic intoxication patients are dissociative patients who give themselves in vivo placebo sodium amytal interviews using pharmacologically insignificant amounts of alcohol. Successful treatment might result from the doctor doing the interviewing, rather than the patient.

EATING DISORDERS

In our series of 236 cases of MPD (Ross, Norton, & Wozney, 1989), 16.3 percent had a previous diagnosis of an eating disorder. I think that this is a gross underestimate of the prevalence of pathological eating behavior in MPD, which must be present in over 50 percent of cases, and probably over 75 percent. Eating disorders are one of the hierarchically lower disorders within chronic trauma disorder and are related to sexual abuse in general (Goodwin & Attias, 1988; Goodwin, Cheeves, & Connell, 1988) and to MPD in particular (Torem, 1986, 1987, 1988).

Anorexia and bulimia can both occur as nonspecific behavior within chronic trauma disorder, or they can have specific dissociative mechanisms. Goodwin and Attias, (1988) have described such specific dissociative mechanisms with great depth and clarity. The distortion of body image in anorexia nervosa can have a dissociative basis and can be caused by the copresence of an alter personality in some cases. Somatic memories and behavioral enactments of specific abuse incidents can underly binging, vomiting, purging, and other behaviors.

I am not going to say much about eating disorders and dissociation, other than to note that there is undoubtedly a large subgroup of eating-disordered patients who are dissociative in nature. Some of these have frank MPD, some don't. These patients are an excellent population for study because they have discrete behavioral symptoms that can be monitored in treatment. The efficacy of dissociative and abreactive interventions could be readily demonstrated in a subgroup of patients in treatment for eating disorders.

I have emphasized the concept of a dissociative subgroup of eating disorders because there is likely an affective subgroup, among others. As in all sections of DSM-III-R, the challenge is to identify specific diagnostic subgroups that respond differentially to different well-defined treatments. One of the subgroups that should be considered throughout psychiatry is the dissociative.

PSYCHOSEXUAL DISORDERS

Many of the psychosexual disorders are dissociative disorders. Take the man who is impotent with his wife, but not with his mistress, during masturbation, or while dreaming. There is nothing wrong with his penis or with the nerves and hormones connecting his penis and his brain. He has dissociated his ability to have an erection in one particular social context.

The same is true for psychogenic frigidity in a woman who reaches orgasm easily with a lover or vibrator. Such a woman has dissociated her ability to be aroused and fulfilled sexually. Impotence and frigidity occur on a spectrum. At one end of the spectrum are pure biological forms, at the other pure psychological forms, and in the middle are mixed forms. This is analogous to the classification of asthma as intrinsic, extrinsic, or mixed.

The psychosexual disorders of arousal and orgasm are like conversion disorder and psychogenic pain: Psychogenic impotence is clearly dissociative, whereas dyspareunia (painful intercourse for the female) may be. The disorder of absent function is clearly dissociative, whereas the disorder of abnormal pain is not so clearly dissociative.

Another group of psychosexual disorders involve sexual orientation and gender identity. In the absence of any research data, I can only speculate that ego-dystonic homosexuality and transexualism are dissociative in nature. Evidence in support of this possibility is the frequent existence of homosexual and opposite-sex alters in MPD. This does not mean that a substantial proportion of transsexuals are dissociative, but the possibility is worth investigating. I have assessed one man with an incorrect diagnosis of schizophrenia who wants a sex-change operation. His female personality is easily contacted and wants to get rid of the male host, everything he stands for, and his genitals. The female alter sees this as a power struggle for control of the body.

The most important possibility is that many sex criminals have dissociative disorders. Bliss (1985) has provided preliminary evidence that this is the case, but no definitive study has been conducted. We know that many abusers were themselves abused. It would make sense that many sexual criminals have chronic trauma disorder with MPD. One such man is described in the discussion of schizophrenia. Enough is now known about dissociation that it is *imperative,* from the point of view of the social responsibility of the psychiatric profession, to investigate whether sexual criminals are often dissociative and whether treatment techniques from the MPD literature would reduce recidivism.

MANIC-DEPRESSIVE ILLNESS

Manic-depressive illness is called bipolar affective disorder in DSM-III and DSM-III-R. I believe that, like schizophrenia, it is a biological brain illness, that the primary treatment is medical, and that psychosocial interventions are required. This is the majority, mainstream view in contemporary psychiatry. Manic-depressive illness is a disorder of switching. Patients with the disorder switch states in a pathological manner. Their problem is several-fold: They switch into states, switch out of states, and get stuck in states in an abnormal manner.

There is a severe discontinuity of mood, speech, thought, and behavior across states. What about identity? And memory? A distortion in memory is characteristic of depression, and depressed patients ignore their positive achievements and qualities while selectively focusing on the negative (Beck et al., 1979) when in the depressed state. Little attention is paid to the discontinuity of identity that must occur across states, as patients switch from depression to mania. This is an interesting area for research in itself.

I am not suggesting a reclassification of mania or depression as dissociative disorders. They are affective disorders. But the discontinuity of identity across states in MPD might shed light on the switch process in manic-depressive illness. Frank Putnam (1989), I'm sure, has written about this extensively in his book. The situation might be a little different with nonpsychotic unipolar depression. This disorder might have prominent dissociative mechanisms.

I have done successful classical cognitive therapy with a few unipolar depressive patients. In my experience, which is representative, depressed patients can be transiently converted to a normal affective state with cognitive interventions even in the first few sessions. Often less than 10 sessions are required to switch the patient out of depression for a long period of time. What does this say? It tells us that the normal mood, thoughts, and behavior of depressed patients are not lost. They are not simply absent due to a chemical deficiency in the brain. In fact they can be recovered psychotherapeutically quite quickly.

This is like the recovery of normal mood in MPD by switching from a depressed to a nondepressed alter, and it suggests to me that in unipolar depression the patient's normal mood is dissociated. It must be, otherwise how could one get it back so quickly? The machinery that maintains the separateness of alter personalities can be analyzed cognitively, and many of my interventions in MPD are cognitive. Perhaps in unipolar depression the depressogenic cognitions are the psychic machinery for maintaining a dissociation of normal mood. Dismantle the machinery, and the normal mood comes back. This is what happens in cognitive therapy, according to Beck (Beck et al., 1979).

A corollary of this view of unipolar depression is that the antidepressants are actually antidissociatives. The standard view of the antidepressants is that they work by correcting a deficit. The deficit is thought to be a deficiency in noradrenalin or serotonin function in the brain. Maybe tricyclics actually work by dampening down and suppressing an excess of dissociation. Neurochemically, this would mean that the antidepressants reduce levels of one or more neurotransmitters. This could occur by an actual reduction in synthesis or release of transmitter, an increase in reuptake or degradation, or a modulation of receptor density or sensitivity. Both mechanisms, dissociative and depletive/depressive, could be at work in subgroups of affective illness, which would account for the contradictory results in biological marker studies—dissociative depressed patients have an excess of transmitter, nondissociative have a deficiency. Some patients presenting with depression, of course, actually have MPD (Frances & Spiegel, 1987).

This reasoning is an example of how the study of MPD can lead to novel hypotheses in biological psychiatry. These hypotheses could lead to experimentation and insight at the basic and clinical levels. The view that the antidepressants are actually antidissociatives would make sense of the fact that chlomipramine, a tricyclic antidepressant, is effective for obsessive-compulsive disorder (Ross, Siddiqui, & Matas, 1987), which is dissociative in nature in at least a large subgroup. This line of thought leads to the opposite prediction of that made in the section on obsessive-compulsive disorder: Chlomipramine could be most effective in the dissociative subtype of obsessive-compulsive disorder, rather than least effective. The two possibilities could be studied in the same clinical trial.

A similar trial could be carried out for unipolar depression. Depressed patients without chronic trauma disorder could be divided into high- and low-dissociators on the DES and DDIS. Half of each group could be given imipramine, and half chlomipramine, in a randomized double-blind fashion.

Imipramine is less effective for obsessive-compulsive disorder than chlomipramine, but the two are equally effective, overall, for depression. If obsessive-compulsive disorder is dissociative in nature, and if chlomipramine is the most antidissociative tricyclic, then chlomipramine should be more effective than imipramine in the high-dissociative depressed group and equally effective in the low-dissociative depressed group.

Similarly, if cognitive therapy is an antidissociative treatment, it should be more effective in high-DES unipolar depression. I want to emphasize that I am advocating a way of thinking about psychopathology and classifying psychiatric illnesses that leads to testable hypotheses in both biological and psychological psychiatry and eradicates Cartesian dualism.

A final additional speculation. Methylphenidate (Ritalin®) is effective in slowing down hyperactive children, although it is a stimulant. This is paradoxical. Similarly, some people react to benzodiazepines, which are sedatives, with hyperalertness, arousal, and agitation. Why should a stimulant slow down a hyperactive child? Perhaps the children are hyperactive because they can't dissociate irrelevant stimuli effectively. Perhaps methylphenidate helps them dissociate better.

As for the people who fly into a rage on diazepam, perhaps the drug interferes with their ability to maintain their rage in a dissociated state. This would make sense, because sodium amytal increases the ease with which one can access dissociated states, and it is a sedative. Similarly, one can sometimes transiently reverse catatonia in a schizophrenic with benzodiazepines like diazepam and lorazepam.

Clinically I've had the experience of *curing* the catatonic state of a woman with a psychotic unipolar depression in 5 minutes with sodium amytal. This woman had been unable to eat or drink, was mute and fearful, and was catatonically posturing in the seclusion room. Within 5 minutes of starting the intravenous sodium amytal, she began tearfully but coherently giving me a full history of the prodrome and onset of her depression. After the interview she went to the washroom and had lunch. I attempted to but could not engage her voice in conversation. Such dramatically effective interventions arise from looking at the world through dissociative-colored glasses.

CONCLUSION

In this chapter I have argued for a major reorganization of DSM-III-R. Many disorders currently scattered around DSM-III-R should be reclassified within either the trauma disorders or the dissociative disorders. Others have dissociative aspects that should be studied scientifically. Thinking dissociatively also leads to novel testable hypotheses in both biological and psychological psychiatry. The reorganization is consistent with the existing data, conceptually consistent, and obedient to the dictates of Occam's Razor. It also overcomes Cartesian dualism.

This latter quality of the reorganized diagnostic system is not an accident. DSM-III-R is a specialist document of interest to psychiatrists, but it is an anthropological artifact as well. DSM-III-R reveals the philosophical, cultural, and ideological foundations of modern psychiatry. Psychiatry is in turn a microcosm of the modern world. The philosophical foundation of the modern world is Cartesian dualism, as one learns reading DSM-III-R. DSM-III-R is a product of complex unresolved historical forces as much as, perhaps even more than, it is a scientific document. For instance, egosyntonic homosexuality has been defined as not being a psychiatric disorder in DSM-III-R because of political lobbying, not because of definitive scientific evidence.

The cure for Cartesian dualism in psychiatry is the study of dissociation. Why? Because Cartesian dualism is the philosophical expression of a dissociative disorder underlying Western civilization. This historical-cultural dissociation is the subject of the next chapter.

CHAPTER EIGHT

Multiple Personality and Nonclinical Dissociation

The mind of an individual psychiatric patient is embedded in the collective mind, language, and history of his or her culture: Clinical dissociation arises out of the everyday, nonpathological dissociation occurring in a given society. This means that multiple personality disorder (MPD) is a microcosm of our culture and that history must be taken into account in studying MPD (Carlson, 1981, 1984; Drew, 1988; Hawthorne, 1983; Rosenzweig, 1988). When I say "our culture," I am talking about urban literate English-speaking North America of the late 20th century.

The philosophical foundation of our culture is Cartesian dualism. The evolution toward this dualism, which is a fundamental dissociation of mind and body, began in ancient Greece. The dualism is fundamental in the sense that it is the *dynamic,* living foundation of our culture. It is concretely present in our art, science, and religion. The philosophical doctrine expounded by Descartes is not the *cause* of this dualism—it is an expression and a reinforcer of it.

In conjunction with this basic dualism, the history of Western civilization is a history of increasing fragmentation and specialization of function. The shaman has dissociated into many fragments, including doctor, priest, poet, entertainer, weather forecaster, psychotherapist, and politician. The fragmentation is not all bad: It has led to modern medicine and the highest material standard of living in human history. It is also not all good.

In this chapter I am going to examine the Cartesian dualism in Freudian psychiatry and Christianity; the relationship between extrasensory perception and clinical dissociation; and everyday nonclinical dissociation. The purpose of this chapter is to embed the study of MPD in a broad, general context. The thesis of the first section of the chapter is summarized in Figure 8.1.

DUALISM AND DISSOCIATION IN FREUD AND CHRISTIANITY

There is no dissociation in the thought of pre-Socratic philosophers like Heraclitus. Dual forces in the early Greek universe were in a unified dynamic relationship with each other. Heraclitus's mind is different from the modern unconscious mind, which contains the waste products of dissociated mental

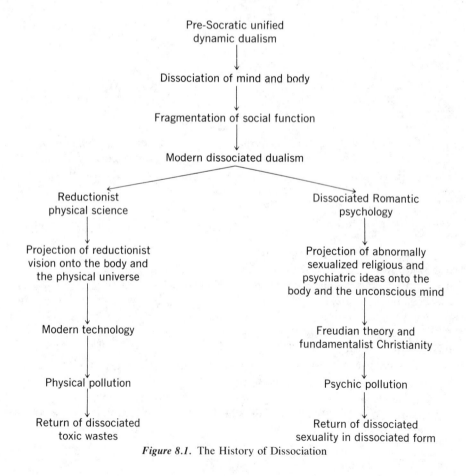

Figure 8.1. The History of Dissociation

function. As outlined in Figure 8.1, the history of Western civilization contains a fundamental theme of dissociation, the full explication of which would require a separate book.

In brief, a dissociation of mind and body occurred in Western peoples, observable in the ancient Greeks, followed by a fragmentation of social function. This occurred over millenia, at different rates in different peoples. Eventually modern dissociated dualism evolved, in which the split between mind and body was entrenched. The dissociated mind underwent a secondary split into two complementary fragments, reductionist physical science and Romantic psychology. Both these fragments were based on a prior disconnection of body and mind. One camp projected its vision of mechanistic function onto the body and the physical universe, the other either sentimentalized the natural world, or projected abnormally sexualized ideas onto the body and the unconscious mind. The outcome of this history is evident in contemporary psychiatry.

Freud suffered from the underlying dissociative disorder of our culture, but he failed to analyze it. His understanding of the unconscious is based too much on the unconscious mind of modern industrial Europe. Freud was a water quality expert who analyzed the pollutants in rivers and lakes and came to erroneous conclusions about the nature of *water* (in North America we treat our unconscious mind the same way we treat our environment: We project onto both the waste products of our mental life). The triad of dualism, dissociation, and projection is a basic dynamic of both psychoanalytic theory and contemporary fundamentalist Christianity.

Reductionism, as a philosophical doctrine, began in ancient Greece with the atomism of Democritus and Leucippus. According to these men, the world is composed of indivisible particles called atoms. The movement of these particles accounts for all the phenomena of nature. The soul was composed of more rarified atoms in this philosophical system, but both body and soul existed in a mechanistic universe. Greek atomism was basically Newtonian in principle, as are DSM-III and DSM-III-R (see Chapter 7). In DSM-III, psychiatric disorders tend to be related to each other like independent mechanical particles.

By the 19th century, with the work of Newton, Galileo, and others behind him, the Frenchman Laplace asserted that if the positions and momenta of all the particles in the universe could be determined for a single moment of time, all future configurations of matter could be calculated. This was impossible logistically, but it communicated a vision of a purely mechanical universe. Nineteenth-century physicists were so confident that they had a complete account of the universe at hand that a professor advised the young Max Planck not to go into physics, on the grounds that there was no more fundamental work to be done in the field. This advice was scientifically mistaken.

Descartes was an advocate of the complete independence of mind and body: He dissociated the two. Physical scientists, both before and after

Descartes, discarded the mind and went on to develop reductionist science, with its technology. In the other half of the secondary split, students of the psyche became increasingly idiosyncratic. They became Romantic dreamers. Freud's metapsychology is like a pale moonlit dream recounted by a Romantic poet. It is disconnected from the reality of the human psyche: Freud's early patients had their symptoms because of childhood sexual abuse, not because of disarray in the complex psychic machinery he *invented* and projected onto them.

After Freud, psychiatry became divided into mechanistic biology and psychoanalytic dreaming. The analytic dreamers did not so much study reality as project their fixed theories onto it. This is evident in the typical analytic case history, in which the patient is nowhere in sight. In this regard, analytic ideas about somatization and psychosomatic illness are a projection of mental ideation onto the physical body and do not represent a counter of dualism.

Our psychiatry is dualistic, and so is our religion. Christianity is based on the rejection of the body. The body, in the Christian vision, especially in its sexuality, is evil and its energies are demonic. The Christian fights against the temptations of the flesh and punishes the body, with the eventual aim of discarding it. Christianity and Freudian theory are both based on the projection of unhealthy theory onto the body, and on a dissociation of body and mind. They are subsets of a common dualistic culture. Historically, Christianity was initially grafted onto pagan religion and retained much of its natural vitality for many centuries, but that natural health has not been maintained. I am not idealizing pagan culture, which was often barbaric and superstitious.

In our society Christianity no longer provides a unifying vision. It is no longer a great religion in urban North America. Our society is secular and individualistic, the product of the triumph of technological reductionism over Romanticism, of one side of the secondary split over the other. Our society has become secular thanks partly to Freud, who "explained" religion, thereby destroying it. However Freud's explanation of religion was anthropocentric and explained only dualistic contemporary Christianity. The dualism of Western civilization underlies Freudian psychiatry as much as it does late Christianity. Both suffer from the same dissociative disorder.

Freudian theory and late Christianity have much in common. Both view the body as the source of energies resisted by the mind. Freud states that in the ideal mind there is no resistance to libido: This is an unattainable ideal. Both Freud and late Christianity look into the unconscious and see demons, perversion, sickness, and horror. In both instances, the discarded products of mental consciousness in dissociated form are what is being observed. The natural unconscious does not contain toxic by-products of industry.

The Western mind projects the products of its own function onto the unconscious and mistakenly concludes that they originate there. Hell and the unconscious are the same thing, named differently by two philosophical systems that are identical in their basic dynamics. Because these projected ideas are dissociated, they take on a life of their own and are perceived as demons or perverse drives.

It is not true that normal children literally, consciously want to have intercourse with their opposite-sex parents. That is a dirty-minded view of the unconscious and children, not because intercourse is dirty, but because the theory defines normal children as sexual perverts. In terms of the suppression of public awareness of child abuse, Oedipal theory provides a rationale for blaming the victim. Freudian theory offers an "out"—the abuser can be excused as the victim of his child's projective identification and/or unresolved Oedipal conflict. That is one reason why Freudian theory caught on; its unhealthy sexualized projections onto the unconscious mind were "culture-syntonic."

Freud did to the unconscious mind, with his theories, what New York City does to the ocean with its garbage. Instead of listening to the tales his patients were telling him about childhood trauma, Freud projected his theories onto them to "explain" their symptoms. Freud wasn't fluent in the language of the unconscious, so he didn't hear what his patients were telling him. Or rather he heard, but he couldn't bear to listen. Being a theoretician of genius, Freud had to invent a philosophical system that justified his not listening. Being a great clinical observer, though, he managed to hear some of what his patients were telling him, despite his theory. Freud described the mechanism of projection but was not fully aware of his own pathological projection.

Modern Christianity is similarly dissociated. Sexual perversion and fundamentalist Christianity are intertwined in our culture. This could be demonstrated demographically. It is no accident that contemporary evangelical preachers are so often chronic, frequent users of prostitutes. They are highly dissociated men. Their religion is disconnected from their sexuality. Although they preach monogamy, their sexuality is promiscuous, because they have attempted to repress and control it in an unnatural way. Consequently it has been distorted and leaks back in an unhealthy form.

The parents of MPD patients are often "religious," but their religion is a dissociated religion practiced only by their host personalities. It is the epitome of the kind of religion Freud analyzed and promiscuous evangelists practice. The sexually abusive alters of the parents of MPD patients, for which the parental host personalities are amnesic, are the "demonic" representatives of distorted sexual drive. They are the projections of unhealthy Christian doctrine coming back to torment the world. Contemporary television evangelists do not have MPD, I assume, but they exemplify a culture-specific dissociative disorder.

Freud's vision of the unconscious was also distorted and abnormally sexualized. He said that the unconscious is composed entirely of libido, and he sexualized all of human activity. This is incorrect and unhealthy. The unconscious mind contains sexual energy (if it didn't we wouldn't be here), but it is not *exclusively* sexual. The unconscious mind contains many forms of energy. The human body, in which the mind is rooted, is composed of physical matter, like the rocks, trees, stars, and wind. The body participates in their order of reality and gives different forms of that reality to the mind. The reductionists are correct when they state that the mind is rooted in the body.

But the reductionists have made the other great error of our civilization. They have denied the reality of the psyche. In fact the universe contains both soma and psyche. That would seem to be obvious enough—we have minds, and they are part of the universe. Yet we have evolved a physics that doesn't take mind into account. Our physics is the physics of half the universe. Freud analyzed God and found him to be a projection of the human mind; reductionism is equally a projection of the human mind. The two are opposite sides of the same dissociated coin.

Freud was correct as far as he went, in analyzing modern Christianity, but he was limited by the duality of his own psychology. He couldn't analyze what his patients' fathers had done to them, nor what our civilization has done to the unconscious mind, because he was socially embedded in both forms of pollution. He had a cultural countertransference problem: The incestuous fathers were his friends, neighbors, relatives, and colleagues. Freud used analytic theory to block out awareness of their criminal behavior.

A healthy relationship between mind and body is not a dualistic one in which the mind regards the body as its personal machine and takes care of it. Nor does the healthy mind regard the bodies of children as sexual objects. William Blake, a Christian, had the unified vision Freud never achieved: "Man has no Body distinct from his Soul; for that call'd Body is a portion of Soul discern'd by the five Senses" (1966, p. 149). Psychiatry needs to recover from the dissociative disorder of our culture, which affected Freud as it affects sexually promiscuous evangelists today. MPD patients offer an antidote to one of the abnormally sexualized projections of the modern dualistic mind (Freud's repudiation of the seduction theory and replacement of it with Oedipal theory). One of the paradoxes of Freud's genius is that he provided tools for analyzing his own psychopathology, but he left it to others to use them. We need to recover Freud's original insight into post-traumatic dissociative disorders.

Thinking in terms of dissociation, as well as familiarity with MPD, leads to a critique of Freud: Freud's analysis of religion, and of his patients, was impaired by his own dualism and dissociation, maladies from which psychiatry still suffers today. It would be a mistake to try to "throw out" either Freud or Christianity because both are interwoven with the foundation of our culture. I think we need to recover the original vision of both. Because this is a clinical book, I am only briefly sketching my thesis about dualism, dissociation, and projection in Western culture. The main point is that MPD must be understood in a broad context and in terms of the basic dynamics of our culture. Freudian psychiatry is neither universal nor complete. It cannot provide a technique for full psychoanalysis, because it is too determined by the dualism of our culture.

EXTRASENSORY PERCEPTION AND DISSOCIATION

The exclusion of extrasensory perception (ESP) from serious mainstream psychiatry is an artifact of our cultural history. There are only two possibilities concerning ESP experiences: Either they are real or they are illusory. If ESP is real, excluding it from psychiatry and mainstream science is prejudice masquerading as science. If ESP is not real, there is no more reason to exclude it from phenomenological study than any other set of delusions, including Schneiderian first-rank symptoms. Why did ESP experiences get excluded from mainstream psychology and psychiatry, then?

ESP was discredited along with hypnosis because of its historical connections with charlatans and cranks. Mainstream scientists rejected both the individuals involved in ESP studies and the paranormal as a field of academic inquiry. The exclusion of ESP from mainstream psychiatry was thus culture-specific and determined by the social prejudices of a particular phase of our civilization. ESP was also rejected because of scientific conservatism in much the same way that the stethoscope, smallpox vaccinations, and the circulation of the blood were initially rejected by the medical establishment.

Before ESP was banished to the fringes of psychology, subjects with dissociative and paranormal experiences were widely studied in Europe (Rogo, 1986a). In the 19th century many leading physicists and psychologists devoted a lot of time and energy to the study of ESP. Among these men was Carl Jung, who wrote a thesis in medical school dealing with the paranormal and dissociation, although he didn't use those terms (Jung, 1902).

The 19th-century mediums displayed many features of MPD. This doesn't mean that they had MPD—we don't know whether they had abuse histories and created alter personalities to cope with it. But there is a close relationship between MPD and mediumship. The young women studied by Jung entered trances, during which "controls," dead people, and other entities took executive control of their bodies. Some of the women had somatic and other "hysterical" symptoms outside their trance states.

The paranormal phenomena of 19th-century spiritualism can be readily understood as purely psychological in nature. Late 20th-century MPD patients often have alter personalities who claim to be dead people, spirits, astral beings, or other entities. It is clear that these are dissociated parts of the patients' minds. Often, though, the alters provide an initially compelling picture of paranormal power. The demons can be very chilling, until one discovers that they too are abused children.

It is peculiar that an expert in the paranormal like Rogo (1986b) can write a book on poltergeists, spend hundreds if not thousands of hours tracking them, yet never once have witnessed a poltergeist firsthand. That's a bit like my writing a book on MPD, never having met an alter personality. If poltergeists exist, why are they so hard to document?

ESP experiences are a dimension of psychological experience that has been arbitrarily banished from modern psychology. This is unfortunate because many people believe they have such experiences. ESP experiences should be viewed as subjective psychological data, and their relationship with other psychological phenomena should be studied systematically.

In analyzing the relationship between ESP and dissociation, the first step is to establish that dissociation and paranormal phenomena coexist in people. This is evident from 19th-century spiritualism, as documented in Jung's thesis. As a preliminary study, we (Heber, Ross, & Fleisher, unpublished data) interviewed 11 nontraditional therapists and 17 psychiatry residents with the DDIS and DES. The community-based therapists could not have an advanced degree, could not be in a group practice with an M.D. or Ph.D., and had to identify themselves as alternate healers or therapists.

Neither group exhibited a notable degree of psychopathology. For instance no individuals in either group met criteria for somatization disorder or borderline personality disorder. The item that most clearly differentiated the nontraditional healers from the psychiatry residents was ESP experiences, which were very common in the community-based group. The two groups both had low rates of childhood abuse.

This preliminary study suggests that ESP experiences occur in otherwise healthy, high-functioning individuals in our culture. They are not linked to childhood trauma or substance abuse and represent a dimension of experience that is not linked to psychopathology. This does not prove that ESP is real, but it means that a dimension of psychological experience is being left out of modern psychology.

ESP experiences also differentiate MPD from a variety of other clinical groups. There are strong links between childhood trauma, dissociation, and ESP in clinical populations. It may be that ESP experiences are a form of nonclinical dissociation. ESP experiences may occur spontaneously in the absence of trauma in some people. When such individuals are traumatized in childhood, the rest of the phenomenology of chronic trauma disorder with MPD appears. In other words, ESP experiences may be a marker of a dissociative trait, MPD being a dissociative state disorder. It follows from this speculation that the relationship between ESP and hypnotizability should be studied carefully.

An observation that needs to be made is whether integrated MPD patients lose their ESP experiences. They lose much of their psychopathology. If the ESP goes with it, does that imply that it was pathological in nature? If the ESP remains, does that mean it is real, or should one infer that the patient is incompletely treated? A third possibility is that the state disorder has been cured while the trait marker remains.

I now have a number of papers in press that include data on ESP experiences (Ross, Heber, Anderson, et al., 1989; Ross, Heber, Norton, & Anderson, 1989a; Ross, Norton, & Fraser, 1989). To my knowledge these are the only empirical data on ESP in the contemporary mainstream psychiatric literature. If ESP is delusional, it is important that we study it like any other psychopathology. If ESP experiences are common and not linked to psychopathology in the general population, they are still worthy of serious study.

Extrasensory perception is a legitimate area of clinical study. In view of the enthusiasm in our culture for trance channelers, ersatz enlightenment, and levitation in six easy lessons, scientific caution in the endorsement of ESP as a field of study is necessary. On the other hand, ideological rejection of ESP as a clinical phenomenon is just that, ideology, not science. A concluding vignette will illustrate the problems of dealing with ESP in inpatient psychiatry.

A single Eskimo man in his late 20s was admitted under my care because of suicidal ideation. He belonged to the highest risk group for suicide in the Canadian Arctic: acculturated, educated, single, Eskimo males. He had several severe psychosocial stressors and a diagnosis of adjustment disorder with depressed mood. I discharged him after a few days, and he was still alive 2 years later.

This man's father and paternal grandfather were both shamans. He himself had experienced the bending of plants with his mind, several other forms of telekinesis, and several episodes of clairvoyance. There were no psychotic features or hallucinogen abuse. He wanted me to take away his suicidal ideation and to prevent him from having any more ESP experiences. On one level, he seemed to perceive me as a powerful shaman who could cure his symptoms of craziness. My attempts to normalize his experiences as culturally acceptable, to explain that many people from all cultures and races believe in the reality of such experiences, and to point out that they are not necessarily symptoms of mental illness did not seem to impress him.

I was thus in the position of being requested to denigrate his culture in order to make him feel better, while being aware that the denigration of his culture and its shamanism was a major factor in his emotional disturbance. I think that clinicians should be perplexed and uncertain about how to handle ESP experiences in their patients, except in the most floridly psychotic patients. We should not devalue these experiences, because that is bad medicine, akin to the devaluating of trauma histories as Oedipal fantasy.

EVERYDAY NONCLINICAL DISSOCIATION

Anxiety, depression, and dissociation are common features of everyday life. Dissociation isn't recognised as much as the other two, just as dissociative disorders are diagnosed less often than anxiety and affective disorders. Before reviewing some of our research data on nonclinical dissociation,

I am going to provide several examples of nonclinical dissociation. These will provide a feel for the importance and prevalence of dissociation as a major aspect of normal mental function. As for any psychiatric disorder, understanding of clinical dissociation must be embedded in a more general psychology of normal mental function.

At a movie theater one can get so absorbed in a movie that one enters a dissociative state. While dissociated, the moviegoer is unaware of being in an altered state. It is only when the movie hits a dull patch, someone gets up to go for popcorn, or the person in the next seat makes a romantic hand maneuver, that one comes out of trance (the third example can provoke a rapid switch to another altered state). The experience is a bit like waking up and then realizing that you have been asleep but are now awake.

Another example is the dissociation that occurs while reading a child's book aloud for the hundredth time. The child and the other parent can be attentively listening to the story and may not notice the slightest change in the reader's voice. The reader suddenly returns to consciousness, aware that he has completely blanked out for the last three pages, without any interruption in his reading. This doesn't happen with new books and is more likely to happen at the child's bedtime in a dim room, lying on a bed, with a bedtime book.

I remember hearing that a well-known Canadian folk singer is amnesic for all of every performance. This is an extension of the normal process of reading several pages in a trance, with posttrance amnesia. Of course the singer might have MPD, which is a further extension of normal dissociation. Similarly, everyone who drives has had the experience of coming to, suddenly aware that he or she is amnesic for the last few blocks. This can be dangerous at night on a lonely road if the trance state shifts into sleep.

Dissociation can increase an individual's functional level. I remember walking long distances in Rome while visiting a friend there in the 1960s. I didn't have a map and didn't know the city. I found my navigation more effective when I paid less attention to it, letting my unconscious slide along the grooves I had cut during previous walks. Every athlete is aware of this process and of the need to cultivate it. A light trance state with diversion of attention from the task at hand can produce a better performance.

Concerning athletes, Wayne Gretzky is probably the greatest athlete Canada has ever produced. Apparently he scored lower on a battery of tests of athletic ability than all other members of the Edmonton Oilers. He might rank a little higher on the Los Angeles Kings. But he doesn't look like an athlete. He is slight. What makes him such a superior hockey player, then? I think Gretzky is a genius at entering a special state. There is a qualitative difference between the state he is in and that of other players on the ice.

Watching Gretzky is always entertaining; at any time he can shift into a level of skill that makes the other players look as if they come from a different league. Indeed, every year there are only a small number of players in the National Hockey League who score half as many points as he does. One of his most effective strategies is to position himself behind the net—when he gets the puck there, he often seems to mesmerize the opposing team. The other players also enter an altered state momentarily, in which they are frozen and confused.

One can observe this special psychology during power plays. Gretzky will have the puck for a sustained period of time, during which the other players just don't know what to do. They are lost. Because the other players are excellent athletes, these induced trance states are brief. But they are there. One can tell a trance state is at work because of the calm, control, and fluidity of Gretzky's motion during these intervals, compared to the stilted, anxious, hesitant movements of the opposing players.

I have seen Gretzky, Kurri, and Anderson control the puck for 20 seconds uninterruptedly, swooping, swooping, swooping around the goal, passing, and shooting, passing and shooting again, recovering each rebound. They may take four or five shots on goal during such an interval, while the opposing players seem to be standing around. Then suddenly there is a shift of state, one of the three loses the puck, the other team seems to wake up, and one is back to normal hockey. It is hard to know how long these intervals last because they involve time distortion for the observer.

I think that Gretzky possesses a primordial skill that must have been used by ancient hunters to mesmerize game, or by warriors to put their opponents in trance. He is the supreme embodiment of this psychological skill in our culture. That is why he is Canada's greatest living sports hero. The problem with our society is that this higher, more evolved, more ancient state of mind–body unity has no role outside sports. Athletes who can achieve it command great fame and riches.

Everyday dissociation occurs at a more mundane level. Divided consciousness is required, for instance, to talk on the phone, scan the newspaper, and stir the spaghetti sauce at the same time. Everyone daydreams, which is a dissociative state. There are several multibillion dollar industries in North America that exist because their products induce altered states related to daydreaming. The products include novels, magazines, movies, television, pornography, alcohol, and cocaine. In fact most of the crime in North America is driven by the desire to enter altered states of consciousness, primarily through drugs and sex. This could be called the social pathology of artificially induced dissociation.

The desire for intense dissociated states is built into our DNA: Without the desire for orgasm, the race would not be propagated. Such states are wonderful, desirable, and healthy, in their natural form. But there is nothing wonderful about the chemical ecstasy of the heroin-addicted ghetto prostitute. This is why there is a psychiatry of dissociation, the goal of which is to substitute healthy, normal altered states for self-destructive, painful ones. The goal of the treatment of MPD is not to produce someone who never dissociates. That would be like giving people a lifetime prescription for an antidepressant to prevent them from feeling sad when loved ones die. Such a prescription would be a clinical error for two reasons: It is a misconceived ᵍoal of treatment; and the antidepressants don't have that effect anyway.

Studies have established that hypnotizability, which is closely linked to normal dissociation, is distributed on a bell-shaped curve in the general population (Berg & Melin, 1975; Gordon, 1972; Laurence, Nadon, Nogrady, & Perry, 1986; Morgan & Hilgard, 1973). Only about 10 percent of people are excellent hypnotic subjects. High hypnotizability has nothing to do with being gullible, easily influenced, hysterical, or dumb. It is a skill that requires conscious focusing and willing participation, except in highly charged situations like a hockey game, war, sustained brainwashing, natural disaster, or sexual assault, during which an individual becomes vulnerable to spontaneous trance or the induction of trance by others.

It is also well established that hypnotizability declines with age, peaking in early adolescence, and that men and women are equally hypnotizable. We found similar results when we gave the DES to 168 adolescents aged 12 through 14 years and to 345 college students with a median age of 24 years (Ross & Ryan, unpublished data; Ryan, 1988). The curve of scores in the college students is shown in Figure 8.2. Most people do not have many dissociative experiences, and the ones they do have tend to be experiences of absorption in a task or entertainment. This results in a left-skewed distribution of DES scores, with only a small number of people being highly dissociative. I say small, but there are probably at least 30 million highly dissociative individuals in North America with DES scores above 20. One cannot extrapolate from our two studies to the entire population of North America, so 30 million is a mere guess.

The point is that there are probably millions of people in North America who hear dissociative voices and have a highly dissociated experience of self. Many of these people probably have no history of childhood trauma.

The median DES score at age 12 in our sample is 20.2. At age 14 it has declined to a median score of 14.8. The difference between the 12- and 14-year-olds is significant at $p = .0001$. In both the adolescents and the college students, there is no difference in DES scores between males and females. This means that if MPD is the outcome of an interaction between dissociative ability and trauma, the female:male ratio for MPD should be the same as the female:male ratio for childhood trauma. The ratio in clinical series of MPD is 9:1, which is probably higher than the trauma ratio. This suggests that males with MPD are missing from clinical practice, as discussed in earlier chapters.

I think that contemporary psychology has underestimated the amount of dissociation in the normal population and in clinically disturbed individuals. Dissociation is not irrational: There is nothing "irrational" about Wayne Gretzky's scoring statistics in the National Hockey League or about his income. Both are derived from measurable performance in the physical world. Everyday dissociation needs to be thoroughly studied, in its pathol-

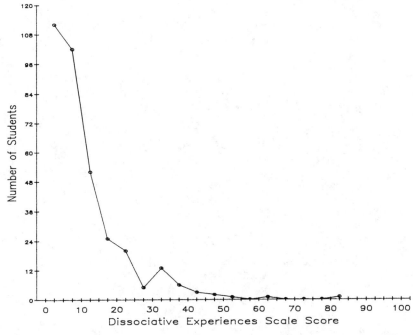

Figure 8.2. Dissociative Experiences in 345 College Students (From Ryan, 1988)

ogy, in its mundane aspects, and in the superior performance of gifted individuals. It is as if modern academia has a blind spot for one of the major themes of human psychology, an amnesia, one might say. MPD patients are providing the stimulus for the reversal of this amnesia in North America in the late 20th century.

PART THREE

Treatment of Multiple Personality Disorder

The treatment of multiple personality disorder is complex, difficult, and rewarding. This section deals with treatment outcome, general principles of treatment, and specific techniques. The techniques are described in detail. The treatment of MPD is psychotherapy, but many adjunctive interventions including hospitalization, medications, working with social agencies, and group therapy may be used. The treatment must be embedded in sound general principles of psychotherapy and must have a foundation of trust, safety, and a solid treatment alliance. These are all conflicted issues for the victim of severe child abuse.

The techniques of treatment are suitable for both inpatient and outpatient psychotherapy. They can be used by therapists of any professional background working in any setting. Only a small part of the discussion focuses on hospitalization, medications, physical restraints, and other interventions not available to the community-based nonmedical therapist. MPD can be treated to stable integration without hospitalization, although the hospital can be a valuable resource.

There are many techniques and treatment issues unique to MPD, but I want to emphasize the need for the therapy to be based on good general skills. The work is best thought of as "regular" psychotherapy with a number of special techniques blended into it. It is technically eclectic but is guided by an understanding of the nature and function of the personality system. The MPD patient has used dissociation in a complex way to cope with childhood trauma: In the therapy she must recover and integrate the conflicts, feelings, and memories arising from the abuse.

The MPD patient also needs to learn how to be a single person. This involves unlearning an overreliance on dissociation and acquiring a new set of flexible, adaptive coping strategies. Most of the treatment in the late and postintegration phases of therapy is no different from the therapy of an adult victim of child abuse who never developed MPD. This work is less technically challenging but as important as the earlier phases.

MPD is the most severe psychiatric disorder that can be cured with psychotherapy. The cognitive-behavioral treatment of panic disorder can result in long-term remission, but MPD is much more complex than panic disorder. There is in fact no other psychiatric disorder of comparable severity that carries such a good prognosis. The prognosis depends, however, on the availability of specific intensive psychotherapy for the disorder.

The purpose of this section is to describe the techniques and principles of MPD psychotherapy in sufficient detail that the reader can begin using them.

CHAPTER NINE

Treatment Outcome

Strictly speaking there are no treatment outcome data in the literature. There have been no randomized controlled trials of any method of treatment for multiple personality disorder (MPD). Nor have there been studies of the treatment of one of the subdiagnoses of chronic trauma disorder with MPD, such as depression. It would be possible, for instance, to conduct a standard study of the efficacy of tricyclic antidepressants in treating the depressive symptoms of MPD patients.

An adequate study of the psychotherapy of MPD would involve a number of measures, not all of which are available. There would have to be valid and reliable diagnostic assessment with standardized instruments at the beginning of the study. The DDIS and DES would be satisfactory for this purpose. Next there would have to be good measures of the target symptoms: These would have to be sensitive enough to track treatment response. It would be necessary to have a well-defined treatment protocol and to demonstrate that the therapists in the study were in fact delivering the protocol. These are requirements of any psychotherapy outcome study for any disorder. They may sound straightforward, but they present major logistic and measurement problems for investigators.

Although there are no outcome data according to these strict criteria, in fact quite a bit is known about the treatment of MPD and its outcome. There is a large body of collective clinical experience accumulating in North America, and an uncertain number of therapists have treated the disorder to stable integration. I would estimate the number of therapists in North America who have treated MPD to stable integration at between 50 and 300.

Richard Kluft has provided virtually all of the literature on treatment outcome, based on careful observation of his own caseload (Kluft 1982, 1983, 1984a, 1984c, 1985a, 1985b, 1985c, 1985d, 1985e, 1985f, 1986a, 1986b, 1987a, 1988d, 1988e). In this chapter I will review the requirements for the first multicenter treatment outcome study of MPD; then I will review Kluft's treatment outcome data; then I will discuss childhood MPD and its treatment outcome; and I will conclude by describing the treatment results we have had in Winnipeg.

REQUIREMENTS FOR A MULTICENTER TREATMENT OUTCOME STUDY

A multicenter treatment outcome study is required for a number of reasons. It is already known that the treatment of MPD is often highly effective, and we have a basic outline of what needs to be done in therapy. There are two kinds of research: The first is a bookkeeping kind of effort to demonstrate what is already known, in order to convince others of its correctness. An example of this would be doing a systematic study to determine whether child personalities often hold abuse memories. This is something that everyone who works with MPD knows, so there isn't much intellectual excitement in documenting it. However, it would be useful to be able to say that in a series of 100 cases of MPD, there were so many child alters, such-and-such a percentage had abuse memories, and such-and-such a percentage of other types of alters held abuse memories.

In practice, the logistic effort required to produce such data is so big compared to the payoff that researchers are unlikely to devote scarce time and resources to that particular piece of work. The other kind of research involves finding out what is going on when it is really unknown. An example of this is the study we did to find out how clearly MPD can be differentiated from temporal lobe epilepsy with the DDIS and DES (Ross, Heber, Anderson, et al., 1989). We really didn't know what we would find in this study and weren't predicting results as clean and unequivocal as those we got.

Globally, MPD treatment outcome studies are more like the former, bookkeeping kind of research. They are necessary to establish scientifically the efficacy of a therapy already known to be highly cost-effective. This is in turn necessary to legitimize the field and to ensure that treatment will be paid for by third-party insurers. There is no reason that third-party insurers should continue to fund expensive treatments indefinitely in the absence of solid outcome data. The history of medicine is replete with examples of officially sanctioned ineffective treatments.

A treatment outcome study would be very challenging and interesting to conduct. There would be numerous problems demanding innovative and creative solutions, ranging from logistic to psychometric, to transference–management issues. The first step would be to assemble a sufficient number of therapists who were willing to commit themselves to the paperwork involved. The study would last at least 4 years if subject enrollment took 6 months, treatment 2½ years, and follow-up a year. Because each therapist could enroll only a small number of subjects during the 6 months, at least 20 therapists would be involved.

I am not an expert in the design of treatment outcome studies. What I am going to do in this section is present a few ideas about how an MPD treatment outcome study might be done. There are undoubtedly many other possible designs. I want to emphasize that the following are preliminary considerations only.

It is standard procedure in any treatment study to start with pilot projects that do not involve randomization or control groups. In study of a new medication the first stage, called Phase I, involves animal experimentation and administration of the drug to healthy human volunteers to ensure safety. Phase II involves dose-finding studies and uncontrolled, nonblinded investigations that provide initial data on efficacy, followed by the first double-blind studies. Phase III involves full-scale multicenter randomized, double-blind placebo-controlled studies in a number of different countries. The data from the first three phases are required to get permission to market the drug. In Phase IV, which occurs after permission to market the drug has been obtained from a given government, further studies of possible new indications and applications, new preparations, and so on are conducted.

Generally, to move a new drug from discovery in the test tube to market takes 10 years and 100 million dollars. This description of the development of new medications illustrates the minute amount of time and money society is investing in the treatment of MPD. The treatment of MPD, though, is actually in Phase II despite the lack of resources, and it is only 5 years since the major burst of publications in 1984.

In terms of intake criteria, all subjects should score above 20 on the DES, and at least 75 percent should score above 30. All should meet DSM-III-R criteria for MPD, all should have histories of childhood physical and/or sexual abuse, and therapists must have contacted alter personalities directly. In addition, all subjects should fit the pattern of chronic trauma disorder with somatic symptoms, substance abuse, depression, Schneiderian and borderline symptoms, secondary features of MPD, and ESP experiences. I don't have enough data yet to suggest cutoff scores on the subsections of the DDIS, but these will be forthcoming in the near future.

All cases of MPD in early pilot studies should have more than five personalities, there should be at least some amnesia, and no cases should be polyfragmented. Less than five alters, lack of amnesia, and polyfragmentation should be absolute exclusion criteria because simple and polyfragmented cases are atypical and might respond to treatment differently from cases of complex MPD. Concurrent schizophrenia, organic brain syndrome, serious medical illness, ongoing victimization or perpetration of abuse, pending criminal charges, and lack of a stable fixed address should also be exclusion criteria. These items are all necessary to provide a reasonably stable setting for therapy free of confounding variables and secondary gain.

No subjects should pay for their treatment. This is necessary because some will not, therefore none can, and because subjects in research studies usually don't pay for their treatment in any case. It would not be a fair test of the treatment if some subjects had to drop out for financial reasons. Sessions should be a minimum of once a week and should not exceed three sessions a week with the primary therapist except for time-limited periods of crisis. This is necessary for standardization and to approximate usual clinical practice. There is no use in demonstrating the efficacy of a treatment if 14 hours a week of therapist time are required for each patient.

The next requirement is adequate measures of treatment response. These are not available. Outcome measures would have to include symptoms, diagnoses, parasuicidal behavior, employment status, social function, use of emergency departments and inpatient services, and stable integration of alters, as defined by Kluft (1984c). General measures of psychopathology like the SCL-90 could be used, as could a Global Clinical Impression Scale rating the overall status of the patient on a five-point scale. There would be a lot of work to do preparing standard forms for therapists to complete, because these do not exist.

In terms of the treatment package, the therapists would have to document whether they had performed specified therapeutic tasks. Geri Anderson and I have devised a Therapist Checklist for this purpose that has not been validated or studied psychometrically (see Appendix B). In the pilot studies it would be possible only to monitor the therapy loosely. In later more ambitious studies, assessment of randomly chosen videotaped sessions by independent raters using a reliable rating instrument might be required. The field is not at this point yet, nor are the funding agencies.

After completion of the pilot studies, the problems of randomization and control groups would have to be tackled. I doubt that a truly rigorous controlled study of the psychotherapy of MPD will ever be conducted. The ethical and logistic problems of randomization and controlled treatment are insurmountable because of the long duration of treatment, its efficacy, and the morbidity experienced by untreated patients. It would be inhumane and unethical to assign an MPD patient to a waiting list or placebo control for 2 or 3 years.

One potential solution would be to compare two effective treatments, say cognitive and psychodynamic treatment protocols. The problem there is that adequate differentiation of the two treatments is probably not possible, because both contain substantial nonspecific elements and elements of each other. The other possible approach is to compare the outcome of treated patients to their own pretreatment status. This would involve a single-subject experimental design. I am far from being an expert in single-subject research methodology, but I think it provides the only viable, practical methodology for MPD treatment outcome studies. Parallel group designs are just not feasible.

Comparing subjects who enter treatment with those who decline would be worthwhile but would not provide definitive data because those who decline may be quite different from those who accept. Later, more methodologically rigorous studies would utilize better validated dependent measures and more careful documentation of the treatment. There would be more therapists in more centers. Because the treatment lasts years, it will be difficult to follow larger multicenter studies with attempts to dissect out the active and inactive components of the treatment package. This can be done economically for treatment regimes that last 10 or 20 sessions, but not for a treatment that requires hundreds of hours. I think, though, that rigorous enough studies can be done to convince third-party insurers of the efficacy and cost-effectiveness of the treatment of MPD.

It is vitally important for the subspecialty of dissociative disorders, for psychiatry in general, and especially for patients, that treatment outcome studies be started within the next few years. Such studies, along with other research, continued vigor in the life of the International Society for the Study of Multiple Personality and Dissociation (ISSMP&D), and the annual Chicago MPD meetings, are essential if dissociation is to enter the mainstream. It is still possible that dissociation could fall into obscurity again, as it did early in the 20th century.

TREATMENT OUTCOME DATA IN THE LITERATURE

Treatment outcome data on MPD are provided entirely by Kluft except for one paper by Coons (1986d). All other outcome data consist of single case studies (Carlson, 1984; Cutler & Reed, 1975; Hall, LeCann, & Schoolar, 1978; Lipton & Kezur, 1948; Rosenbaum & Weaver, 1980; Sizemore & Pittillo, 1977). I mentioned treatment outcome in three cases (Ross, 1987). Coons (1986d) reported on a series of 20 cases of MPD followed for a mean of 39 months after intake. He found that 5 (25 percent) were integrated, 2 had achieved unstable integration prior to redissociating, and 2 were partially integrated.

In addition Coons reported that 100 percent of the 20 patients had accepted their diagnosis, and 77 percent had developed coconsciousness. He devotes most of his attention to events within the therapy, describing transference, countertransference, and therapeutic modalities in detail. Kluft has been publishing detailed studies of his caseload for much of the 1980s and has described by far the largest individual caseload of any investigator. The rest of this section deals with Kluft's data.

Kluft (1982, 1984c) has provided an operationalized definition of integration that could be used in treatment outcome studies. He defines fusion or integration as requiring the presence of 3 stable months of

1. Continuity of contemporary memory
2. Absence of overt behavioral signs of multiplicity
3. Subjective sense of unity
4. Absence of alter personalities on hypnotic reexploration
5. Modification of transference phenomena consistent with the bringing together of personalities
6. Clinical evidence that the unified patient's self-representation included acknowledgment of attitudes and awarenesses which were previously segregated in separate personalities

I fully endorse these criteria except for the fifth one, which I would drop. The transference criterion is insufficiently operationalized, depends too much on the observer's ideology, and would have little or no interrater reliability. An individual psychoanalytically oriented therapist might want to retain this criterion in his own practice, but it could not be part of a scientific study. This criterion could be reintroduced if it was adequately operationalized.

Kluft's (1984c) outcome data are based on 171 cases he saw over a period of a decade. Of these he treated 117, and in addition he was able to monitor the treatment of another 6 patients who reached integration, making a total of 123. Of the 123, 20 were still in treatment, 10 had interrupted treatment, and 10 cases were unsuccessful, leaving 83 cases (67.5 percent) treated to stable integration. Based on these data one can say that two thirds of MPD patients entering treatment should reach stable integration.

However, Kluft excluded 50 of the 83 patients from his final report for a variety of reasons. Seven were excluded because the full protocol for demonstrating stable integration (Kluft, 1985g) was not used or the therapists were inexperienced in treating MPD; 16 had not been stable for long enough; 20 were lost to follow-up or had not yet been followed up; 2 patients were of questionable reliability; 4 had partially relapsed or shown dissociative features after integration; and 1 had died.

The remaining 33 patients met more rigorous criteria of 27 months of stable integration (2 years following the initial 3 months). The 33 patients consisted of 25 females (75.8 percent) who had a mean age of 36.1 years at fusion, a mean of 13.9 personalities, and an average duration of treatment of 21.6 months. Putnam et al. (1986), analyzing these data, found that the number of personalities correlated with the time to reach integration at $p = .004$.

This figure of 21.6 months to reach integration is one of the key pieces of information in the field. It means that MPD is a treatable disorder in the majority of cases and that the duration of treatment is reasonable given the amount of work to do: In only 8 cases (24.2 percent) was the length of treatment longer than 30 months. This means that three quarters of MPD patients can be treated to integration in less than 2½ years. Of the 33 patients, only two (6.1 percent) took longer than 3½ years to reach integration.

The 21.6 months may not be representative of the treatment of MPD across North America for several reasons. Most important, no other therapists have the experience of Kluft, so few if any will have his level of skill to offer. In addition, Kluft's patients may not have been as sick as the average North American patient with MPD. Kluft (1982) reported that of his first 70 patients treated to integration, only 22.8 percent "had strong borderline features" (p. 233). In comparison, of 40 cases we interviewed with the DDIS (Ross, Anderson, Heber, et al., in press), 67.5 percent met DSM-III criteria for borderline personality disorder, and of 33 patients reported by Horevitz and Braun (1984), 70 percent were DSM-III borderlines.

In addition, only 45.5 percent of Kluft's (1984c) 33 integrated cases had been hospitalized prior to diagnosis, whereas 6 were hospitalized during treatment: Kluft does not report whether these patients overlapped. Of the 236 cases reported to us (Ross, Norton, & Wozney, 1989), 74.6 percent had been hospitalized. Patients in Kluft's practice are seen in a private office setting; the hospital-based clinical experience of Braun and me probably includes more severely borderline patients.

I have noticed an unexpected negative therapeutic reaction in patients who were told by me that the average duration of treatment to integration is 21.6 months, based on one series. Patients who are not going to make the deadline may become discouraged, think of themselves as failures, and blame themselves for not getting better on schedule. Having seen this a couple of times, I now tell patients that with hard work the duration of therapy may be in the range of 2 or 3 years but that this is variable.

It is important to understand that 21.6 months was arrived at by one therapist with one case load. The length of time to integration is affected by the skill of the therapist, difficulty of the case, availability of social supports, life stage and situation of the patient, amount of treatment delivered per week, luck, and probably a host of unrecognized factors. Therapists should not become preoccupied with their "stats." For instance our team treated the polyfragmented woman mentioned in earlier chapters to stable integration in less than 21.6 months but more than half of the first year was inpatient work. This patient received more than 500 hours of psychotherapy from me, my cotherapists, and ward nurses in a year. Without that she might have taken 5 years to integrate. There is no way that a solo outpatient psychotherapist could treat such a case to integration in less than 2 years.

Treating MPD to stable integration is a bit like running a marathon. There is only so fast you can go. I could run 100 miles a week for a year and still not reach a 2:30 marathon: My physiological endowment limits me to a maximum life goal of sneaking in under 3 hours, if I ever get the training time. Similarly, in the psychotherapy of MPD, the most skillful therapist in the world could not take the patient faster than her maximum rate. It is humanly impossible to recover and deal with so much trauma in a brief psychotherapy. In fact if you go too fast you end up going more slowly, because the patient creates symptoms and resistance to put on the brakes.

Multicenter treatment outcome studies will confirm Kluft's finding that the majority of MPD patients can be treated to integration within 2 or 3 years. The reason I say this with some confidence is that a growing number of therapists throughout North America have treated MPD successfully in this kind of time period. The treatment delivered by Kluft has not been described in sufficient detail to attempt a replication of his methods, but he has described its general principles and many of its techniques. Most successful therapists probably have at least 80 percent of their interventions in common because they practice good generic psychotherapy, and because there are certain things, such as negotiation between alters, that you just have to do in treating MPD.

MULTIPLE PERSONALITY DISORDER IN CHILDHOOD

Like the literature on treatment outcome, most of the work on childhood MPD has been done by Richard Kluft (1984b, 1985b, 1985c, 1986e). In a review of the literature, Vincent and Pickering (1988) identified 12 reported cases of childhood MPD: Of these, 1 was reported in the 19th century by Despine (Fine, 1988), 4 are cases of "incipient MPD" (Fagan & McMahon, 1984, p. 26) and 5 are Kluft's cases. Since then an additional case in a 3-year-old has been reported by Riley and Mead (1988). This means that of eight modern cases of full MPD in childhood, five (62.5 percent) are reported by Kluft, whereas Malenbaum and Russell (1987) report one, Riley and Mead (1988) one, and Weiss, Sutton, and Utecht (1985) one.

This is a very unusual situation in the history of a childhood psychiatric disorder, when you consider that we accumulated a series of 236 adult cases in one questionnaire survey. There are a number of probable reasons why so few childhood cases have been identified. For one thing, most MPD specialists are adult mental health professionals. MPD is less well developed in childhood and doesn't present with a 20-year history of chronic trauma disorder, secondary features of MPD, extrasensory experiences, and other features that raise the diagnostician's index of suspicion. Kluft has pointed out that the external behavioral manifestations of MPD are more muted in childhood because children don't have the finances, mobility, or independence to develop alters with different sets of friends, clothes, and interests. Many of the secondary features arising from the activities of alters may therefore not be present.

In addition, it may be difficult to differentiate switches of personalities from developmentally normal discontinuities of state that occur in children. Kluft (1985b) has listed seven reasons for the difficulty of identifying childhood MPD. These are, in summarized form:

1. No index of suspicion by professionals
2. Symptoms suggest some other disorder
3. Fluctuation of symptoms suggests other disorders
4. Other explanations for behavior invoked, such as lying
5. Child is unaware of his or her circumstances and/or condition
6. Child withholds data
7. Childhood MPD has different features

As Dell (1988a, 1988b) has pointed out, professional skepticism about MPD is often extreme to the point of overt hostility. It may manifest itself as "malicious harassment, contemptuous ridicule, and deliberate interference in the medical care of the patient" and it may be "uninformed, instantaneous, reactive, and unyielding" (Dell, 1988a, p. 537). Such not uncommon responses go far beyond the limits of reasonable skepticism defined by Bliss (1988), Hilgard (1988), and Spiegel (1988) in discussion of Dell's paper. Cases of childhood MPD may evoke such extreme reactions more commonly because there is less literature on childhood MPD and because the abuse is ongoing.

Despite the limited data base, Kluft (1985b) has devised a list of predictors of childhood MPD that could form the basis of a screening instrument. Many of the items on the list also occur in adult MPD, including intermittent depression, trance states, voices, Schneiderian passivity experiences, disavowed behavior, and fluctuating mood and behavior. Because I have no direct experience with full MPD in childhood and the literature is so sparse, I am not going to say any more about the phenomenology of childhood MPD, except to emphasize that cases can present with the full classical features of the adult form.

What is most important to understand is the treatment outcome in childhood MPD. Childhood MPD seems to be treatable to long-term stable remission with short-term psychotherapy. This probably means permanent cure. For this to happen, the abuse must stop. In fact it is unethical to try to treat childhood MPD in the face of ongoing abuse, because the treatment would rob the child of his or her way of coping. The data on the treatment of MPD suggest that primary prevention of the disorder is possible.

This is the most important goal of the field, to identify and cure MPD in childhood. If that could be done on a large scale, incalculable but huge savings in dollars and suffering would result. There would be a major interruption of the transmission of abuse to future generations. This could happen. If as much money were allocated to MPD research and treatment as for AIDS, we could diagnose and treat tens of thousands of children, if not more, to stable integration in North America. I am not suggesting that MPD is a more important public health problem than AIDS: It definitely isn't. But a budget of hundreds of millions of dollars could be spent effectively on the diagnosis and treatment of MPD in North America.

The treatment of childhood MPD to stable integration takes 5- to 10 sessions in many cases. The longest treatment in the literature consists of 30 sessions over 5 months. The shortest took 1 session. It would be hard to imagine a more cost-effective preventive intervention in all of medicine, other than vaccinations. The ease of treatment of childhood MPD, compared to the painful and arduous course of adult treatment, is evidence that MPD is entrenched and reinforced in an extremely powerful way by physical, sexual, and emotional abuse.

The preliminary data on the treatment of childhood MPD is so important that it *must* be followed up with good research and clinical investigation. No other disorder in psychiatry could be prevented on such a scale with methods already available.

TREATMENT OUTCOMES IN WINNIPEG

I diagnosed my first case of MPD in 1979 as a medical student, my second in 1982 as a resident, and my third in 1985 as a staff psychiatrist. At that time, in 1985, I couldn't comprehend how Kluft, Braun, Caul, Bliss, and others could accumulate so many cases. However in the last 3 years we have been diagnosing MPD at a rate of over one new case a month. This has occurred in a city of 600,000 people during a period in which I had extensive teaching, writing, and research commitments as well, so was not carrying a full clinical load.

At our Dissociative Disorders Clinic we have seen 50 cases of classical MPD. Of these, 22 have entered active specific treatment, which includes 3 cases treated outside the hospital by colleagues. The breakdown of outcomes for these 22 patients is as follows:

Outcome	No.	Percent
Integrated	6	27.2
Reached unstable integration, relapsed	2	9.1
Treatable, left the province unintegrated	2	9.1
In treatment, expected to integrate	5	22.7
In treatment, outcome uncertain	4	18.1
Dropped out, unintegrated	3	13.6

If one adds the integrated, expected-to-integrate, and one of the integrated-relapsed patients who will reach stable integration together, this makes 12 out of 22 patients (54.5%) who will reach integration, as a conservative estimate. The other integrated-relapsed patient has been lost to follow-up. This is a conservative estimate because the 4 patients rated as "In treatment, outcome uncertain" could reach integration if things go well. If this proved to be the case, 16 out of 22 (72.7 percent) of our caseload could reach integration. The two patients from out of province who have been treated by us as inpatients would almost undoubtedly reach stable integration if a skilled therapist was available where they live, which makes 18 out of 22 (81.8 percent).

It is important to remember that out of the first 40 patients we saw, 27 met DSM-III criteria for borderline personality disorder. Our sample is from a tertiary care hospital-based practice and therefore may be more disturbed than the average MPD patient in North America. On the other hand the most severe cases may be in the prison system, so our case load might be less disturbed than average. Of the 6 patients we have treated to integration to date, 5 had clinical diagnoses of borderline personality disorder and met five or more DSM-III criteria on structured interview. Borderline features do not appear to be a predictor of poor outcome.

Combined with Kluft's (1984c) outcome data on a larger series followed for longer, these figures suggest that MPD is a treatable disorder. A 70 percent response rate is as good as any treatment for any complex disorder in psychiatry, be the treatment biological, psychotherapeutic, or behavioral. MPD, I believe, is as common as schizophrenia and more treatable. MPD is the only complex mental disorder that can be cured with currently available techniques.

In conversations our experience has been confirmed by others in two regards: Many therapists find MPD to be treatable to stable integration; equally important, collective experience is that chronic trauma disorder without MPD or with partial MPD is much more difficult to treat and carries a poorer prognosis. Many people have said this to us, although they haven't used the term chronic trauma disorder.

When I am assessing a patient with the features of chronic trauma disorder and can contact preexisting alter personalities, I feel good because I know what to do and have an effective treatment to offer. When there are no alters, I feel much less happy. Some might say this is an iatrogenic self-fulfilling prophecy. I think it's just a fact that for chronic trauma patients without MPD, psychiatry has little to offer other than trials of medication and supportive therapy. Social service referrals, group therapy, academic upgrading, support groups, family therapy, and other interventions may be worthwhile, but I don't have a sense that *anyone* can do for the chronic trauma patient without MPD what a skilled therapist can do for the classic multiple.

This leads to a paradox: MPD is both the most terrible and the most hopeful mental disorder to have. No other group of patients has anything approaching the degree of trauma to remember and work through. But, unlike lithium-nonresponsive manic-depressives, schizophrenics, persons afflicted with delusional disorders, and many other mental patients, the person with MPD can escape from the mental health system. MPD can be cured. The treatment of MPD is both the most difficult and the most rewarding work I have done in psychiatry.

CHAPTER TEN

General Principles of Treatment

The basic principle of the treatment of multiple personality disorder (MPD) is that it is the treatment of a person. Technical wizardry, creative ingenuity, accurate empathy, extrication from double binds, deep hypnotic repair of trauma, spontaneous play with child alters, these and other interventions are worth nothing if the *person* does not get better and live better. The operation was a success but the patient died—that saying describes a potential error in the treatment of MPD, which is as detailed and delicate as any work done by neurosurgeons.

The goal of the treatment of MPD is not palliation. It is cure. Lesser outcomes may be all that is possible in certain cases, but they are not cures. It takes an artistic temperament to treat MPD successfully, and it also takes spiritual discipline. The treatment is prolonged and difficult, and many subtle traps lie in wait for the therapist. This makes the treatment of MPD challenging and rewarding work.

The treatment of MPD can be medical when medications and an inpatient ward are used. Except for these two components, an M.D. confers no advantage or special expertise in the treatment. The psychotherapy of MPD can be done by any qualified psychotherapist, of any professional background (Lego, 1988). The physician need not be the primary therapist and can play an adjunctive role even in cases that require medication and admission.

In this chapter I am going to describe the broad general principles of treatment. There are three hierarchical layers to this discussion, the lowest level comprising Chapters 11 and 12. First there are principles that apply to any psychotherapy, and to MPD in an overall way. The second hierarchical level contains general principles of treatment that apply to many psychotherapies, but the entire pattern or package is unique to MPD. For instance, contracting is done in many forms of treatment, including behavioral containment of inpatient psychotic behavior, but contracting with alter personalities is unique to the treatment of MPD. The third hierarchical level consists of the actual techniques, interventions, and strategies that form the microcosm of treatment.

AN OVERVIEW OF TREATMENT

In some residency programs future obstetricians are required to do a year of general surgery, in order to learn basic principles and techniques of surgery. Similarly in psychotherapy, there are common skills that all therapists must possess. No one should treat an MPD patient as a first training case, because the treatment requires general skills and experience. Robert Mayer (1988) eloquently describes the uncertainties of starting to work with MPD patients in a hostile and unsupportive environment.

One of the reasons I am writing this book is to contribute to a literature that will help therapists who find themselves with a case of MPD and no prior experience. The MPD patient will test, test, test, and retest the therapist. It is impossible to treat severely borderline multiples without getting angry at them, wishing they would die, and dreading to come to work at times. I think it is also impossible to work with such patients and not act out against them a little bit once in a while, at a minimum. That doesn't mean such acting out is "okay," and it certainly needs to be minimized. But it is humanly impossible never to act out in therapy, I believe. If you don't have a basic positive feeling for the persons you are treating, I don't think you will be able to tolerate the projective identification pressure they exert, and you will therefore not be a good therapist.

Trying to work effectively with an MPD patient you don't like must be a bit like trying to spend 6 months in a skylab with someone you can't stand. One consequence of this reality of human social contracts is that hateful patients may be less likely to get good treatment, or any treatment. The MPD therapist must be able to tolerate uncertainty and strong "unacceptable" countertransference feelings including hate and erotic arousal, all admixed with plenty of hysteria. Psychiatric jargon supplies ample terminology for covert expression of the hostile countertransference aroused by MPD patients.

The main thing to ask oneself is, "Who wouldn't be like this, with that childhood?" Defining the patient's bad behavior as "characterological" reinforces negative feelings in the therapist, because it attributes causality to the patient's character, rather than to the abuse. This raises a second trap, which is displacement of negative countertransference onto the abuser. Many fathers of MPD patients are extremely hateful, or at least their abusive alters are, and the therapist can't help but feel angry. In the end, the therapist just has to be able to handle the intense feelings that are part of therapy, without acting out in any direction.

It is very helpful to have supportive colleagues and administration. Running the Dissociative Disorders Clinic is like running a heart transplant service. There are more people in need of hearts than there are available organs. Not everyone who is a good candidate for transplant can have one. Unfortunately, someone has to decide who will get a transplant and who won't. This means that someone has to decide who will live and who will die. No matter how many objective criteria are used, and how many consultants and committees get involved, a decision has to be made. This is easier emotionally and less dangerous medicolegally if it is a committee decision. But in the end, someone gets a heart, and someone doesn't.

Similarly, in our Dissociative Disorders Clinic we have to decide which treatable patients are going to get therapy and which aren't. There are far more patients than therapists. We try to apply inclusion and exclusion criteria, but there is no avoiding the decision. It would be easier for us emotionally not to do consults, because then we wouldn't have to meet people who aren't going to get adequate treatment. The untreated would just be statistics. Doing consults is doubly difficult because the patients know that the therapists understand them and have more to offer therapeutically.

A final general caution: You shouldn't treat MPD if you have an empty, lonely personal life or if you are married to someone with a severe personality disorder or unresolved chronic trauma disorder. It just isn't possible to do the work at work, then come home and have to do it at home. If your life is empty, the drive to fill it with overinvolvement in therapy will be too great. Although no one in late 20th century urban North America is truly healthy, the MPD therapist must "have it all together" to a reasonable extent. This is so because the patients don't.

GENERAL CONSIDERATIONS

General principles of treatment have been enunciated by Braun (1986a) and Kluft (1985f). These build on earlier statements by Bowers et al. (1971) and Allison (1974), as well as collective experience and the MPD literature as a whole. The main recommendation of Bowers and his coauthors was that the therapist should stay within the limits of his competence. Although this is true, it only part of the truth. Even expert therapists will be stumped at times: Everyone will make some mistakes, no matter how experienced.

There should be a balance between intimidating beginning therapists with the need for "expertise" and an anything-goes attitude. I am particularly mindful of the first error, having met psychiatrists who misuse countertransference comments on trainees for power, intimidation, and control. Experts in the treatment of MPD should not erect false criteria of expertise for the purpose of establishing themselves as gurus. Thankfully the field is free of such wise men to date.

George Greaves (1988) has written with great restraint about some of the incredible therapeutic errors he has encountered as an MPD consultant. When I talk about the inevitability of making errors, I am referring to "small potatoes" mistakes compared to breast-feeding a patient or taking a patient on holidays as a babysitter. There is a hierarchy of severity of errors: The most extreme example Greaves cites is a therapist who treated an MPD patient by day and abused her in a cult by night. Such behavior is so pathological that it can't even be classified as an error. Until I read Greaves's paper, it never even occurred to me that therapists might breast-feed their patients' child alters under the title of reparenting.

Bowers enunciates 12 principles of treatment that Kluft (1985f) says have "stood the test of time" (p. 5). These are, restated in my words:

1. The treatment goal is integration.
2. Help each alter personality to understand that she is one part of a whole person.
3. Use the alters' names as convenient labels, not licenses for irresponsible autonomy.
4. Treat all alters fairly and empathically.
5. Encourage empathy and cooperation between personalities.
6. Be gentle and supportive. Remember the severity of the trauma.
7. ECT is contraindicated.
8. Stay within the limits of your competence.
9. Use hypnosis judiciously.
10. Treat the person in her social context and intervene systemically when necessary.
11. Group therapy may help.
12. Do not dramatize symptoms such as amnesia.

These are sound principles of therapy. The problem is, given these principles, what do you actually do? The therapy of MPD is a problem-solving, practical therapy, requiring countless specific interventions.

Consistent with recent trends in psychiatry and psychotherapy research, Braun (1986a) has provided a more operationalized set of guidelines than those of Bowers. Braun's 13 steps are roughly sequential and have the feeling of chapter headings in a treatment manual. They are as follows:

1. Developing trust
2. Making and sharing the diagnosis
3. Communicating with each personality state
4. Contracting
5. Gathering history
6. Working with each personality state's problems
7. Undertaking special procedures
8. Developing interpersonality communication
9. Achieving resolution/integration
10. Developing new behaviors and coping skills
11. Networking and using social support systems
12. Solidifying gains
13. Following up

The linear sequence of these steps exists only as an abstract outline of therapy. In practice, much like the stages of dying, all the issues are worked and reworked throughout therapy. For instance, trust remains a major issue even after the system is completely mapped.

I don't think that Braun's outline of the treatment of complex MPD in late 20th-century North America can be improved on: It can only be elaborated. A century from now major modifications may be required if the phenomenology of MPD has changed significantly, and modified protocols would probably be required in other cultures. I think, though, that these are probably sound principles of treatment for therapists throughout the world.

It is important to bear in mind Braun's observation (cited in Kluft, 1985f) that therapists of different schools do similar work with MPD patients, despite their differences in vocabulary and theory. Effective treatment of MPD seems to demand a common set of techniques and interventions, based on the patient's symptoms, conflicts, and needs. No matter what your theoretical orientation, for instance, you will have to negotiate between alters because they will get into destructive, disruptive arguments.

In the remainder of this chapter I am going to discuss inclusion and exclusion criteria for treatment and limit-setting, before going on to the core techniques and strategies in the next chapter.

INCLUSION AND EXCLUSION CRITERIA FOR TREATMENT

The first set of inclusion and exclusion criteria, outlined in the preceding section, apply to the therapist. The second set apply to the patient. They are broad and based on common sense. The patient must want therapy and must give informed consent to it. This means she must be aware of the goal and the difficulties of treatment. An immediate problem arises: How many alters should agree to treatment? The host *must,* and beyond that the more the better is a good rule of thumb. The presence of initially hostile alters is common and is not a contraindication.

If the patient is willing to work hard, appears genuinely motivated, and can stay within the treatment contract, that is really all that is required. These principles alone are insufficient, though, because they don't help one decide who to treat and who to refer back to the referral source. The problem with the further guidelines I will provide is that none are based on data, and all are contradicted by our own clinical experience.

You would think that a history of chronic involvement with the mental health system, welfare, the courts, drug abuse, and prostitution would be a contraindication to treatment. But we have treated such patients with good results. Long-term treatment with injectable antipsychotic medication, and first psychiatric hospitalization in childhood might suggest a difficult case, but such patients can be treated to integration. Actually it is hard to define good exclusion criteria.

The ones we use hinge on the severity of the trauma and any history of violence by the patient. Patients with severe prolonged cult abuse, those who have witnessed multiple murders, and those who have committed murders are difficult. One patient referred to us used to masturbate his mother intravaginally with a loaded gun during his early adolescence, following which she would perform fellatio on him. He had been sexually abused by nuns and priests, had witnessed murder, and had dreams and flashbacks containing large amounts of blood. He had a male alter whose sole sense of masculinity was derived from pounding his penis with a brick. Society just doesn't provide us the security or resources to work safely with such a man. The treatment would be too dangerous and traumatic for the therapists, let alone the patient.

Another exclusion criterion is the patient whose function is precarious but whose world might be destroyed by therapy. Mental health professionals with MPD sometimes belong to this group. Such people are probably best served by a slow-paced supportive therapy with very gradual engagement of alters and abuse memories (Kluft, verbal communication, 1988). Anyone starting to treat a mental health professional must obviously be extremely careful about confidentiality.

I spent a number of sessions with an articulate professional person (she is not in a mental health or medical field) deciding whether to start therapy. The final, correct decision was that at her stage of life, and in her life situation, her total amnesia for experience before the age of 12 was best left intact. The alters I spoke with all agreed on this point and made the decision in consultation with me.

Similarly, a separated mother with a major depressive episode could not remember anything before the age of 14. She was not a professional but was stretched to the limit coping with her current stresses. I left her amnesia barrier intact and referred her back to her social worker without a word about any dissociative disorder. She has never had any secondary features of MPD, but even if she had I would have made the same decision. Recent involvement in major crime is a contraindication for therapists not already involved in forensic work. I think it would be a mistake to leap into a forensic case while working in a system that does not otherwise handle forensic patients, just because the patient has MPD. Involvement in such a case would require prior consultation with administration and colleagues, at a minimum.

Another group of patients are the ultrasevere borderlines who have been in the system as borderlines for years. Such patients are known to every resident, emergency room, and inpatient ward. Several in our city have MPD but are not receiving treatment in our Dissociative Disorders Clinic, and will not. There is no need to become a masochistic dumping ground for untreatable borderlines who have been caught up in the system for years. As ambassadors for MPD in the profession, it would be a coup to take over and cure such patients, but the likelihood of success is low. Failure would only reinforce uninformed hostility toward MPD and its treatment. Making "heroic" efforts with untreatable patients is bad medicine, not heroism. It deprives other more treatable patients of valuable finite resources. On the other hand, one must remember that "bad borderline" multiples can often make substantial treatment gains.

Related to this consideration, patients should not be accepted primarily because of pressure from colleagues to take over their most troublesome cases. The pressure can take many forms.

In our Dissociative Disorders Clinic we weigh all of these factors using our clinical judgment. The availability of therapists comes into the equation, as do the educational needs of residents. We also have to time our treatment intakes in relation to the progress of patients already in treatment. We can't have all our patients in the intense midphase of treatment at the same time, partly because we can't admit too many patients at one time. This means that some people have to wait for others to get better. The patients already in treatment figure this out, which becomes an added complication. Dealing with a patient's guilt about not getting better fast enough or her desire to take a flight into health is slightly compounded by the fact of our waiting list.

Because the treatment is long-term, even sabbaticals and possible pregnancies must be considered. If there are therapists who do not have permanent positions, that adds another problem. Because we have an inpatient unit with skilled MPD nurses, we have accepted some patients from out of province. Experience has taught us that they *must* have a therapist at home who is willing to follow up with them. Lack of such a therapist is an absolute contraindication to admission. This is necessary because otherwise we get in the position of trying to function as long distance telephone therapists, which doesn't work. We have felt our way into these guidelines by trial and error, reading, consultation, and attendance at conferences.

Whatever the guidelines suitable for a particular setting, it is important to think carefully about who you are going to treat and why; this will become more crucial as more mental health professionals diagnose more cases. The number of diagnosed cases suitable for treatment is likely to run further and further ahead of the available treatment slots over the next 5 years.

We work in a setting in which we can be primary therapists for our patients on an inpatient and outpatient basis and can cover for each other on holidays. We work as cotherapists with almost all patients, with no one seeing a patient by himself. The isolated therapist with no supportive colleagues will have to apply all of the exclusion criteria more stringently. I cannot consult on the specific difficulties of community-based private practice treatment of MPD, because I have no direct experience of anything other than hospital practice.

LIMIT-SETTING

An organism that cannot establish boundaries and set limits will quickly die. If this happens at the organ level within a human being, death may occur at all hierarchical levels in the system from cells to the whole person. This will in turn have a harmful effect outside the person in broader systems. The point is that limit-setting is not an optional aspect of therapy. The only questions are what limits, and how rigid are they?

I have a few absolute limits. No patients come to my home. No patients have my home phone number. No patients touch me sexually. I will never talk about my wife or my feelings about her. The only one of these I insist on for all therapists is the no sex rule. Not talking in detail about intimate aspects of the therapist's marriage is an absolute rule for all therapists in my book, but I am willing to concede that other therapists might have different rule books on this point that are correct for them and their patients. Many therapists have their offices in their homes and give out their home numbers, and I don't see anything wrong with this. I need the boundaries personally in order to function without burning out.

There are other limits. Patients can't barge in on other people's sessions, and I rarely see an outpatient more than twice a week, for instance. There are many such rules, most of which are common sense or logistically based and don't have to be mentioned to the patient.

Combined with these rigid boundaries is permeability in others. Hugging is fine, as are small gifts, home visits, and going for walks in sessions. All of these "techniques" might be frowned on by other schools. I think it's important to discuss the sickness of social systems, including the health care system, in therapy, and I am prepared to discuss my political views with the patient if she wishes. I limit this to my views on systems directly relevant to the therapy, however. I wouldn't talk about foreign policy in session because it isn't relevant. Generally, I am willing to express my thoughts and feelings about the therapy, the patient's life, transference, and countertransference in an open manner.

One thing I don't set limits on is what the patients can call me. Some call me "Colin," some "Dr. Ross." I also get referred to as "the doctor," "doc," "my shrink," and "my psychiatrist." All of these are fine with me. I don't see any reason to make a big deal about what the patients call me. Some patients call me "Dr. Ross" sometimes and "Colin" sometimes.

I think of limits as being rigid in the sense that the cell wall of an amoeba is rigid. The cell wall *has* to stay intact if the organism is to survive. That is very different from being inflexible. In fact the cell wall must be fluid, permeable, and constantly in flux in order to perform its function. This is how limits work in therapy.

We regularly set limits on our availability, on the amount of ownership of the patient's problems we are prepared to undertake, on the length and number of sessions, on the duration and intensity of abreactions, on the amount of written material we can review, on the degree to which we are prepared to be the patient's "friends," and a host of other issues. Once in a while we might hold a 3-hour session or read 50 pages, but not most of the time.

The balance between being a friend, parent, and therapist often requires limit-setting. I think it devalues the meaning of friendship to pretend to be the patient's friend, and it also reduces therapy to rent-a-friend, which is distasteful. I didn't go to school for 10 years after high school to be a rent-a-friend, and I could have generated a lot more lifetime income by now with an M.B.A. I prefer the role of expert technical consultant on MPD and general consultant on life. This doesn't preclude fondness for the patient, without which therapy might not be as effective.

It helps to like the patient in order to do 2 or 3 years of intense work with her. But it is not necessary to be the patient's friend. I make no attempt to present a neutral facade and in fact tell patients I like them. I also tell them when I am finding them irritating and advise them that such behavior is likely to drive away anyone but the most dedicated masochist. Patients have to accept that the relationship is limited to the therapy and that this makes it an artificial, largely one-way relationship. We discuss this.

Therapists working with their first case or two may get into trouble because of insufficient limit-setting. To some extent this is unavoidable because the patients are so interesting and needy. I doubt that there is a single MPD therapist in North America who hasn't gotten overinvolved in some way or other at some point. It's easy to spot overinvolvement with hindsight, but not so easy when the patient is hurting badly and in crisis. Criticism of insufficient limit-setting is difficult to accept and difficult to deliver diplomatically. The main thing to remember is that the patient, at some level, feels stifled by the overinvolvement and is relieved when healthier limits are set and maintained.

Limits are more important on the ward than in outpatient work. This is because of the powerful regressive forces that are activated by an inpatient admission, both within and outside the patient. The high-functioning MPD patient might be treated to integration entirely as an outpatient without much discussion of limits. This doesn't mean that patients who do get admitted are lower down on the evolutionary tree—that they have primitive defenses. Often patients are admitted because of their life situation, lack of supports, degree of hostility in the persecutors, severity of trauma, or location of their home, rather than because they have primitive character structures. I would like to watch an advocate of the term *primitive defenses* use it to a patient's face, then defend the terminology.

Limits also have to be set on colleagues and social institutions, and on oneself. It is important not to think of limits as punitive measures directed solely at the patient. In this chapter I am discussing general principles, and that is the case here. There is no formula for limit-setting. The main thing is to view limits as necessary and positive aspects of therapy that increase the effectiveness, efficiency, and humanity of the treatment. It is not kind to allow a disturbed patient to be all over the map. Lack of limits can result in deterioration into iatrogenic brief reactive psychosis.

SUMMARY

The main point of this chapter, which I will repeat again, is that good therapy of MPD is good generic therapy. The patient is a person, not a diagnosis, not a group of people in one body, and not a diversion for the therapist. Complex MPD patients challenge all the skills, staying power, and self-discipline of the therapist. At the same time they have the most to teach and are the most rewarding, by far, of any patients I have worked with. I have not met a person with MPD who did not impress me as a human being with great courage and faith in life.

CHAPTER ELEVEN

Specific Techniques of Treatment: The Initial Phase of Therapy

The treatment of multiple personality disorder must be based on good general principles of psychotherapy. This poses a problem for psychiatry because of the current swing of the pendulum away from psychotherapy training and toward diagnosis and medication as the special expertise of the psychiatrist. In some residency programs in North America trainees are not receiving adequate instruction in psychotherapy, according to secondhand reports I have heard. This means that many young psychiatrists will not have the general skills and experience to treat MPD successfully.

The psychiatrist who is going to treat MPD must be a diagnostician, physician, and psychotherapist. This is especially the case if inpatient work is going to be done. Of the triad, the physician is the least important, although medications can be helpful during the middle phase of therapy in many cases. Medical training provides an advantage, though, in assessing the physical complaints of the MPD patient, which can be complex. As for any psychotherapy patient, an adequate physical assessment is necessary, but the same person rarely does both the therapy and the physical examination.

Most MPD patients will not receive their psychotherapy from physicians. Therefore the emphasis in psychotherapy training should be on students in social work, psychology, and nursing. It simply isn't realistic or cost-effective to expect psychiatrists to do most of the work. Nor is there anything about medical or psychiatric training that uniquely prepares one to be an MPD psychotherapist.

For psychiatrists to be an optimally effective component of the treatment team, however, they must be skilled psychotherapists as well as diagnosticians and prescribers of medication. This is how our team at the Dissociative Disorders Clinic works: My cotherapists can treat MPD to integration, but they can't prescribe medications and aren't trained in the differential diagnosis of mental disorders. I am enough of a professional chauvinist to maintain that the psychiatrist-psychotherapist has the most comprehensive range of skills of any mental health professional.

It is also true that many patients are best treated as clients in community-based agencies staffed entirely by nonmedical personnel. This is particularly true for MPD clients who have had abusive treatment from hospital-based psychiatry in the form of misdiagnosis and mismanagement. As I explained in the Introduction, I am referring to people with MPD as patients in this book and have adopted a convention of the patient being female and the therapist male. This is because I am a male hospital-based physician who treats females mostly and because the female:male ratio in clinical series of MPD is 9:1. I am aware of the political, legal, social, philosophical, and economic aspects of the terms *client* and *patient*. The social context of the treatment has a strong effect on the tone of the therapy and on the nature of the therapeutic alliance.

The special techniques I am going to describe can be used by any therapist of any background. Those techniques that require a ward setting or medical training will be discussed as such under separate headings. I want to emphasize again though, that most of the work is good general psychotherapy. It involves supportively helping the patient to recover her memories, deal with them, and learn to live in a way that is not self-destructive. The psychotherapy of MPD is an *enabling* therapy in the feminist sense.

I am going to describe the techniques in detail because the literature does not describe them fully and does not provide a grip on what to do, beyond general principles. In this regard I take two texts on cognitive therapy as my model (Beck & Emery, 1985; Beck et al., 1979). One can't instantly become a fully trained cognitive therapist just by reading these two books, but they provide detailed strategies and techniques for actual implementation.

It is important to provide a similar catalog for MPD treatment because there are far more patients than therapists. Therapists who already have good general skills should be able to learn the special techniques of MPD work without too much difficulty. The danger in describing these techniques in detail is that inadequately trained therapists will start using them in therapies that are out of control. Ideally everyone should have close supervision from an experienced therapist at least on his first case. Thereafter less intense consultation may be all that is required. This is so partly because one complex

MPD patient is a better teacher than 20 "regular" cases. It is possible to become familiar and comfortable with most of the specialized techniques and principles of MPD therapy in the course of taking one person to integration.

A fact of life in North America is that not all therapists will get adequate supervision on their first case of MPD. Robert Mayer's (1988) experience will be repeated by others in years to come, though others are unlikely to describe it with such eloquence. This means that there must be a compromise between compelling patients to go without treatment because of the shortage of trained therapists and advocating that "anything goes."

Another consideration is that MPD patients often get into treatment before they are diagnosed and can't just be dropped. One patient was diagnosed after she spontaneously switched to a child alter on the ward. She was effectively in instantaneous therapy for MPD, because I had to deal directly with a frightened personality who feared I would assault her. Often it just isn't feasible to "put a lid on it" and continue with supportive therapy. Often the lid comes off and stays off. When the therapist has no prior experience, can't find adequate supervision, and can't transfer the case, there is a problem. I hope this chapter will be of some help to therapists who find themselves in this situation.

As a brief general outline of therapy, I think that the patient needs to recover her abuse memories, come to terms with them, integrate into one person, and learn how to live effectively without pathological dissociation. I don't think there is any need to get into hairsplitting arguments about how integrated a "normal" person is. Most people feel as if they are one person most of the time, and so do integrated MPD patients. It isn't necessary to advocate a mythic unity of self never attained by non-MPD people. Nor does MPD provide an earth-shaking challenge to usual concepts of the self and individual responsibility. MPD is a dissociative *disorder*. When it occurs as chronic trauma disorder with MPD, it is a dysfunctional adjustment that needs treatment.

It is important, I emphasize again, not to lose sense of general principles and common sense in the treatment of MPD. The first intervention in the treatment is to say hello to the patient. The second is to introduce oneself. These simple acts set the context of therapy: The participants are human beings, and therapy is a conversation. If it can begin as such, things are off to a good start.

The more MPD therapy I do, the less gimmicky I become. At first I thought that I had discovered a gold mine. I thought that there would be no limit to the clever techniques, creative interventions, and tricky maneuvers I could come up with. I envisioned an endless series of papers on special techniques. Rather than being sadder but wiser, I am now happier and wiser. Special techniques are important, but not as important as general ones. Indeed "techniques" can get in the way if they detract from the core reality, which is two human beings in conversation. The therapeutic conversation has a context, rules, and rituals that I will describe. So does talking with a bank teller or engaging in any other human transaction.

In this chapter and in Chapter 12 the special techniques of MPD treatment are discussed under a number of headings, with techniques peculiar to inpatient work described separately in Chapter 13. This chapter focuses on techniques used predominantly in the initial phase of therapy.

THE MODEL OF TREATMENT

Many models of psychotherapy are after-the-fact accounts dressed up in jargon. On the other hand, good therapy can't consist only of the application of techniques, with no overall sense of their purpose. What is MPD therapy for and how does it work?

I practice a psychotherapy that is a mixture of psychodynamic, cognitive, and systems techniques and formulations. It is a pragmatic, active therapy in which I do a lot of talking. When people describe the work I do with MPD patients as "long-term psychotherapy," I reply that that is not what I do. I do short-term therapy that goes on for a long time. The difference is important.

Long-term psychoanalytic psychotherapy is characterized by things I don't do, and I do many things that are not "allowed" in strict psychoanalytic psychotherapy. From an analytic point of view, there are more "parameters of treatment" in my work than treatment. I don't think of the things I say as "interpretations." I talk a lot, offer advice and personal opinions, make political comments and jokes, try to reduce the transference rather than augment it, prescribe medication, see other people with the patient, and bring cotherapists, medical students, and nurses into sessions (just as cotherapists bring me into sessions). I try hard not to be "deep." In the treatment of MPD it is important to be as shallow as possible. There is no need for "deep" exploration because the most important material is immediately available on the surface, though the surface is dissociated into separate compartments.

I remember a colleague saying to me that MPD is important because it proves the existence of the unconscious. I take the opposite view. For me MPD demonstrates that the so-called unconscious is not unconscious at all—it is wide-awake and cognitive in nature, but dissociated. The unconscious no doubt exists, but I don't deal with it much in therapy. I interact with the alters and find that I can do the work of therapy by sticking to what they consciously know.

For example, a patient misses a session and is amnesic for 2 hours starting 10 minutes before the session was to have begun. The last thing she remembers is walking across the hospital parking lot on the way to our building. To find out what happened, there is no need for months of exploration or convoluted hypotheses about Oedipal and pre-Oedipal conflicts. An alter, if he or she agrees to come out and talk, will readily explain his or her motivation for taking executive control prior to the session and ensuring that "she" missed it. The work of therapy is to understand the cognitive errors behind the alter's behavior, their dynamic origins in childhood abuse, and their current protective function, then to negotiate an alternative strategy. The alternative strategy will usually be a step towards coconsciousness, cooperation, and eventual integration.

MPD therapy is an "up front" kind of therapy, as I practice it. I give the patient lots of feedback, am frank about what I am thinking, and encourage what the cognitive therapists call "collaborative empiricism." This involves patient and therapist working together in a pragmatic, hypothesis-testing, problem-solving fashion to reach the goals of treatment.

My model of therapy is no more than this: The patient has developed chronic trauma disorder with MPD in response to childhood abuse. She needs to integrate. After integration she needs to learn how to function as an integrated person. The next three chapters are a set of guidelines and suggestions for helping the complex multiple reach that goal.

THE PHASES OF PSYCHOTHERAPY

The psychotherapy of MPD can be divided into four phases: initial phase, middle phase, late phase, and postintegration work. Integration may occur anywhere from halfway to nearly at the end of therapy. Post-integration work will be described separately at the end of Chapter 13.

Like the stages of death and dying, the phases of MPD therapy are only a rough linear map of the work: There is much going back, reworking, premature going ahead, and simultaneous presence of more than one stage. Just as it is important not to reify the alters into people, it is important not to view the phases as more than rough guidelines. With that caution, certain tasks and techniques predominate in different phases of therapy.

The initial phase is often preceded by a lengthy involvement in the mental health system. Often patients have worked for extended periods of time with other therapists. There are two ways to think about this previous work, which are not mutually exclusive. One is to belittle the previous therapist who did not make the diagnosis and view the previous therapy as a waste of time.

Usually, however, I find that previous diagnostically nonspecific therapy has been essential preparation for the MPD work. The previous therapist may have established a good treatment alliance, done extensive supportive work, involved appropriate services and agencies, helped in coping with friends, relatives, and children, shored up weak life skills, worked through some of the incest, and carried out other necessary tasks. Often the patient was not personally ready or was not in a life situation to do the intense definitive work. A medical analogy would be the internist who treats a number of metabolic and infectious illnesses in order to prepare a patient for surgery. Without the surgery the patient would die, but without the preparation the surgery couldn't be done. Sometimes the referral source is a therapist who has been doing good work and has a good treatment alliance. Because we rarely have new treatment slots available in our clinic, we usually suggest in consultation that the previous therapist continue his or her work but gradually shift into MPD therapy with ongoing consultation/supervision available from us. Occasionally we transfer a case from the referral source to us, if the consultation includes a request to take over the case.

In such cases we make a straightforward explanation to the patient: She is transferred to us for specific psychotherapy for MPD because that is our area of subspecialty expertise. The transfer has the same rationale as transfer of the metabolically stabilized patient from internist to surgeon. In some cases we act as cotherapists with the referring person, which is analogous to the internist managing the diabetes during the surgical admission: Consultant and consultee function as a team.

The transfer of a patient can be rocky at times. In one case, an MPD patient maintained a delusion that her previous therapist was dead for several months after transfer, lamented the loss of the "only good mother she had ever had," spoke of joining her previous therapist by suicide, and idealized and devalued both the new and old therapists. The delusion could have been rated correctly as a diagnostic criterion for a psychotic depression on a structured diagnostic interview, except that a major depressive episode was not present. The delusion responded to time, support, clear statements that the previous therapist was not dead, empathic discussion of the loss, formation of a positive transference with the new therapists, small doses of trifluoperazine, and psychotherapeutic work dealing with the patient's childhood. The only component of this multimodal treatment package for the delusion I would have felt comfortable about dropping was the antipsychotic medication.

The initial phase of therapy begins with the first diagnostic assessment session. The major tasks of this phase include making the diagnosis; sharing the diagnosis with the patient; educating the patient about dissociation and abuse; proposing a treatment goal of full integration; negotiating a treatment contract; and beginning to map the system. Because mapping involves contacting alters who are hostile, many of the techniques of the middle phase quickly come into play. The initial phase of therapy is best thought of as the preliminary phase of a stage that encompasses both it and the middle phase.

The middle phase of therapy includes the most painful recovery of abuse memories and the abreactions. There is further mapping of the system, extensive negotiation, dismantling of amnesia barriers, and sometimes several integrations or fusions of alters. This is the period of therapy during which specialized techniques are most required.

The late preintegration phase is less intense. It involves reworking, final negotiations between alters, and a lot of work that will be carried into the postintegration period. One can think that therapy is in late preintegration, then discover another layer or group of personalities, and go through the stages of therapy all over with that layer. It is important to realize that different groups of alters may move through these stages nearly independently and can be integrated as groups. In the treatment of MPD, nothing follows a simple linear progression.

After the final alter personality has been integrated, there is still a lot of work to do. Some patients just seem to be better and have no major difficulties postintegration. Others make a transition from multiple personality disorder to posttraumatic stress disorder in a single personality. Such patients may have intense flashbacks and continue to be suicidal, unstable in their mood, and self-destructive in their manner of living for a long period of time postintegration. For some the outcome may be resolution of their MPD, with a residual untreatable personality disorder.

As a generalization, though, postintegration work is much less intense, requires few if any specialized techniques, and has a greater supportive component. Although progression through these stages is not linear in any simple way, one can see definite increments of progress throughout therapy. There are many milestones on the way from diagnosis, to the first partial removal of an amnesia barrier, through the first integration, to full resolution of the MPD. I will go through the therapy describing each of the techniques in our Therapist Dissociative Checklist (see Appendix B).

ESTABLISHING TRUST AND SAFETY

These two items are closely linked together. Both are issues throughout therapy and have to be reworked with newly encountered alters or groups of alters. The therapist establishes trust by being trustworthy. That may seem self-evident, but it is an example of the empirical approach I take and recommend to the patient. It is important to remember that the complex MPD patient has had her trust in loved ones violently broken countless times. She has developed a complicated system of protectors, persecutors, and other personalities to deal with problems of trust and safety: The total personality system simply won't accept "caring" statements about how much the therapist can be trusted. There are often dangerously naive and trusting child or other alters who have been ruthlessly exploited by a variety of people.

As always in MPD, one must be alert for paradox and contradiction. There will be alters who are too trusting and ones that don't trust enough. In his workshops and talks Richard Kluft always emphasizes the need to treat all personalities in an "even-handed" fashion. That is a correct and necessary principle. Being even-handed, however, doesn't necessarily mean acting the same with all alters: I couldn't act the same with all alters even if I wanted to, anymore than I could act the same with children, colleagues, friends, and enemies.

To establish trust and safety with some frightened child alters, it is important to tell them in a gentle, straightforward manner that it is safe. I might say, "It's all right. You're safe now. I'm a doctor and I'm not going to do anything to hurt you. I just want to talk to you." The alter might reply, "You promise you're not going to hurt me?" I would then go on to explain that the bad things happened a long time ago, her daddy is far away now, and the nurses and doctors are going to help the alter to feel better. I might say, "I promise I'm not going to hurt you. I completely, completely promise. You can believe me and I wouldn't lie to you. You'll see. We'll just talk and everything will be okay."

When child alters are hiding in the corner, shaking, screaming, trying to bang their heads, or scratching themselves, physical restraint may be necessary. Usually very little force is required, and it is more a comforting, holding form of restraint than an aggressive control or containment. A hand on the shoulder may help. When touching any alter, it is usually best to get permission first, unless it is an emergency situation, because some alters are very frightened by touch and perceive it as assaultive. With child alters one might explain, after getting permission, "I'm just going to hold your hand now to stop you from scratching yourself. We're not going to let anything bad happen to you here. You're not allowed to hurt yourself, and we won't let any of the others hurt you either."

Trust and safety are complicated in MPD because the therapist has to protect some alters against persecutory attacks by others. Alters may take control of an arm in order to scratch, slash, hit, or otherwise hurt the patient. With an adolescent or adult alter, simple reassurance may help only a little bit at most and may be ridiculed. With more cognitively advanced personalities I often give a set speech about how it is smart not to trust people. This is similar to paradoxical interventions made by a family therapist.

I tell the alter that it is true that many people broke her trust in the past and that there are many untrustworthy people in the world. I congratulate her for her "street smarts," her advocacy of a nontrusting position, and her wariness. This is an excellent and necessary survival strategy in our world, I say. If there is another alter who has repeatedly been exploited because of being too trusting, I agree with the protector that this is dangerous. But I then go on to say that, although she may not have met many, there are in fact many decent people in the world. Without being self-aggrandizing, I simply tell the patient that she can trust me but that I don't expect her to believe this right away.

I then recommend an empirical test of the hypothesis that I am trustworthy. I tell the alter to keep an eye on me and see if I do anything abusive. More than that, I ask the alter to tell me right away if I am doing anything she doesn't like. I recruit untrusting, hostile, and persecutory alters as consultants in the therapy at the first opportunity and try to get their opinions

on things. This technique for establishing trust delivers a number of therapeutic messages, many of which the patient has never received in a sustained
consistent fashion. These include the following: Your opinion is worth something; you have a right to protest; abusive behavior is not acceptable; you
already have many positive skills; I can't solve all your problems, but I am
willing to help; and, I would like to talk with you at length.

Some patients bring transitional objects to sessions. This is fine with me.
Some alters would not be able to work if they did not have a teddy bear
with them. Also, some patients benefit from a transitional object given to
them by the therapist. Patients can be highly resourceful at securing transitional objects; for instance, one patient kept her appointment slips under
her pillow during the most difficult period of therapy. Such behavior might
be abhorred as "regressive" by some therapists. It is just a temporary
technique for one phase of therapy, and the patient will soon enough leave
it behind. If she doesn't soon enough leave it behind, then that becomes a
problem in its own right, which be solved.

Being available for phone calls is another way of establishing trust and
safety. I have an absolute policy of never giving my home phone number
out to any patients, and I have an unlisted number. If any patient obtained
my phone number and started abusing it, I would get a new phone number
and deal with the transgression in therapy. A major part of creating safety
is establishing limits. However, I am available for phone calls at work during
the day, although I explain to patients that most of the time I can't get back
to them immediately.

Because I work at a teaching hospital, my patients are covered by the
on-call staff as a general departmental policy. Recently our department has
placed psychiatric nurses in the emergency department, who work with the
emergency physicians. These nurses have experience at switching alters and
are an excellent backup resource (as well as a source of new cases they
diagnose themselves). In general, the more educated staff are about MPD,
the safer the environment for the patients.

Creating trust and safety is something that is done by both therapist and
patient. Child alters will often stake out a corner of the office, or a chair,
as their territory. They feel safer there. As I do most of the time in therapy,
I discuss trust and safety in a straightforward, open, problem-solving fashion.
This will often involve joint strategy making in consultation with a number
of alters. Child alters may also make good use of inner safety techniques.
They may simply leave, or they may seek to be close to a protector inside.
One group of ritually abused children were safe if they could get to a tree
in an inner landscape: There, the father-alter could not harm them.

Inumerable imaginative, magical forms of protection can be given to the
patient or may already have been created. I have sent alters into dream
landscapes to bring back abuse memories: In such cases, the alters have felt
braver because a light, luminous rope was tied around their waists. I held
the rope in my hand as they entered the frightening rooms of their memory,

and I could pull them out if necessary. Or I have marked alters with magical retrieval markers that allowed me to retrieve them by calling their names. In the magical world of inner hypnotic reverie, anything is possible, but all is not fantasy, for there are terrible memories of real trauma hidden behind the amnesia barriers.

I will discuss hospitalization and limit-setting under separate headings, although they are key tools for establishing safety. All of the techniques overlap, interdigitate, and reinforce each other. I discuss them as if they were separable only for clarity.

If it came down to a choice between my dying or the patient's dying, I would choose to live. The safety of the therapist must be protected as well as that of the patient. Therapists who work with cult-abused patients know that the risks to the therapist are not theoretical. Safety for the therapist depends on limits and toughness. It is not kind to the patient, therapist, therapist's loved ones, other MPD patients, or the institution, to allow the therapist to be harmed. Such events would only impede the treatment of other MPD patients.

The first way to protect the therapist is not to accept patients with convictions for violent crimes except in a secure forensic or hospital setting able to handle non-MPD forensic cases. That is simple. A more common problem is to uncover past or ongoing violence, witnessing of murder, severe physical and sexual abuse by pimps, and other violent acts during therapy. In this situation the therapist has formed a treatment alliance, has "taken the lid off," and would feel badly about dropping the patient. The patient would be at high risk of suicide and would have difficulty trusting anyone in the future if disclosure of such violence resulted in termination of therapy.

If therapy is to continue with the previously violent patient, appointments should not be scheduled for evenings. There should be other professionals nearby. Sometimes two therapists will have to see the patient jointly. There must be a written contract not to bring weapons to the sessions. If there is a suspicion that the patient is carrying weapons, she must consent to being escorted to the security station for a weapons search. Searches may be required prior to each session. If the patient persists in bringing weapons, therapy should be unilaterally terminated without arrangements for transfer to another therapist. These rules tell the patient that abuse is unacceptable and that safety is going to be ensured for both participants in therapy.

If the therapist is nervous enough to even faintly consider having a weapon of his own in the office because of a particular patient, consultation is *mandatory*. It is foolhardy and stupid to try to handle such cases without consultation. In some cases contact with the police may be required, and if so, the safety of the therapist overrides patient confidentiality. That is a personal and therapeutic opinion of mine, not a legal or professional-ethics statement. I would rather be sued and alive than dead and a virtuous protector of patient confidentiality.

One useful technique for therapist safety is to implant a posthypnotic suggestion and to reinforce it periodically. David Caul told a story at a workshop of freezing a patient in midair with a posthypnotic signal, as the patient was lunging at him with a knife. In one case we used a posthypnotic suggestion for a patient to go into a catatonic trance whenever a staff member yelled "Time out!" and made a time-out hand signal. A nervous evening nurse unnecessarily froze the patient in front of the nursing station one night, with no untoward effects on the patient. We were reassured by this impromptu test and were able to treat the Evil One to stable integration, partly because of our own sense of safety.

There is nothing unprofessional about opening the door of the office and standing near the door if it seems necessary. One can ask the patient to sit on the floor, giving the therapist an escape advantage if a hostile alter cannot be contained. If such techniques are required more than a few times, hospitalization, termination, and consultation should all be considered. The basic principle is that you have to do what you have to do to stay safe.

A single threat against my family by any alter is grounds for immediate termination of therapy.

There are hundreds of thousands of individuals with MPD in North America, and most of them can be treated with safety. MPD therapists are a scarce resource and must be protected. Handling MPD patients is often like handling misbehaving children: Limits, toughness, strict rules, and consistent enforcement are the kindest and most effective treatment. Not everyone agrees with that parenting approach, but the patients will eventually teach it to most therapists who are committed to effective, efficient treatment. Within such rules, good MPD therapy can be fun and curative.

DEVELOPING A TREATMENT ALLIANCE AND DISCUSSING THE DIAGNOSIS

I have linked these two aspects of therapy because they depend on each other. In discussing the diagnosis, a balance must be struck between a matter-of-fact approach similar to that for any medical diagnosis and traumatizing the patient with a flood of information. I set the grounds for the diagnosis by normalizing dissociation, then explaining the link between trauma and dissociative disorders. Some patients will already know their diagnosis and its etiology, but most will not. The way in which I discuss the diagnosis also depends on whether it is a diagnostic consultation or an early treatment session.

In consultation I am usually comfortable explaining MPD in a general way and giving the patient the actual term MPD as a diagnosis. It is important to demystify the symptoms, put them in a framework, explain that they are common and treatable, and to emphasize that MPD is not a form of insanity. I often use an educational metaphor, saying that treatment involves unlearning highly effective dissociative defenses used in childhood, which are now maladaptive, and learning new ones. I never use words like "defense, trans-ference, or libido" with patients. Instead of talking about defenses I usually talk about strategies, ways of coping, or similar generic ideas.

I tell patients that MPD is just a label we use for having other parts inside that are so separate they feel like different people. I state that they are not other people, that they are all parts of one person, and that the goal of therapy is integration. I think that integration is the best goal and that not trying for it cheats the patient. This is analogous to striving for cure in all cases of childhood leukemia, while being prepared to abandon that goal in unresponsive cases for whom the treatment is worse than the illness. MPD is as serious and real as leukemia, though real in a different way.

I also talk about prognosis and the probable duration of therapy, being careful to make only ballpark estimates and to advise the patient that con-trolled studies have not been conducted. Overall, there isn't that much difference between the way I discuss etiology, diagnosis, treatment, and prognosis in panic disorder, schizophrenia, and MPD. I review what is known and what I recommend in each illness. When explaining schizophrenia to patient or family, I make a point of clarifying that most psychiatrists view it as an illness of the brain, but that definitive research proof is still lacking. In panic disorder I review a mixed biological-cognitive-behavioral model of etiology and treatment in which I believe.

Discussing the diagnosis is not something that is done once or twice at the beginning of treatment, then dropped. Throughout therapy one will be educating the patient about the nature of her disorder, as more of its com-plexities unravel. Dissociation will have to be explained over and over with newly encountered alters. Like the emotions and memories, the cognitive information about the diagnosis has to be processed and reprocessed throughout therapy. The patient has to discover the meaning of MPD for herself, which will have unique qualities and nuances. We call this "education and infor-mation processing" on our Therapist Checklist.

I am a strong advocate of diagnosis and differentiated treatment protocols. Some people view this approach as distastefully medical, but I see it as correct and humane. It is ill-advised for a community-based psychotherapist capable of only one generic treatment modality to attempt to treat panic disorder, MPD, and schizophrenia. I don't believe that there is one model or school that can account for all forms of emotional disorder. Without giving a formal lecture, I communicate a flexible, technically eclectic treatment plan to the patient and emphasize that treatment will be collaborative but not democratic. The patient is the patient, and I am the doctor. We are not friends, and I am the only one getting paid.

Some patients insist on being "equals" in a way that undermines therapy and is a resistance to getting on with the work. Patients are not "equals" in the social contract of therapy. Neither are they subordinates. In therapy I expect patients to make their own decisions and be responsible for them-selves, but at times they must defer to my greater experience and insight.

This doesn't mean I am being paternal, it just means that I am a professional with skills. People don't get insulted or insist on being treated as "equals" when an architect makes decisions about structural details for their house. The same applies in psychotherapy.

The frame of psychotherapy in North America is often too personal, intimate, and private. The frame should be more like the consultation with an architect on house plans. It is the client's house and life; the architect has special skills; and the client can't design a house alone. In my architectural practice I build whole selves in ongoing consultation and collaboration with my clients, who are called patients for sociological reasons extrinsic to the work. When the therapy contract is thought of in this way, the whole issue of being "equal" becomes irrelevant. That is the atmosphere I try to create in therapy, as a corrective to an excess of intimacy.

Of course, building a self is a far more important, difficult, and personal project than building a house. No effective therapy with an MPD patient has ever been dry and technical. I think it is reasonable to say that creative work in architecture engages the architect in a direct, personal way, just as MPD therapy does. The difficulty in advocating a more "professional" stance in therapy is that it will be perceived as cold and insensitive. In practice, nobody can treat a significant number of multiples in an overinvolved, over-personalized way without hurting patients and burning out. Zen-like detachment is necessary. With these remarks I am trying to convey a sense of the tone of the treatment alliance.

It is essential to establish a treatment alliance with as many alters as possible. With some this will be very difficult. The host and rational adult personalities can be worked with on an adult level. With the child alters a formal treatment contract doesn't have much meaning. With the children the alliance is closer to that of play therapy, except that the play involves intense abreactions of abuse memories. Often it is necessary to do safe things with the children in a kind of systematic desensitization. Reading books, playing cards, drawing, or going for walks may be necessary beginning steps.

These activities, described in more detail in Chapter 12, are dangerous in that therapy may deteriorate into prolonged atherapeutic play. The play is only a means to an end, which is the recovery of abuse memories and integration. It is easy to lose track that one is treating an adult and helping an adult to live better in the world. The therapist must also form a treatment alliance with the hostile alters, who will quickly dispel the illusion of delightful children.

As mentioned earlier, it is helpful to recruit the persecutors as consultants to the therapy. This may involve cognitive techniques aimed at challenging the destructive behavior. For instance, attempts to kill the host through overdose or slashing are often viewed as helpful euthanasia by the persecutors. The first step in forming an alliance is to point out that both the persecutor and the therapist have the same goal: They only differ on means. Both want the suffering to end. I often make a little speech acknowledging that the treatment is increasing the host's suffering, but insisting that it is a necessary stage of therapy. I agree that if things could not improve, the therapy would be harmful and futile.

Persecutors are often very resentful of the therapist's interfering and treading on their turf. They see therapy as implying that they are failures at taking care of "her." This cognitive error can be addressed directly. Simple statements to the effect that everyone needs a hand sometimes can help. I acknowledge that the persecutor has far more knowledge of the patient and ask for permission to draw on that expertise. A good strategy is to move quickly to a practical problem in which the persecutor can act as a protector. The therapist might ask the persecutor to come out in a predictable social situation in which some other aggressive or potentially abusive person has to be dealt with.

Alternatively, one layer of persecutors may be recruited as enforcers to keep another layer of hostile alters, who will not yet enter therapy, from harming vulnerable alters. Both internal and external tasks can be set. The most powerful way to form a treatment alliance with hostile alters is to divine their pain and sadness and comment on it. They too are suffering children and adolescents. One Evil One turned out to be a child who declared, "I don't want to hurt anybody," during her integration ritual. Most hostile alters act tough but want to be loved.

Globally, the best way to form a treatment alliance is to know what you are doing and form a sensible plan of action. Patients can tell if you know what you are doing. The best way to undermine the treatment alliance is to fake expertise or certainty that isn't there. MPD patients have received extensive training in detecting lies. I have found that MPD patients are forgiving of the therapist's errors if the mistakes are acknowledged openly. It is also important not to promise what you can't deliver, because such promises will come back to haunt you and will weaken the alliance.

Usually forming a treatment alliance is not too difficult, although there will be strong resistance and hostile alters providing protection for the patient. Most patients are so relieved to meet a therapist who understands their disorder and seems to know what to do that a working relationship is readily established. The alliance is far from static, though. It varies from alter to alter and fluctuates throughout therapy. With some patients I have never gotten to first base therapeutically and haven't been sure what went wrong. Some patients just don't seem to be ready to work, and sometimes the patient and I don't seem to click. It is important not to be personally offended if a patient can't work with you—sometimes they will come back later.

A STATED GOAL OF INTEGRATION

I am using a separate heading for this technique to emphasize its importance, having already discussed it to some extent. Although it is important to state this goal of therapy at the outset and to contract for it at least informally with the host personality, overemphasizing integration can create unnecessary hostility in many of the alters. The alters view integration as dying. "You just want to get rid of us" is a statement I have heard many times. One of the ways to soften this resistance is to adopt the patient's metaphor of integration, rather than imposing one of your own.

For some patients an explanation of integration in terms of computer circuitry seems to make sense. I say that the patient's mind is like a computer in which certain areas of the grid are disconnected from each other. The free flow of information and coordination of function is impeded by these short circuits in the system. The goal of therapy is simply to repair the short circuits, not to remove or replace parts. Other patients may prefer an image of divided streams rejoining into one full, strong river. Leaves with their dividing veins and common stem, or trees, can provide a good metaphor, as can baking a cake, in which no ingredients are lost, and a new whole is created. Richard Kluft (1987, Oct. 24) has a videotape of an integration ritual involving melting snows on a mountain flowing down to join together.

The essential principles of integration metaphors are that nothing is lost, all aspects of the self have their value and place, and a whole greater than the sum of its parts is created. I also include a statement at the beginning of therapy that for this particular patient full integration may not be a desirable goal. For instance one patient retired from her career unintegrated but felt that occasional blank spells were now tolerable, because the threat of losing her job or publicly embarrassing herself was gone. For health and life-stage reasons, and because of the quiescence of most alters, she did not feel it would be beneficial to do the work required for full integration. Kluft (1988d) has described the need to go slowly in the older patient and to be satisfied with a nonintegrated outcome in some cases.

Throughout therapy, integration is mentioned and discussed, but the work does not usually focus directly on it. One way to avoid unnecessary resistance to integration is to focus on the barriers between personalities, rather than on joining them together. If the amnesia is gradually dismantled, and feelings, attitudes, and memories are increasingly shared, the patient will approach integration without having to be talked into it. By the time every personality is aware of everything about everybody else, many will spontaneously consent to integration or will even integrate outside therapy. Movement toward integration should not be forced. Rather it should be viewed as the final outcome of work that deals directly with other issues. This approach sidesteps potential conflict between therapist and patient.

CONTACTING ALTER PERSONALITIES

The idea of contacting alter personalities directly seems to "spook" many professionals and make them leery of trying to treat MPD. Actually contacting alters is usually fairly simple. The difficult part is figuring out what to do with and say to them once they are out. In teaching beginning therapists about contacting alters, I sometimes make a comparison with learning how to start IVs in medical school. In medical school students are expected to start difficult IVs with minimal training. In fact when the IV nurse, who has started thousands of IVs, can't get one started, the medical student, who may have started 10 or 15, is often called. The same situation occurs when the technicians can't draw blood: They may have been doing blood draws daily for years, but when they have trouble, the medical student gets called.

Most medical students get very anxious starting IVs at first, then become skilled and confident quite quickly. As a purely technical skill, calling out alters is easier and safer than starting IVs. A number of medical students doing 2 months of inpatient psychiatry on my ward have called out alters. They watch me several times, do a few under direct supervision, then often carry on independently. To do this they must have a solid grip on the issues of therapy and have specific limited therapeutic goals in mind. If there is any trouble, ward nurses who are experienced in MPD work are available.

One medical student did supervised integrations of personalities as well. This young man had no previous experience in psychiatry and was not planning on going into psychiatry as far as I was aware. If medical students can learn this skill, I don't see why most mental health professionals can't. Calling out alter personalities is a skill that could be learned by all medical students in a 2-month rotation if there was enough opportunity.

These remarks apply to reasonably straightforward calling out of alters. In some cases there is greater technical difficulty. The point is that lack of experience with the technical aspects of MPD work is only a minor barrier to the training of new therapists. Experiential workshops, videotape demonstrations, and limited direct experience would be sufficient training for most purposes.

As in much of the therapy, one good way to proceed is to ask the patient how her switching works. Some patients already know how to induce a switch, and can do so on request. In such cases, the therapist just asks to talk to a certain personality and the switch occurs readily. Virtually all patients learn how to switch on demand during therapy. When switching is well practiced, I just say, "Okay, could I talk to Mary now? Mary." This is followed immediately by a brief head nod, eye closing, and emergence of Mary. Naturally I make such requests in a context, with prior discussion, so that the timing makes sense to the patient.

I'm uneasy about making the calling out of personalities sound so simple, for fear that inexperienced therapists will call out hostile, frightened, or other alters they can't handle without adequate preparation of the patient, themselves, or the therapy. It may be simple to call out a screaming head-banging child, but not so easy to deal with her or get her to go back inside. Calling out of alters can be traumatic for both patient and therapist.

The first step in contacting alters may involve indirect methods described in the section on interviewing voices in Chapter 7, in the discussion of schizophrenia. The first attempt at contacting alters is always based on some reason for suspecting their existence. Usually this is a history of blank spells, and this history is usually accompanied by voices and other secondary features of MPD. The patient must be given a clear rationale for what is being done for what reason. Usually this will involve an explanation that the therapist is trying to help the patient recover missing memories.

After the necessary history-taking and an explanation that the missing memories may be recoverable, I might say the following:

> What I want to do is try to contact the part of your mind that knows what happens during the blank spells. To do this I want you to be as relaxed as possible, so in a moment I'm going to ask you to close your eyes. This helps with the relaxation. You don't have to be worried, this is perfectly safe and nothing frightening will happen. All I am going to do is talk and help you try to relax, then I'll just ask to speak to the part of your mind that remembers what happens during the blank spells.

> I'd like you to close your eyes now and sit as comfortably as possible in the chair. Good. Now I want you just to concentrate on my voice, trying not to think about other things. Just focus your mind on the sound of my voice. Simply by listening and concentrating on my voice, you will find that your body begins to become more and more relaxed and comfortable, just a pleasant, warm, natural sensation of relaxation and calmness as you listen to the sound of my voice.

> Now it will be as if a blank spell is starting. Just like when there is a blank spell in your life outside. You will find that the memories of the blank spells are coming forward so that I can talk with the part of the mind that holds them. That part of the mind will be here and be able to talk with me directly. While this is happening, your body will stay sitting in the chair, comfortable and relaxed. Everything will be perfectly safe and you will not get up out of the chair.

> Now it's like Susan is starting to have a blank spell. The part of the mind that remembers will come forward and be able to talk with me. While that other part of the mind is talking, Susan can listen and be wide awake if that is safe. She can remember as much as she is ready to remember. Or else Susan can be like she's asleep inside and not remember anything, just like during the blank spells. Susan will be able to hear and remember as much as she feels ready to, and it will be all right if she doesn't remember anything at all.

> Now in a moment I want you to open your eyes, and when you do it will be that other part of the mind that is in control and talking to me, the part of the mind that remembers what happens during the blank spells. Open your eyes please, as soon as you are ready.

This procedure can have several outcomes. One is that nothing happens: The patient just opens her eyes and says that nothing happened (if this is the end of the procedure, it is important to realize that the patient may nevertheless be in trance, so a suggestion to come out of trance must be given). With consent, I might next go on to a longer induction with heavier sleep and safety suggestions, and try again. If this is unsuccessful, I would then go to indirect techniques. A second outcome is that the patient talks lucidly in a hypnotic state, but there is no alter personality present. This is the case in simple psychogenic amnesia in which memories are recovered with hypnosis. In highly hypnotizable subjects the procedure can result in the recovery of memory without creation of alters.

Often a lucid, cooperative alter emerges, and I begin taking a history from her, as described below. Sometimes there is a brief switch of executive control, but the alter only stays out for a few seconds. Usually in such situations, a hostile alter tells the therapist to get lost. Sometimes the patient won't open her eyes, but a different voice will say, "There's no one here," or "We're not coming out." In that case I might say:

> I understand that you don't want to talk to me right now. That's fine. I'm certainly not going to try to force you to talk to me, because I don't want to do that. Anyway, I couldn't force you to talk even if I wanted to.
>
> Let me explain why I would like to talk to you. I just want to get to know you a bit and spend some time with you. I'm not going to try to get you to do anything you don't want to do. In fact one reason I would like to talk to you is to get your opinion on things. Maybe there's something I'm doing that you don't like, that I could change if you told me about it.
>
> What I was thinking was, maybe if you don't feel like talking with me, you could write me a note. Maybe when Susan is at home she could leave out a pad and pen for you. Then you could come out at home and write me a note, and Susan could bring it to the next session. Or there might be some other way you could communicate with me without coming out right here. I'd like you to think about it.
>
> So let me ask again if there's anybody there, any other part of the mind, who would like to talk with me.

This approach can be used later in therapy when part of the system has been mapped, but there are alters who are reluctant to enter therapy. Depending on the degree of certainty as to whether alters are present, I will personify the absent part of the mind in my requests. If I am virtually certain that there is an unidentified alter, I will ask to speak to "someone I haven't talked to yet." If it appears to be a case of psychogenic amnesia, I will use generic referents like "the part of the mind that remembers," or "the part of Susan's mind that holds the memories." This is done to avoid suggesting multiplicity when it is not present.

If an alter or alters will not come out, indirect conversation, ideomotor signals, inner conferences, automatic writing, and other techniques can be used. Often one just has to wait till the other personality states are ready. There are a number of different hints of an alter being nearly ready to take executive control or of "someone being there," which can guide the therapist. Sometimes a given technique for calling out an alter seems to be working incompletely. In such cases, one can just try harder with the same technique or try later, rather than switch techniques.

Often the host personality has a feeling of another personality being close to emerging. The host may feel anger, sadness, or another emotion rising to the surface, or may just have an inner intuition of someone being there. She may hear a voice or get bits of memory that seem to be coming from an alter. The patient may feel spaced out, "funny," depersonalized, or partially in trance. Or the host may feel herself starting to go inside, but the process stops.

The therapist may observe subtle facial changes. The patient may start to close her eyes or nod her head. She may look tranced out. Or there may be a subtle change in facial gestalt that looks like the beginning of a switch. Sometimes the patient will enter a phase of uncontrolled trance switching without anyone taking executive control. The therapist may observe changing voice, face, and body language, without anything coherent being said or any distinct entity taking executive control. The patient may toss her head, moan, or call out "Stop!" These episodes can sometimes reach a high level of drama.

Sometimes an alter will take control of a hand and arm and throw something, start scratching, or perform some other motor act. If the patient is holding a pad and pen for automatic writing, the hand may drop the pen when the therapist asks if there is anyone there. Alternatively, an alter may inflict pain on the host when the therapist touches on a delicate theme or asks for a switch to occur. Sometimes the hostile alter in the background will cause a sudden headache, abdominal cramp, or other symptom that has been plaguing the patient for months. This is a handy demonstration of the psychogenic nature of the symptom and allows the therapist to form initial hypotheses about its associated cognitions and dynamics.

As soon as such activity starts in sessions, the alters have declared themselves and are unwittingly in therapy. One can be confident that they will enter further into the work in a stepwise fashion. I might say at this point:

I see that whoever is there can cause Susan to feel a lot of pain. It is clear that you have a lot of power to cause symptoms and that there's nothing Susan or I can do to stop that. So I'm not even going to try. If you're so powerful, it seems to me you should have nothing to fear from coming out and talking to me directly. But it seems you're scared to do that. I wonder why. If you are scared, let me point something out: If you did come out and talk to me, you could always go back inside anytime you felt like it. So there's no way I could do anything to you. You'd just disappear. But maybe you're too scared to try that.

This may be responded to with silence, increased headache, obscene gestures of the arm and hand, or a switch of executive control. It is helpful to keep a sense of humor about all this and to share it with the patient. An alter may emerge, glare at the therapist, and declare, "I'm not scared of anybody." I always try to sidestep the power struggle and confer control and power on the hostile alter. Like Janet (Ellenberger, 1970), I am willing to exploit the vanity of the demons.

It isn't necessary for an alter to be in executive control for it to be in therapy. One can talk through the personality in executive control to ones listening in the background at any stage of therapy. Sometimes uncontacted alters interact with the known personalities in dreams or inner hypnotic reveries, and sometimes these can be guided by the therapist. If all of the technical efforts to contact personalities directly, assuming it is a case of MPD, are unsuccessful, the options left are a sodium amytal interview or waiting. I think of sodium amytal as a crude battering ram for entering an otherwise closed system and usually use it for that purpose. Once I'm in, I proceed psychotherapeutically much as I would without sodium amytal.

Contacting alters is only half the problem in therapy. The other half is getting alters to go back inside, which can sometimes be difficult. This is particularly the case in outpatient work, when the patient has to find her way home, go to school or work, or otherwise function outside the office. It may be near the end of a session, and a child who can't drive and doesn't know where she lives may be refusing to go back inside. Or the alter may be abreacting, hostile, or intent on getting picked up after the session, taking drugs, or doing something else the therapist and host personality would not like.

Let me make a brief digression here, because of that last sentence. I can't treat complex MPD in an acting-out patient by taking a morally neutral position. I tell patients that my treatment goals for them include getting off drugs, out of prostitution, and out of the mental health system. I tell them that I view prostitution, substance abuse, and wrist slashing as unhealthy and undesirable components of an unhappy life. Some people may think this means I am imposing my view of the universe on patients. I think it is impossible to do therapy without advocating a worldview. I feel fine about advocating that the patient get off the street. On the other hand, I rarely if ever talk with patients about my own religious beliefs.

The first step in trying to get a reluctant alter to go back inside is to find out why she doesn't want to go away. There may be a simple misunderstanding or some finite issue that can be at least partially resolved. One can contract for a set amount of time out for that alter in the next session. If time is running short or an agreement can't be reached, gentle force may be required. Remember that other parts of the system want the switch to occur and that it is in the best interests of the whole patient. It is important not to get embroiled in disputes about alters' rights and to keep the interests of the whole patient in focus.

It is countertherapeutic to allow alters to run amok, even in a pleasant childlike fashion. Sessions must come to an end in a reasonable time, and often on a predetermined schedule. If too many allowances or concessions are made, the rest of the therapist's caseload will suffer, the institutional system will start to act out against the MPD patient, therapy will be out of control, burnout will begin, and the therapist's family will be unhappy. So the child must go back in.

This is where the hypnotizability of MPD patients comes in handy. Usually the alter can be put to sleep. Once negotiation has failed, the therapist takes control and speaks in a firm but authoritative voice, giving repeated suggestions for sleep. Often these will be effective in a few seconds. Once the alter goes to sleep, it is useful to plant a posthypnotic suggestion for immediate switching in future sessions as soon as the therapist tells whoever is out to go to sleep. Then the host is called out.

If the physical setting allows and it is safe, I sometimes leave the office if the patient refuses to leave. This works only if the setting is safe and if the therapist can outwait the patient. In such cases I set the next appointment and tell the patient she can leave when she is ready. Or the patient might be able to wait elsewhere in the building until a switch occurs. The principle involved is that practical solutions to bringing the session to a close must be found, in order to preserve the therapy. Like any problem in therapy, if this becomes persistent, it may be grounds for consultation. There is probably an unresolved conflict in the therapy.

The suggestion to go to sleep can be amplified with forehead touches or other cues. It is rare for this problem to get seriously out of control in a therapy that is otherwise proceeding reasonably well. Usually the alter agrees to go in or spontaneously switches in a reasonably short period of time.

Another problem is patients for whom the return of the host personality seems to be psychophysiologically difficult. Some host personalities just seem to have a harder time coming back. In such cases the difficulty in switching seems to be a property of the system and isn't linked to any particular alter, resistance, or dynamic. In such cases one just has to work at it longer. Lengthy monologues by the therapist can help, as can physical touch or the holding of a special object like a teddy bear, amulet, or diary.

With such patients I give suggestions that the therapist's voice will pull the patient back. We give repeated instructions to focus on physical reality and orient the host personality to where she is and who the therapist is. This can sometimes take 10 or 20 minutes. The worst that can happen, in our experience, is a longer delay than planned for.

A final problem is cases in which alters seem to shift rather than switch. In some patients the personality system is not distinct and structured, or there may be structured and amorphous regions. Sometimes neither the patient nor the therapist is sure who is out, or who was just out. If nobody can tell, it may not matter much as long as there is coconsciousness. The only way to deal with this kind of fuzziness in a system is to ask for clarification and work with the parts that are clearest. Things may become clearer over time. Another observation of Janet's (Binet, 1986, p. 147) may be helpful: Giving an alter a name may "crystallize" it and make it more distinct. This may be a therapeutic form of iatrogenic modification of the phenomenology if used sparingly.

In summary, the calling out of alter personalities, as an isolated technical intervention, is not the most difficult part of therapy. It can be learned easily by medical students and nurses. Most patients learn to manage their switches during therapy, so that alters can be called out with a simple request. When switching or lack of switching becomes a prolonged problem in therapy, this is usually an indicator of some other unresolved problem, rather than a purely technical difficulty. The therapist will have to keep the number of switches per session under control in order to provide structure within sessions; also, too much switching is stressful for the patient.

MAPPING THE PERSONALITY SYSTEM

It is impossible to treat MPD without mapping the system. Mapping can be done formally with diagrams or informally, with the therapist constructing a mental map of the system as he goes along. I am going to talk about formal mapping because it illustrates the principles of both the formal and informal approaches. We draw diagrams in some but not all cases, and some but not all patients like to use maps in their diaries and treatment sessions.

Mapping and gathering a history of the personality system are intertwined and done at the same time. A full map includes the name, age, time of appearance, function, degree of amnesia, position in the system, internal alliances, and any other relevant traits of each alter personality. Like most of the treatment, mapping is done in a straightforward way by asking the patient and consulting with the known alters.

The first step is to ask the amnesic host personality what she knows. Often this will be no more than a description of the voices, but the description can yield valuable information. Often the patient knows the sex of some voices and can divide them into friendly and hostile voices. Collateral history of the patient's behavior during blank spells will yield clues as to the types of alters in the system, as will objects missing and present. Samples of unfamiliar handwriting can be important both in content and in penmanship.

An active MPD diary will usually contain at least five or six different scripts. There will be hostile, furious scratchings with swear words and threats. A frightened childlike communication in block letters is common. There is often a microscopic script that may belong to an observer. Alters may identify themselves by name in the diary and will reveal their conflicts and concerns. Such information is like an advance reconnaissance prior to the first guerrilla infiltration of the personality system by the therapist.

Some patients will describe with astonishment the out-of-character clothing they find in their closets and drawers. They may describe typical street prostitute garb. This always makes my heart sink a bit, because I know how hard the work is going to be. Others may find toys, teddy bears, or other items purchased for child alters in their home and not know how they got there. Sometimes the patient "just has a feeling" that there is a little girl there, someone who is very angry, or someone who wants to help. The more prior information, the more specific and safe the first request for an alter will be.

Once the first alter emerges, it may be clear that she is an alter. There may be a dramatic shift in gestalt, and a charming child may announce with a smile, "Hi! I'm Susie." I then reply, "Hi, Susie. Nice to meet you. How are you?" Depending on how the child is feeling, and what she understands, I will then begin taking a history from her. As long as she is comfortable with this, I explain that I am going to ask a few questions, and that she is free not to answer any of them.

Soon after the emergence of a new alter, I ask who the alter is and if she knows who I am. If it is unclear whether a switch has occurred, I may ask, "Can you tell me whom I'm talking to right now?" If the patient answers, "Susan," I then clarify that she knows who I am and ask, "Are you the same Susan who I was talking to before I asked you to close your eyes?" If she is, then I ask whether she remembers anything that she can't usually remember. If she can't, it is probably the host personality. Sometimes there will be a coconscious alter with the same name or an alter behind an amnesia barrier with the same name, and these two possibilities must be inquired about directly.

The initial questions after calling out an alter are the point in therapy at which iatrogenic creation of MPD is most likely to occur, if it ever occurs. Therefore one must take great care in a forensic assessment not to ask leading questions, suggest multiplicity, or create artifacts. The way of proceeding just outlined might have to be modified for forensic work. Once I am clear enough that I am talking to an alter, I make no further effort to phrase every question meticulously in such a way as to avoid iatrogenesis, because I don't believe that *de novo* creation of alters occurs in this stage of clinical work. It can occur later in therapy, however.

If the alter is cooperative and comfortable, history taking proceeds much as in any psychiatric assessment. One is serially interviewing members of a family about themselves and the family as a whole. Only in this family, some members know all about everybody, some know about only themselves, and others have varying combinations and degrees of amnesia. Mapping the system is like interviewing a family at its home. In an MPD house, not all rooms connect to all others; some are connected by one-way mirrors, some by intercoms, some by open doorways; and some do not connect to anywhere but the outside world. The therapist has to find out who lives in what rooms, and what other rooms they can enter in what way.

Usually I ask the name and age of the alter early on. I then ask what the chronological age of the body was at the time of the creation of the alter. If the alter knows about the host, I ask, "How old was Susan when you were first there?'' Then I ask why the alter came at that time, and what she has been doing since. Next I want to know how much time this alter has been in executive control since her creation, and how much she knows about what happens during the host's blank spells.

Having gathered this information, I then ask if there is anyone the alter talks to inside, or anyone else that she knows about. The answer to this may be "There's Alice and Mary too," or "I'm not allowed to talk about that." Following the former response, I find out everything that Susie knows about Alice and Mary, then ask if she thinks either of them would be willing to talk to me and whether it would be safe. This may be followed by calling out Alice and repeating the sequence of questions with her. In a complex multiple this process may be repeated more than 50 times throughout therapy, and the therapist may introduce himself to the patient numerous times.

A statement that an alter is not allowed to talk communicates important information. It is paradoxical because it reveals that there is an untrusting, hostile, controlling, persecutory alter in the background. This way of revealing hidden information is similar to a deep gruff voice announcing, "There's no one here." I usually tell the alter in control that I understand that she can't talk and clarify that I'm not angry or disappointed. This is done in order to avoid making the alter feel guilty, and to avoid creating a tug-of-war between therapist and background alter, which the therapist will lose.

Mapping the system is not a cut-and-dried process. It takes place piecemeal over the entire preintegration phase of therapy. The mapping may proceed very slowly while abreactions occur, conflicts are resolved, and crises are survived. The picture I have presented is accurate, but not for all personalities or all patients. It may take a great deal of finesse to learn why the frightened child alter can't talk, who she is frightened of, and who could help protect her. There are often discontinuities in the mapping process that occur when an entire new layer of personalities is contacted. All the previously known personalities may be completely amnesic for the newly encountered layer, so one begins the questioning anew.

In complex MPD it is often necessary to write down the names of the personalities because there are too many to remember. This can get especially confusing when there are a number of complex multiples in the therapist's caseload. Different alters in different patients will have the same names, for one thing. As well, during the phases of therapy when alters are being fused, the products of the fusions may have new names or names compounded from previous alters, which increase the mnemonic challenge to the therapist. Patients may be hurt and offended when the therapist gets mixed up about who is who.

Every system has its own structure, which must be recorded on the map. Different types of systems are described in Chapter 5. Mapping is not an end in itself, and the diagrams are just helpful ways of remembering and filing information. It is easy to get overexcited about mapping and to see it as an interesting diversion in its own right. It is that on a research basis, but in therapy the therapist must focus on helping the patient get better and live better. When the therapist gets caught up in the phenomenology or in fascination with techniques, the therapy suffers.

TREATMENT CONTRACTS

As I mentioned earlier, with increasing experience I have become less gimmicky and technique-oriented in therapy. However one technique has become more central and important in my work as time goes on. That is contracting, which is linked to limit-setting. I will discuss limits separately later. Therapy is not a love affair, an educational seminar, a spiritual journey, or a friendship. It is a specific type of collaborative work done within the boundaries of a social contract. The purpose of MPD therapy is to cure the chronic trauma disorder and to help the patient live better. "Better" means more happily, more adaptively, at a higher level of function, more freely, and in a more whole and centered way. These are intrinsically worthwhile goals.

It is impossible to work without a contract, though the contract may be implicit and unconscious. Because I work within a universal health care scheme, the issue of fees doesn't come up in my contracting. There are two major contracts in therapy, of which the first is more informal. The first agreement is for a diagnostic assessment and a subsequent recommendation for treatment.

The following example illustrates the procedure for the first contract: A woman in her 20s was admitted to the hospital because of depression and suicidal ideation. She had been chronically depressed, met criteria for dysthymic disorder, and had a superimposed major depressive episode of several weeks' duration. She was completely amnesic for her life prior to age 15. Her retrograde amnesia extended backward in time from a point 2 or 3 days prior to a rape at the age of 15. She also had ongoing blank spells that lasted minutes or hours.

She denied auditory hallucinations. Positive secondary features of MPD included disremembered objects being present and the patient being told of disremembered events. She was raped by her stepfather at the age of 24, had a brief abusive marriage, and had a recent abusive heterosexual relationship. The stepfather had been on the scene since her childhood.

After taking the history, I outlined the decision tree of therapy with her, emphasizing that the goal was as short an admission as possible. There were three main problems: First was her depression for which the treatment options were medication and/or psychosocial treatment. The second was her suicidal ideation, which made no passes outside the hospital a necessary initial intervention. Treatment for suicidal ideation would also involve medication and/or psychosocial work. The third problem was her memory blanks.

Possible approaches to the memory blanks were to leave them alone, to try to recover some memory of the ongoing amnesia, or to go full tilt at dismantling all the amnesia. The last option was presented to her only for completeness. She was told that this would be a long-term project, that the amnesia was probably highly protective, and that the work would likely involve recovering painful, difficult memories. I told her that such work might interfere with her function as a mother and student. I was advising her as to the possible benefits, risks, and side effects of all treatment options, in order that she could give informed consent.

She had fewer secondary features of MPD than most undiagnosed MPD patients and scored only 22.0 on the DES. The next step was to contract for an attempt to contact an alter, under the guise of "talking to the part of the mind that holds the memories of the blank spells." In this patient the attempt would be analogous to exploratory surgery under general anaesthesia. If cancer was found, a decision as to its operability would have to be made, and further surgery, chemotherapy, or irradiation contracted for postoperatively. The alter would be contacted under the protective veil of hypnotic amnesia.

A hypnotic induction was contracted for, and a diagnosis of psychogenic amnesia was confirmed. In trance the patient contracted for recovery of the memory of a number of recent blank spells, which occurred posthypnotically. The next step was to debrief the patient with a general explanation that additional memories were there, but that a decision would have to be made as to how to proceed. Next multidisciplinary discussions were held as to which therapists, counselors, and support persons might carry out which tasks. Other agencies were contacted, and a tentative treatment plan was drawn up. This was then discussed in detail with the patient and a verbal contract for therapy that would leave the childhood amnesia intact was made, with a proviso that definitive work might be undertaken in the future if the patient's life situation permitted.

When a diagnosis of MPD is made and a decision to go ahead with definitive treatment has been agreed to, a specific MPD treatment contract is required. Usually in outpatient work this is a verbal contract, but for inpatient treatment the contract is always written and signed by the patient, by me, and by at least one other team member. One or more alters may sign the contract. A detailed explanation of written inpatient contracts is given below because they embody all principles of contracting. Other aspects of hospitalization are discussed in Chapter 13.

We have found with experience that inpatient admissions go much better if they are carefully planned. The more structure, the less acting out. We have therefore developed a number of forms and procedures for inpatient admissions. These are all used in elective admissions, and most are used in a more rapidly activated sequence for emergency admissions.

The first form is our Pre-Admission Assessment Worksheet for MPD Patients (see Appendix C). The pre-admission assessment is self-explanatory. Its main purposes are to ensure that adequate support, placement, and follow-up are going to be available; to plan for any potential violent acting out; and to set specific goals of therapy. The more operationalized and behaviorally defined the goals, the better. There is no use setting a treatment goal like "feeling better," because no specific plan follows from it, and the team will never be able to tell if the goal has been reached in a definable way.

The pre-admission assessment involves a meeting of at least me, the Dissociative Disorders Nursing Research Assistant, any cotherapists involved in the case, and the head nurse on our ward. Usually a primary nurse for the admission is chosen, and she will attend at least some of the pre-admission meetings. In more difficult cases, the Director of Nursing for our department, and the Head of the Department, a psychiatrist, may be involved, as may the police, hospital lawyer, or other agencies. Some consultation with the Medical Director of the inpatient unit may also be required: This usually focuses on timing of the admission, coverage, and ward caseload.

All of this illustrates the need for carefully planned treatment contracting. We go into the formal contracting meeting with the patient with a well-defined team consensus as to how to proceed. During the admission procedure this is the first major intervention in controlling the splitting that will occur. Contracting is not a fully democratic process, and the patient does not have the last word. If the patient cannot agree to certain nonnegotiable terms, then there will be no admission.

During the contracting session a full discussion of every point and its rationale is undertaken. Points are drafted and redrafted until they reach a form acceptable to patient and staff. This process can get out of control and needs to be focused. Patients may digress into legalistic nitpicking, attempt a power confrontation on a side issue, or berate staff for their attitudes. The session has a defined goal of resulting in a signed treatment contract.

We have found that contracts are more effective and therapeutic the simpler and clearer they are. Contracts with numerous subclauses and contingency plans quickly become unworkable. Convoluted contracts invite constitutional challenges by the patient that distract from the treatment goals. The following treatment contract illustrates most of the principles of inpatient MPD treatment plans.

Treatment Contract

The treatment contract is for Mary (including all her parts) and the staff of M3. The contract is in effect at the time of admission and throughout Mary's stay on M3.

The terms of the contract are as follows:

1. Mary's voluntary admission will be for approximately 3 weeks.
2. Mary will be seen in therapy by Dr. Ross and Sharon Heber approx-

imately 1–2 times per week, by Pam Gahan 1 hour per day, by her primary nurse and other nursing staff for a minimum of 15 minutes per shift on days and evenings.

3. Because of the angry and potentially aggressive part, "Fighting Mary," planned therapeutic sessions may be held in the seclusion room as deemed necessary by treatment staff and Mary. Mary may also request to go to the seclusion room if in need of a safe place.

4. Aggressive and threatening behavior is not acceptable on the unit, for example, damaging or threatening to damage self, others and/or property.

5. Consequences for such behavior will be dealt with as per unit guidelines, for example, Mary will be asked/ordered to go to the seclusion room for a time-out period voluntarily. If staff assess Mary's control to be minimal or absent, Mary will be physically assisted to the seclusion room and may need to be restrained for a period of time. In the seclusion room the door will be locked, and Mary will remain in seclusion for 30 minutes. The last 15 minutes must be settled or additional periods of 15 minutes will be added until behavior is settled. Prn medication may be used as per Doctor's orders.

6. Angry Mary will notify a responsible person before acting on suicidal feelings.

7. All of Mary's personalities are expected to be honest and open and are encouraged to talk about feelings with the treatment team.

8. Mary is expected to follow general unit guidelines as outlined in the patient information booklet.

9. Mary requests that all staff give her space and do not touch her when her BACK OFF sign is posted in her room.

This contract is flexible and negotiable approximately once every week. The contract will be renegotiated by Mary and a core treatment team member.

Signed: _____   Date: _____

The contract is accompanied by general unit guidelines provided for all patients. The Department has specific guidelines for use of the seclusion room, with which our contracts are consistent, but these are not given to the patient. In addition we have Guidelines For Containment/Protection of Aggressive MPD Patients, General Unit Guidelines for MPD Patients (see Appendix D), and guidelines for inpatient staff that deal with etiology, theory of dissociation, inpatient rules, and a variety of MPD issues. These are discussed in the section on hospitalization in Chapter 13.

The function of the contract is to help therapy be safe and effective. This function is carried out both by the content of the final contract and by the process. The process is good for both staff and patient. It has a quasi-legal aura to it that combines rights and enforcement. The process tells the patient that she is taken seriously, that staff have thought carefully about her, that every effort will be made to keep her safe, and that acting out is unacceptable. In addition an expectation for settled behavior and nonspecial treatment compared to other patients is instilled.

The more violent the past behavior of the patient, the tougher the contract must be. Some items are specific to an individual patient and are included at her request. For instance one patient had been injected with medications prior to participation in child pornography films: Her victim alter was terrified of needles, so a "no-I.M." meds clause was included in her contract. For another patient items about confidentiality or some other issue might be helpful. A contract should fit on one page.

There will be minicontracts at a verbal level throughout therapy. These may include agreements to put an alter to sleep for a while, changes in frequency of sessions, rules about phone calls, or countless other matters. One of the most difficult aspects of the therapy is the suicidal drive of the patient (Ross & Norton, 1989b). No-suicide contracts can be drawn up with specific alters much as they would be for a non-MPD patient.

We have found no-suicide contracts to be somewhat helpful, but not a panacea. When they are effective, it often seems to be because of the scrupulous honesty of the patient. Many MPD patients have a strict code of honor and truthfulness and will not break a promise. The problem is getting the persecutory alter to agree not to harm anyone. Once the promise is truly made, though, it is often kept. Alters may discuss openly the difficulty they are having sticking to the agreement and may only be able to contract for short periods. When suicide is viewed as euthanasia, the alter responsible for the self-destructive behavior may be unwilling to relinquish that option on a long-term basis. Sometimes the system is just out of control, and contracting is meaningless. As a general rule, a short-term contract is better than no contract.

Therapy can also go wrong when the contract between the therapist and the institution is faulty. This usually doesn't involve the therapist's job description or job contract, although it may when too many hours are being devoted to one patient. More often subtle, unspoken agreements in the institution are violated by the therapy. These may be ideological or may involve treatment modalities. Renegotiating with the institution can be a far more formidable task than settling differences with individual patients.

ESTABLISHING INTERPERSONALITY COMMUNICATION

Interpersonality communication is an essential interim goal of therapy and a step toward integration. Patients enter therapy with a wide range of types and degrees of interpersonality communication in place. There is also great variability from phase to phase of therapy and from one region of the personality system to another. In the broadest sense, communication between personalities includes somatic memories, Schneiderian symptoms, dream intrusions by alters, and other MPD phenomena that are symptoms as well as communications.

In our series of 236 cases (Ross, Norton & Wozney, 1989) 71.7 percent heard voices arguing and 66.1 percent heard voices commenting. Voices are a form of interpersonality communication that is encouraged and cultivated during therapy. MPD therapy is the only form of psychiatric treatment in which auditory hallucinations are deliberately amplified. As described in Chapter 7, voices can take many forms.

The host personality often experiences voices as frightening signs of insanity at the beginning of treatment. Personalities in the background will simultaneously view them as conversations in a matter-of-fact way. This illustrates the necessity of understanding the meaning of any given communication for all personalities who are party to it. Once a treatment alliance has been formed with the host and another alter, the next step is to begin working toward open communication between them. Because the alter in the background may have traumatic memories to give back, this must be done carefully.

If the host is completely unaware of the other personality, one can begin breaking down the amnesia barrier using neutral, nonthreatening material. This could begin with writing exercises (see below), whispering, or transmission of visual images to the host. The idea is to desensitize the host personality to the process of communication, in order that she can eventually receive the difficult content. This can be conceptualized in behavioral terms as the construction of a hierarchy for systematic desensitization.

I might get an agreement from the host that the alter will try to send her messages. I then ask the alter, who is coconscious behind a one-way amnesia barrier and with whom I have previously discussed the exercise, to say a number or to say, "Hello." The host listens and writes down the message. I then switch to the alter and check as to whether the message has been received correctly. Step by step I then have the alter transmit more complex neutral messages, until a conversation is established. Because the background alter is coconscious and can hear the host easily, the desensitization is unidirectional: where there is two-way amnesia, the desensitization must be done in both directions at once.

If the patient has trouble opening up the communication channel, formal hypnotic suggestions can be given to help. It is important to suggest that amnesia barriers will dissolve away at a safe pace and that only as much communication as can be tolerated will occur. I can't see experimenting with flooding techniques in MPD treatment, because patients can barely handle the degree of flooding they experience spontaneously. Such techniques might work with Vietnam veterans, but their trauma occurred in adulthood in a foreign country. Flooding a person with war memories is not the same as flooding someone with incest memories.

Once the host can hear the alter's voice, I might ask the alter, with the host in executive control, if there is anything she wants to say to the host. The therapist can prompt therapeutic conversation, knowing the fears and concerns of the alters. For instance the alters are often afraid that other alters won't like them, will be mad at them, will blame them, or will not be satisfied with their performance. A direct simple statement by the host that she likes the hidden child and wants to talk with her can ease the child's fears. It also makes the host feel better.

If there seems to be excessive trouble establishing communication between two personalities, there is a good chance that someone else is blocking it. In this situation it is necessary to explore further and try to deal directly with the blocking alter, who will have a rationale for what she is doing. I might say:

> I have a feeling that there's someone else there who's blocking the conversation between Susan and Susie. If there is, there's probably a good reason for the blocking. I'd like to find out what it is so I'd know what to do. Is there anybody there who knows about that who could talk to me?

If an alter comes forward, I ask for as much information as possible, then work to solve whatever problem is motivating the blocking. This could be a fear that Susan will go crazy if she learns too much. I deal with this by contracting for gradual establishment of coconsciousness and ongoing consultation with the blocking alter as to how it's going. If a more unreasonable, hostile motive is at work, I might postpone further communication between Susan and Susie until the hostile alter is onside.

Once two personalities are able to talk freely, communication will continue outside therapy. If Susie holds abuse memories, the next step would be to begin working on coconsciousness for Susan. Abreactive work with Susie will already be ongoing behind the amnesia barrier, so that Susie is somewhat desensitized to the memories before they are transmitted to Susan. As in the procedure for voices, coconsciousness begins as an in-session phenomenon, with neutral content.

I get permission from both alters for a trial of coconsciousness, then switch to Susie. Prior to the switch I may do a formal hypnotic induction with suggestions for removal of the amnesia barrier. A typical instruction would be:

> In a moment Susie will open her eyes and be here. This time, though, Susan will be awake and listening. Susan will be in the background but she will be awake and listening and watching. Susan will be able to hear and understand everything that's said. Then after I'm finished talking with Susie, Susan will come back and she will keep the memory of the conversation with Susie. The memory will not be lost. Susie can you be here now?

I keep the discussion on a safe topic, then switch back to Susan. Before going back to Susan I will give an instruction for selective amnesia for any material touched on in the conversation with Susie that would be too difficult. This usually works very well. Once Susan is comfortable with coconsciousness, we then move toward more difficult content, and eventually Susan is fully coconscious for Susie's abreactions of abuse. Susan will have a partial abreaction herself while watching Susie's reliving of the trauma, then may have a complete abreaction herself when she returns to executive control. Sometimes Susan does not complete her final abreactions of Susie's memories until after Susie has been integrated with her.

During the early phases of establishing coconsciousness, it is helpful to ask Susie to talk to Susan while Susie is out. Susie can then report to the therapist on Susan's responses. This gives Susan experience at being a background alter, and seems to help free up the communication channel. The same procedures can be used for all forms of communication between all combinations of personalities.

One can contract for return of memories through internal images, diaries, dreams, or any other technique the therapist can invent. The metaphor of the family living in an MPD house provides the frame for this work. The therapist has to move back and forth from room to room and deal with everyone's anxieties and fears about talking with everyone else. Prior to direct communication between personalities, the therapist acts as a messenger and interpreter. Before exercises with Susie and Susan can begin, Susan will have been filled in on Susie's name, age, function, character, and concerns. This is the first step in desensitization.

As personalities begin to communicate more and more, a process of generalization sets in. The amount of information leakage across the amnesia barrier begins to increase in many ways. Feelings that have never been directly addressed in therapy leak from Susie to Susan, making Susan feel small and frightened. At the same time Susie may start to feel a bit bigger, stronger, and braver. Sometimes the therapist will notice "slips" at this stage of therapy that raise a suspicion of malingering. Alters may know things they are supposed to be amnesic for and may try to claim amnesia for information they have disclosed. I view this more as trouble adjusting to coconsciousness than malingering and usually let it slide by without much comment. The main thing to remember is that such slips are a phase-specific phenomenon in therapy that remits prior to integration.

As the alters move closer to integration they come to a point where everybody knows and feels everything, and decisions are made democratically. The entire system does not arrive at this point en masse, however. In complex layered cases, it is common to successfully integrate some personalities before others are even suspected. Establishing coconsciousness is usually done simultaneously with establishing interpersonality communication, because the two reinforce each other reciprocally. The purpose of coconsciousness is communication, and the purpose of communication is coconsciousness.

Interpersonality communication is reinforced by the therapist in a number of ways. One is by modeling communication for the patient, which occurs when the therapist requests switches and debriefs alters on conversations held behind amnesia barriers. I give lots of "strokes" for progress in therapy and lots of reassurance. Also, I'm explicit about the goals of therapy and my investment in them as a therapist. At some point in therapy, most patients berate me for being narcissistically invested in curing them. I deal with this by acknowledging that indeed I did go into medicine to heal people and that I get much more personal and professional satisfaction from successes than from failures. I then ask the patient if she would prefer to have a doctor who was committed to curing her and willing to work hard toward that goal, or one who didn't care one way or the other and saw her for 15 minutes once a month. I point out to the patient that my narcissistic investment in her outcome is an asset for her, not a liability.

There is no need to be apologetic for commitment to the goal of integration and the specific techniques that help the patient get there. The patient will stall and resist the work toward interpersonality integration in countless ways. This is as it should be for someone who has survived extreme trauma thanks to dissociation.

SUMMARY

The preceding sections describe the principal techniques used in the initial phase of therapy. If a new layer of alter personalities is discovered late in therapy, these techniques may be used again at that stage. Similarly, many of the techniques described in the next two chapters can be used in the initial phase of therapy. The dividing of techniques into phases of therapy is a rough guideline only.

CHAPTER TWELVE

Specific Techniques of Treatment: The Middle and Late Phases of Therapy

The middle and late phases of therapy are long and involve most of the work. During this part of the treatment many patients will feel, at times, that the effort is not worth it. Within a short-term perspective, this may be an accurate assessment. The patient will often experience more distress as her dissociative defenses are being dismantled. Numerous symptoms of a posttraumatic stress nature will occur and the ability to cope on a day-to-day basis may deteriorate. Fortunately this does not last forever, and eventually the patient moves into the less volatile, later stages of treatment.

The techniques in this chapter, like those in the last, can be used throughout therapy but are characteristic of the middle and late phases.

ABREACTING ABUSE MEMORIES

Disclosing abuse memories at an informational level is the first step towards abreaction. Abreaction is not an end in itself and is extremely painful for the patient. It is also stressful for the therapist, and in fact some therapists develop full DSM-III-R posttraumatic stress disorder from working with severely abused multiples. If someone could develop a method for treating multiple personality disorder (MPD) that circumvented the abreactions, it would be wonderful. The problem is that intense reliving of abuse in the presence of a therapist seems to be part of getting better, much like inflammation is part of the natural healing process.

In a surgical analogy, the abuse memories are like foreign bodies: Unless they are removed, the abscess cannot be definitively treated. This does not mean that every single abuse incident requires full abreaction. Such work would take far too long. Generalization occurs in abreactive work, as in other aspects of the therapy, so that reliving key representative traumas cleanses the entire system.

Observing and guiding the abreactions is emotionally intense, technically delicate work for the therapist. The therapist must "be on his toes." To do the work, it is essential not to be too involved and not to take the abreactions too literally. The patient will experience an abreaction as an exact copy of the original experience, which it isn't. An abreaction is a highly stylized enactment of the memory of a real trauma. It is not a video playback of reality. The therapist is not really watching a rape, and the abreacting patient is not really a child.

Abreactions, though, are sincere, genuine experiences for patients. They are very dramatic and can be exploited and embellished for secondary gain. Abreactions convince the therapist of the reality of the childhood abuse. There is just no way that clinical abreactions by multiples are faked. They are dissociative recreations of the original trauma and are important healing rituals. To be healing, the ritual must have a frame and a meaning and must be debriefed.

Abreactions can be countertherapeutic and destructive if not handled properly. Especially during inpatient work, when multiples may regress behaviorally, the reliving of childhood trauma can take the form of malignant abreaction. Malignant abreaction consists of chaotic uncontrolled runs of screaming, self-abusive, or regressed behavior during which the patient may switch repeatedly. There is no learning or transfer of meaningful information to other personalities. Malignant abreaction exhausts the patient, ward staff, and therapists, and can be stressful for other inpatients.

Malignant abreaction must be suppressed with behavioral techniques, medication, and/or hypnosis. Left uncontrolled, it may destroy the therapy. Between such extreme chaos and the staged, contracted abreactions of outpatient psychotherapy, there is a spectrum of abreaction. Often it will be difficult to tell when an abreaction should be limited and when the therapist should allow it to run its course.

There is another spectrum from a purely informational recall of trauma to full abreactive reliving in the present. As in other MPD work, a desensitization approach is often useful. This can sometimes be contracted for directly with the alter who holds the memories. In such cases a treatment alliance has already been formed with a child and the child has done several abreactions behind an amnesia barrier. It is now time for the host personality to learn about the trauma.

The first step is to tell the host about the alter and establish neutral communication as described previously. The host is told that the child alter was created at the age of 6 to be the victim of sexual assault by her father. A contract is made for the child to abreact an assault with the host coconscious in the background, then the child alter is called out. The child is asked to begin describing the scene just prior to the assault, and usually an abreaction will begin spontaneously. If it doesn't, hypnotic suggestion that the abuse will be relived can be made.

It is usually not hard to tell that an abreaction is occurring. The alter speaks as if the abuse is happening in the present, and there is a vivid recreation of the event. Facial expression, body posture, tone of voice, and autonomic state leave no doubt that an intense experience is occurring. A therapeutic abreaction has a curve with which the therapist becomes familiar and usually lasts 5 or 10 minutes at peak intensity. The abreaction begins with a preamble about the setting, who is present, and where the father is at the moment. This progresses through an approach phase, during which fear mounts, then the overt sexual assault begins.

During this phase, the child may cry out, plead with the father to stop, clutch her pubic area, try to push the father off, attempt to spit out semen, or curl up in the corner. After the peak intensity there is a denouement during which the child may whimper or express sadness. This is accompanied by a transition back to the present, as the alter reorients and realizes that the abuse happened long ago. The abreaction has an outline that parallels the arousal curve of the father. Following the abreaction there is a debriefing with the child and the host. "Debriefing" is not a dry, technical intervention and may involve touch, holding, reassurance, and hypnotic suggestions for sleep, calm, or safety.

If an abreaction does not follow this curve, it may have been therapeutic, but the therapist should consider the possibility that not enough work has been done. If the abreaction seems to go on too long at peak intensity, this is a cue that the patient is stuck in it and that there will be no therapeutic benefit. Successful abreactions often involve cuing by the therapist, with inquiries like, "What happened next?" or "And then what?" The therapist can use the past tense while the patient uses the present tense, without reducing the intensity or completeness of the abreaction. Patients seem to handle this incongruity easily with trance logic.

If the alter is stuck in the abreaction, the therapist must intervene. A hand on the shoulder and firm hypnotic commands that the child will go to sleep often work. The child is put to sleep, safety suggestions are given, and the host is called back. A suggestion for amnesia for the host may be inserted, if necessary. Alternatively, a malignant abreaction may be converted to a therapeutic one, which will then run its course. This is done in a fashion similar to termination of an abreaction, except that suggestions for progression through the memory are given. A short speech about the therapeutic purpose of the abreaction can be made, and this may be heard by an inner self helper or the system generally. It is important to remember that hypnotic suggestions can be given to the whole person at any time in therapy: During a malignant abreaction such suggestions help martial rational, adult resources.

In an extreme case, an injection of 2–5 mg of lorazepam may be required. This is the best medication to use because it is a benzodiazepine and is therefore much less toxic than antipsychotic medications. Other benzodiazepines are not as well absorbed intramuscularly. A private practice nonmedical therapist will not have this strategy available, so must try and try again with hypnotic suggestions and commands. Sometimes abreactions are very difficult to turn on or off. If there is too much uncontrolled switching and abreacting, consultation and/or admission may be required.

The recovery of abuse memories may occur in many ways. Memories may initially come back as flashbacks, dreams, hallucinations, vague premonitions of upcoming flashbacks, inner reveries, overheard conversations between alters, diary entries, or physical symptoms. If anyone of these channels seems to be becoming overactive and crowded with transmissions, that may be a clue that an alter is moving toward abreaction. Alters that have not entered therapy often make themselves known in this way.

For instance, hallucinations of blood, accompanied by fear and feeling small, may occur. There may be an alter in the background who is deliberately causing the hallucinations. One then asks to talk to "Someone I haven't met before who knows about the blood Susan has been seeing." If an alter comes out, she can usually explain why she is causing the hallucination and describe the original bloody trauma. One then attempts to contract with the alter to stop the hallucinations and concurrently work toward controlled recovery of the trauma. Often an alter will give a casual rationale for the hallucinations along the lines, "I thought she should know about it." Another motivation might be to make the host disturbed enough to be admitted, so that the work can be done in safety. Alternatively the motive might be hospital dependency. Often the hallucinations are caused by a persecutor alter who reasons that the host is bad and should be punished.

Sometimes one can contract for a more controlled recovery of memory through dreams or flashbacks without directly contacting the responsible alter. Some abuse memories seem to be held in a general unconscious and are not linked to any one alter. These may be recovered by the host with the help of hypnosis, and the host may then abreact. Another variation is a trance memory held by a specific personality. This can be recovered by hypnotizing the alter, who then abreacts the abuse she originally experienced in a trance state. This abreaction occurs in trance, so the alter must be brought out of trance in the session, prior to switching to anyone else.

When an alter has gone into trance during a trauma, she may be amnesic for it after the abreaction. In this situation gradual or sudden recovery of the trauma can be contracted for hypnotically, in the same way as is done for the host. In our caseload one alter had repeatedly gone into her parents' bedroom in the middle of the night during childhood, in a trance state, but had never used the knife she carried in a raised hand. All known personalities were amnesic for these episodes, but the alter remembered feeling as if she was going into trance prior to the onset of the blank spells. The abreaction of this event did not follow the curve of an incest abreaction. The curve I described earlier is observed during abreactions of paternal incest and would have a different shape for abreaction of other forms of trauma.

Following any abreaction, much of the debriefing involves working on associated cognitive errors. Often the historical origin of the cognitive error can be identified during the abreaction: This seems to help the cognitive therapy be more focused and effective. During debriefing I review the purpose of abreaction, congratulate the alters for their courage, repeat that it is safe now, and discuss the need for future abreactions. A balance must be struck between comforting a child who has just been assaulted and working with a rational adult. Just as patients can get stuck in abreactions, so can therapists.

It is not helpful to treat the patient exclusively or predominantly like a child or to spend years repeating abreactions and simply comforting the child alter afterward. Abreactions will occur spontaneously during the active phases of therapy, and these should also be controlled and debriefed. I suspect that one of the most widespread therapeutic errors involves patient and therapist getting stuck in abreaction and comfort cycles.

Abreaction is hard work and very stressful. Therefore it is an aspect of therapy that requires particular care and structure. It is that—an aspect of therapy—and should be considered as such, despite its drama. Except in MPD cases without severe abuse histories, the therapist should be uncomfortable if intense abreactions are not occurring and should not be lulled into a false sense that things are going well. Clinical experience to date is that severely abused multiples must relive their trauma in a meaningful way in therapy in order to get better.

AGE-APPROPRIATE ACTIVITIES WITH CHILD ALTERS

Working with child alters can be a lot of fun. That is why it can be difficult. The therapist could spend hundreds of hours playing with child personalities in a countertherapeutic fashion. Play can seem more pleasant than recovering memories and helping the patient take responsibility for herself as an adult. Throughout therapy child alters should be worked with but not indulged. Despite childish handwriting, facial expressions, and body posture, they often function at a cognitive level far beyond their years and may have a more complete and mature understanding of the personality system than the host does at the beginning of therapy.

Child alters can be more seductive than overtly seductive, sexually acting-out adolescent and adult personalities. They can be lonely, sad, or frightened and can evoke parental and protective instincts in the therapist. They can be delightfully spontaneous, childlike, and trusting, giving the therapist powerful positive feedback for playing games with them. One of the functions of the child may have been to divert the father from incest, and she may divert the therapist from the painful work of therapy in a parallel process.

No matter how frightening the abreactions or confrontations with persecutors are for the children, the purpose of therapy is recovery, not play. The therapist needs to push gently at different times throughout therapy, while listening carefully to advice to slow down. Within the necessary framework, age-appropriate activities with child alters can be highly therapeutic. They have a number of different purposes, which are served by both process and content.

It is impossible to work at peak intensity all of every session. Like a play, novel, or movie, there is a rise and fall in the action of therapy, and interludes of different intensity are required. Both patient and therapist can benefit from a break. The break, which may be a walk, a visit to McDonald's, a card game, or any other mutually enjoyable activity, is still part of therapy. Irrespective of what is said during a break, it provides the patient an experience of normal child–adult interaction. This will have value as corrective emotional experience and as modeling of parental behavior for the patient, who may have children. Such interludes help build trust and safety both with the child and with hostile alters in the background.

If a trip out of the therapist's building is made, it may have an important desensitization component. The outside world often seems very big and frightening to child personalities. As well, the therapist has an opportunity to make in vivo observations, which may be useful later in therapy. Just being together in a happy way can help both parties to the social contract prepare for abreactive work. The interlude shows that the therapist values the child and acknowledges his or her subjective experience of self and the world. This in turn indirectly validates the child's perception of the abuse as wrong and traumatic.

Sometimes a child personality does not believe that many years have passed and that she is now in a different city. One child was convinced that this must be true by looking at her hands and looking out the window at the snow: The patient grew up in a city that never had snow. Such educational interventions may progress to a walk in the snow, which consolidates the new cognition through touch, sound, smell, and even taste if the child eats a handful of snow.

One adolescent alter was extremely shy and nervous and could only stay out for brief periods of time. She held a key position in the personality system and could communicate with many personalities at different levels in the system, so I wanted to be able to talk with her at greater length. Playing cards seemed to help her to relax and increase the length of time she could stay in executive control. Reading stories to children is another way of drawing them out into the therapy, especially when they have been severely abused.

Formal play therapy is a modality we don't use much in our Dissociative Disorders Clinic, partly because we don't have much experience with it in non-MPD therapy. However, therapists at other centers have extensive experience with the use of dolls, sand trays, dollhouses, and other toys. These props are used in much the same way as they would be in work with an actual child, for establishing trust, disclosing abuse memories, resolving conflicts, and defining issues for verbal therapy. My feeling is that most of the work can usually be done without the props, but I am ready to believe that I underutilize toys.

Patients may bring shawls, teddy bears, blankets, or other transitional objects into therapy, and these should be talked about explicitly by the therapist. If the therapist doesn't comment, the child may conclude that the therapist doesn't like her, or her bear. Sometimes the bear becomes a co-patient in the therapy. This occurs when the child alter projects onto the bear so intensely that the bear is alive. When this happens, the transference to the bear is extremely charged and plastic, and important work can be done. The child may divulge abuse secrets that only she and the bear knew about or may enter a long monologue addressed to the bear in which she defines key issues in therapy.

The therapist may comment on how brave the bear is, how lucky the bear is to have the child with him, and how glad the therapist is that the bear was willing to share these memories. A promise may be made to have the bear back for future sessions. By working with the bear, the therapist can deal with displaced and projected material that would be too painful for the child to discuss directly. Talking with teddy bears can be very useful and shouldn't be omitted because it isn't "proper" technique. The negative aspects of the transference will also come out in this work, and the bear will be at risk of being stabbed, burned, drowned, lost, or otherwise abused between sessions. Abuse of the bear should not be allowed during sessions if possible, because the therapist who allows the bear to be hurt will be perceived as condoning child abuse.

There is no need to be concerned that talking with teddy bears will reinforce regression, promote psychosis, reward maladaptive behavior, or have similar harmful effects. MPD patients understand the conventions of therapy perfectly well and can make good use of this technique. If work with transitional objects does become counterproductive, then that is a problem in therapy that must be discussed, understood, and resolved, like any other.

One of the devices we use most often in working with child alters is drawing. The children can talk about the abuse through drawings in a deep, intense way. They can often say more with crayons than they can with words. Most of the time no fancy skills are required to interpret the drawings. They will contain anatomical portrayals of particular abuse incidents, often with red blood. Knives appear frequently, as do confining rooms, views of houses from outside, and simultaneous views of various rooms in houses with abuse occurring in some. The drawings may be obviously disturbed at a glance, with furious circles of black and a chaotic welter of angry lines. I make a point of striving for common sense in commenting on drawings in therapy and in discussion with colleagues. I find stereotyped Freudian interpretations of drawings distasteful: Such "interpretations" too often have the primary purpose of making the interpreter look clever.

The drawings can be done in session, between sessions, or in the occupational therapy department if there is an interested occupational therapist. We have also had child alters scheduled for occupational therapy (O.T.) during inpatient admissions. The children go to O.T. on the understanding that they will act like the host personality, answer to the host's name, and ask to leave if the artwork is too stressful. If possible, patients should never switch or act like children in front of other patients.

A problem arises when a patient asks the therapist to display her artwork on an office wall. This is a no-win situation for the therapist. The least harmful option is probably to decline most of the time in most cases. For one thing, most of the artwork is not skillful or attractive and will soon become a sore point for the therapist, who has to look at it every day. MPD patients want and need to be "special" and will get into a competition with other patients for Number 1 status, via displayed artwork. This needs to be nipped in the bud. I keep a file in my office, separate from the hospital outpatient chart, for each MPD patient, in which I save drawings, cards, notes by me, and other artifacts of therapy.

There is nothing intrinsically wrong with displaying patient artwork in the office, as long as the therapist is aware of the implications and complications of doing so and is prepared to deal with them. Most of the time, putting artwork on the wall will be a "big deal" for the patient, and depending on the degree of conflict in the system, it may make some alters very angry. I prefer not to create more problems in therapy when there are already many to deal with. There are, however, only a few absolute rules in therapy, and *Display no artwork* is not one of them.

Age-appropriate activities with child alters are a useful component of therapy that can easily get out of control. It is probably better for a beginning therapist to err on the side of too few such interventions rather than too many. I have heard tales of incredibly bad therapies perpetrated in the name of "reparenting," which I would describe as gross malpractice if called to testify. The therapist is a therapist not a parent, and the patient is a patient not a child. Age-appropriate activities with child alters are an aspect of therapy that could easily bring the treatment of MPD into disrepute. It is equally true that there is nothing wrong with the therapist's inner child participating in therapy, as long as the participation is therapeutic.

The particular props or techniques used in such activities are probably less important than the process of interaction at a childlike level. The techniques do not need to be described in detail, as with calling out alters or dismantling amnesia barriers, and are mostly nonspecialist in nature. The therapist needs to view his play as serious work, the way children do, then his work can become serious play.

WORKING WITH AGGRESSIVE AND PERSECUTORY PERSONALITIES

Working with persecutors, who were present in 84.0 percent of our series of 236 cases (Ross, Norton, & Wozney, 1989), is one of the most difficult aspects of therapy. Dealing with these personalities is technically demanding, emotionally stressful, and potentially dangerous. Some MPD patients who have committed violent crimes and been in prison might be untreatable because of their aggressive personalities. In regular clinical work, however, the angry personalities can usually form a treatment alliance and achieve stable integration.

I have discussed techniques for establishing trust and safety earlier, and these are often used with the aggressive internal states. It is a general principle of MPD work that one should always gather as much information as possible before contacting a new alter and, in fact, at all times throughout therapy. If the therapy of MPD is viewed as a strategic-military exercise, then reconnaissance is essential for effective planning.

The first hint that an aggressive alter is present is often a disclosure of internal intimidation by a frightened personality. The identified personality will give out information in small parcels and repeatedly emphasize that "there's going to be trouble." The trouble can take the form of wrist slashing, headaches, internal bullying, increased blank spells, interference with function, or imposition of unpleasant states on the host personality. The strategies for dealing with such problems vary a great deal from situation to situation and case to case.

Hostile personalities tend to belong to one of a few different subgroups. How the therapist deals with them is determined partly by the subgroup. Some uncooperative personalities are not violent or frightening for the therapist and represent a more benign resistance to therapy. For instance, one adolescent personality began making the patient miss sessions by taking executive control before the patient could leave home and not relinquishing it until after the scheduled time was over. I dealt with this situation by using a paradoxical intervention.

The adolescent alter came out in a session at my request and made it clear that there was nothing I could do to ensure that the patient made her appointments. I therefore stopped making appointments with the host personality altogether and said I would only make appointments with the adolescent at her request, which I did. This made it impossible for the alter to exert power through dissociation and gave complete control to her. I already knew that this alter wanted to be in therapy herself, so I made her the patient. The host personality thought this was very unfair—"Why should *she* have appointments and not me? *I'm* the one who's in therapy." I replied that it was too bad, but that was how I was going to handle it. The adolescent alter didn't miss any more appointments, quickly became a helper in the therapy, and has since been integrated.

As I stated earlier, the therapist should always avoid power struggles because they are impossible to win. I always give power to the patient, including persecutors, in such situations, within clear limits. Self-abusive or destructive behavior is not acceptable. The main point is this: The patient has to be more invested in recovery than the therapist. If the opposite is true, the therapist, being desperate to cure someone, will be outmaneuvered and outpowered over and over. The therapist must relinquish all power and investment in outcome at the direct transactional level, in order to secure it at a metalevel.

Another type of aggressor is usually adolescent, feels mostly or exclusively anger and rage, and assaults the host personality and the therapist. Such personalities usually feel bad about themselves and are misguided helpers. Working with them involves firm behavioral limits and a focus on cognitive errors, including the delusion of having separate bodies, described later in this chapter. One of the key early interventions is to get such persecutors to acknowledge that they experience a broad range of feelings, because they often view themselves as exclusively angry. Telling jokes is a good way to do this, as the alters usually have a good sense of humor. Once the alter begins kibitzing, the therapist can point this out.

I have found it helpful simply to tell the persecutor that I view her as part of the whole person and I assume she is there for a good reason. I also thank her on behalf of the whole patient for carrying the anger. The persecutors usually feel rejected, unloved, and feared internally because of their anger. It is a novel experience for them to listen while the therapist explains to the host personality the invaluable work the persecutor has done on her behalf by holding the anger. A revolution in self-concept can occur for the persecutor when the host agrees and expresses thanks. Many persecutors are sad. It is a relief for them when someone understands the burden of carrying all that anger, and it is a further relief when the anger is normalized and legitimized. I always tell the patient that it is normal and inevitable to be extremely angry about the abuse and that it would be abnormal not to be angry. Persecutors often think they are bad for being angry.

Standard techniques for dealing with anger such as devising alternate strategies for handling it, using controlled ventilation, interrupting transactional sequences with an endpoint of anger as early as possible, and reinforcing control are as useful for the MPD patient as for anyone, though their implementation can be complicated.

If such personalities attempt to attack the therapist, they must be physically restrained. Earlier on in our work, when we were inexperienced, we had to do this more than we do now. One of the errors I made in an early case was to certify a patient after a hostile alter abruptly left the session. I think this fed into the alter's self-perception of being dangerous and volatile and put us in a position of coming on as "the law," which stimulated further aggression. In a similar situation I would now be much more likely to let the patient stay in control and simply wait for her to phone or to appear at the next appointment time.

A good way for the therapist to stay out of trouble with hostile alters is not to do anything. This is a technique I learned in general adult inpatient work and on call. If there is a crisis, the best intervention is often to do nothing for a while. Then when the therapist finally calls the patient or comes down to the ward, the whole thing has blown over. This takes judgment, because there can be real emergencies or minor problems that are best dealt with quickly and simply. Overall I think it is more therapeutic to be under-available for the patient than overavailable. The hostile alters won't have to test and push as much if the therapist is less reactive. This is different from being "neutral" as a general stance, which is unacceptable in MPD work because it is unethical to be neutral about the abuse.

Another type of persecutor is the internal demon, the alter identified as the incestuous father, and other paranormal alters. These are more difficult. They often require containment and outmaneuvering. One way to do this is to work with the other alters in the system, who are often severely intimi-dated. The therapist works with the host and the frightened children to develop magical shields, safe places, and protective formulas to ward off the persecutor. Usually one is dealing with a school playground bully who really wants to be contained and loved.

One explains to the children that the alter is not really the devil or the father but is just pretending in order to scare them. The persecutor listens to all this intently and fumes and rants in the background. Again, one can be paradoxical: "The more he tries to scare you, the more frightened he is to talk with me. You'll know if he says lots of mean things and tries to scare you, that he really wants someone to pay attention to him and love him. He was hurt too." This puts the persecutor in a paradoxical position of dem-onstrating his vulnerability by acting tough. "Maybe if he was really tough, he would be brave enough to talk to me, instead of just acting tough and scaring the children." It is tougher to be vulnerable than to be tough, as the patient learned from the abuse.

These strategies are a way of taking the wind out of the persecutor's sails. This is done by creating a more benign perception of him in the rest of the system.

The persecutor may come out in a session and heap scorn on the thera-pist's paradoxical strategies, claiming to see through them. That is a sign that they are working, because the alter has slipped to a backup level of resistance and is debating with the therapist rather than refusing to talk. I reply that there is no trick involved and that my statements are simply the truth, which they are. It is the context that contains the paradox, and I don't comment on that. It is important not to get too elaborate and tricky and to "play it straight" most of the time. Sometimes it just takes a long time and a lot of repetition to stop the persecutory behavior. The therapist has to be able to tolerate superficial wrist slashes, minor overdoses, and other self-abuse in order to preserve the long-term goals. This behavior should be tolerated but not condoned, even implicitly. Sometimes I acknowledge that I would like the self-abuse to stop, but that I can't make it stop.

A comment similar to a transference interpretation can be made. The patient didn't deserve the abuse as a child, she doesn't deserve the abuse now, and the therapist doesn't deserve abuse from the patient. As a child the patient could not stop the abuse, but the therapist is an adult, won't tolerate abuse, and will stop the therapy if the assaultive behavior can't be contained. The therapist has to be prepared to lose the patient in order to treat her.

The farthest I have been pushed by a persecutor is to part ways in front of the hospital late in the evening: I went to my car, and the patient went running off barefoot to jump in the river and drown herself. The next day there were headlines on the front page of our newspaper, describing an incident in which a woman claiming to have 33 personalities was pulled off the bridge at the last moment by a passerby. Only the passerby was interviewed by the reporter. The police had brought the patient back to the hospital from the bridge twice that evening before we parted. Some might say that it was an unacceptable gamble to take, under any circumstances. I say that my ability to go that far saved an otherwise untreatable patient.

The therapist who is desperate to "save" the patient and is incessantly worried and frightened won't be able to tolerate the work. His patients will either drop out, become chronically infantalized, or act out destructively. MPD can be a malignant and untreatable illness because of the unrelenting destructiveness of the persecutors. It is not kind to engage such patients in an ineffective therapy that adds to their conflicts and suffering. All you get is an unhappy patient who has to overdose more often than she would without therapy, because of her therapist's holidays. Having said that, I have to emphasize that it is difficult, if not impossible, to predict which patients should not be treated, other than in extreme and obvious cases.

Dealing with persecutors may require elective hospitalization, which is discussed in Chapter 13. The overriding concern in work with persecutors of all kinds is to establish a treatment alliance with them. I usually do this by hiring them as consultants to the therapy. I tell the persecutor that I assume she has a good reason for what she is doing and that her behavior makes sense from her point of view. I ask her to explain why she is abusing the other personalities emotionally and physically, so that I can understand. In conjunction with that I ask the persecutor to tell me right away if I am doing anything she doesn't like. I don't promise to stop whatever it is immediately, but I agree to discuss, negotiate, and seriously consider changing my approach. I tell the alter that I don't claim to be perfect and that in fact I am guaranteed to misunderstand and do the wrong thing once in a while.

By treating the persecutor as a valued colleague, the therapist gives her a revolutionary experience: being respected as an adult. This is similar to work done with acting-out adolescents who have been branded as bad actors and are fulfilling the prophecy. I establish a collaborative empirical contract with the persecutor to consider alternate strategies for reaching her goals. Discussion thereby replaces confrontation.

Many persecutory alters are hostile to therapy because they think it will increase the host personality's suffering, which in fact it will transiently. As soon as this motive is identified, I acknowledge that the hostile behavior is actually protective and that it has been very helpful over the years. I remind the persecutor that it is smart not to trust me too much, because others who seemed trustworthy in the past have been abusive. This reminder is essential with patients who have been sexually abused by previous therapists. I go on to acknowledge that if the whole person really couldn't get better, recovering abuse memories would not be worth it. I agree with the persecutor's negative short-term cost–benefit analysis, but I predict a positive long-term outcome.

Once the persecutor has agreed to monitor the therapist and collaborate on protecting the host, most of the behavioral problems will have been solved. Persecutors, like helpers who present as cooperative and benign, often resent the therapist's intrusion in the system. They feel that it implies that they did a poor job taking care of the patient. The persecutor must be reassured that this is not the case. I usually emphasize that I am only available for brief periods every week, and that the alters have full-time responsibility 24 hours a day. It is logistically impossible for me to usurp their role, and in fact I want to help them to be more effective.

Persecutors often present as tough and uncaring, but this is nearly always a facade. Pointing out that their apparently destructive actions are actually meant to be protective softens the tough stance. It also helps to reduce the level of fear and alarm in the rest of the system. One way to demonstrate the advantage to the persecutor of bargaining with the therapist is to negotiate a deal with other alters that is directly beneficial for the persecutor. An alter who controls switching might agree to let the persecutor go to a bar if the persecutor agrees to stop fooling around with razor blades and scaring the children, for instance. David Caul referred to this kind of work as "horse trading," a good term.

Most persecutors can be brought into the therapy without extreme difficulty. They have a number of positive qualities including energy, commitment, staying power, assertiveness, and toughness in which the host personality may be deficient. They often have a frank, honest, no-nonsense approach to life. Integrated, the persecutors donate these valuable qualities to the host personality. In forensic cases persecutors may be sadistic sex murderers who have committed numerous crimes and be beyond rehabilitation. The therapist should always enter negotiations with persecutors cautiously, and with eyes and ears open.

COGNITIVE RESTRUCTURING TECHNIQUES

The purpose of this book is to help trained mental health professionals learn how to diagnose, understand, and treat MPD. It is not to create therapists out of lay people. Similarly, the purpose of this section is not to create cognitive therapists *de novo* in a few pages. Cognitive interventions in MPD work should be grounded in an understanding of the cognitive therapy of anxiety (Beck & Emery, 1985) and depression (Beck, 1976; Beck et al., 1979). Because the cognitive therapy of MPD is innovative and systems oriented, additional reading is recommended, specifically *New Directions in Cognitive Therapy* (Emery et al., 1981) and *Cognitive Therapy with Couples and Groups* (Freeman, 1983). Courses and workshops in cognitive therapy are available at a variety of professional meetings.

There is an unresolvable controversy in the field as to whether cognitions cause affects, or affects cause cognitions. Psychoanalytic therapists tend to feel that drives and feelings are primary and that dealing with cognitions is too superficial and "intellectual" to result in real insight. The opposite dogma is that affects are epiphenomena of cognitions. My view is that the therapist intervenes in a *field,* one in which cognitions and affects are interconnected by a complex variety of causal chains, feedback loops, and other regulatory mechanisms. Cognitions are one potential point of therapeutic entry into the field. I don't think that the debate over the relative primacy of affect and cognition will ever be fruitful, therefore I don't concern myself with it much.

In doing cognitive work it is necessary to provide a rationale for the patient that makes sense, however. This is different from a theory or model. I tell patients the following story, if I feel that an explicit rationale is necessary:

Sometimes what you feel is determined by what you think. When this is true, the best way to change how you feel is to change how you think.

Let me give an example. Imagine you are upstairs in your bedroom at bedtime, alone. You hear a noise downstairs. You think to yourself, "A burglar has broken in and he's going to come upstairs and rape me." You will react with feelings of fear, panic, and alarm, and your behavior may be to hide, call the police, or get a baseball bat. On the other hand if you hear exactly the same sound and think to yourself, "The dog knocked over his water dish," your reaction will be very different. You may feel annoyed or not feel anything in particular at all. Your behavior may be to get up and check on the water dish, or if you're tired, you might decide to leave it till morning and go to sleep.

This illustrates how different thoughts can result in very different feelings and behaviors in exactly the same situation. Part of the work we're going to do together is going to involve looking at your thought patterns in detail to see if they are causing you to feel upset, anxious, or depressed and to see if you can learn to feel better by changing your thought patterns. Let me tell one other story to explain how this will work.

Think about what happened when you learned to ride a bike as a kid. At first you had to think to yourself, "I have to put my left foot here, then I swing my other leg up, then I do this, then I do that." You had to think very laboriously about each little step in what you were doing. Soon, though, bicycle riding became automatic, and you didn't have to think about it at all. The same is true with the thought patterns we're going to be looking at in therapy. You've repeated the patterns so many times that they've become second nature, almost like they're automatic.

Because of this we're going to try to reverse the process of learning to ride a bike. We're going to take the automatic thoughts, make them fully conscious again, examine them in detail, like I said, change some, and then see if that helps you feel and live better. In your case most of the thoughts were ingrained in you by the abuse, as we've been talking about.

Most of the time I don't provide a rationale for the cognitive interventions, I just blend them into the therapy. The patients have no trouble understanding what is being done. I rarely use the technical terminology of cognitive therapy in the sessions, except perhaps to refer to automatic thoughts, cognitive errors, or errors in thinking. With MPD patients, pointing out cognitive errors can be experienced by the patient as blaming or belittling, so one has to continuously check for the effects of cognitive interventions. This is true with all techniques used throughout therapy.

The classical cognitive errors such as catastrophizing and selective generalization are common in MPD. They can be dealt with using standard strategies. The cognitive therapy of MPD is different from that of depression or anxiety primarily because incompatible and contradictory cognitions are held and endorsed by separate personalities. Mapping the cognitions involves calling out the different alters and dealing with them psychotherapeutically at the same time. Because of the dissociation, pure, classical cognitive therapy is impossible in MPD, and the work must involve noncognitive techniques never discussed by Beck and his colleagues. I don't think it makes sense to speak of the "cognitive therapy" of MPD as a method entirely distinct from systems or psychodynamic work.

An exhaustive explication of the use of cognitive techniques in the treatment of MPD would require a separate monograph. Therefore I am going to be illustrative. In our paper (Ross & Gahan, 1988a) on the cognitive analysis of MPD, the first assumption we list is *Different parts of the self are separate selves* (see Chapter 5). One of the cognitions this leads to is the erroneous belief that different alters have different bodies. This is a crucial error to address in therapy because it helps maintain the self-destructive behavior of alters, who in effect attempt to commit murder of the self.

I might challenge this belief in a number of ways. The first step is to take a full life history of the alter who is claiming to have a separate body. Often she will endorse several other subcognitions including the belief that the abuse never happened to her and that the host's parents are not her parents. The belief in a separate body is usually part of a more massive denial and dissociation of the reality of the abuse. Having taken the cognitively oriented history, I might then go on to focus on the time and mechanism of origin of the alter.

Different alters claim to have different origins. Persecutors sometimes state that they were discarnate entities floating in the ether prior to entering the patient's body. In such cases, the persecutor will usually acknowledge that the body is the host's body, and she will claim to have an unaffected astral body, which is not harmed by the cigarette burns or wrist slashes. In this instance I would then explore the cognitions in the second set, derived from the belief that the victim is responsible for the abuse.

When an alter claims to have a separate physical body, I might ask about where she lives, what she eats, where she buys her clothes, and how all of these differ from the host personality's activities. The alter can rarely give a satisfactory account of these day-to-day matters, so the questioning plants the first seeds of doubt. I then restate the alter's perception as a logical proposition and get her to make an experimental prediction, which I know will be refuted by the facts.

The classical example of this strategy involves recent wrist slashing. Through Socratic questioning I get the alter to endorse a chain of cognitions: I have a separate physical body → I forced the host to slash her wrists → I did this because the host is bad → the host is bad because she caused the abuse to happen → she deserves to be punished → I was never abused → I'm not bad → I don't deserve to be punished → the slashing doesn't affect me → there are no slash marks on my arm. I then ask the alter to roll up her sleeve. When she sees the same slash marks the host inflicted on herself on her own arm, the entire chain of cognitions is shaken.

It is important to link together as complex and central a group of cognitions as possible, to maximize the impact of the intervention. I then review the empirical findings. The alter acknowledges that there are slash marks on her arm, that they look just like the ones on the host's arm, and that she doesn't know how they got there. Next I propose an alternate hypothesis to account for the findings, namely that the two personalities are dissociated aspects of the same mind. This hypothesis is then discussed, the alter provides arguments in favor of the old theory of separate bodies, and these are analyzed, weighed, and refuted as persuasively as possible.

Alters usually abandon their cognitions in a stepwise fashion. The demonstration involving slash marks may rapidly result in an acknowledgment of a shared body, but the alter will still insist that the abuse never happened to her. "It happened to this body, but it didn't happen to me" is a common statement. I may not challenge that belief. Instead I might acknowledge it and say that the belief in separateness was an effective and necessary survival strategy during childhood. I emphasize that I appreciate that the psychological reality for the alter is that the abuse did not happen to her. I say that this is as it should be.

I then divert attention to the fact that the persecutor has a stake in the welfare and survival of the body she inhabits. If the body dies, she dies. If the alter acknowledges this, a contract for no self-harm may be possible. Other persecutors will restate their conviction that they are discarnate entities with no stake in the survival of the physical body. In that instance I then proceed to an examination of the alter's motives for self-abuse. My intention is to try to redefine the slashing or overdosing as helping strategies that could be improved upon. If this can be done, then a contract may be negotiated for a moratorium on self-harm while alternate strategies are being considered.

Often one has to nibble away at the cognitive fortress like a mouse trying to break into a castle made of cheese. The personality system will have an elaborate rationale in place for its self-destructive behavior, but there are always flaws in the logic somewhere. Once these are located, they can be chewed away at until a sizable breach has been established. The cognitive work also has a computer-game feel to it, as the therapist analyzes the system and tries to figure out the entry codes. The cognitive interventions are like viruses inserted into the system, which then replicate and dismantle it from within.

The dysphoria and self-abuse are largely driven by the assumption *The victim is responsible for the abuse* (see Chapter 5). This error in reasoning originated in early Piagetian stages of development, but the patient now has a mind capable of formal operations, which can unlearn the earlier modes of thought. There are a number of strategies I use for this problem. The narcissistic quality of the belief that "I must be bad" can be challenged. Using a Socratic approach I get the target alter to review her beliefs about children in general. Usually she will agree that children in general are not capable of adult responsibility for what happens in their lives.

If a child gets sick, that is not her fault. If a child's father dies in a car accident, that is not the child's fault. But it is understandable how a child might reason incorrectly and conclude that Daddy died and went away because he didn't like her, and it was her fault. As adults we can understand the child's reasoning and know that it is mistaken. I then ask the patient how she feels about the little girls in our city who are currently being sexually abused by their fathers. Is it their fault? The patient will usually insist that there is no way it could be the girls' fault and will add that she would like to rescue them.

I then clarify that in general children are not responsible for traumatic things that happen to them. In particular little girls who are being abused today are not responsible. The adult is fully responsible, and the behavior is criminal. If these things are true for all children in the world, why aren't they true for the patient? Is she so special and different that she's the one child in the world who is responsible for her abuse? This line of questioning puts the patient in the position of being grandiose if she claims responsibility for the abuse. Because she feels worthless, the logical structure has to break down. Its internal inconsistencies have been revealed.

Such interventions do not work instantaneously. It takes a great deal of repetition, abreaction, negotiation, and other work for the cognitive errors to be cured. Additionally, one can ask the patient as an adult to review all the strategies available to her as a child to deal with the abuse. She could tell, but nobody would believe her, and she would be abused even worse. She could fight, but that would be ineffective and would escalate the abuse. She couldn't run away at 4 years old. She didn't know how to kill herself. She could try to be perfect, but that didn't work. So she dissociated, the best and most brilliant strategy.

In conjunction with a review of strategies, I examine motive. Did she enjoy the abuse, did she ask for it, did she want it? Does she think that girls who are being abused today like it and want it? So how could it be her fault? She may restate her arguments that it would have stopped if she had been perfect. I then ask if it is reasonable to bring children up in an environment where they will be raped if they don't vacuum well enough. At some point, tears will break through, then anger, then a declaration that the father is a bastard and the patient wants to kill him. I respond to this by evoking memories of the positive aspects of the father and the feelings of alters who were treated well by him. The patient must learn to tolerate ambivalence without dissociating, and in any case I want to discourage murder.

This set of interventions can be complicated if the alter enticed the father into bed in order to divert him from a sister in another bed, when he crept into the bedroom at night. This was honorable and courageous behavior and didn't prove that the patient wanted or deserved the abuse. Often the patient will have experienced sexual arousal during the abuse and will cite this as proof that she is bad, dirty, to blame, and really wanted it. I deal with this by asking the patient how her fingertip would react if she placed it on a hot stove. It would blister if she didn't pull it away quick enough. Blistering and reflex withdrawal occur independently of our thoughts and motives and are natural bodily responses to stimuli.

Similarly, the human body is designed to be sexually aroused by certain stimuli. This has been very useful in evolution to ensure the propogation of the species. It's why vibrators work. "The fact that your body found the abuse pleasurable doesn't in the least prove that you wanted it or enjoyed it emotionally," I say, "anymore than blistering proves you like getting burned." Much of the cognitive work is educational in nature, and only some is more formally argumentative.

A difficulty can occur in patients with highly structured, layered personality systems. One can deal with and disarm hostile, abusive alters with cognitive and other techniques in one layer, then encounter similar alters in another layer who have observed the "mind games" and declare that they aren't going to be taken in by them. My cognitive interventions have also been called "hocus-pocus" by alters in such systems. Despite this I have found that the same strategies seem to work layer by layer, even though the bag of tricks has already been used.

The third set of cognitions (see Chapter 5), based on the assumption *It is wrong to show anger,* is susceptible to cognitive restructuring. Part of this involves a short lecture on the utility and natural beauty of anger, the right-eousness of anger, the energy value of anger, anger as a motivator, and so on. The patient's anger must be redefined as legitimate and healthy, but in need of containment and channeling. Anger is not desirable in itself, and it occurs in a transactional context. Neither is it intrinsically undesirable. It just is. Anger gets bad press in our culture, and many patients have been subjected to severe ideological suppression of their anger by "religious," sexually abusive parents.

I borrow a page from the feminist handbook and point out that much of the social change brought about by the women's movement was motivated by healthy anger. I also work hard to get the patient to see that the abusers controlled and abused the patient by cognitive brainwashing, in which the patient was told she was bad for having normal angry responses to abuse. Concerning the fact that several alters contain all the anger, while others have never been angry, I review the utility of dissociation once again. The goal of the therapy is to remove the boundaries that keep thoughts, feelings, memories, behaviors, and skills compartmentalized in separate personality states. In part, the cognitive errors are the intrapsychic machinery that maintains the dissociation: When the errors are corrected, the leakage of anger and other feelings from alter to alter increases.

I might ask, "Who says anger is bad? How do you know that?" knowing full well that the parents said it. A common reply is, "I just know it's bad." I counter, "How do you know that? Did you find some stone tablets with *Never Get Angry* written on them? Is *Never Get Angry* a scientific law that you studied in physics?" *Reductio ad absurdum,* playful parody, and ex-aggeration, even sarcasm can be useful techniques. The patient then might say, "I know it's bad to get angry because I always got beaten up if I got angry at home." I go on, "Oh, I see. You're saying that your parents are healthy, well-adjusted people and that you value their opinions on how to raise children. If they said anger is bad, they must be right. They were right that it was okay to abuse you, they were right that it was okay to kill your cat, so they must be right about this too. Is that it?"

The next comment by the patient might contain several four-letter words. This is good because it mobilizes the patient's anger, and I point this out and approve of the anger. There has just been a revolutionary transactional sequence for the patient. I push patients hard on their cognitive errors.

Another way to work with cognitions is to get alters who endorse incom-patible cognitions to state them out loud while the others are listening. The alters then have a disagreement among themselves that they have to resolve. This provides practice in internal democracy. The conversation generates irrefutable evidence that the patient as a whole does not endorse any of the cognitive errors, that the whole is greater than the sum of its parts, and that the alters exist to ensure that ambivalence is experienced as certainty. Life is both simpler and more complicated after integration. With coconsciousness the alters can begin to understand directly how they function as a dissociative system with complex linkages between subregions, rather than as separate, independent people.

Because cognitive therapy is always cognitive-behavioral, graded exercises are useful. These can be applied to the fifth assumption, *The primary personality can't handle the memories* (see Chapter 5). Through graded return of memories and gradual attainment of coconsciousness, this assumption and its cognitions are experimentally refuted. This assumption is an example of dichotomization: The options at first appear to be complete amnesia, or complete recovery of memories with insanity. Fears that one alter won't like another can be disconfirmed by having the fearful alter listen in while the issue is discussed with the other personality.

In parallel to what occurs in the therapy, many of the cognitive techniques are scattered throughout other sections of this chapter. Cognitive interventions interact and synergize with other techniques.

It isn't only patients who make cognitive errors. The resistance to MPD among mental health professionals can be analyzed in terms of cognitive errors. For instance Fahy (1988) in a review that is dismissive of MPD as a legitimate nosologic entity, says that the failure to define a personality is a major weakness of the DSM-III criteria. He then characterizes MPD as "hysterical" (p. 604) without defining that term. This is an error of reasoning and analysis. Something approaching closer to a classical cognitive error is the incorrect belief that a diagnosis of MPD provides the patient with a license for irresponsibility.

Once this assumption is made, a set of attitudes and behaviors hostile to MPD follows logically. If the assumption is dismissed, the attitudes and behaviors simply melt away. Cognitive therapy has a Zen flavor to it in that one doesn't so much teach patients what to do, as teach them what not to do. Once they stop doing what they shouldn't be doing, everything works well and naturally. This is, however, only a part truth about the therapy of MPD. The main point the reader should carry away from this section is that cognitive interventions are only one "personality" within the entire therapeutic system, not a freestanding entity.

NEGOTIATING WITH ALTER PERSONALITIES

Some of the principles and techniques of negotiation with alters have been referred to previously. The therapy of MPD can be thought of globally as analogous to labor–management negotiations. The therapist alternates between roles of mediator and arbitrator. Arbitration occurs with involuntary hospitalization, violation of absolute rules of therapy, use of hypnosis for putting alters to sleep, hiring of alters as internal enforcers to keep other personalities in line, and similar unilaterally enforced actions. These are temporary measures in an ongoing process of therapy, unless termination occurs. Even unilateral actions by the therapist have been negotiated with some other part of the system.

A goal of treatment is to convert the patient from a dysfunctional, war-stricken state to a more functional political organization. The patient enters therapy with hostile, uncooperative, frightened, abusive, and hidden personality states that have limited coordination with each other. The role of the therapist is to analyze the system, identify the specific conflicts and problems, and negotiate solutions with the involved parties. This is similar to a consultant to a large corporation who generates a plan for improved corporate function. As a system, the MPD personality system is often as complex as a large company.

Businesses have problems similar to those of the MPD patient: Marketing does not communicate with finance; payroll is having trouble converting to a new system; the lines of communication are unclear; one vice-president has an alcohol problem; another is pursuing his career goals at the expense of the corporation; the company is reacting in a self-destructive way to certain market forces; the original structure of the company cannot adapt to a changed business environment; a hostile takeover by a corporate raider is feared; the secretaries are unhappy with office noise levels; cash flow is down; and so on. The systems analyst has to take numerous types of problems into account.

Anyone who can analyze and treat complex MPD could learn to improve the function of large corporations: The logic of the analysis is the same. The MPD therapist would have an advantage over most consultants because of his awareness of the emotional determinants of system dysfunction. For instance if I were asked to consult to a corporation, I would make a point of interviewing the secretaries personally. In my experience they often have a unique and profound insight into the function of systems in which they are employed, one which you cannot get from management. This is analogous to interviewing everybody in the MPD personality system.

In MPD treatment the therapist has to talk to everybody, find out what the problems are, and then work out solutions. For example, a woman was recently admitted for intensive inpatient work. She complained that a record of "Old McDonald Had a Farm" was playing over and over in her head. She found this very distressing and feared she was going insane. Brief inquiry easily established that an older male alter was playing the records for a frightened child, who liked them. The male agreed to try to learn how to play the records without the host hearing them, with hypnotic help from the therapist. The next strategy would be to have the male find out what tapes the child would like to listen to, ones that the host would also enjoy. The patient could buy these and play them on her Walkman, and the child could listen to them.

This negotiated solution would remove the symptom, demonstrate to the child that it is safe to enter therapy, reinforce the protective role of the male, establish coconsciousness of nonthreatening, pleasurable experience, demonstrate to the host that she is not insane and that her symptoms are treatable, and provide a concrete example of the benefits of negotiation. Yet it is simple and practical and does not involve any "deep" theories or exploration. The involved alters could consent to the intervention as is, or they could propose and negotiate modifications.

Negotiation is a pervasive aspect of therapy that, once grasped in principle, is used in a pragmatic fashion. The method of therapy, I can't repeat too often, is to ask and find out, then problem solve. Sometimes the therapist will feel as if he is dashing around chaotically putting out fires, without an overall direction. This can be an inevitable stage of therapy or a sign of inadequate analysis and problem priorization. But most of the work goes on at a microlevel and involves solving countless little problems such as the auditory hallucination of "Old McDonald Had A Farm."

USING METAPHORS, RITUALS, IMAGERY, AND DREAMS

This is a rich and imaginative set of interventions. There are neuropsychological links of some sort between abuse, dissociation, and visual imagination. MPD patients often have very intense visual modes of thought. They are good at thinking in metaphors and using guided imagery techniques. These interventions can be so creative and interesting for the therapist that they become countertherapeutic: It is important to keep a clear focus on current function in the real world.

Some patients have highly structured internal environments in which the alters can move around. Bringing a frightened child into therapy may involve, with the therapist's guidance, a helper personality's hypnotic expedition to a distant room in an internal house. One patient had a child alter who was locked in a room. The other personalities were terrified to open the door of the room and let the child out because they knew something bad was going on in there. A great deal of work was done fusing some of the alters, putting some to sleep, negotiating with adult alters to protect other child personalities, and preparing for the therapist to open the door.

The other personalities could smell a pinelike odor coming out of the room, which seemed to be from a cleaning agent called Pinesol. With hypnotic preparation I went into the building, opened the door, and called the alter over. She was in a room in which pornographic movies were being made. She and other children, many drugged or drunk, were taking part in hardcore sex while being filmed. I was able to accompany the child out of the room because nobody but her could see or hear me. In the hall there was a struggle as she tried to get away, and we were able to escape from the building. I brought her to the hospital and she found a safe place to be in her inner world. The door to the room was reported to be permanently closed, but the memories were not lost. They were now memories of the past rather than ongoing abreactive experience. The odor of Pinesol was from actual Pinesol used as a cleaner by the pornographers. With this intervention a range of frightened, agitated, and highly anxious behavioral states went into remission.

My office contains a number of amulets, medicine bundles, and shamanic power objects that testify to my authority and healing power and reveal to the patients that therapy is a prolonged spiritual ritual. I have magically transformed these possessions into objects consistent with the cultural expectations of my patients. Nonshamanic people who enter my office see only degrees on the wall, filing cabinets, professional books, and a computer. I, however, know that all therapy is a mysterious ritual.

Therapy can be guided by both global metaphors and micrometaphors. The patient's personal metaphor of integration provides organization and direction for all the work. An example of a micrometaphor occurred in therapy with a patient who could not understand why there was so much commotion in her personality system, with alters constantly changing alliances and positions. Because a number of child and adolescent alters were involved, I pointed out to the patient that there was trouble on the school playground. She grasped this immediately.

The metaphor seems simple but it is complex. It brings to bear on the therapy a wealth of assumptions, tacit knowledge, cultural expectations, and direct experience about the social structure and function of playgrounds. There are bullies, shy kids, outcasts, older kids, younger kids, and a few protective teachers who also know how to spoil the fun. Commotion on the playground, rather than being a sign of mental illness, is evidence of exuberant life. Changing alliances and positions are part of the natural order of playground life, and not necessarily cause for anguish or alarm.

The patient immediately set about the task of organizing the playground a little, getting someone to look out for the young children, finding a friend for the lonely adolescent, and putting limits on bullying. Therapists sometimes put alters to sleep, frequently call out alters, and talk about eventually terminating therapy: All of these are metaphors, the last communicating sinister but unacknowledged feelings about patients. Is therapy really something to be "terminated"? Why don't we talk about metamorphosing patients out of therapy, or transmigrating them? Why have we chosen an official term that evokes extinction?

Particular metaphors or imaginative rituals should not be reified, or blown up into a method or school of therapy. They may make an interesting case presentation or clinical tip and can be the subject of a 15-minute conference presentation. Usually they should not be more. Rituals can be borrowed from whatever mythology the therapist and patient find congruent. I might tell an alter that I am going to get tough with her or set limits: more metaphor. This paragraph contains metaphors involving the following words: reified, blown up, school, tip, borrowed, congruent, get tough, set limits, and contains.

Therapy is no more metaphorical than molecular biology, however. I remember noticing in premedical studies that the scientific study of DNA is almost all metaphorical. In a single paragraph one finds metaphors about genetic blueprints, mapping DNA, transcribing DNA, messenger RNA, the genetic code, cellular architecture, bonding, reading DNA, information encoded on chromosones, and the gene pool, to give a sample of the basic vocabulary of genetics. Science is as fundamentally metaphorical as poetry, but the metaphors of science are connected to physical reality in a special way that yields modern technology. The metaphors of MPD therapy are connected to reality in ways that dramatically modify observable behavior, including suicide, abuse of children, and expensive utilization of societal resources. MPD therapy deals with ''facts'' just as much as molecular biology, in fact with more important facts.

I make these remarks to indicate that the use of metaphor in MPD therapy is not soft, hazy, romantic, or poetical, in the usual current senses of those terms. These are techniques that are used for specific purposes, the effects of which need to be monitored.

The interpretation of dreams as I do it in MPD work is very different from psychoanalytic dream work, although other therapists are much more analytic in their MPD dream work (Marmer, 1980). Basically I work with dreams as a staging area for the recovery of accurate memories of real childhood trauma. This does not mean, as I said in the section on abreaction earlier in this chapter, that the memories are videocopies of past reality. Other than using them as a vehicle for recovering memories, I don't ask about or comment on my patients' dreams that much. This may be a limitation of mine, and I should probably do a wider variety of dream work. Actually I am more interested in studying paranormal properties of dreams than their personal psychological meaning.

For MPD patients dreams are like hallucinations. Freud understood this connection but overextended it and, with the repudiation of the seduction theory, went astray. He incorrectly believed that dreams, childhood thought, hallucinations, and the experience of ''savages'' are all evidence of primary process thinking and that the unconscious is irrational. In dissociative patients with childhood trauma histories, dreams and hallucinations can be intrusions of real memories. In MPD it is possible to contract with the ''unconscious,'' which is composed of conscious alter personalities with whom the therapist can converse directly. Staged recovery of memories can occur through dreams, hallucinations, internal movies, abreactions, and flashbacks in much the same way as negotiating anything else in life.

Getting memories back through dreams is a safe, rational way of doing things. MPD trauma dreams make sense. Often a particular alter deliberately sets the pace with which memories are recovered through dreams, both in terms of the number and intensity of dreams and the timing of the dreams in therapy. New dreams can precede the uncovering of a new layer of personalities in highly structured patients. Like the process of negotiation about "Old McDonald Had A Farm," there is nothing "deep" about the therapist's comments or interpretations. The kind of dream work I am describing and classical analytic or Jungian dream work are not mutually exclusive and can be done in the same therapy.

The picture of the mind that emerges from MPD work is different from the psychoanalytic vision. I see what Freud called the "unconscious" as dissociated conscious mind. Some alters function at developmentally earlier levels of cognition but are not therefore less conscious. What is actually unconscious is the physical body, but it, too, is highly structured and rational. There is nothing "irrational" about catching a ball, digesting food, transporting oxygen to tissues, or developing inflammation, all of which are done with little or no "conscious" control. This is the sense of things I get from my patients.

To do MPD dream work the therapist should proceed on the hypothesis that the images and events make sense and that it will all eventually fit together. This will set the correct tone for clinical inquiry. If dreams are coming too fast or are too disturbing and direct contact with the alters in the background has not been established, several techniques might be helpful. Hypnotic suggestion might help, or the therapist can talk to "whoever is controlling the dreams" by talking through the host or whichever alter is in executive control at the time.

I might say:

I'm talking to whoever is controlling the dreams about blood that Susan has been describing. I don't know for sure, but going on how it has worked in the past, this probably has to do with something bad that happened. If that's true, it's good that the memories are coming back. The problem is they're coming back a bit too fast and causing Susan a lot of distress. So I'm asking whoever is giving the memories back to slow things down a bit. Actually, I'd like to talk directly with whoever it is, if that's possible.

I might then try ideomotor signals, the alter talking to the host, or other indirect techniques for contacting the dream controller. I might also make reassuring or other statements to the presumed alter in the background.

Hypnotic interventions, audiotapes, and benzodiazepine medications may all help to control traumatic dreaming, but often the patient just has to tough it out. When I make shamanic expeditions into a patient's dreamworld, through guided imagery techniques, I can enter landscapes reported from spontaneous nocturnal dreams. There I may meet an alter for a specific task, as described above. Alternatively I may stand at the edge of the dreamworld awaiting an alter's return from a task journey. This provides a sense of control, safety, and protection. Another variation is to place a magical marker on an alter as a tracking and retrieval device.

For instance, a child personality may run away into a dark place and not know how to get back. If a marker has been placed on her beforehand, the therapist can give a hypnotic suggestion that because of the marker his voice is bringing the child back to the therapy room. In this instance I would give relaxation instructions and say:

> I'm calling for Susie now. Susie is far away and nobody knows where she has gone, but it's safe now for her to come back. I'm calling now for Susie, and because of the marker I gave her, my voice can reach her and bring her back. My voice is traveling out into the darkness, guided by the marker, and is bringing Susie back to talk. Susie, you feel yourself coming back now, everything is safe, it's Dr. Ross calling you and bringing you back to talk. My voice is traveling out into the darkness to find Susie and bring her back.

This is a cultural equivalent of the circumpolar shaman sending spirit guides out over the arctic landscape to locate game. Patients can be given any of an infinite variety of objects to carry with them, for numerous purposes. One of my cotherapists gave a patient an ornamental rock that she held in order to guide herself back to the office, after her child personality had been out. She was a patient who had a prolonged, foggy state during switches back to her host personality. Another therapist gave a patient a pen of his to carry for strength, a gift that crystallized erotic and other transferences. That it was a standard issue hospital pen taken from our supply cupboard did not detract from the therapeutic power of the gift.

One of the most important rituals is the actual integration ritual, described in Chapter 13. There is no need to list countless examples of metaphors, rituals, and imagery because they all conform to general principles. The information transmitted through dreams is often fragmentary at first. To clarify it, the therapist uses other techniques, focused on contacting the alters who hold the memories consciously. I will conclude by describing a technique used by George Fraser that I have heard him teaching in workshops.

A good way to map the system, resolve issues, and recover memories is to hold inner board meetings. The patient relaxes with a brief hypnotic induction, and the host personality walks into the boardroom. The patient is instructed that there will be one chair for every personality in the system. Then a general suggestion is given for all members of the system to enter the boardroom and take a seat. Once this is done, the therapist chairs the meeting, takes roll call, and coordinates negotiations between board members. Often there are empty chairs because some alters aren't ready to enter therapy. The empty chairs provide useful information, and those present can be asked what they know about the missing people. There should be a number of doors in and out of the boardroom because some alters might not feel safe using the same entrance as others.

The boardroom contains a projector and screen on which abuse memories can be replayed. Alternatively, selected alters can adjourn to a separate screening room. Watching the abuse on a screen is done with specific hypnotic suggestions that the host will see the movie but not feel the feelings. This allows for safer, staged recovery of memories prior to full abreaction. Such internal meetings can be held in a variety of settings. They are a way of rapidly establishing coconsciousness and cooperation for selected issues and material.

Another common use of guided imagery is to find safe locations for the children in the inner landscape. This can include safety from memories, external abusers, and persecutory alters. Children can be asked to go away and play while particularly difficult adult work is being done. This set of interventions is high on the list of targets for ridicule by skeptics. Rituals, dreams, metaphors, and imagery directly tap the hypnotic/dissociative virtuosity of the patients and teach them that their gift can be used for recovery and improved function. As I said at the beginning of this section, though, these techniques can get out of control if the therapist becomes more interested in his own creativity than in the patient.

HYPNOSIS AND RELAXATION TECHNIQUES

Richard Kluft (1982, 1985c) has written specifically on hypnotic techniques in the treatment of adult and childhood MPD. He has also published a very interesting paper on the use of hypnosis to recover lost objects (1987c). This paper provides circumstantial evidence that Kluft's use of hypnosis in MPD treatment also results in the recovery of real memories. It is a bit difficult to provide a catalog of the uses of hypnosis in MPD work because it can be used to augment virtually any intervention (Gruenewald, 1971; Howland, 1975; Schafer, 1986). In one sense, everything done prior to integration is a hypnotic intervention, because some part of the patient has been continuously in trance since early childhood.

When people ask me if it is necessary to use hypnosis to treat MPD, I usually say "No," because I don't want them to think they can't do anything with these patients without years of experience in hypnosis. I also point out that the aim of therapy is to bring the patient out of trance, not to put her in it. All this becomes a bit semantic, but I think that anyone who is making massive ongoing use of dissociation is in some sense continuously hypnotized. The idea that MPD is a disorder of autohypnosis is also a bit arbitrary, because the original induction was probably done by the abuser.

One adult patient was not getting better as she should have been, despite the integration of 50 alters and her apparent substantial strengths. I then discovered that her father was still having intercourse with her at least twice a week and had been doing so continuously since childhood. The final layer of alters contained a mute victim alter, and was divided into a good and a bad side. The father would knock on the door, and the host would switch to one of three enabling alters under the control of the leader of the bad side, who would open the door. Once the father entered, the bad leader would switch the patient to the victim. When the father (actually the father's alter, because the father's host personality was amnesic for the abuse) interrogated the patient for information about whether the ongoing abuse had been disclosed in therapy, the bad leader had one of the enablers talk for the mute victim-alter, without a switch of executive control.

However the leader of the good side temporarily took all memories of disclosure in therapy out of the minds of the enablers at the moment they began to reply to the father. When the father left, the patient switched back to her host personality, who was amnesic for the entire episode. Attempting to decide which parts of this patient are in trance at which times is a scientifically impossible and therapeutically irrelevant task. One could say, for instance, that the host personality is hypnotized by the father, while the enablers are hypnotized by the leader of the good side; that the entire personality system is in autohypnosis; or that only the host has gone into autohypnosis on the grounds that only she experiences amnesia. This doesn't resolve who is putting the father in trance: Would feminists object if I suggested it could be the mother, who does not have MPD?

I don't think it is true that the host is awake and the alters are in a trance state when in executive control, as some people assume. Some people seem to think that when the therapist is talking to any alter but the host, the patient is in trance. This is an arbitrary distinction with no empirical basis. Besides, different alters can be the host at different times. This means that it isn't necessary to do a hypnotic induction in order to contact an alter. In fact the reverse can sometimes be true: You have to hypnotize an alter to get the host back.

Another problem in deciding what is and what isn't a hypnotic intervention is the difficulty distinguishing between a relaxation exercise and a hypnotic induction with MPD patients. I remember one patient with whom I wanted to call out an alter for the first time. I explained what I was going to do then said, "Now I want you to close your eyes and be as relaxed and comfortable as possible." She closed her eyes and immediately exclaimed, "Boy! Do I feel relaxed!" I hadn't even started my relaxation procedure yet! Two more sentences from me and she would be in deep trance.

MPD patients can go into trance states instantly in response to innumerable internal and external cues. In some sense my patients probably go into trance walking across the hospital parking lot to get to our building: I probably never see them fully awake till after integration. I think that advocates of the theory that MPD is an artifact of hypnosis have to be extremely careful how they define an induction. As I proposed in Chapter 8, Wayne Gretzky "hypnotizes" hockey players on opposing teams. Does this mean his scoring records are an artifact of hypnosis? What meaning does the word *artifact* have in such a theory?

It is known that there are awake, alert hypnotic states and that induction procedures need not involve relaxation, sleep, focus, or fatigue imagery. Given this, one has to be aware that most interventions in MPD may have a hypnotic component. A formal induction procedure is rarely required. I usually use formal inductions longer than 15 seconds only early in therapy or when getting into a new layer of personalities. The main use of the lengthier inductions seems to be anxiolysis. The personality in executive control and the alter about to emerge are nervous about switching and need calming and reassurance about it for a while.

Otherwise, formal inductions serve only to mobilize the patient's dissociative skills for particular therapeutic purposes. I use a relaxation and warming up induction out of personal preference. I like it because it gives permission for hypnotic amnesia through sleep suggestions, is anxiolytic, can be generalized for relaxation training, is pleasant, and involves the entire body. A danger of hypnotic induction techniques reported to me by Pam Gahan, is induction of trance in the cotherapist.

I ask the patient to sit as comfortably as possible, relax, close her eyes, and get ready. I then advise the patient that I want her to do three things: Concentrate on the sound of my voice, pay attention to the meaning of the words, and imagine the things I ask her to imagine. With repeated suggestions to focus on the sound of my voice I then warm up the feet, then both legs, then the hands, the arms, then redo the hands, feet, arms, and legs. I then do the back, stomach and chest, and all internal organs (I don't actually name the individual organs), before doing the neck, the top of the head, and finally the face. Then I suggest, "The mind too is warm, calm, relaxed, and tired, just a pleasant, natural feeling of warmth and relaxation and tiredness as you listen to the sound of my voice."

And now as you sit reading this book you begin to notice that your body is a little more relaxed and warm and comfortable than usual, as you listen to the sound of my voice. You aren't disturbed by any other thoughts or sensations, you're able just to focus on the words, understand their meaning, and feel yourself calm and comfortable and relaxed. And the more you read, the deeper and deeper you go into this pleasant, relaxed, natural state of calmness and tiredness, as you listen to the sound of my voice. This feeling of calmness and relaxation becomes stronger and stronger with every word you read, until, at the beginning of the next paragraph you will be in a deep hypnotic state, perfectly relaxed and calm. This will last for 30 seconds or until you read to the end of the paragraph, whichever comes first. Then you will be wide awake, fresh, and alert, feeling calm and confident and ready to continue reading.

You have just undergone a hypnotic induction of greater length and formality than that required for the treatment of MPD to integration. All that a lengthier induction would do for you is intensify the effect. If you are highly hypnotizable, you may have entered a hypnotic trance from which you are going to awaken now, feeling fresh, alert, calm and confident, and ready to continue reading. You are now fully awake and alert.

In case you have reservations about the ethics of including such a hypnotic induction in a book, I want to point out that reading always occurs in a trance state. You were already hypnotized by the act of reading, which is itself an induction ritual of great hypnotic power, before you reached the preceding paragraphs. Think of it, millions of commuters on morning trains using their newspapers to dissociate! For me, writing induces an even deeper trance state than reading. Those readers who are not hypnotizable will be impressed by the ineffectualness of the so-called hypnotic induction. That is a useful lesson for them because it demonstrates the difficulty of attributing so much complex phenomenology to such a simple intervention, as the hypnosis-artifact theorists do. I wonder whether professionals who dismiss MPD as an artifact tend to be nonhypnotizable individuals and therefore do not understand the limitations of hypnosis.

Hypnosis can be used for adjunctive pain relief, improved sleep, and general relaxation. I fairly often make audiotapes for MPD patients with an induction and whatever suggestions are suitable. This may include increased confidence, reduced stomach pain, or any other instruction. I have reviewed the use of posthypnotic suggestions for safety in an earlier section. Inductions are most often used to facilitate contact with alters, increase interpersonality communication, stop malignant or unproductive abreactions, and retrieve memories. Hypnosis should not be thought of as a technique in itself which one either uses or does not use. Although an induction can be done at a specific point in time to augment another intervention, hypnosis is never something one does for its own sake.

There is therefore no need to list further examples of the use of hypnosis in MPD work. It can facilitate many or all aspects of the work, but patients can be treated without a defined verbal induction ever being done. Schafer (1981) has written an interesting paper illustrating the use of hypnosis in dissociative individuals who do not have MPD.

AGE PROGRESSION AND AGE REGRESSION

Personalities can be made older or younger for many purposes. Both age progression and age regression are good examples of techniques that can be augmented by a formal hypnotic ritual. Staff at the Royal Ottawa Hospital (Bornn, 1988) sometimes make specialized use of prolonged, massive age regression in selected inpatient cases. I don't do that, and I am not going to talk about such extraordinary interventions. I also do not do intrauterine or past life work, although either could be useful therapeutic rituals. MPD patients often have spontaneous past life intrusions among their other paranormal experiences.

I have watched a non-MPD patient age-regress to the intrauterine state and complain about an unsuccessful illegal abortion, but I have a lot of trouble believing in this as a real memory of an event that occurred at 2 months' gestation. Such memory is physiologically impossible and could be explained only by reincarnation theory. The patient certainly experienced the abreaction as intense and real, however, and it clearly symbolized chronic feelings of being unloved and rejected.

I use age progression more commonly than age regression. Age regression can be used to take an alter back to before the time of a trauma that is causing an otherwise untreatable symptom. One child alter was constantly screaming inside about a murder witnessed many years earlier. This screaming and an associated conversion symptom went into temporary complete remission when the alter was regressed to an age 2 years earlier than the murder. This was only a temporary technique until a more definitive solution could be worked out, the alter integrated, and the symptoms cured.

In either direction, the change in age is suggested hypnotically with a magical explanation to the child. The alter may say that she doesn't know how to get older. I reassure her that I know how to do that for her, and all she has to do is listen. I then simply instruct her to grow up to the desired age and tell her it is happening. I then say that in a few seconds she will open her eyes, be the desired age, and not be frightened. Because she is older, she will understand that the trauma happened a long time ago. It is in the past now, she is safe, and she understands better and can talk about it.

Such age progression is useful for infant alters, frightened children who are stuck in the past, lonely alters without friends, and others who could benefit from the ability to function at the level of formal operations. Age progression demonstrates that alter personalities are not people, psychologically or legally. Age progression can be done rapidly, at a decade in less than a minute in some cases. In other cases it may be necessary to stop every year for a brief birthday party, or other alters may hold an internal birthday party every few days to help the child grow up quickly. Age progression can be spread out over minutes, hours, days, or weeks.

I age-progressed a child alter for one patient because she didn't feel it made sense to integrate that personality with her adolescent protector if they were different ages. Some therapists make a point of growing up alters to the chronological age of the patient prior to integration with the host, but I haven't found this to be necessary. The vast majority of the work can be done with the alters at their presenting ages, but age progression has been very effective and helpful in some cases. Before age progression is undertaken, there must be consultation with the necessary alters, including the one to be aged, the host, and often a protector/observer.

WRITING EXERCISES

Some patients write volumes and volumes in their journals, diaries, and notebooks, and bring in a far greater amount of material than the therapist can possibly read. This requires limit-setting. One of our patients likes to write in session, which seems to work well for her. There is a wide variety of ways in which written materials can be used. Writing can be used for both diagnostic and therapeutic purposes, as illustrated by a case I consulted on.

A young woman was inflicting serious knife slashes on her face during the night and was completely amnesic for the behavior. Nocturnal epilepsy with automatisms? No. In consultation I recommended that she leave a note pad and pencil by her bed on a night table and that she write a request for anyone there to send her messages on the note pad. Such messages began to appear and resulted in entry into her personality system and eventual extinction of the slashing.

Similar requests can be made of alters who are known but who are reluctant to participate in therapy. These requests can be made by talking through the host in session and asking the alter to write at home. The host can either leave a set of specific questions for the alter to answer or an open-ended request to talk may be sufficient. This may result in furious scratchings or rational conversation. In either case important information is transmitted, and the process of communication has begun. With hostile alters, it may be safer for the therapist to begin communication in this indirect way with the hostile personality taking executive control at home rather than in the office.

Daily journals can be a forum for coconsciousness, with alters taking turns writing, and commenting on what others have had to say. The penmanship can vary dramatically from personality to personality (there is a good study waiting to be done on handwriting analysis of MPD scripts). I described the use of writing exercises in the section on establishing interpersonality communication.

Another way in which writing can be of benefit in MPD work is encouraging creative writing, such as poems, stories, and autobiographical sketches. A considerable number of poems by people with MPD have been published in *Integration,* the newsletter of the Canadian Component Society of the International Society for the Study of Multiple Personality and Dissociation. The MPD support group in Ottawa has also published a lot of creative writing by patients in their newsletter *Reaching Out.* I see such work as healthy, normative, and therapeutic. Although their poetry is not technically advanced, it is much more interesting than most of what I've seen in literary magazines. This is so because of the seriousness of the MPD subject matter and the integrity of the expressed feelings.

The purpose of this section is to highlight writing exercises as a distinct set of therapeutic techniques. There is no need to provide further detail or examples, because the principles are readily grasped. I have already discussed artwork in a previous section, so will not say more about it now, although it is listed separately in the Therapist Dissociative Checklist (Appendix B).

USE OF AUDIOVISUAL MATERIALS

Everything that applies to using videotapes in therapy also applies to the use of audiotapes, except that the impact of video is greater. The only exception to this is prescribing audiotapes for relaxation, better sleep, and symptom relief. For such purposes I generally make a new tape for each patient during a session: The patient supplies the blank tape. The reason I make the tape in session is that hearing it live the first time seems to heighten the efficacy of the tape. Because of the therapeutic relationship, a tape with my voice, rather than a packaged tape by a stranger, is probably more effective.

I frequently request permission to videotape for educational rather than therapeutic purposes. I use the tapes at workshops and talks. So far I haven't had any trouble with this, and patients have been happy to contribute to the education of other mental health professionals. Patients are aware of the difficulties in modern society that act as a barrier to MPD diagnosis and treatment, and they like contributing to public education. Some patients would like to do so but can't for confidentiality reasons; I respect this. In an indirect way making such educational videos is healthy for the patient, but this is a minor side benefit, and I clearly define it as such. Actually, patients are happy to do this favor, but because they are vulnerable to exploitation of all kinds, it is necessary to be sensitive and careful about the matter. Written consent for videotaping for educational purposes is essential.

The other main uses of video are to facilitate interpersonality communication and to give everyone a chance to observe the switching and different alters from the outside. I only use video for such purposes on an occasional basis, and I consider the medium to be inessential and adjunctive. Like everything else in the therapy, video should be used in a planned, negotiated way. Severe reactions of panic, fear, agitation, and distress can occur if material is observed for which the host is not ready or if the host thinks she looks crazy on tape. Such reactions are often dealt with by spontaneous amnesia for the watching of the videotape. Therapists need to understand clearly that they can't force premature coconsciousness through audiovisual materials because protective amnesia barriers will be created. This will be countertherapeutic, will slow the pace down, damage trust, and create iatrogenic complications in a therapy that is already too complicated.

Another use of videotape is having patients watch educational programs about MPD. This can be helpful and may act as a kind of vicarious group therapy if the patient gets to see a tape of someone else switching. Anyone planning to do a workshop on MPD must realize that there may be diagnosed and/or undiagnosed MPD patients in the audience, among the lay or professional attenders. Provocative tapes may stimulate switching, panic, emergency trips to the washroom, or other reactions in audience members. When I know there are multiples in the audience, I may ask all the children and any other alters who would be frightened to find a place inside and not watch or listen while the monitor is on.

An application of audiovisual technology I have recently begun using is live telelinkage to professionals outside Winnipeg for ongoing consultation. This is probably the way of the future, although difficulties about consultant billings have to be worked out. I haven't yet done an assessment of a patient by telelink, but I think this could be done as long as the consulting therapist was present throughout and the patient's anxiety was not too high. When the pragmatic alternative is no direct observation by the consultant at all, this may be the most effective way of proceeding. Psychiatry, like cardiology, needs to be in the space age; cardiologists can instantaneously read EKGs done hundreds of miles away.

In one antidepressant study I was involved in, computerized EKG analyses were fed back to me from the United States within 5 minutes through the phone system. They had to be overread by a cardiologist in the United States if there were abnormalities of questionable importance, but I could immediately include or exclude the majority of subjects. The computerized analyses were deliberately conservative and yielded false positives rather than false negatives. With similar provisos and precautions, there is no reason that expertise in MPD cannot be tapped effectively with remote video technology.

MEDICATIONS

There are many problems about the use of medications in MPD. The most common error is incorrect, countertherapeutic prescribing in undiagnosed patients. MPD patients get a lot of medications. In our series of 236 cases (Ross, Norton, & Wozney, 1989), 63.3 percent had received a benzodiazepine, 59.5 percent a nonbenzodiazepine sedative, 68.9 percent antidepressants, 54.5 percent antipsychotics, 21.9 percent lithium, and 12.1 percent electroconvulsive therapy (ECT). We don't know how many of these prescriptions were warranted or how many helped. There is no indication for ECT in the treatment of MPD. Most courses of ECT are probably prescribed for MPD patients who do have depressions, mixed with dissociative Schneiderian symptoms. An important study would be a retrospective analysis of the efficacy of courses of ECT given to MPD patients prior to their diagnosis. The efficacy is probably the same as it would be for sham ECT.

This is an important issue because ECT is a humane and effective treatment that I have prescribed to selected nondissociative patients with dramatic benefits. If an MPD patient does actually have a psychotherapy and medication-nonresponsive psychotic depression, then ECT could be properly indicated for that depression. However I doubt very much that there has ever been such a course of ECT administered to a patient who has failed to respond to adequate trials of both medication and specific psychotherapy. ECT is absolutely contraindicated as a treatment for the MPD itself.

Likewise there is no indication for the use of lithium in MPD. It could be prescribed properly only for concurrent bipolar affective disorder. In practice that would be next to impossible because of compliance problems. I have prescribed lithium to one MPD patient on a trial basis, during the active phase of her psychotherapy. It had no beneficial effect. This woman had a 10-year history of classical rapid-cycling manic-depressive illness, as well as MPD. Since integration the manic-depressive illness has been in complete remission on no medication for 18 months. As a single-subject study this is an extremely powerful finding. I have to emphasize that the manic-depressive history was a vividly clear textbook description of rapid cycling illness.

There have been no systematic or controlled studies of the use of any medication in MPD. This means that there is no sound basis for any prescription written for an MPD patient and that every prescription is an empirical trial without scientific foundation. This applies to both benefits and side effects. It is important not to make exaggerated claims for either the efficacy or the harmfulness of medications in MPD in the absence of data. A recent report by Loewenstein, Hornstein, and Farber (1988) provides the first small-N open-label pilot study of the psychopharmacology of MPD.

Most MPD patients develop clinical depressions, so the question of antidepressant medication comes up frequently. I have not seen a clear example of beneficial response to an antidepressant in my practice. A general rule of thumb is that medications have a better chance of working if the symptoms are spread across the entire personality system. If only one or two alters are depressed and others are euthymic, in my opinion that is a contraindication to a trial of antidepressants.

The tricyclic antidepressants are extremely dangerous in overdose. Some people will die from ingestion of 2 weeks' supply of a therapeutic oral dosage of tricyclic. If such a medication is to be tried, the absolute maximum to be dispensed at one time is a week's supply. This will not guarantee that the patient is not stockpiling. Compliance can be monitored with blood levels, but there are no data on possible differences in therapeutic blood levels for depressed MPD patients, compared to people with nondissociative depressions.

If an antidepressant is to be tried, one of the newer antidepressants such as trazodone, with fewer anticholinergic side effects, should be considered. The problem with these medications is that they may be too expensive for many patients. As with all medications, unusual, idiosyncratic responses seem to be the norm in MPD. With the tricyclics, just getting to a therapeutic dosage is often an insurmountable problem. In the face of all these difficulties, I have suspended the prescribing of antidepressants to MPD patients altogether. I would rather admit someone and treat her psychotherapeutically as an inpatient than give an antidepressant. Exceptions to this approach are probably few in number.

This does not mean that prescribing antidepressants to MPD patients is necessarily incorrect. Others may have seen good responses on an anecdotal basis, but such reports would not convince me to change my prescribing habits.

I am a little bit more liberal with the antipsychotic medications, but I have almost entirely dropped them out of my MPD practice. I gave one patient a tardive dyskinesia from a prescription for 25 mg of thioridazine at bedtime. Her dyskinesia of the diaphragm and periocular muscles took a number of months to resolve. I think that antipsychotic medications can dampen down auditory hallucinations in some MPD patients through nonspecific sedation, which produces an illusion of specific antipsychotic effect in the undiagnosed patient.

The antipsychotics have numerous side effects to which MPD patients are often highly sensitive. They do not appear to have any specific antidissociative action. On our inpatient unit they have been entirely replaced by benzodiazepines, which are safer, more effective, less toxic, and easier to administer. I never prescribe nonbenzodiazepine sedatives to any patients, so won't discuss them. MPD is a strong relative if not an absolute contraindication to the prescription of barbiturates. In any case the barbiturates have only a handful of proper indications in medicine.

This leaves the benzodiazepines, which I think are wonderful medications. MPD patients are at high risk of benzodiazepine dependency and abuse prior to integration, and this is a constant problem. Anyone who is going to prescribe these medications to MPD patients must have a clear plan of action, in terms of dosage, rate of dosage increase, maximum dosage, and dosage reduction schedule. This need not be spelled out in obsessive detail in advance, but there should be a clear decision tree in place for each contingency.

I have found that MPD patients can tolerate enormous doses of benzodiazepines. Triazolam is usually prescribed at a dosage of 0.25 or 0.5 mg as a sleeping pill. I have taken an MPD patient from zero milligrams of triazolam at admission, up to 25 mg per day and back down to zero in a 3-month admission. I used triazolam because this was the benzodiazepine with which the patient felt most comfortable, and I used diazepam for the withdrawal period because of its long half-life. This regime was administered without excessive sedation or any physiological signs of withdrawal. Based solely on anecdotal experience with a small number of patients, I am impressed by the efficacy of benzodiazepines in easing anxiety, acting out, chaotic switching, and demanding behavior on the ward.

The contribution of the ultrahigh doses of benzodiazepine are difficult to assess because we have tightened up our contracting, ward management, and doctor–nurse teamwork extensively during the period of experimentation with high-dose benzodiazepines. Nevertheless my clinical impression is that they are very helpful.

For inpatient work the benzodiazepine of choice is lorazepam. This is because it is the only benzodiazepine that is well absorbed orally, sublingually, and intramuscularly. It is also inexpensive. If a patient is assessed as being unlikely ever to need an I.M. injection, then any of the medium- or long-acting benzodiazepines could be chosen. If short-acting agents are to be used, frequent administration around the clock will be required.

A typical prn order for lorazepam for an inpatient is 2–5 mg po or I.M. prn up to a maximum of 20 mg/24 hours. This can be given as often as every 30 minutes until the desired effect is achieved. A base dosage of lorazepam can be added to this prn regime at admission or later on depending on requirements. For instance a patient who receives at least 10 mg of prn lorazepam a day for the first week of admission should then get 10 mg/day in divided doses as a non-prn prescription. Prns are then added onto this as required, and the base dosage is worked upward from there. The goal is to have as few prns as possible with the maximum benefit. So far, I have started putting on the brakes when I get over 25 or 30 mg/day of lorazepam, but this may not be necessary in some cases.

In prescribing ultrahigh doses of benzodiazepines to inpatients, one has to calculate the fastest rate of withdrawal possible and the maximum dose one is willing to prescribe postdischarge. If this dosage is exceeded during admission, withdrawal to the discharge dose has to begin far enough in advance of the projected discharge date to be physiologically acceptable. It may be difficult to predict either the discharge date or the acceptable maximum outpatient dosage, but miscalculations may result in a prolonged admission just for dosage reduction.

In some cases I deliberately oversedate the patient with benzodiazepines if acting out, self-abuse, verbal abuse of staff, and/or assaultive behavior get too far out of line. This can be done with complete safety, whereas the neuroleptics are fraught with complications and side effects. Ten milligrams of IV diazepam can save the hospital several shifts of constant care nursing, the patient a lot of bruises, and the patient–staff relationship a lot of damage. In some instances I deliberately attempt to put the patient to sleep until the next morning. This can be achieved with IV diazepam supplemented by oral or I.M. lorazepam should the patient wake up during the night.

I think that IV diazepam is underutilized on inpatient units in favor of neuroleptics. It is extremely useful in anticholinergic delirium for instance, and for any behavioral disturbance that cannot be managed with more conservative techniques.

Most MPD patients experience panic attacks. It is usually not a realistic goal to strive for complete blockade of panic with benzodiazepines, as one would in a nondissociative panic patient (Walker, Norton, & Ross, in press). The goal is to reduce both general and panic anxiety to a level that allows psychotherapy to be productive. We usually try to get a lot of work done during an admission, so the pace is stepped up, and anxiety is inevitably greater. Medication is always an adjunct to the psychotherapy in cases being treated with active specific techniques.

Two types of clinical trials should be conducted in MPD: One is the blockade of outpatient panic with alprazolam or clonazepam. These two agents are effective in panic disorder. The point of the trial would be twofold: to determine the phenomenology of panic in MPD, and to compare the response to medication to that in the panic literature. The other trial is a comparison of lorazepam and placebo in inpatient treatment of MPD. For the inpatient trial the targets would be general anxiety, panic, spontaneous switching, involuntary seclusion, disturbed behavior in general, and global clinical impression. Some of these items would be difficult to measure, and in fact measures would have to be developed for some.

In view of Loewenstein, Hornstein, and Farber's (1988) report of the efficacy of clonazepam in the adjunctive treatment of posttraumatic stress symptoms in MPD, and because of its apparent efficacy in a variety of psychiatric disorders as well as its long half-life, clonazepam is probably the benzodiazepine of choice for a moderate-dose outpatient trial. As these authors point out, specific target symptoms must be identified and tracked, and a subgroup of responders must be identified within the entire MPD population.

I would recommend against a trial of tricyclic antidepressants in outpatient MPD panic because of the risk of overdose and difficulties with tolerance. There is probably room for study of high-dosage buspirone (Ross & Matas, 1987) as an alternative to inpatient lorazepam as well.

Another common problem in MPD is insomnia, which is often untreatable prior to integration and has numerous causes. I may use usual sedative doses of benzodiazepines for insomnia but do not go to ultrahigh doses for that purpose. I don't know of a good chemical solution to MPD insomnia but favor audiotapes as probably having the best cost–benefit ratio. Small doses of neuroleptics may induce dyskinesias, and small doses of tricyclics may cause surprisingly strong anticholinergic side effects. The physician should always be concerned about stockpiling for overdose even with prescriptions for small amounts.

The other medication that can be useful in MPD work is sodium amytal (Dysken, Chang, Casper, & Davis, 1979; Dysken, Kooser, Haraszti, & Davis, 1979; Hall, LeCann, & Schoolar, 1979; Marcos & Trujillo, 1978; Marcum, Wright, & Bissell, 1986; Naples & Hackett, 1978; Pellegrini & Putman, 1984; Perry & Jacobs, 1982; Ruedrich, Chu, & Wadle, 1985). Sodium amytal is a short-acting barbiturate that is administered intravenously. I mix 500 mg in 10 cc of sterile water and administer it at one cc per minute through a #23 butterfly needle. The medication is injected until the patient is drowsy, which may occur by 300 mg and almost always by 500 mg. I have never gone above 500 mg, although this can be done. The patient can usually walk well by one hour postinfusion, which means she can go for a cup of coffee, then go home, although she shouldn't drive until the next day.

If the medication is administered at 50 mg/minute, the only complication that occurs is excessive sedation. If it is administered too fast, the patient will stop breathing and die unless respiration is assisted. I always do my sodium amytal interviews on the ward, where a crash cart and hospital paging system are immediately available. If excess sedation occurs, it wears off quickly, and the interview is then continued. Patients concurrently taking monoamine oxidase inhibitors may require lower doses of sodium amytal and may get profoundly sedated by usual doses.

Sodium amytal is a chemical alternative to verbal hypnosis. It seems to overcome resistance more effectively, by massive anxiolysis combined with anesthesia of cortical function. Sodium amytal is an anesthetic. I use it to put resistance to sleep. I almost always try verbal hypnosis first, and I usually combine a verbal hypnotic induction with the administration of the sodium amytal. I time suggestions for warmth, relaxation, and hypnosis to the expected onset of the narcosis, which usually starts after 2–3 cc and is pronounced by 4–6 cc.

Another metaphor for sodium amytal is that it is a battering ram. It gets the therapist into the system. I use sodium amytal interviews in MPD for contacting difficult-to-call-out personalities and to gain access to otherwise hidden regions of the personality system. The drug can only be used a few times for such purposes because serial administration may create a craving for barbiturates. The physician may create a feedback loop in which the system will reveal an alter only if rewarded with barbiturate.

Like IV diazepam, sodium amytal is underutilized in general psychiatry. It can be used to switch a patient out of catatonia, panic, delirium, and an alter personality state. The effect on delirium is transient and really only switches the patient to a behaviorally quieter delirium. In fact sodium amytal can be thought of as a state switch facilitator. As interest in dissociation increases, there will be a resurgence of interest in sodium amytal in general psychiatry.

The following is an example of the use of sodium amytal in inpatient MPD work. The rapid-cycling patient referred to earlier in this section had been on the ward for months with no therapeutic progress. She had four identified personalities including the host, a helper, an abreacting child, and a self-abusive, grunting, spitting, biting state. She spontaneously switched to the child and abuser a number of times per day, but we were unable to effect any change in the behavior of either alter. Patient and staff were getting drained by the frequent physical restraint and the repeated X rays. On one occasion she was transported to emergency in a neck collar with spinal immobilization.

At a complete therapeutic impasse, I tried a sodium amytal interview not expecting much benefit. The interview readily opened the door into her polyfragmented personality system, and she reached integration within 5 months. Prior to sodium amytal she appeared to be untreatable, in fact worse than prior to diagnosis, and in need of permanent institutionalization. Sodium amytal should be considered when other techniques have failed or when temporary access to an unavailable alter is required. Anyone using the medication should be aware that artifactual dissociated states can be created that do not exist outside the narcosis. Any apparent alter contacted under sodium amytal should then be called out and worked with in the usual way in subsequent sessions.

Another caution is necessary. Sodium amytal is not truth serum. Patients can lie, confabulate, get lost in fantasy, and distort their memories under sodium amytal, just as under verbal hypnosis. Sodium amytal interviews are useful therapeutically only if they yield information that can be followed up on in later sessions.

The overall guiding principle for the use of medication in MPD is *first do no harm.* The greatest harm is probably done through prescriptions for antidepressants, neuroleptics, and benzodiazepines for undiagnosed patients thought to have schizoaffective disorder, atypical bipolar affective disorder, borderline personality with brief reactive psychosis, and similar diagnoses. In diagnosed MPD patients the cost–benefit calculations for medication can be complicated and can vary from time to time within one patient, and between patients. Medications are always adjunctive for patients receiving specific intensive psychotherapy.

If medication is to be prescribed, it should be given in an adequate dosage for an adequate duration, with adequate definition and tracking of target symptoms, as for any patient. There is no scientific justification for idiosyncratic regimes in the treatment of MPD, but there is room for a well-planned empirical trial of any medication, if there is a reasonable rationale for its use for a particular problem. No more rigorous guidelines are possible because no real research on the use of medications in MPD has been done. The use of medication in MPD has been reviewed by Barkin, Braun, and Kluft (1986).

PHYSICAL RESTRAINTS

The use of physical restraints in MPD has been discussed in detail by Walter Young (1986). I use them sparingly but have found them to be invaluable in a few cases. If physical restraint is required regularly or considerable physical effort is required, an inpatient admission is probably necessary. The only form of physical restraint we use on an outpatient basis is light holding that requires little effort.

There is a spectrum of physical restraint from gently restraining an alter's arm from scratching, to straitjacketing and sheeting in a seclusion room. It is easy to hold a child's arm gently but firmly, while repeating that self-abuse is not acceptable and that the office will be kept safe for everyone. Scratching, light headbanging, hitting oneself with a closed fist, and similar behavior can be explored for their motivation and meaning with minimal physical energy expenditure by the therapist. Such behavior may have components of abreaction, Schneiderian passivity experience, or testing of the therapist.

The next level of self-abusive behavior may require more vigorous holding by the therapist. The patient may flail aimlessly in a way that is easy to contain. Sometimes we have to work a bit hard in outpatient sessions to restrain a headbanging alter, and a therapist's hand may get bumped between head and wall. Once the behavior escalates above this level, though, there should be at least two therapists in every session, and an admission is imminent. A prolonged requirement for mild outpatient restraint may be an indicator of something wrong in the therapy.

On the inpatient unit severe acting out should be anticipated and planned for. We try to discourage it by selecting patients for therapy carefully, by contracting for no self-abuse or assault prior to or immediately upon admission, and by setting firm limits and clear consequences, including possible discharge. I am prepared to charge patients with assault or support nurses in making such charges if I feel it is warranted. MPD patients do not have a right to assault staff, and they do not *have* to assault staff. MPD is neither a necessary nor a sufficient cause of assault, in hospital or out. Many complex MPD patients with severe abuse histories pose no behavioral problems.

The best kind of physical restraint is preventive. When prevention fails, planning is the next best strategy. On the ward the most common form of physical restraint involves four or five male staff members carrying an acting-out patient to the seclusion room, where she receives an I.M. injection. Unpleasant as this is, and as much as it recreates the abuse scenario, without such physical restraint some patients cannot be treated. Many times we have used these restraints on MPD patients who have gone on to stable integration.

One preventive technique that often works is to start a psychotherapy session in the seclusion room with the patient sitting on the floor in the far corner from the door. The therapists stand near the door, which is just ajar. This provides for quick escape and locking of the door. Outside the room are three to five male staff. The patient, including the assaultive alter, is aware of this. The presence of muscle often prevents assaultive behavior and allows a treatment alliance to be formed with the persecutor, who can later be worked with easily in solo outpatient sessions. If the therapists have to exit the seclusion room quickly because of threatened assault, the patient may begin self-abuse, at which point the five male staff enter and pin her down. A drawback of this strategy is that it sets an expectation for acting out and communicates a perception of the alter as volatile and dangerous, which may become a self-fulfilling prophecy.

MPD is the only psychiatric disorder in which planned, contracted physical restraint is used. When we want to work with an alter who we know is going to be violent, we may contract with the host to enter physical restraints prior to calling the alter out. This may involve a straitjacket, wrist and ankle straps, or sheeting in varying combinations.

One patient had a personality called the Evil One who threatened to attack anyone who attempted to restrain her. She tried to break seclusion room windows with her fist and leave the ward. The patient was very big and strong and could have killed staff members by hand. The Evil One was coconscious with the host but not for a cooperative alter. In this case we had to contract for the physical restraint with the helper personality, plan the session, and then call out the helper several days later when the interview with the Evil One was to be done. We then placed the helper in a straitjacket and sheeted her to the bed.

The next step was to call out the host and explain the procedure to her. After this we talked with the Evil One, who was eventually integrated in a prolonged session held with full restraints. These sessions are difficult and draining for staff and would raise the ire of some patients' rights advocates. The more satanically abused patients enter the mental health system, the greater will be the need for such procedures. Some forensic MPD patients, such as serial killers, could probably be worked with only in a jail with armed guards, billy clubs, physical restraints, and large doses of medications, if at all. Anyone undertaking such work would have to give consideration to the potential risks for himself and his family.

I think that tighter contracting, high-dose benzodiazepines, firm limits, and more therapeutic experience have combined to reduce the need for inpatient physical restraint, but this is hard to determine because of variations in the individual patients admitted to our clinic. Physical restraints are a humane and effective treatment modality, without which some people would not have the possibility of curative treatment. As much as we try to present restraint in this manner as a technique for safety, patients are angry and frightened by it. Feelings about the restraint often must be talked about at length in calmer periods, including after discharge.

SUMMARY

These are the principal techniques of the middle and late phases of the treatment of MPD. The assignment of techniques to different phases is somewhat arbitrary and could have been done differently from the presentation in these three chapters. The main point to remember is that all the interventions described here must be embedded in a sound treatment based primarily on general principles of psychotherapy.

CHAPTER THIRTEEN

Other Therapeutic Considerations

This final chapter includes a number of techniques that are not related closely to specific phases of therapy or that are miscellaneous in nature. This does not imply that they are unimportant, but they do not form the core of treatment. In addition there is a discussion of integration and postintegration work.

Integration rituals are unique to the psychotherapy of multiple personality disorder (MPD). They can be done using whatever imagery, metaphor, and terminology is suitable for both patient and therapist. I have provided a detailed description of the kind of integration ritual I usually do, because most therapists do not know how to do this part of the work. Then the chapter concludes with some final remarks about the treatment and the patients.

HOSPITALIZATION

In our series of 236 cases of MPD (Ross, Norton, & Wozney, 1989), 74.6 percent had received inpatient psychiatric treatment. We did not ask specifically, but most of these admissions were probably prior to diagnosis. Once the diagnosis is made, inpatient admissions can be either elective or emergency. The two types of hospitalization can involve quite different purposes, goals, and treatment modalities. Like any effective medical intervention, hospitalization of the MPD patient can be beneficial or destructive. Some patients should be kept out of the hospital as much as possible, even in the face of severe suicidal ideation, because they regress quickly and extremely on the ward.

Many nonmedical therapists are envious of our Dissociative Disorders Clinic, which is a vertical service setup. If we admit our patients, I am their admitting psychiatrist, and they see their outpatient therapists throughout. When patients of other professionals get admitted onto our service, we are available as ongoing postdischarge consultants. However, having hospital beds can be a mixed blessing. Some patients jockey to get into the hospital, and this can become a tiresome power struggle that diverts attention from the therapeutic focus. The jockeying can lead to serious acting out. A nonmedical therapist with no admitting privileges can simply sidestep all of this.

In addition we have to turn down out-of-province referrals and referrals from other hospitals because of limited manpower. None of these decisions are easy. Working on an inpatient unit requires an extensive educational and process-oriented effort. Many hours have to be spent with nursing staff, administration, medical students, residents, psychologists, occupational therapists, social workers, chaplains, family members and friends, agency workers, medical consultants, and other professionals. Much of this would be nonbillable time for the private practitioner. For me it is time away from writing and research.

Anyone planning to begin intensive inpatient therapy of MPD should plan very carefully. Administration must support the project. The patients will place a major strain on the nursing budget, the emotional resources of nursing staff, and the therapists. This is especially true if the unit is a general adult psychiatric ward without much psychotherapy expertise. Few psychiatric nurses have hired on with a job expectation of working with MPD patients. Nurses could earn the same pay with far less emotional expenditure than occurs listening to abuse stories and restraining alters. In addition, they are at risk for compensation injuries. These are real and legitimate concerns.

A further complication occurs when ward staff have unresolved abuse histories of their own. Cycles of overinvolvement, rejection, staff acting out, disbelieving the diagnosis, and burnout may ensue. Nurses are most at risk for such reactions, not because they are more unstable than other staff, but because they have the most intensive and prolonged exposure to the patients. Nurses cannot retire to the quiet of the outpatient department after a session. Our nurses, after much trial by fire, now function at a high level as MPD specialists and are expert at switching alters, providing supportive care, setting limits, and reading the dynamics of a situation.

Splitting is a major issue, as Braun (1986a) has pointed out. Splitting occurs within the patient, between patient and staff, staff and staff, other patients and other staff, in fact in all imaginable combinations and permutations.

Without processing by staff, chaos will occur. Patients will attempt to recreate the abusive environment of childhood, just as they do in their personal relations outside the hospital. I can't emphasize enough the need to meet and talk, meet and talk, meet and talk. The MPD psychiatrist can expect to be the repository of large amounts of negative displaced affect. All of this can stimulate serious reconsideration of career planning. As the nurses point out, I get to publish and give papers, all they get is to go home bruised and tired.

In profit-driven hospitals in the United States, MPD patients may become sought-after if they are covered by insurance plans. There are many MPD patients, and they often need long admissions. In a universal health care scheme such as we have in Canada, profit doesn't come into play. Our services are limited by financial resources, though. We never have enough adult beds, there are too few staff, and there are too few psychotherapists.

A small team can handle only a small number of MPD inpatients at a time. With trained nurses, me, a half-time resident, a full-time nurse, and a social worker we can handle two MPD cases at a time with reasonable comfort, given our research and other commitments. Three stretches us. At four some of us would start burning out within a few months, depending on who was doing the most work, and all would be emotionally blunted and detached from work within 6 months. To handle more patients, more full-time staff and more specialist nurses would be required.

I strongly recommend that anyone starting up an MPD inpatient unit begin with one elective admission of a patient who doesn't act out too much. The only exceptions should be for experienced groups who have received major funding to set up a specialty unit. The problems tend to increase exponentially with the number of patients, because of staff fatigue. We have found that some patients interact badly and others beneficially. Some MPD patients who are higher functioning can bring up the general tone of the other patients, whereas ones who are particularly prone to splitting, manipulation, and acting out can bring the tone down.

Some MPD patients spend a lot of time with MPD copatients, some stick to themselves. When two or three acting-out patients are on the ward at the same time, a behavioral contest for therapist and nursing attention can begin. Much of this is based on legitimate need in the middle of difficult psychotherapeutic work, but some is not. There is no general rule of thumb about how MPD patients are going to affect each other on the ward.

We expect our patients to follow regular ward guidelines and procedures. They do not have special rooms, they eat with the other patients, and the consequences for unacceptable conduct are generally the same as for other patients. Switching is not allowed out on the unit, and child alters are not allowed to be in executive control outside sessions. If spontaneous switching occurs, it is dealt with quickly, and the patient is moved out of the public area as soon as possible.

We also specify the times and amount of intensive psychotherapy as much as possible. For most patients we limit the intensive psychotherapy to specified sessions with the OPD therapists and the primary nurse. All other nursing staff are available for supportive and general nursing care only. This arrangement limits unrealistic demands for nursing time, reduces switching, and results in better organized therapy. These rules are tighter, the greater the need for behavioral control.

The elective admissions are usually planned in order to do a specific piece of psychotherapeutic work. They are positive events. We might learn from an alter of a new set of horrific abuse memories, for instance, and judge in consultation with the alters that the host personality could not handle them on an outpatient basis. Another common indication is to work intensively with a persecutor who might act out on an outpatient basis. This is most likely to happen when the therapy is breaking through the facade of meanness to the persecutor's pain. Emergency admissions, on the other hand, are usually for suicidal ideation, suicide attempts, or internal chaos and anxiety.

Kluft (1984a) has provided guidelines for inpatient management of MPD with which I largely agree. Especially on the ward, MPD patients must be managed as well as treated. I disagree with Kluft on the advisability of a private room because I think it increases the specialness of the patient, encourages autism, reduces grounding in the present, and is in any case impossible most of the time on most units. A seclusion room can function as an elective time-out room if required. I agree with Kluft that the patient should be called whatever she wants to be called at any given time, with a proviso: In public on the ward all alters must answer to the same name and call themselves by the same name.

We have found that MPD patients readily accept the need to act "like normal people" on the ward and that this procedure does not cause internal resentment or rebellion of major proportions. We place a high value on rules, limits, and control on the ward and are much more laissez faire and relaxed in the outpatient department.

The goal of the elective admission is to deal with the therapeutic issue as fully as feasible, then discharge to immediate continued work on an outpatient basis. These two agenda items have to be traded off against each other. The goal of the emergency admission is to do whatever has to be done to discharge the patient safely as soon as possible. In all cases there is an emphasis on early discharge. It is healthier to be out of the hospital than in, and psychiatric wards are not good places in which to seek sanity.

I have discussed many of the principles and techniques of inpatient work in previous sections on medications, physical restraint, treatment contracting, and so on. It is only in inpatient work that a medical degree is required. Comprehensive inpatient treatment requires medical investigations, medications, a physical examination, and smooth function within the hospital administrative hierarchy. Hospital wards are places in which doctors are required. Without a doctor in charge, the admission may run into problems because of dysfunction in the team. This is largely an artifact of the organizational structure of the modern hospital. A psychologist could as easily be the team leader with a physician as consultant on medications, but this is not how hospitals work.

Inpatient treatment of MPD could be done in a nonmedical institution without nurses or doctors if medications were not required. This might be the best environment for adolescents and would probably be the most cost-effective. In Canada there is no possible way for such an institution to be funded at present. In a nonmedical setting, the patients would be clients or residents, not patients.

The inpatient treatment of MPD is a more intense version of outpatient work, in which greater structure and team coordination is required. The inpatient experience can be very countertherapeutic when the primary therapist is not allowed on the ward to do therapy, the psychiatrist does not believe in MPD, and the institution acts out against the patient and therapist. This is a scenario that gets played out repeatedly across North America. One reviewer advised me, in commenting on a paper I had submitted to a journal, that he had recently instructed nurses not to talk to a patient when she was acting as if she was someone else. The reviewer noted that the "MPD behavior" stopped in 3 days. This was sensitive and informed care compared to the experience of some MPD patients.

So far we have not had a problem with a nondissociative patient trying hard to be diagnosed as having MPD. However, other patients do complain to their doctors about not getting as much time with them as my MPD patients get with me. This causes complications for the other physicians in our department, who have supported my research assistant out of group earnings for 3 years. Subspecialists in other institutions may not receive this kind of response from colleagues. Our experience in our first year of inpatient treatment of MPD is summarized in a paper (Ross, 1987) and touched on in another (Ross, 1988).

GROUP THERAPY

There are only a few publications on the group therapy of MPD (Caul, 1984; Coons & Bradley, 1985; Caul, Sachs, & Braun, 1986). At the Dissociative Disorders Clinic we have little experience with it. Most workers in the field agree that MPD patients do not do well in heterogeneous groups. A possible exception might be incest survivor groups with skilled leaders. Those who recommend group therapy see it as adjunctive.

The first time we held a group meeting for MPD, three patients attended. One, an inpatient, had to go to the seclusion room after the session. One went home and vomited. The third missed most of the session in trance or because a child was out. This experience with patients who we thought were well-prepared convinced us not to explore this modality further.

Groups that appear to be successful have a number of requirements. All patients have to be in individual therapy, and there are usually two group therapists. A minimum of switching is allowed. Patients should not be acting out severely outside therapy and should not be in ongoing abusive relationships if possible. This reduces the number of candidates considerably. Groups must meet for an extended period of time and usually have a fixed enrollment except for replacement of dropouts.

A variant of group therapy is the inner group therapy described by David Caul (1984). This basically involves getting the alters to hold conferences and talk with each other, with the therapist acting as a facilitator. Inner group therapy is a cultivated and refined variant of a technique that is probably used to some extent by all therapists. The concepts and strategies of non-MPD group therapy can be brought to bear on the internal group in such work.

The same holds true for family therapy of the adult MPD patient (Millette, 1988; Sachs, Frischholtz, & Wood, 1988; Schwartz, 1987). It is adjunctive but may provide a useful conceptualization of the inner system of the patient. The denial and scapegoating of any abuse family are present in the MPD case, with the added complication of amnesia in other family members, including at times the perpetrator.

The one type of group we do have experience with is the MPD support group. Our patients do not have a structured support group that holds meetings but a number of them provide each other with considerable support. They are mostly patients who have met on the ward. The group members do not discuss abuse memories with each other or call out each others' alters. I find this informal group to be healthy and helpful. Any minor complications it may have caused are more than made up for by the benefits.

I won't comment further on the group therapy of MPD because of my lack of experience and the lack of operationalization of the modality in the literature. I don't wish to leave the impression that I am devaluing MPD groups, though, because some are conducted by experienced therapists with a thorough knowledge of the MPD literature. One can't be an expert on everything.

INVOLVING SPOUSES AND FRIENDS

Spouses may participate intensively in therapy or may take an informed and supportive but less involved stance. Either can be satisfactory. The spouses need to know the diagnosis and to be educated as to etiology, treatment, and prognosis. In a nonmedical community-based agency that does not work diagnostically, the same thing can be achieved without using the terms MPD or personality.

Formal marital therapy can be conducted using the principles that the therapist would use with a nondissociative couple. These must be supplemented with the techniques described in this book if alters are to be worked with directly during the marital sessions. One approach is to wait until the patient is further along in individual therapy and can work coconsciously in marital therapy without overt switching. We have worked with couples in which the nondissociative spouse, always the male in our practice, has been at ease with switches in session and at home. Often the switching has been going on at home for a long time.

Complex transactional sequences can occur. For instance a hypersexual alter can come out and engage in highly provocative and pleasurable foreplay. Suddenly there is a switch to a crying child. The erotically aroused husband begins to comfort the child, hoping for a quick switch back to the sexual state, when suddenly a hostile verbally abusive alter takes executive control and berates him. Then the host returns, amnesic for the entire sequence and wonders out loud what is wrong with the husband.

In some couples there can be both subtle and overt reinforcement of the dissociation by the husband. This can result in an ongoing incestuous relationship between child alters, who perceive the husband as a paternal protector, and the husband, even if the couple has intercourse only when the wife's adult alters are in control. Complex recreations of the original incestuous family can occur. These are compounded if the husband also has MPD. In such a couple, both spouses would require individual therapy, and couple therapy would also be necessary. Communication and coordination between the therapists would take a lot of time and processing in such a case.

Most of the time the approach taken is educational and supportive work with the husband and intensive individual therapy with the wife. Supportive husbands can also act as effective cotherapists, but doing so may blur their role as husbands and so must be managed carefully. Another marital relationship is one in which overt physical, sexual, and emotional abuse is occurring: This must be dealt with at a practical level as in any nondissociative abusive marriage. One has to track the patient's cognitions and abuse dynamics across the personality system.

Working with couples includes working with homosexual marriages. These are neither inherently wonderful nor inherently unhealthy. Lesbian lovers can be controlling, infantalizing, or abusive. They can also be tender, understanding, and truly intimate. There are extrinsic problems in the homosexual marriage because of society's response to such relationships, but the same basic relationship issues seem to occur as in the heterosexual relationship. The MPD member of the couple has trouble with touch, trust, intimacy, orgasm, limits, dependency, and other issues, whether the other member is male or female.

In one case we had a specific problem that was preventing us from discharging the patient. The patient spontaneously awoke every morning with a psychotic alter in executive control. With a little difficulty, the host could be called out by the nursing staff, and the patient could go to work on a day pass. We had to teach her roommate, with whom she had a platonic relationship, to call out the host, and this had to be practiced on overnight passes before discharge was possible. Spouses, friends, and relatives can be taught specific skills like this depending on the problems that must be solved.

Friends can act as part-time nursing staff both inside and outside the hospital on an informal basis. Their main function is to be there and to be themselves. I tell friends and relatives this and emphasize that their role is not to be the primary therapist. Church groups and other support groups may help avoid admissions by caring for the patient during a rough period. These support people sometimes need a little help to adjust their degree of involvement and to strike a balance between supporting and smothering. Patients need to stand on their own as much as possible.

Some friends provide useful observations and hypotheses about what is going on at different stages of therapy. I treat the friends as intelligent observers who are with the patient far more than I am and who have made extensive in vivo observations. The MPD therapist is usually delighted to get such help, on the grounds that $N + 1$ heads are better than N heads. Consistent with the spirit of the rest of the therapy, spouses, relatives, and friends are involved in the therapy in a flexible, pragmatic fashion. Most of the time I don't feel any need to attempt extremely fancy systemic interpretations of what is going on.

In some cases relatives can be involved briefly to give the therapist a firsthand feel for the family system. The main work of therapy can then be to help the patient extricate herself from an untreatable, abusive extended family. In some cases working with the relatives might involve assisting the police in their arrest. There is no standard stance or goal that is taken with every case. I am sketching this aspect of the therapy in brief because it is based primarily on common sense and general principles of therapy. Some cases require only individual sessions with the patient and no direct contact with anyone else.

The only way of working with relatives and friends that makes me uncomfortable is the situation in which the wife doesn't want her husband to know she is in therapy. I don't think I could contract for such a therapy except in unusual circumstances, if ever, and I never have. The therapy contract would create a pathological secret, for one thing, and it would make it impossible to deal effectively with crises. If the patient ever had to be admitted, how would that be done? The secret would be very unfair for the husband. Particularly for a male therapist seeing a female patient, such secrecy would give "seeing" the wrong meaning.

The more community supports and informed loved ones can be involved in the patient's life, the better for the patient, therapist, and therapy.

WORKING WITH SOCIAL SERVICE AGENCIES

In our paper on treatment techniques (Ross & Gahan, 1988b) we list 20 techniques used in the treatment of MPD. These overlap with Braun's (1986a) general principles of treatment. It may seem odd that techniques and principles overlap, but it is not really odd because the techniques are the principles in operation. One of the headings we discuss is working with social service agencies, which is a vital part of treatment.

The treatment of MPD is unavoidably systemic in nature. The intrapsychic pathology is a family of conflicted selves, the disorder arises in abusive families, team treatment of the individual is widely used, friends and relatives are often involved in the therapy, and wider social systems play their roles in the patient's life. As I outlined in previous chapters, MPD is embedded in the general history of Western culture, which makes it a systemic illness in the broadest sense.

We have worked with a variety of social agencies in a variety of ways for a variety of purposes. Early on, following considerable thought, I decided after consultation with my patients to treat the diagnosis of MPD like any other psychiatric diagnosis with regard to filling in welfare forms, tax benefit applications, insurance forms, and related paperwork. I also bill the health care system for MPD, not adjustment disorder, depression, personality disorder, or some other cover-up diagnosis. This may seem like a small point, but it is part of destigmatizing MPD and treating it like a legitimate diagnosis.

On the other hand, I also withold the diagnosis if I think it might cause trouble for the patient, and there is no need for the institution involved to have it. In such cases I make a generic, vague statement about psychotherapy for emotional difficulties arising from childhood. In letters of this kind I make a point of saying that the patient does not have a psychotic illness, does not require long-term medication, and has a disorder from which she can potentially make a full and permanent recovery. I may offer to send update reports in the future. All of this is not very different from procedures with other disorders.

A good deal of interaction with social agencies is instrumental and straightforward. In addition we provide consultation and educational services to those who request them. These can take the form of written assessments, sending papers, workshops, seminars, or telephone consultations. Our attempts to establish research liaisons with community agencies have resulted in some interesting problems that illustrate the difficulties of working with social service agencies.

In trying to get access to agency clients for structured interviews, we have experienced a full range of responses from open cooperation and support to extreme suspiciousness and guardedness. I have learned a lot about the gulf between a male hospital-based psychiatrist and female community-based feminist therapists. So far I have been unsuccessful at converting died-in-the-wool antilabeling feminist therapists to the view that it is *good* to diagnose MPD and treat it with specific techniques.

Many community-based nonmedical therapists have large collections of horror stories about their clients' involvement with psychiatry. Trying to get untarred can be impossible when one is a white male middle-class hospital-based doctor. Sometimes the ideological gulf is just too big, and one cannot collaborate clinically with such agencies, or vice versa. This can cause trouble for patients/clients/unlabeled persons who are involved with psychiatrists/therapists/unlabeled persons on both sides of the ideological Grand Canyon.

Successful collaboration has to be based on multidisciplinary mutual respect. By far the best glue is a case. So far we have worked in a case-oriented fashion with clergy, lawyers, psychiatrists, nonmedical therapists, police, general practitioners, educators, parents, children, siblings, friends, spouses, homemakers, and crisis home workers; this is probably an incomplete list. Much of what we do is education about the nature of MPD, its etiology and treatability. We make a point of debunking superstition about having more than one person in a single body and advocate a common sense understanding. We always use the starting point of a traumatized child trying to cope.

We have not had to deal with the malicious undermining of treatment that specialists in other cities have experienced. Nevertheless there is plenty of psychopathology in our social systems in Winnipeg. Particularly in postintegration therapy, part of the work is helping patients develop street smarts and survival skills for a disturbed world. Patients often have the fantasy at the beginning of therapy that once they are integrated, they can become "happy" people in a fair and nonabusive world. Patients have to wake up about this if they are going to get better.

The therapy can get complicated when social systems already predisposed to abusive acting out are stimulated by the patient's projective identification. Projective identification is an elaboration of projection. Projection occurs when a person projects her own feelings onto someone else, thereby getting rid of them. A typical example of projection is the person who is angry at the police, then projects her anger onto them and no longer feels angry, but thinks the police are hostile toward her. When this is taken to a delusional extreme, it results in the patient thinking that the CIA are spying on her and planning to kill her. This is a psychotic delusion that is uncommon in MPD.

In projective identification, projection is taken a step further. By body language, manipulation, and other subtle techniques, the patient engineers the situation so that the other person actually experiences the projected feelings. Not only that, the other person is manipulated into acting out those feelings on the patient. The therapist is angry at the patient and treats her abusively, while the patient feels no anger and takes the role of the victim.

The MPD therapist can become a manager of both the pathological defenses of the patient and the pathological counter acting out of a social system. This can easily degenerate into an endless wild-goose chase after primary fault. It can also be very difficult to tell who is acting out and who has a legitimate complaint—patient or agency—in a given conflict. One's primary responsibility is to the patient. In these situations I am supportive and confrontational with the patient and tend to play my cards a bit close to my chest with the agency.

One patient showed excellent judgment by voluntarily placing her child in temporary foster care during her most unstable midphase of treatment. When she tried to get her daughter back, the child protection agency showed good judgment by suggesting a phased-in return of the child: The daughter valued the stability and consistency of the foster home and felt pressured and threatened by the mother to return. The outcome was an adversarial confrontation between mother and agency, which deteriorated into lengthy legal proceedings.

The mother saw the agency as solely interested in its own power and control, and the agency saw the mother as blinded to her daughter's best interest by her own neediness. Neither side was completely right, and neither was completely wrong. My therapeutic role, as I defined it, was to point out repeatedly that the core issue was the relationship between mother and daughter, to which all other parties were accessory; to supportively confront the mother about how she undermined her own best interests; to advocate a calm, strategic stance by the mother; to cultivate a nonadversarial relationship with the daughter and social service agency; to write various clarifying letters to the agency and the mother's lawyer; to facilitate family therapy for the mother and daughter with a nonagency therapist chosen by the mother and approved by the agency; to object to a request in an agency affidavit that the mother's therapy with me, which had been voluntary for 2 years, be ordered by the court as a condition of access; and to maintain my role as the mother's doctor.

Private practice therapists should give careful consideration to how many such cases they can take on, because of the large amount of nonbillable time involved. There is no general formula for how to work with social service agencies. Sachs (1986) has reviewed the different types of agencies with which patient and therapist can be involved. These can include Alcoholics Anonymous (AA) groups, vocational rehabilitation programs, homemaker agencies, Parents Anonymous, incest groups, assertiveness training groups, the clergy, peer networks, vocational counselors, and countless other resources. We have also worked with police, lawyers, child care agencies, universities and colleges, welfare agencies, insurance companies, other hospitals, foster parents, employers, and nonacademic training programs.

Sometimes the therapist's role is to "cool out" the agency worker who is overreacting to the diagnosis of MPD in one way or another, so that the worker can carry on at her normal level of competence. Workers on crisis telephone lines often spend extensive periods of time talking with suicidal MPD patients. We recommend to them, if the patient gives her diagnosis over the phone, that they clearly state that they have no expertise in MPD, that they aren't qualified to talk to the other personalities, and that such discussion should be left for the therapist. Crisis line workers, to the extent possible, should talk with MPD patients just as they would with other callers. Their main responsibilities are to provide support and common human understanding and to send an ambulance in emergencies.

We've found that crisis line workers sometimes have trouble setting limits with MPD patients. Limits are necessary and can be hard to enforce when child alters are abreacting over the phone. Bowers et al's (1971) guideline of staying within your expertise is the main recommendation we make.

In summary, involvement with social service agencies is a frequent part of the treatment of MPD. It can vary from the writing of simple, routine letters to complicated management of acting-out agencies and patients. Throw a disturbed therapist into this mix, and you can have a major problem.

EDUCATING COLLEAGUES

Educating colleagues is both rewarding and frustrating. The most receptive medical personnel are medical students, followed by junior residents, senior residents, nonpsychiatric physicians, junior psychiatrists, and senior psychiatrists, in that order. Among mental health professionals, those who catch on the fastest are therapists who work with abuse victims, hypnotherapists, and therapists who are used to thinking systemically. In my experience the resistance to MPD is greatest in biological reductionists, but creative biological psychiatrists are likely to be more receptive than many psychoanalytic psychotherapists.

There are a number of reasons why it is important to attempt to educate colleagues about MPD. In no particular order, these include the following: to reduce the number of false negative diagnoses of MPD; to increase the likelihood of patients receiving specific treatment; to reduce the amount of iatrogenic illness caused by false negative diagnoses; to increase awareness of dissociation in general psychiatric patients; to garner support for research and clinical work; to ensure availability of informed coverage during absences; to increase awareness of the role of childhood trauma in psychiatric illness; to foster a climate of openness to new ideas, perceptions, and interventions; to reduce hostility to oneself and one's patients; to create a supportive rather than a stressful climate for the work of therapy; to stimulate a more concerted effort to reduce the transmission of abuse to subsequent generations; to emphasize the importance of phenomenology; and to illustrate to colleagues that accepted clinical folklore, such as the rarity of MPD, can be grossly erroneous.

Education takes many forms but is primarily by example. As more publications appear and as more colleagues in more centers make the diagnosis, it will become an inescapable fact that MPD is not rare.

Two major cognitive errors seem to create much of the resistance to MPD. The first is the erroneous idea that the diagnosis provides the patient with a license for irresponsibility. Many colleagues appear to believe that MPD therapists collude with a patient cop-out: "I am not morally, psychologically, or legally responsible because another personality did it." This is a variant of "The devil made me do it." The idea that there are other people inside is a dissociative delusion. The purpose of therapy is to remove the delusion, not reinforce or collude with it.

If I diagnose paranoid schizophrenia, does that mean I am condoning, rewarding, or reinforcing disturbed delusional behavior? No one seems to accuse me of that, in my general psychiatric work. What's the problem with MPD, then? My procedure is to state explicitly an expectation of responsibility, to outline the consequences of unacceptable behavior, to explain that I view the patient as one divided person, and to set a treatment goal of integration. The fixity of the idea that diagnosing MPD means licensing irresponsibility, in the face of a complete lack of supporting evidence, makes me think that it is a defensive rationalization rather than a real reason for distrusting the diagnosis.

The second cognitive error is the theory of iatrogenesis. This idea has caught on without a single supporting study. There is not a single documented case of iatrogenic false positive MPD reported in the entire world literature. Yet iatrogenesis is probably the most widely accepted etiological theory in psychiatry. Because these two major cognitive errors about MPD are so widespread and entrenched, yet supported by virtually no evidence, I can't help but suspect that they are defenses covering a deeper resistance.

The drive to disavow the reality of the child abuse, maintain the abusive status quo, and punish the victim, is very powerful in North America. As a profession, over the last 100 years, psychiatry has been ambivalent about where it stands on abuse. Within psychiatry there have been strong drives to maintain the status quo, with its power relations and economic benefits. Although child abuse is in theory acknowledged as common and pathological, it is often left out of clinical inquiries or its importance is downplayed. I don't think the profession has really got the reality of childhood trauma in North America into focus yet. Feminists will suggest that the profession doesn't want to: I wouldn't go that far, but I wonder about it.

The education of colleagues can take many forms, one of which is writing books. Papers, seminars, workshops, public talks, rounds, consultations, informal conversation, media appearances and interviews, clinical supervision, and demonstrations of diagnostic interviews are all important. Allowing trainees to sit in as observers and cotherapists is extremely important.

It is in fact essential for trainees to sit in on the psychotherapy of MPD. I think it's also healthy for the therapy. Many psychoanalytic therapists cultivate as intense a transference as possible with their patients. In our work we try to dilute the transference, which is too intense. A trainee cotherapist is one effective way of doing this. There is no way that a trainee can learn the nuances and subtleties of interaction and intervention by hearing about them. The importance of having more well-trained therapists is greater than the possible negative effects for the patient in most cases. More important, I think the positive benefits for the patient outweigh the negative. If nothing else, there is the principle that two heads are better than one.

Having two therapists allows for scheduling sessions when one therapist is away; keeps both therapists on their toes and working; diffuses the transference in a healthy way; guards against excessive intimacy and privacy in the therapy; dilutes and defuses countertransference problems, allowing therapists to share the load; debunks mythology about the staffperson as supertherapist and trainee as bumbling beginner; provides the patient with an ongoing second opinion; gives the patient a message that she is important and worthy of double the usual professional input; normalizes and destigmatises MPD by making it "public" in a small and safe way; demonstrates that the staffperson is a teacher and therefore is likely providing good care; generally guards against eccentric therapy; and allows for the possibility of sessions with both therapists separately, thereby increasing the amount of therapy time per week.

I don't see any serious disadvantages to cotherapy, other than the possibility that some patients or alter personalities will feel as if they are guinea pigs for educating residents. This concern can be dealt with in a straightforward way, as part of an abuse dynamic and as a resistance to more serious work. I doubt that the presence of a trainee cotherapist introduces new issues into therapy. It probably modifies or accentuates some conflicts that would have to be dealt with anyway. Once the work is underway, the fact that the cotherapist is a trainee or is less experienced fades out of consideration.

Trainees and colleagues can sit in on sessions in the emergency department, on the ward, or in the outpatient office. In my experience, a number of medical students have done excellent psychotherapeutic work with MPD inpatients, work that has included calling out alters. One student did a number of supervised integrations after observing me do some, during a 2-month rotation in psychiatry. If medical students can put in chest tubes, do bone marrow aspirations, and deliver babies, there is no reason they can't integrate alter personalities. However the treatment of MPD will never be properly described by the medical aphorism: See one, do one, teach one.

It is a logistic and economic fact that most treatment of MPD will have to be carried out by individual therapists in private offices. This doesn't mean that the therapy needs to be excessively private, intimate, and overheated. I think that cotherapy with trainees offers a corrective to a psychotherapy *zeitgeist* which has gone too far in the direction of privacy. This is true for the treatment of MPD and for much psychotherapy generally.

BILLING PROCEDURES

I don't think there is anything about billing procedures for MPD that is specific for the disorder. However there are problems. In Canada we have universal free medical care. The only cap on billing for psychotherapy is that it is limited to 90 minutes per patient per day. The trouble is that psychiatrists are the only MPD psychotherapists covered by the health care system, other than a few nonmedical therapists on salary in institutions. This means that MPD patients do not have universal access to specific psychotherapy, because there are very few psychiatrists providing it. For many patients and therapists in Canada, fees are as much an issue as they are in the United States.

I am supervising the treatment of a woman who has been extensively involved with the mental health system, with a misdiagnosis of schizophrenia, for 25 years beginning in early adolescence. She has had countless admissions. She will reach integration. She pays a fee of five dollars per session, and I do not charge for the supervision. The treatment will save the health care, welfare, and legal systems tens of thousands of dollars. The government would pay if I provided the treatment but will not pay even after special application when I am supervising. This makes no economic or therapeutic sense. Society will get a cured patient and a trained therapist out of the deal.

MPD provides new meaning to the phrase *being sane in insane places*. Generally I think that MPD patients should pay or not pay according to the same rationales that would apply to any patient. I don't see any grounds for making a special case based on the MPD. The main problem is that the treatment will never be for a short term. There is just no way of getting in and out, curatively, in 10 sessions. Even though successful treatment can be extremely cost-effective for society overall, the patient and therapist have to wring funds out of dissociated fragments of society that are not in communication or cooperation with each other. The only other source is the patient's pockets, which are usually shallow. I think it is important for private practice therapists to avoid becoming economic martyrs on behalf of poor MPD patients. Unfortunately this leaves the patients in the lurch and repeats the neglect that contributed to formation of their condition in the first place.

INTEGRATION AND POSTINTEGRATION WORK

Development of new behaviors and coping skills, integration, and postintegration work are in a single section because they are inextricably intertwined with each other. Integration has several meanings. In one sense integration is a slow process that occurs throughout therapy and for years afterward. In another sense, no one is ever integrated, because we all experience some degree of dissociation and have all been highly dissociated at some time in our lives. Every woman who has given birth has been in an extreme dissociative state, for instance.

Integration can also be used as a synonym for fusion. I don't use the term fusion, purely out of personal preference. Integration in the sense of fusion is a discrete event that occurs at a specific moment in time. It is the joining together of two or more alter personalities to become a single entity. Integrations can occur spontaneously, they can be done deliberately by the patient by herself, or they can be assisted by the therapist using a verbal integration ritual. Usually I integrate only two personalities at a time, and usually one of the alters is integrated into the host.

In polyfragmented cases, large numbers of fragments can be integrated at one time to form a more substantial unit. These integration products can in turn be integrated together. This process produces increasingly large fusion products that are eventually combined to form a single self. The process resembles a flow chart with a number of levels: There are several hundred entities at the top, increasingly fewer at each level down, and one person at the bottom.

Integrations are intrinsically meaningful psychic events. I remember in medical school having the opportunity to be first assist on a number of intracranial procedures and second assist on several others. During one procedure the neurosurgeon commented that the moment of peak intensity for him was always the moment of penetration of the dura. I had observed this in the previous operations. The operating theater is usually a sociable place, with technical conversation, as well as bantering and tension-relieving interchanges. The atmosphere is casual, informal, and secular.

In the moments surrounding the opening of the dura, which is a tough membrane surrounding the brain and separating it from the skull, there is a change. Everyone becomes quiet, serious, and still. There is a quietness like the one in small medieval English churches. I saw more devotion and religion in those moments than I have ever experienced in a church service. Then the living brain is revealed, and the operation proceeds. People are moving around and talking again. The penetration of the dura is the only moment of this nature I have experienced in medicine, except for MPD integration rituals.

It's not that the participants impose an *idea* of religion on the event. The event has an intrinsic solemnity and depth of its own, which the observing mind attends to and experiences as significance and meaning welling up from a common human reality. It is not a matter of theory or interpretation. The integration of two personalities is both a death and a birth. There is sorrow in it, and joy. Many alters experience integration with the host as a death, and the host may mourn the loss of her companion.

The actual integration ritual is like a marriage or a burial. It is a landmark for a long process that has finally come to fruition. Before two alters can integrate they must do a large amount of work. They have shared memories, feelings, hopes, and fears, and have learned to work together for the benefit of the whole organism. The actual integration is a ceremony like a wedding, which formalizes everything that has gone before, through the courtship, engagement, practical planning, and all the subtle adjustments and negotiations required to get from the couple's first meeting to the wedding day.

Like a wedding, the integration is the end of one phase and the beginning of another. It is not the end of the therapy. Integrations can be done with any vocabulary and within any framework suitable for patient and therapist.

For me, a purely secular vocabulary doesn't do the ritual justice. This too is analogous to a wedding: I live in a secular world, speaking a secular language, but we had the King James version for my wedding, and I will have it at my funeral. Even with the death of Christianity as the organizing principle of Western civilization, there is still only one text for the most important landmarks in life.

Because of this feeling about the therapy, I do integration rituals as follows, having spoken with both alters to confirm that they are ready:

> You're sitting there now as comfortable and relaxed as possible, with your eyes closed, and I want you to listen to the sound of my voice. Just concentrate on the sound of my voice, and that will help you to relax and prepare for the joining together of Susan and Mary. Even now as I speak that process of joining together has begun, Mary opening herself to Susan, and Susan opening herself to Mary, so that the two can be blended and joined together to become one.

> Nothing will be lost and nothing will be left behind. Everything that was separate before as a separate Mary and a separate Susan will be blended and joined together to become the one Susan, stronger, more whole, and better able to deal with life. Nothing is lost and nothing is left behind. All the thoughts, and memories, and feelings, all the skills, and attitudes that were separate before are blending and joining together to become one Susan.

> Nothing is lost and nothing is left behind. Susan opening herself to Mary and Mary opening herself to Susan, blending and joining together to become one, a complete and final blending and joining together of everything that was separate before. We are thankful that there was a separate Mary and a separate Susan, because we know that helped Susan survive. All the others that are listening and watching give thanks now, thanks that Mary was there to help, and thanks that she is now blending together with Susan to make a stronger, more complete personality.

> That blending and joining together is becoming complete now. A complete and final blending and joining together of everything that was separate before, complete and final and permanent. Nothing left behind and nothing lost. And for this we give thanks. In a few moments now when you open your eyes it will be Susan who is there, and there will never again be a separate Susan and a separate Mary like there was before. There will be the one Susan, stronger, more whole, more complete, and ready for the work that is to come, ready for the future integrations. And this is good.

> In just a moment now you will open your eyes and the integration of Mary and Susan will be complete. As soon as you're ready, you can open your eyes.

The patient then lifts up her head, opens her eyes, and I ask her how it went. If she says that it went well, I congratulate her and ask her what she would like to do now. Some patients like to be alone for a while, some want a hug or a handshake, others may just get on with business. Usually the integration ritual is a little bit longer than the text I have just given because of more repetition. So far no patients have complained that they dislike this style of integration ritual.

Not every integration is successful. This is almost always because the integration was premature and not enough preparatory work had been done. A number of different technical difficulties can occur. Sometimes the integration goes only halfway, and the alter gets stuck. In this situation the host can't take full executive control and neither can the alter. This has happened a couple of times and I have dealt with it by repeating the ritual or by reversing it, finding out what the problem was, solving it, and redoing the integration later.

Sometimes alters will leave a few traumatic memories behind. I've never been able to figure out where these are housed. They seem to be held in a general, nonpersonified unconscious and eventually leak back at some point or may have to be retrieved hypnotically. Various forms of interference can occur, consisting of noise, depersonalization, fear, or other phenomena that break the alters' concentration and discourage them from proceeding. This is usually due to an alter in the background who hasn't been worked with. Sometimes an alter can get cold feet at the last minute, so the integration has to be postponed.

Some therapists make use of trial integrations to desensitize the alters to the process. I don't do this, but I don't see anything wrong with it. I prefer to do all the necessary work and shoot for permanent fusion the first time, but some patients may not accept this approach. Trial integrations can be set up on a try-it-and-see basis for minutes, hours, or days. The patient can be instructed to deintegrate whenever she feels the need to. This procedure involves some tricky trance logic, because an alter may make an independent decision to deintegrate, which shouldn't be possible if she is integrated. When the therapist asks the deintegrated alter how this happened, she may explain "I just decided" without being bothered by the logical difficulties. The same applies to the spontaneous breakdown of what were intended to be permanent fusions.

Kluft (1988e) has been writing about integration throughout the 1980s, and summarizes and extends his work in his most recent paper. This paper is mandatory reading for everyone treating MPD. It builds on his earlier writings on the topic (Kluft 1982, 1984a, 1985e, 1985g, 1986b). I have reviewed his criteria for integration in Chapter 9. He has written more extensively than anyone else on the reasons for relapse following complete integration (Kluft, 1986b).

Patients can relapse for a number of reasons. These are the most common causes:

1. Discovery of a new layer of alters (not a true relapse)
2. Reemergence of previously fused alters
3. Creation of new personality states

4. Feigned integration (also not a true relapse)
5. Recurrence of dissociative symptoms short of emergence of a full alter personality

One reason for relapse is further trauma. If the trauma is severe enough, the drive to reactivate an old personality or create a new one will be strong. In fact it is unethical to remove all the dissociative defenses in the face of known ongoing trauma, because dissociation is such an effective and protective strategy. Any form of trauma can be involved, including death, illness, assault, natural disaster, accident, or war.

Patients may feign integration to please the therapist or to attempt a flight into health. The reasons for this have to be discussed and resolved. Sometimes dissociation can be resorted to transiently out of habit, when the patient could have coped nondissociatively with a little more effort. Some patients may not be prepared to face life as single people and will deliberately relapse with no intention of doing further work. In practice this could be the best possible outcome for some people. I would personally count such an adaptation as a partial treatment success. Probably the most common cause of relapse is that not enough work has been done in therapy. This need not be anyone's fault or a sign of procedural error by the therapist.

When new alters are discovered, this can be discouraging; when there are many layers, it can begin to seem like an infinite regression. The therapist starts wondering if he is being conned and whether the new layer really has been there since childhood. One patient was like this and just wasn't getting better in the way she should have been. The reasons for the layers, and the failure to recover, became clear when ongoing sexual abuse was finally disclosed. One should suspect ongoing trauma in a patient who isn't getting better at the expected pace.

I am not going to write in detail about postintegration therapy because it is the therapy of an individual person. The techniques and principles are no longer dissociative or subspecialist in nature. Much of the work is educational and supportive, with a lot of strategizing and problem solving. Sometimes the integrated patient will have a personality disorder, and sometimes not. If the patient still has posttraumatic stress disorder following an apparently complete integration, this may be a clue to the existence of another layer of alters, and further trauma.

The first year following integration is tough. The patients say that in many ways it is tougher than having MPD, and it is certainly very different. When things get difficult, the patient can't check out and let somebody else handle it. The issues of therapy tend to be broad and general, including sexuality, religion, work, relationships, and common human problems. Upgrading, retraining, and further education may be embarked on. Some relationships will have to end, some will be strengthened, and new ones will form. Some of the abuse-derived cognitive errors will need further work.

As far as termination is concerned, I don't have any fixed time frame, and I don't think there can be one. I personally wouldn't see someone for 5 years postintegration, because I think others could do that work as effectively, freeing me for dissociative work with someone else. I wouldn't have any problem with a year. Between those two markers I go on a case-by-case basis. This is distinct from follow-up, which goes on forever. I am referring to active supportive therapy, which can be hard work. The intensity is not the same as that of the active phase though. In the best arrangement the patient terminates with the therapist through a gradual reduction in frequency of sessions.

Some patients may have ongoing concurrent psychiatric disorders after the remission of their dissociative disorder. This could include anxiety, affective disorders, or other problems, which then might require treatment in their own right. Again, no special skills in dissociative work will be required. Watching a formerly severely impaired individual function effectively and derive personal fulfillment from her life is a wonderful reward for the therapist. The recovered MPD patient sounds a hopeful note in a disturbed civilization.

CONCLUSION

There are many little tricks and techniques derived from a welter of schools of psychotherapy, which can be used in the treatment of MPD. Every therapist will have his own favorite interventions. The only one I want to comment on in conclusion is chatting. I was struck at a workshop by comments on chatting made by a fellow Canadian, Marlene Hunter. I was also struck by how appreciative the audience was of her remarks. Chatting is an excellent therapeutic intervention. I regularly make small talk with my patients, at various points throughout the sessions. I also tell jokes.

Therapy needs to be a natural conversation between two people. It shouldn't be fettered with unnecessary and rigid rules and rituals. Chatting is good not just for a minute or two at the beginning of a session, but as a normal experience for the patient. It creates comfort and trust, and it gives the patient the experience of being regarded as a normal human being. When I reflect on which of my endowments I think is most valuable for my patients, I usually conclude that it is my ability to see them as normal people. The best thing a therapist can do for a patient is spontaneously and naturally perceive her as a normal human being. This is how I see MPD patients. For me, switching is a natural, normal, human thing to be doing if you have been severely traumatized as a child.

The phenomenology of MPD is not weird or bizarre if the therapist knows how to view it. The patients are intensely human, and their symptoms are rooted in thousands of years of history. This perception is best communicated in idle, everyday conversation, which is therefore not idle. The most important technique in the treatment of MPD is not to be caught up in techniques. Although it is necessary to talk about the person with MPD as a patient or client, the important thing is that she is neither. The MPD patient is a suffering human being who can get better with the correct form of psychotherapy.

Multiple Personality Disorder in the 1990s

The decade beginning in 1980 saw an exponential increase in the diagnosis of multiple personality disorder in North America (Kluft, 1988a). This was accompanied by a similar increase in the volume of professional literature, and in conferences, workshops, meetings, journals, newsletters, self-help groups, and professional organizations. Yet mainstream psychiatry has remained relatively untouched by the resurgence of interest in dissociation. What lies ahead in the 1990s? Will dissociation fall into obscurity again, as it did early in the century? Or will it become an established part of mainstream psychiatry, psychology, and social work, on an equal footing with anxiety and depression?

It is likely that the latter outcome will occur, but only in part. I believe, based on preliminary research and clinical experience, that MPD is roughly as common as schizophrenia in North America. I think that 2 to 5 percent of psychiatric inpatients in North America in the late 1980s have full, classical MPD, in addition to a substantial number of outpatients who have the disorder. I think that MPD, psychogenic amnesia, and atypical dissociative disorder together are as common in the general population as the anxiety disorders. There may be good epidemiological evidence to this effect before the turn of the century.

I also believe that dissociation is a prominent aspect of most mental disorders, just as anxiety and depression occur in schizophrenia, dementia, substance abuse, and other conditions without a formal affective or anxiety disorder being present. In some patients psychogenic amnesia may occur as a secondary feature of mania, just as classical panic attacks can occur during a primary depression. By the year 2000 dissociation will no longer occupy an obscure corner of the diagnostic system, and the general psychiatrist will have to be knowledgeable about it to practice effectively.

Over the next 10 years a substantial body of clinical research on dissociation will be generated. This will focus on phenomenology, etiology, treatment, and a variety of psychological measures and diagnostic instruments. Standard psychiatric diagnostic interviews will have to incorporate MPD and psychogenic amnesia in order to be regarded as comprehensive.

If MPD does enter the mainstream in this way, there will be a number of effects on general psychiatry. One is that the funding for psychotherapy outcome research will increase. MPD will provide a much-needed counter to the excessive enthusiasm for biological psychiatry that has dominated the 1980s. From a public health, societal point of view, biological psychiatry has been overfunded in the last decade. MPD will also stimulate new thinking in biological psychiatry.

The study of dissociation could result in revised exclusion criteria for clinical drug trials, studies of biological markers, family studies, and a wide range of research in mental health. It is not good science to fail to mention severe, chronic childhood trauma as either an inclusion or exclusion criterion for a drug study. I suspect that much of the research data gathered over the last 20 years in psychiatry is contaminated by the inclusion of unrecognized dissociative individuals. Exclusion of these people from heterogeneous groups of subjects would result in cleaner data.

MPD will help bring the focus in psychiatry back onto real childhood events that would be disturbing and traumatic for anyone who experienced them. The field has expended too much energy on excessively complex, untestable theories and models. A willingness to diagnose and treat MPD on the part of psychiatry might also help bridge the chasm between hospital-based physicians and community-based nonmedical mental health professionals. MPD is a severe mental illness that is nonbiological, and it therefore straddles both domains.

Specialists in dissociative disorders should look outside psychiatry to establish collaborations with anthropologists and other researchers who have studied phenomena related to North American clinical MPD (Kenny, 1981). For instance, ideas of Luria (1968/1987, 1972/1987) and Jaynes (1976) could stimulate interesting approaches to clinical dissociation, especially disorders of memory and auditory hallucinations.

If dissociation remains in relative obscurity and the above predictions turn out to have been wishful thinking, that will be unfortunate because MPD patients reveal what is happening to many children in our society. We should not forget what so many men and women with MPD have remembered in therapy.

The Dissociative Disorders Interview Schedule

DEMOGRAPHIC DATA FOR DISSOCIATIVE DISORDERS INTERVIEW SCHEDULE

Age: [ ] [ ]

Sex: Male=1   Female=2   [ ]

Marital   Single=1 Married{including common-law}=2
Status: Separated/Divorced=3   Widowed=4   [ ]

Number of
Children: {If no children, score 0}   [ ] [ ]

Occupational
Status: Employed=1   Unemployed=2   [ ]

Have you been in jail in the past?
Yes=1   No=2   Unsure=3   [ ]

Physical diagnoses currently active   [   ]
                                                   [   ]
                                                   [   ]

Current and past diagnoses must consist of written diagnoses
provided by the referring physician or available in the patient's
chart (give DSM-III codes if possible, if not write DSM-III diagnoses
to the right of the brackets).

Psychiatric diagnoses currently active [   ]
                                       [   ]
                                       [   ]

Psychiatric diagnoses currently in   [   ]
remission   [   ]
                                             [   ]

The Dissociative Disorders Interview Schedule is reprinted with permission of Colin Ross and Sharon Heber. Copyright 1988. For additional information on the DDIS see Ross, Heber, Norton & Anderson (1989a).

CONSENT FORM FOR DISSOCIATIVE DISORDERS

INTERVIEW SCHEDULE

I agree to be interviewed as part of a research project on dissociative disorders. Dissociative disorders involve problems with memory.

I understand that the interview contains some personal questions about my sexual and psychological history, however, all information that I give will be kept confidential. My name will not appear on the research questionnaire.

I understand that the information I give to the interviewer will not be available to any doctor, authority, therapist, case worker or other person involved with me. My answers will have no direct effect on how I am treated in the future.

I understand that the overall results of this research will be published and these results will be available to authorities or therapists involved with me.

I understand that the interviewer and other researchers cannot offer me treatment and cannot intervene on my behalf with any authorities or therapists involved with me.

I understand that the purpose of this interview is for research and that I cannot expect any direct benefit to myself other than knowing that I have helped the researchers understand dissociative disorders better.

I agree to answer the interviewer's questions as well as I can but I know that I am free not to answer any particular questions I do not want to answer.

Although I have signed my name to this form, I know that it will be kept separate from my answers and that my answers cannot be connected to my name, except by the interviewer and his/her research colleagues.

I also understand that I may be asked to participate in further dissociative disorders interviews in the future, but that I will be free to say no. If I do say no this will have no consequences for me and my authorities or therapists involved with me will not be told of my decision not to be interviewed again.

Signed: _____   Witness: _____

Date: _____

/df

Dissociative Disorders Interview Schedule

Questions in the Dissociative Disorders Interview Schedule must be asked in the order they occur in the Schedule. All the items in the Schedule, including all the items in the DSM-III diagnostic criteria for dissociative disorders and borderline personality disorder must be enquired about. The wording of the questions should be used exactly as written in order to standardize the information gathered by different interviewers. The interviewer should not read the section headings aloud. The interviewer should open the interview by thanking the subject for his/her participation and then should say:

"Most of the questions I will ask can be answered Yes, No or Unsure. A few of the questions have different answers and I will explain those as we go along."

1. Somatic Complaints

    1. Do you suffer from headaches? Yes=1 No=2 Unsure=3 [ ]

        If subject answered No to question 1, go to question 3:

    2. Have you been told by a doctor that you have migraine
        headaches?   Yes=1 No=2 Unsure=3 [ ]

    Interviewer should read the following to the subject:

    "I am going to ask you about a series of physical symptoms now.
    To count a symptom as present and to answer yes in these
    questions, the following must be met:
    a) no physical disorder has been found to account for the
        symptom.
    b) the symptom does not occur only during a panic attack.
    c) it caused you to take medicine (other than aspirin),
        see a doctor, or alter your life style."

    Interviewer should now ask the subject, "Have you ever had the following physical symptoms for which doctors could find no physical explanation?"

    The interviewer should review criteria a-c for the subject immediately following the first positive response to ensure that the subject has understood.

    3. Abdominal pain (other than when menstruating)
        Yes=1   No=2   Unsure=3   [ ]
    4. Nausea (other than motion sickness)
        Yes=1   No=2   Unsure=3   [ ]
    5. Vomiting (other than motion sickness)
        Yes=1   No=2   Unsure=3   [ ]
    6. Bloating (gassy)
        Yes=1   No=2   Unsure=3   [ ]
    7. Diarrhea
        Yes=1   No=2   Unsure=3   [ ]
    8. Intolerance of (gets sick on) several different foods
        Yes=1   No=2   Unsure=3   [ ]
    9. Back pain
        Yes=1   No=2   Unsure=3   [ ]

10. Joint pain
    Yes=1   No=2   Unsure=3   [ ]
11. Pain in extremities(the hands and feet)
    Yes=1   No=2   Unsure=3   [ ]
12. Pain in genitals other than during intercourse
    Yes=1   No=2   Unsure=3   [ ]
13. Pain during urination
    Yes=1   No=2   Unsure=3   [ ]
14. Other pain (other than headaches)
    Yes=1   No=2   Unsure=3   [ ]
15. Shortness of breath when not exerting oneself
    Yes=1   No=2   Unsure=3   [ ]
16. Palpitations (a feeling that your heart is
    beating very strongly)
    Yes=1   No=2   Unsure=3   [ ]
17. Chest pain
    Yes=1   No=2   Unsure=3   [ ]
18. Dizziness
    Yes=1   No=2   Unsure=3   [ ]
19. Difficulty swallowing
    Yes=1   No=2   Unsure=3   [ ]
20. Loss of voice
    Yes=1   No=2   Unsure=3   [ ]
21. Deafness
    Yes=1   No=2   Unsure=3   [ ]
22. Double vision
    Yes=1   No=2   Unsure=3   [ ]
23. Blurred vision
    Yes=1   No=2   Unsure=3   [ ]
24. Blindness
    Yes=1   No=2   Unsure=3   [ ]
25. Fainting or loss of consciousness
    Yes=1   No=2   Unsure=3   [ ]
26. Amnesia
    Yes=1   No=2   Unsure=3   [ ]
27. Seizure or convulsion
    Yes=1   No=2   Unsure=3   [ ]
28. Trouble walking
    Yes=1   No=2   Unsure=3   [ ]
29. Paralysis or muscle weakness
    Yes=1   No=2   Unsure=3   [ ]
30. Urinary retention or difficulty urinating
    Yes=1   No=2   Unsure=3   [ ]
31. Long periods with no sexual desire
    Yes=1   No=2   Unsure=3   [ ]
32. Pain during intercourse
    Yes=1   No=2   Unsure=3   [ ]

Note: If subject is male ask question 33 and then go to
question 38. If female, go to question 34.

33. Impotence
    Yes=1   No=2   Unsure=3   [ ]
34. Irregular menstrual periods
    Yes=1   No=2   Unsure=3   [ ]
35. Painful menstruation
    Yes=1   No=2   Unsure=3   [ ]

36. Excessive menstrual bleeding
    Yes=1   No=2   Unsure=3   [ ]

37. Vomiting throughout pregnancy
    Yes=1   No=2   Unsure=3   [ ]

38. Have you had many physical problems or a
    belief that you have been sick, for several
    years beginning before the age of 30?
    Yes=1   No=2   Unsure=3   [ ]

39. Have you ever had any other serious physical
    symptoms for which doctors could find no
    explanation?
    Yes=1   No=2   Unsure=3   [ ]

II. Substance Abuse

40. Have you ever had a drinking problem?
    Yes=1   No=2   Unsure=3   [ ]

41. Have you ever used street drugs extensively?
    Yes=1   No=2   Unsure=3   [ ]

42. Have you ever injected drugs intravenously?
    Yes=1   No=2   Unsure=3   [ ]

43. Have you ever had treatment for a drug or alcohol
    problem?
    Yes=1   No=2   Unsure=3   [ ]

III. Psychiatric History

44. Have you ever had treatment for an emotional
    problem or mental disorder?
    Yes=1   No=2   Unsure=3   [ ]

45. Do you know what psychiatric diagnoses, if any,
    you have been given in the past?
    Yes=1   No=2   Unsure=3   [ ]

46. Have you ever been diagnosed as having:
    a)   depression   [ ]
    b)   mania   [ ]
    c)   schizophrenia   [ ]
    d)   anxiety disorder   [ ]
    e)   other psychiatric disorder (specify)   [ ]
    Yes=1   No=2   Unsure=3

    _____

If subject did not volunteer a diagnosis for 46 (e) go
to question 48.

47. **If the subject volunteered diagnoses for (e), did the subject volunteer any of the following:**
   a) psychogenic amnesia   [ ]
   b) psychogenic fugue   [ ]
   c) multiple personality disorder   [ ]
   d) depersonalization disorder   [ ]
   e) atypical dissociative disorder   [ ]
   Yes=1   No=2   Unsure=3

48. Have you ever been prescribed psychiatric medication?
   Yes=1   No=2   Unsure=3   [ ]

49. Have you ever been prescribed one of the following medications?
   a) antipsychotic   [ ]
   b) antidepressant   [ ]
   c) lithium   [ ]
   d) anti-anxiety or sleeping medication   [ ]
   e) other (specify) _____   [ ]

   Yes=1   No=2   Unsure=3

50. Have you ever received ECT, also known as electroshock treatment?
   Yes=1   No=2   Unsure=3   [ ]

51. Have you ever had therapy for emotional, family, or psychological problems, for more than 5 sessions in one course of treatment?
   Yes=1   No=2   Unsure=3   [ ]

52. How many therapists, if any, have you seen for emotional problems or mental illness in your life?
   Unsure=89   [ ] [ ]

   If subject answered No to both questions 51 and 52, go to question 54.

53. Have you ever had a treatment for an emotional problem or mental illness which was ineffective?
   Yes=1   No=2   Unsure=3   [ ]

IV. Major Depressive Episodes

The purpose of this section is to determine whether the subject has ever had or currently has a major depressive episode.

54. Have you ever had a period of depressed mood lasting at least two weeks in which you lost interest or pleasure in all or almost all usual activities and past times and felt depressed, blue, hopeless, low, down in the dumps or irritable?
   Yes=1   No=2   Unsure=3   [ ]

319

If subject answered No to question 54, go to
question 62.

If subject answered Yes or Unsure, interviewer
should ask,"During this period did you experience
the following symptoms nearly every day for at
least two weeks?"

55. Poor appetite or significant weight loss (when
    not dieting) or increased appetite or significant
    weight gain.
    Yes=1   No=2   Unsure=3   [ ]

56. Sleeping too little or too much.
    Yes=1   No=2   Unsure=3   [ ]

57. Being physically and mentally slowed down, or
    agitated to the point where it was noticeable
    to other people.
    Yes=1   No=2   Unsure=3   [ ]

58. Loss of interest or pleasure in usual activities,
    or decrease in sexual drive.
    Yes=1   No=2   Unsure=3   [ ]

59. Loss of energy; fatigue.
    Yes=1   No=2   Unsure=3   [ ]

60. Feelings of worthlessness, self-reproach, or
    excessive or inappropriate guilt.
    Yes=1   No=2   Unsure=3   [ ]

61. Difficulty concentrating or difficulty making
    decisions.
    Yes=1   No=2   Unsure=3   [ ]

62. Have you ever had recurrent thoughts of death,
    suicidal thoughts, wishes to be dead, or
    attempted suicide?   [ ]
    Yes=1   No=2   Unsure=3

    If you have made a suicide attempt, did you:
    a) take an overdose   [ ]
    b) slash your wrists or other body areas   [ ]
    c) inflict cigarette burns or other self injuries [ ]
    d) use a gun, knife, or other weapons   [ ]
    e) attempt hanging   [ ]
    f) use another method   [ ]
    Yes=1   No=2   Unsure=3

63. If you have had an episode of depression as described
    above, is it: [ ]
    currently active, first occurence =1
    currently in remission   =2
    currently active, recurrence   =3
    uncertain   =4
    due to a specific organic cause   =5

V. Schneiderian First Rank Symptoms

64. Have you ever experienced the following:
    Yes=1   No=2   Unsure=3

    a) voices arguing in your head   [ ]

    b) voices commenting on your actions   [ ]

    c) having your feelings made or controlled by
       someone or something outside you   [ ]

    d) having your thoughts made or controlled by
       someone or something outside you   [ ]

    e) having your actions made or controlled by
       someone or something outside you   [ ]

    f) influences from outside you playing on or
       affecting your body such as some external force
       or power   [ ]

    g) having thoughts taken out of your mind   [ ]

    h) thinking thoughts which seemed to be someone
       else's   [ ]

    i) hearing your thoughts out loud   [ ]

    j) other people being able to hear your thoughts
       as if they're out loud   [ ]

    k) thoughts of a delusional nature that were very
       out of touch with reality   [ ]

If subject answered No to all Schneiderian symptoms, go to
question 67, otherwise, interviewer should ask:

"If you have experienced any of the above symptoms are
they clearly limited to one of the following:"

65. Occurred only under the influence of drugs, or
    alcohol.   [ ]
    Yes=1   No=2   Unsure=3

66. Occurred only during a major depressive episode.   [ ]
    Yes=1   No=2   Unsure=3

VI. Trances, Sleepwalking, Childhood Companions

67. Have you ever walked in your sleep?
    Yes=1   No=2   Unsure=3   [ ]

If subject answered No to question 67, go to question 69.

68. If you have walked in your sleep, how many times,
    roughly?
    1-10=1   11-50=2   >50=3   Unsure=4   [ ]

321

69. Have you ever had a trance-like episode where you stare off into space, lose awareness of what is going on around you and lose track of time?
Yes=1   No=2   Unsure=3   [ ]

If subject answered No to question 69, go to question 71.

70. If you have had this experience, how many times, roughly?
1-10=1   11-50=2   >50=3   Unsure=4   [ ]

71. Did you have imaginary playmates as a child?
Yes=1   No=2   Unsure=3   [ ]

If subject answered No to question 71, go to question 73.

72. If you had imaginary playmates, how old were you when they stopped?   Unsure=0   [ ] [ ]

If subject still has imaginary companions score subject's current age.

VII. Childhood Abuse

73. Were you physically abused as a child or adolescent?
Yes=1   No=2   Unsure=3   [ ]

If subject answered No to question 73, go to question 78.

74. Was the physical abuse independent of episodes of sexual abuse?
Yes=1   No=2   Unsure=3   [ ]

75. If you were physically abused, was it by:
a)   father   [ ]
b)   mother   [ ]
c)   stepmother   [ ]
d)   stepfather   [ ]
e)   sibling   [ ]
f)   male relative   [ ]
g)   female relative   [ ]
h)   other male   [ ]
i)   other female   [ ]
Yes=1   No=2   Unsure=3

76. If you were physically abused, how old were you when it started?   Unsure=89. If less than 1 year, score 0.   [ ] [ ]

77. If you were physically abused how old were you when it stopped?   Unsure=89. If less than 1 year, score 0. If ongoing score subject's current age.   [ ] [ ]

322

78. Were you sexually abused as a child or adolescent?
    Sexual abuse includes rape, or any type of unwanted
    sexual touching or fondling that you may have
    experienced.
    Yes=1   No=2   Unsure=3   [ ]

    If the subject answered No to question 78, go to
    question 85. If the subject answered Yes or Unsure
    to question 78, the interviewer should state the
    following before asking further questions on sexual
    abuse:

    "The following questions concern detailed examples
    of the types of sexual abuse you may or may not have
    experienced. Because of the explicit nature of these
    questions, you have the option not to answer any or
    all of them. The reason I am asking these questions
    is to try to determine the severity of the abuse that
    you experienced. You may answer Yes, No, Unsure or
    not give an answer to each question."

79. If you were sexually abused was it by:
    a)   father   [ ]
    b)   mother   [ ]
    c)   stepfather   [ ]
    d)   stepmother   [ ]
    e)   sibling   [ ]
    f)   male relative   [ ]
    g)   female relative   [ ]
    h)   other male   [ ]
    i)   other female   [ ]
    Yes=1   No=2   Unsure=3   No Answer=4

 If subject is female skip question 80. If male skip
 question 81.

80. If you are male and were sexually abused, did the
    abuse involve:
    a)   hand to genital touching   [ ]
    b)   other types of fondling   [ ]
    c)   intercourse with a female   [ ]
    d)   anal intercourse with a male - you active   [ ]
    e)   you performing oral sex on a male   [ ]
    f)   you performing oral sex on a female   [ ]
    g)   oral sex done to you by a male   [ ]
    h)   oral sex done to you by a female   [ ]
    i)   anal intercourse - you passive   [ ]
    j)   enforced sex with animals   [ ]
    k)   pornographic photography   [ ]
    l)   other (specify) _____   [ ]
    Yes=1   No=2   Unsure=3   No Answer=4

81. If you are female and were sexually abused, did the
    abuse involve:
    a)   hand to genital touching   [ ]
    b)   other types of fondling   [ ]
    c)   intercourse with a male   [ ]

```
        d)   simulated intercourse with a female          [ ]
        e)   you performing oral sex on a male             [ ]
        f)   you performing oral sex on a female           [ ]
        g)   oral sex done to you by a male                [ ]
        h)   oral sex done to you by a female              [ ]
        i)   anal intercourse with a male                  [ ]
        j)   enforced sex with animals                     [ ]
        k)   pornographic photography                      [ ]
        l)   other (specify) _____       [ ]
        Yes=1      No=2      Unsure=3      No Answer=4
```

82.   If you were sexually abused, how old were you when
      it started? Unsure=89. If less than 1 year,
                    score 0.   [ ] [ ]

83.   If you were sexually abused, how old were you when
      it stopped? Unsure=89. If less than 1 year,
                    score 0. If ongoing score subject's
                    current age.   [ ] [ ]

84.   How many separate incidents of sexual abuse were you
      subjected to up until the age of 18?
      1-5=1   6-10=2   11-50=3   >50=4   Unsure=5 [ ]

85.   How many separate incidents of sexual abuse were you
      subjected to after the age of 18?
      0=1   1-5=2   6-10=3   11-50=4   >50=5
                                          Unsure=6   [ ]

VIII. Features Associated with Multiple Personality Disorder

For questions 86-95, if subject answers Yes, ask subject to
specify whether it is occasionally, fairly often or frequently,
excluding question 93.

86.   Have you ever noticed that things are missing from
      your personal possessions or where you live?
      Never=1   Occasionally=2   Fairly Often=3
      Frequently=4   Unsure=5   [ ]

87.   Have you ever noticed that there are things present
      where you live, and you don't know where they came
      from or how they got there? e.g. clothes, jewellery,
      books, furniture.
      Never=1   Occasionally=2   Fairly Often=3
      Frequently=4   Unsure=5   [ ]

88.   Have you ever noticed that your handwriting changes
      drastically or that there are things around in
      handwriting you don't recognize?
      Never=1   Occasionally=2   Fairly Often=3
      Frequently=4   Unsure=5   [ ]

89. Do people ever come up and talk to you as if they
    know you but you don't know them, or only know
    them faintly?
    Never=1   Occasionally=2   Fairly Often=3
    Frequently=4   Unsure=5   [ ]

90. Do people ever tell you about things you've done or
    said, that you can't remember, not counting times you
    have been using drugs or alcohol?
    Never=1   Occasionally=2   Fairly Often=3
    Frequently=4   Unsure=5   [ ]

91. Do you ever have blank spells or periods of missing
    time that you can't remember, not counting times you
    have been using drugs or alcohol?
    Never=1   Occasionally=2   Fairly Often=3
    Frequently=4   Unsure=5   [ ]

92. Do you ever find yourself coming to in an unfamiliar
    place, wide awake, not sure how you got there, and not
    sure what has been happening for the past while, not
    counting times when you have been using drugs or
    alcohol?
    Never=1   Occasionally=2   Fairly Often=3
    Frequently=4   Unsure=5   [ ]

93. Are there large parts of your childhood after age
    5 which you can't remember?
    Yes=1   No=2   Unsure=3   [ ]

94. Do you ever have memories come back to you all of a
    sudden, in a flood or like flashbacks?
    Never=1   Occasionally=2   Fairly Often=3
    Frequently=4   Unsure=5   [ ]

95. Do you ever have long periods when you feel unreal,
    as if in a dream, or as if you're not really there, not
    counting when you are using drugs or alcohol?
    Never=1   Occasionally=2   Fairly Often=3
    Frequently=4   Unsure=5   [ ]

96. Do you hear voices talking to you sometimes or talking
    inside your head?
    Yes=1   No=2   Unsure=3   [ ]

If subject answered No to question 96, go to question 98.

97. If you hear voices, do they seem to come from
    inside you?
    Yes=1   No=2   Unsure=3   [ ]

98. Do you ever speak about yourself as "we" or "us"?
    Yes=1   No=2   Unsure=3   [ ]

99. Do you ever feel that there is another person or
    persons inside you?
    Yes=1   No=2   Unsure=3   [ ]

If subject answered No to question 99, go to question 102.

100. Is there another person or persons inside you
     that has a name?
     Yes=1   No=2   Unsure=3   [ ]

101. If there is another person inside you, does he
     or she ever come out and take control of your body?
     Yes=1   No=2   Unsure=3   [ ]

IX. Supernatural/Possession/ESP Experiences/Cults

102. Have you ever had any kind of supernatural
     experience?
     Yes=1   No=2   Unsure=3   [ ]

103. Have you ever had any extrasensory perception
     experiences such as:
     a) mental telepathy   [ ]
     b) seeing the future while awake   [ ]
     c) moving objects with your mind   [ ]
     d) seeing the future in dreams   [ ]
     e) deja vu (the feeling that what is happening to
         you has happened before)   [ ]
     f) other (specify) _____   [ ]
         Yes=1   No=2   Unsure=3

104. Have you ever felt you were possessed by a:
     a) demon   [ ]
     b) dead person   [ ]
     c) living person   [ ]
     d) some other power or force   [ ]
     Yes=1   No=2   Unsure=3

105. Have you ever had any contact with:
     a) ghosts   [ ]
     b) poltergeists (cause noises or objects
                      to move around)   [ ]
     c) spirits of any kind   [ ]
     Yes=1   No=2   Unsure=3

106. Have you ever felt you know something about past
     lives or incarnations of yours?
     Yes=1   No=2   Unsure=3   [ ]

107. Have you ever been involved in cult activities?
     Yes=1   No=2   Unsure=3   [ ]

X. Borderline Personality Disorder

Interviewer should state, "For the following eight questions,
please answer Yes only if you have been this way much of the time
for much of your life. Have you experienced:"

108.   Impulsive or unpredictable behavior in at least two
        areas that are potentially self-damaging, e.g., spending,
        sex, gambling, substance use, shoplifting, overeating,
        physically self-damaging acts.
        Yes=1   No=2   Unsure=3   [ ]

109.   A pattern in which many of your personal
        relationships tend to be intense, but unstable and
        short-lived.
        Yes=1   No=2   Unsure=3   [ ]

110.   Intense anger or lack of control of anger,
        e.g., frequent displays of temper, constant
        anger.
        Yes=1   No=2   Unsure=3   [ ]

111.   Feeling uncertain about your identity, which may
        include problems with self-image, self-awareness,
        sexual identity or career choice. e.g. because
        you feel uncertain about who you are, you may try
        to imitate different people in an attempt to
        discover which identity fits best for you.
        Yes=1   No=2   Unsure=3   [ ]

112.   Frequent mood swings: noticeable shifts from normal
        mood to depression, irritability or anxiety.
        Yes=1   No=2   Unsure=3   [ ]

113.   Feeling uncomfortable being alone, e.g. frantic
        efforts to avoid being alone, depressed when alone.
        Yes=1   No=2   Unsure=3   [ ]

114.   Physically self-damaging acts, e.g., suicidal
        gestures, self-mutilation, recurrent accidents
        or physical fights.
        Yes=1   No=2   Unsure=3   [ ]

115.   Chronic feelings of emptiness or boredom.
        Yes=1   No=2   Unsure=3   [ ]

XI. Psychogenic Amnesia

116.   Have you ever experienced sudden inability to recall
        important personal information or events that is too
        extensive to be explained by ordinary forgetfulness?
        Yes=1   No=2   Unsure=3   [ ]

If subject answered No or Unsure to question 116, go to 118.

117.   If you answered Yes to the previous question was the
        disturbance due to a known physical disorder (e.g.,
        blackouts during alcohol intoxication, or stroke)?
        Yes=1   No=2   Unsure=3   [ ]

XII. Psychogenic Fugue

118. Have you ever experienced sudden unexpected travel
away from your home or customary place of work, with
inability to recall your past?
Yes=1   No=2   Unsure=3   [ ]

119. Have you ever assumed a new identity (partial
or complete)?
Yes=1   No=2   Unsure=3   [ ]

If subject answered No to one or both of questions 118
and 119, go to 121.

120. If you answered Yes to both the previous two questions
was the disturbance due to a known physical disorder?
(e.g., blackouts during alcohol intoxication, or
stroke)?
Yes=1   No=2   Unsure=3   [ ]

XIII. Depersonalization Disorder

121. Interviewer should say, "I am now going to ask you
a series of questions about depersonalization.
Depersonalization means feeling unreal, feeling as
if you're in a dream, seeing yourself from outside
your body or similar experiences."

a) Have you had one or more episodes of
depersonalization sufficient to cause
problems in your work or social life?
Yes=1   No=2   Unsure=3   [ ]

b) Have you ever had the feeling that your feet
and hands or other parts of your body have
changed in size?
Yes=1   No=2   Unsure=3   [ ]

c) Have you ever experienced seeing yourself
from outside your body?
Yes=1   No=2   Unsure=3   [ ]

d) Have you ever had a strong feeling of unreality
that lasted for a period of time, not counting
when you are using drugs or alcohol?
Yes=1   No=2   Unsure=3   [ ]

If subject did not answer Yes to any of 121 a-d,
go to question 123.

122. If you answered Yes to any of the previous questions
about depersonalization was the disturbance due to
another disorder, such as Schizophrenia, Affective
Disorder, Organic Mental Disorder (mental disorder
with a physical cause), Anxiety Disorder, or epilepsy?
Yes=1   No=2   Unsure=3   [ ]

XIV. <u>Multiple Personality Disorder - NIMH Research Criteria, consisting of DSM-III (123-125) criteria plus two further criteria (126-127)</u>

     123. Have you ever felt like there are two or more very different personalities within yourself, each of which is dominant at a particular time?
         Yes=1   No=2   Unsure=3   [ ]

     If subject answered No to question 123, go to question 128.

         Do any of the following apply to you?

     124. The personality or part of you that is dominant at any particular time controls your behavior.
         Yes=1   No=2   Unsure=3   [ ]

     125. Each individual personality is complex and has behaviors and social relationships that are not shared by the other personalities.
         Yes=1   No=2   Unsure=3   [ ]

     126. Two or more different personalities, have been in control of your body on at least three separate occasions.
         Yes=1   No=2   Unsure=3   [ ]

     127. Some type of amnesia or combination of types of amnesia exists among the different personalities.
         Yes=1   No=2   Unsure=3   [ ]

XV. <u>Atypical Dissociative Disorder (Dissociative Disorder Not Otherwise Specified)</u>

     128. **Subject appears to have a dissociative disorder but does not satisfy the criteria for a specific dissociative disorder. Examples include trance-like states, derealization unaccompanied by depersonalization, and those more prolonged dissociated states that may occur in persons who have been subjected to periods of prolonged and intense coercive persuasion (brainwashing, thought reform, and indoctrination while the captive of terrorists or cultists).**
         Yes=1   No=2   Unsure=3   [ ]

XVI. <u>Concluding Items</u>

     129. **During the interview, did the subject display unusual, illogical, or idiosyncratic thought processes?**
         Yes=1   No=2   Unsure=3   [ ]

130.   **If the subject is assessed as having a multiple**
       personality disorder, and answered Yes to
       question 1., the interviewer should ask, "In your
       opinion are the headaches I asked about earlier
       part of your problem with different personalities
       controlling you?"
       Yes=1   No=2   Unsure=3   [ ]

131.   **If the subject is assessed as having MPD, and**
       has also received the diagnosis of depression
       (question 63), the interviewer should ask:
       " In your opinion is the depression I asked about   [ ]
       earlier:"
       Confined to one personality=1
       Affects most or all personalities=2
       Unsure=3

        Interviewer should make a brief concluding statement telling
subject that there are no more questions, and thanking the subject for
his/her participation.

SCORING THE DISSOCIATIVE DISORDERS
INTERVIEW SCHEDULE

The Dissociative Disorders Interview Schedule is divided into 16 sections.
Each section is scored independently. All DSM-III diagnoses are made according to the rules in DSM-III.

There is no total score for the entire interview. However, average scores
for 20 multiple personality disorder (MPD) subjects on selected subsections
are given below.

Following presentation of scoring rules for each section, you will find a
description of a typical profile for an MPD patient. The DDIS has been
administered to over 300 subjects without a confirmed false positive diagnosis
of MPD.

Structured interview data on 100 MPD subjects from across North America are in the process of being collected. These will provide average scores
for MPD that may differ somewhat from the scores presented here. However,
other studies have shown that the 20 MPD subjects whose scores are given
here are typical of MPD as it presents throughout North America.

I. Somatic Complaints

This is scored according to DSM-III rules. To be positive for somatization
disorder, the subject must answer "yes" to question 38; in addition, the
subject must answer "yes" to at least 14 questions if female and 12 questions
if male, from questions 3–37. We prefer to use the DSM-III-R criteria, which
require 13 "yes" answers for either sex, from questions 3–37.

A history of somatization disorder distinguishes MPD from schizophrenia, eating disorders, and controls, but not from panic disorder. The average number of symptoms positive from questions 3–37 for MPD is 13.5.

II. Substance Abuse

We score the subject as positive for substance abuse if he or she answers "yes" to any question in this section. A history of substance abuse differentiates MPD from schizophrenia, eating disorders, panic disorder, and controls: 11 out of 20 MPD subjects were positive.

III. Psychiatric History

This is a descriptive section that does not yield a score as such. In a questionnaire study (Ross, Norton, & Wozney, 1989) we found that in 236 cases of MPD, the average patient had received 2.74 other psychiatric diagnoses besides MPD.

IV. Major Depressive Episodes

This is scored according to DSM-III rules. To be positive the subject must answer "yes" to question 54. He or she must answer "yes" to 4 questions from 55–62.

A history of depression does not discriminate MPD from other diagnostic groups: 17 out of 20 MPD subjects were positive for major depressive episode at some time in their life.

V. Schneiderian First Rank Symptoms

In this section we score the total number of "yes" responses. The total number of Schneiderian symptoms positive discriminates MPD from all groups tested except schizophrenia. The average number of positive symptoms in MPD is 6.6.

VI. Trances, Sleepwalking, Childhood Companions

Each of these items is scored independently. The subject is positive for sleepwalking if he or she answers "yes" to question 67, positive for trances if "yes" to 69, positive for imaginary playmates if "yes" to 71. Each of these items discriminates MPD from schizophrenia, eating disorders, panic disorder, and controls.

VII. Childhood Abuse

The subject is scored positive for physical abuse if he or she answers "yes" to question 73. Other data are descriptive. History of physical abuse discriminates MPD from schizophrenia, eating disorders, and panic disorder: 15 of ?0 MPD subjects were positive.

The subject is positive for sexual abuse if he or she answers "yes" to question 78. Sexual abuse also discriminates MPD from the other three groups: 16 out of 20 MPD subjects were positive.

VIII.   Features Associated with Multiple Personality Disorder

The responses in this section are added up to give a total score. A positive response in this section is either "yes," or else "fairly often" or "frequently," depending on the structure of the question. "Never" and "occasionally" are scored as negative. Secondary features discriminate MPD from the other three groups: Average number of features positive in MPD is 8.3.

IX.   Supernatural/Possession/ESP Experiences/Cults

In this section the positive answers are added up to give a total score. These experiences discriminate MPD from the other groups. Average number of positive responses for MPD is 5.5.

X.   Borderline Personality Disorder

This is scored by DSM-III rules. The subject must be positive for 5 items to meet the criteria for borderline personality. Borderline personality does not discriminate MPD from other groups tested to date, except for panic disorder and controls. However, the average number of borderline criteria positive does discriminate MPD from schizophrenia, eating disorders, and panic disorder. The average for 20 MPD subjects is 5.3.

XI.   Psychogenic Amnesia

This is scored by DSM-III rules. The subject must be positive for question 116 and negative for question 117. Psychogenic amnesia discriminates MPD from the other three groups: 13 out of 20 MPD subjects were positive. According to DSM-III-R rules, a positive diagnosis of MPD means that one cannot have a diagnosis of psychogenic amnesia. That makes sense to us. However, using DSM-III rules, psychogenic amnesia provides an additional discriminating section.

XII.   Psychogenic Fugue

This is scored by DSM-III rules. The subject must be positive for questions 118 and 119, and negative for 120. This diagnosis also discriminates MPD from the other three groups: 7 out of 20 MPD subjects were positive. As for psychogenic amnesia, DSM-III-R rules state that a diagnosis of MPD prevents a concurrent diagnosis of psychogenic fugue.

XIII.   Depersonalization Disorder

This is scored by DSM-III rules. The subject must be positive for question 121a, and negative for 122. Questions 121b–d are further DSM-III-R examples that are not required for the DSM-III diagnosis. This diagnosis discriminates MPD from other groups very poorly. It is also the only DSM-III diagnosis in the interview schedule with a low interrater reliability ($r = .56$). We consider depersonalization to be a symptom, not a diagnosis, and recommend that it be ignored in interpreting the results of structured interview.

XIV.   Multiple Personality Disorder

The criteria given are the NIMH criteria, of which the first 3 are the DSM-III criteria. The subject must be positive for all 3 items to meet the DSM-III criteria for MPD. The diagnosis of MPD discriminates MPD from all other groups tested to date with no false positives, and two false negatives out of 20. The interrater reliability for MPD is ($r = .78$), the sensitivity is 90 percent, the specificity is 100 percent, and the clinical validity is excellent, in our initial study.

Translation of DSM-III criteria into DSM-III-R criteria is problematic because of the wording in the two manuals. We therefore recommend a conservative DSM-III diagnosis. Subjects who meet the first two criteria only are probably true multiples, however.

XV.   Atypical Dissociative Disorder

This is scored positive based on the interviewer's judgment. A patient can be positive for atypical dissociative disorder only if he or she does not have any other dissociative disorder.

XVI.   Concluding Items

This is a descriptive section and is not scored.

Most MPD patients will meet the DSM-III criteria for MPD and all should meet the first two. Anyone who does not meet the first two criteria is unlikely to have full MPD unless he or she has a high score on secondary features. This may be the case in the first few assessment sessions, before the diagnostician has contacted alter personalities directly. We never make a diagnosis of MPD until we have contacted alter personalities directly. If alters have not been contacted directly or reported by a reliable observer, one can say that the subject almost certainly has MPD based on interview results, but a conclusive diagnosis is not possible.

Most MPD patients will have numerous somatic symptoms; a history of substance abuse and major depressive episode; a number of Schneiderian symptoms; sleepwalking, trance states and/or imaginary playmates in childhood; a history of physical and/or sexual abuse; borderline personality disorder, or at least 3 borderline symptoms; numerous extrasensory experiences; other dissociative diagnoses; and a history of numerous past diagnoses and treatments.

Not all MPD patients will have all of these features, but most will have a substantial proportion of them. MPD subjects with particularly severe abuse histories appear to have higher scores and more items positive, but we do not have sufficient data yet to say that for sure.

Therapist Dissociative Checklist

Therapist Dissociative Checklist

Client's Initials _____   Age _____

Client Number _____   Sex   M   or   F
                                 (please circle)

1. Time period for which you are rating the checklist.

    From (date) _____   To (date) _____

2.   Please indicate which phase (s) of therapy you have been working
        in   during this time period. (see guidelines for the therapist)

    a. Preintegration:

        Initial _____   Middle _____   Late _____

    b. Post-integration _____

3. How long have you been seeing the client in therapy?

    _____ months or weeks (please circle)

4.   How often have you been seeing the client since you last filled
        out this form or since you started working with the client?

    _____ average number of hours/week

    _____ average number of sessions/week

5.   Has the Dissociative Disorders Interview Schedule (DDIS) been
        administered?

     yes   or   no   (please circle)

6.   Has the Dissociative Experience Scale (DES) been administered?

     yes   or   no   (please circle)

Therapist Dissociative Checklist

Please indicate with a ( ) how often the following techniques have been used or addressed during the given time period. (see guidelines for the therapist)

	Never	Occasion-ally	Fairly Often	Frequen-tly
	0	1	2	3
1. Establishing trust				
2. Establishing safety				
3. Developing a treatment alliance				
4. Discussing diagnosis				
5. Education and inform-ation processing				
6. Stated goal of integration				
7. Contacting alter personalities				
8. Gathering a history of the personality system				
9. Mapping the personal-ity system				
10. Treatment contracting or re-negotiating				
11. Establishing inter-personality communica-tion				
12. Establishing co-consciousness				
13. Disclosing abuse and traumatic memories				
14. Abreacting abuse memories				
15. Debriefing of mem-ories and feelings				

	Never	Occasion-ally	Fairly Often	Frequen tly	
	0	1	2	3	
16. Age appropriate activities with child alters					
17. Working with aggressive/ persecutory alters					
18. Cognitive restructuring techniques					
19. Negotiation					
20. Using Metaphors, rituals, imagery, or dreams					
21. Hypnosis					
22. Relaxation techniques					
23. Age progression					
24. Age regression					
25. Writing exercises					
26. Audiovisual					
27. Using expressive arts					
28. Medications					
29. Physical Restraints					
30. Hospitalization					
31. Group therapy					
32. Involving other support agencies					
33. Involving spouses, friends or relatives					
34. Limit-setting					
35. Developing new behaviours and coping skills					

	Never	Occasion-ally	Fairly Often	Frequen tly
	0	1	2	3
36. Integration				
37. Post-integration work				
38. Other (please list)				
_____				
_____				
_____				
_____				

GUIDELINES FOR THE THERAPIST DISSOCIATIVE CHECKLIST

Phases of Therapy

Initial

The assessment and planning phase of therapy. In the treatment of MPD it involves contacting alters, mapping the system, developing a treatment alliance.

Middle

The working phase of therapy. In the treatment of MPD it involves establishing interpersonality communication, breaking down amnesic barriers, disclosing memories, abreaction.

Late

The evaluation and consolidation of gains made in the middle phase of therapy and further reworking of memories. In treatment of MPD it involves preparation for and carrying out of the integration of alters.

Postintegration

The work following the resolution of the major abuse issues and memories, such as developing and applying new coping skills, adjusting to new feelings and memories. In treatment of MPD it involves grieving the loss of alters.

TREATMENT TECHNIQUES

For further discussion of some of these techniques, see Ross and Gahan's (1988b) "Techniques in the Treatment of Multiple Personality Disorder."

1. *Establishing Trust.* Addressing the issue of trust directly or applying specific interventions in developing trust
2. *Establishing Safety.* Directly addressing the issue of safety or applying specific interventions in developing safety
3. *Developing a Treatment Alliance.* Beginning to establish a working relationship with the client and defining mutually agreed upon goals; the client making a commitment to treatment
4. *Discussing Diagnosis.* Presenting the client with a diagnosis and explanation of his/her dissociative process
5. *Education and Information Processing.* Educating clients about dissociative disorders, offering clients reading materials or additional resources
6. *Stated Goal of Integration.* Explicitly stating to the client that a goal of treatment is integration
7. *Contacting Alter Personalities.* Making direct contact with alter personalities
8. *Gathering History.* Learning the history of each alter, for example, who they are, when they came about, why they appeared, where they fit in the personality system, what function they serve
9. *Mapping the Personality System.* Representing in a drawing or chart how the client perceives his/her personality system or internal world
10. *Treatment Contracting or Renegotiating.* Formulating a written or verbal treatment agreement between the therapist and the client to determine duration of treatment, identify consequences for self-destructive or violent behavior and identify other types of treatment expectations
11. *Establishing Interpersonality Communication.* Establishing internal communication between the personality states; sharing information and knowledge among the personalities, including indirect work with alter personalities
12. *Establishing Coconsciousness.* Using techniques designed to allow the host personality to remember when the other alters are "out" and to remove amnesic barriers
13. *Disclosing Abuse and Traumatic Memories.* Revealing sexual, physical, emotional abuse or other traumatic memories that have been dissociated; usually occurred in childhood or adolescence and were

not previously known to the host personality or to the presenting part of the client

14. *Abreacting Abuse Memories.* Reexperiencing abusive events both physically and emotionally as if they are happening in the present

15. *Debriefing of Memories and Feelings.* Exploring and processing thoughts, memories, and feelings surrounding the abuse

16. *Age Appropriate Activities with Child Alters.* Adjusting treatment approaches or interventions to correspond with the developmental stage of a younger personality

17. *Working with Aggressive/Persecutory Alters.* Adjusting treatment approaches or adopting specific interventions when directly talking to or working with aggressive or persecutory personalities

18. *Cognitive Restructuring Techniques.* Using cognitive therapy strategies to challenge the alter personalities' distorted beliefs and perceptions, especially of being separate selves, including cognitive dissonance (see Ross & Gahan, 1988a)

19. *Negotiations.* Encouraging decision making and discussions among the alters about positions in the system, conflicts, or decisions of daily living, for example, taking a vote among the alters.

20. *Using Metaphors, Rituals, Imagery or Dreams.* Using creative elements such as metaphors, rituals, imagery or dreams in the therapy process to recover memories, ensure safety, or process information

21. *Hypnosis.* Using formal induction of hypnosis to contact alter personalities, recover memories, integrate personalities, reduce symptoms, or accomplish other purposes

22. *Relaxation Techniques.* Applying specific relaxation techniques or exercises to help the client relax

23. *Age Progression.* Using hypnotic suggestions to age progress an alter to an older age

24. *Age Regression.* Using hypnotic suggestions to age regress an alter to a younger age; usually used to assist with the recovery of memories

25. *Writing Exercises.* Using diaries or journals to assist in the recovery of memories or to assist in processing memories, thoughts, and feelings; or using writing as a way to communicate with alter personalities who may be reluctant to come out

26. *Audiovisual.* Using audio or videotaping to assist in convincing the client of the diagnosis, to help reduce the client's fears of the other parts, or to assist the client to get to know the other parts across amnesic barriers

27. *Using Expressive Arts.* Using music, drawing, or movement as an alternative to verbalizing feelings and expressing self

28. *Medications.* Using medications as an adjunct to therapy to relieve symptoms of depression or anxiety

29. *Physical Restraints.* Physically restraining the client to avoid injury to self and others

30. *Hospitalization.* Requiring inpatient treatment to protect the client's safety or to work through a crisis in therapy

31. *Group Therapy.* Using group therapy as an adjunct to individual therapy, for example, an incest group

32. *Involving Other Support Agencies.* Involving outside agencies such as social services, AA groups, assertiveness training, vocational counselors, or social support groups as a part of the therapy process to help the client meet various needs

33. *Involving Spouses, Friends, or Relatives.* Educating friends and relatives and involving them as support persons when a client is in the therapy process

34. *Limit Setting.* Setting limits around the pacing of therapy, behavior, personal boundaries for the client and therapist, or the uncovering of painful material

35. *Developing New Behaviors and Coping Skills.* Learning and practicing new responses, changing old coping patterns, and developing new ways of dealing with conflict without dissociating

36. *Integration.* Joining together the various personalities into a single self; Different personalities will be ready to join at different times throughout therapy

37. *Postintegration Work.* May include grieving the loss of the alters, adjusting to new feelings, accepting new memories, increasing self confidence and self esteem, and exploring future plans

38. *Other Techniques.* List any other treatment techniques or approaches used in working with the client who experiences any form of dissociative disorder including MPD

Pre-Admission Assessment Worksheet for MPD Patients

PRE-ADMISSION ASSESSMENT WORKSHEET FOR M.P.D. PATIENTS

1. A pre-admission conference will be held prior to admission of all M.P.D. patients.

2. The patient will be informed of admission after the conference.

3. To be initiated by physician and completed during the pre-admission discussion.

Name : _____

D.O.B.: _____

1) Education:

_____

2) Employment Status:

_____

3) Current living accommodation: _____

   a) How long? _____

   b) Will same be available and feasible on discharge? _____

4) Community resources, personal support system, and family situation.

_____

_____

_____

5) Safety issues: a) Patient's history of violence and describe:

_____

_____

           b) Family history of violence and describe:

_____

_____

           c) Suicidal ideation (active, inactive):

_____

_____

PRE-ADMISSION ASSESSMENT WORKSHEET FOR M.P.D. PATIENTS

- 2 -

    d) Potential for aggressive behavior; potential
       for self-control.

_____

_____

6) Past and/or present criminal history:

_____

_____

_____

7) Lifestyle (past and present):

_____

_____

_____

8) Therapy history (where, who, length, reasons for termination):

_____

_____

_____

_____

9) Goal (s) of inpatient treatment (long, short, expected length of stay):

_____

_____

_____

_____

10) Description of known alters:

_____

_____

_____

_____

General Unit Guidelines for MPD Patients

GENERAL GUIDELINES

1. The MPD patient is to use birth or usual legal name on unit, no matter which alter is out. Alters may be called by appropriate names in individual sessions. Amnesic parts may need reorientation to name expectation when out on unit.
   Rationale. It is less disruptive and less confusing to copatients or casual staff.

2. Child alters are not to walk around the unit, only adult alters. Child alters will have individualized time spent with them or may be taken to a private area when a therapeutic decision is made to allow a child alter to be out.
   Rationale. The patient needs to be able to function as an adult when she/he leaves hospital. It is too disruptive to the mileiu of the unit to see an adult walking around sucking her thumb.

3. Refer to alters as "parts." Reinforce that each is part of a whole.
   Rationale. It maintains consistency in use of vocabulary and helps patient understand the concept that the alter is a part of a whole person.

4. Use multidimensional and multidisciplinary approach. Each staff member deals with specific issues. Divide up the workload so that no one worker has to do everything, for example, psychotherapy, activities. Plan ahead to spend time with child alters in play, and so on. Some patients are not predictable enough on their switching. The ward staff may do work with coping in everyday living issues, whereas the therapist works on integration.
   Rationale. Because of the intensity and time that therapy takes, utilizing a multidisciplinary approach is very effective. Each staff member can deal with specific issues.

5. Nurse are cotherapists.
   Rationale. Nurses are with the patient the most and can take a very active role in therapy.

6. MPD patients are not involved in psychotherapy groups. They are encouraged to participate in ward meetings and can be involved in task-oriented groups such as recreation, projective, and social or learning groups.
   Rationale. Heterogeneous psychotherapy groups can be very difficult and can be a negative experience, especially with an MPD patient who is struggling with individual therapy. However, homogeneous MPD groups can be helpful and are planned.

7. Encourage the MPD patient to be involved in the milieu of the unit and to follow general unit expectations for all patients.
   Rationale. Decreases "specialness." Expectations are the same for all patients.

8. Nursing staff set their own frame for one on one interactions. A minimum of 15 minutes is essential for MPD patients, as for any patient. It is not necessary to spend time every shift with each "part." Patients' urgency to spend increased time on quick integration may need to be paced.

   Rationale. Time frameworks establish boundaries for the nurse and the MPD patient. The patient knows how much time she/he will have for interactions. Time must be realistic but sufficient for meeting patients' basic emotional needs. Pacing of integration allows time to heal and prevents staff burnout.

9. When a patient is rapidly switching, each newly emerging alter can be out without staff orienting her/him to the external environment. Orientation may become necessary when there are signs of confusion or disorientation in a newly switched alter.

   Rationale. Staff avoid reinforcing the switching and decrease manipulative switching.

10. Hold regular conferences with treatment team, especially when dealing with a difficult patient. A pre-admission meeting may be necessary to determine the terms of treatment contract.

    Rationale. Conferences help maintain consistency of care, assist in problem solving, delegate specific tasks, provide support, open doors to communication. Good communication will be enhanced by use of verbal and written exchange in charts, progress notes, communication book, and reports. Progress notes may be used to "flag" important events such as emergence of new alters, integrations, and so on.
    A pre-admission meeting will enable staff to know history of patient, discuss anticipated difficulties, and establish treatment strategies. The charge nurse should facilitate debriefing after a crisis, for all those involved in the crisis.

11. Contract with the MPD patient prior to admission or at admission. Written contract is the most effective. It is important to contract with as many personalities as possible around aggressive, violent behavior and suicidal behaviors.

    Rationale. Contracts establish expectations of staff and patients, establish ground rules, and set limits.

12. Establish a personal support system or groups, that is, mutual staff ventilation and support, use of management and education resources; accessing counseling services when needed.

    Rationale. Support groups provide teaching, cohesion, assistance in recognizing and dealing with transference and countertransference. They allow the team to integrate ideas and avoid splitting, provide an opportunity to discuss ethical, administrative, and political issues, and assist in educating nonbelievers. Counseling services offer off-the-job opportunities to clarify individual responses to both the content and process of dealing with the MPD patient.

References

Alexander, V. K. (1956). A case study of a multiple personality. *Journal of Abnormal and Social Psychology, 52*, 272–276.

Allison, R. B. (1974). A new treatment approach for multiple personalities. *American Journal of Clinical Hypnosis, 17*, 15–32.

Allison, R. B. (1984). Difficulties diagnosing the multiple personality syndrome in a death penalty case. *International Journal of Clinical and Experimental Hypnosis, 32*, 102–117.

Allison, R. B. (1985). The possession syndrome on trial. *American Journal of Forensic Psychiatry, 6*, 46–56.

American Psychiatric Association. (1980). *Diagnostic and statistical manual of mental disorders. DSM-III.* (3rd ed.). Washington, DC. Author.

American Psychiatric Association. (1985). *DSM-III-R in development. Draft.* Washington, DC. Author.

American Psychiatric Association. (1987). *Diagnostic and statistical manual of mental disorders. DSM-III-R.* (3rd ed.–Rev.). Washington, DC. Author.

Anderson, G. (1988). Understanding multiple personality disorder. *Journal of Psychosocial Nursing, 26*, 26–30.

Anderson G., & Ross, C. A. (1988a). A model for psychiatric nurses in working with patients who have multiple personality disorder. *Canadian Journal of Psychiatric Nursing, 29*, 13–18.

Anderson, G., & Ross, C. A. (1988b). Strategies for working with a patient who has multiple personality disorder. *Archives of Psychiatric Nursing, 11*, 236–243.

Andorfer, J. C. (1985). Multiple personality in the human information-processor: A case history and theoretical formulation. *Journal of Clinical Psychology, 41*, 309–324.

Atlas, G. (1988). Multiple personality disorder misdiagnosed as mental retardation. *Dissociation, 1*(1), 77–83.

Atwood, G. E. (1978). The impact of *Sybil* on a patient with multiple personality. *American Journal of Psychoanalysis, 38*, 277–279.

Barkin, R., Braun, B. G., & Kluft, R. P. (1986). The dilemma of drug therapy for multiple personality disorder. In B. G. Braun (Ed.), *Treatment of multiple personality disorder* (pp. 107–132). Washington, DC: American Psychiatric Press.

Beahrs, J. (1982). *Unity and multiplicity*. New York: Brunner/Mazel.

Beck, A. T. (1976). *Cognitive therapy and the emotional disorders*. New York: New American Library.

Beck, A. T., & Emery, G. (1985). *Anxiety disorders and phobias: A cognitive perspective*. New York: Basic Books.

Beck, A. T., Rush, A. J., Shaw, B. F., & Emery, G. (1979). *Cognitive therapy of depression*. New York: Guilford Press.

Benner, D. G., & Evans, C. (1984). Unity and multiplicity in hypnosis, commisurotomy, and multiple personality disorder. *Journal of Mind and Behavior, 5*, 423–432.

Benner, D. G., & Joscelyne, B. (1984). Multiple personality as a borderline disorder. *Journal of Nervous and Mental Disease, 172*, 98–104.

Benson, D. F. (1986). Interictal behavior disorders in epilepsy. *Psychiatric Clinics of North America, 9*, 283–292.

Benson, D. F., Miller, B. L., & Signer, S. F. (1986). Dual personality associated with epilepsy. *Archives of Neurology, 43*, 471–474.

Berg, S., & Melin, E. (1975). Hypnotic susceptibility in old age: Some data from residential homes for old people. *International Journal of Clinical and Experimental Hypnosis, 23*, 184–189.

Bernstein, E. M., & Putnam, F. W. (1986). Development, reliability, and validity of a dissociation scale. *Journal of Nervous and Mental Disease, 174*, 727–735.

Binet, A. (1977a). *Alterations of personality*. Washington: University Publications of America. (Original work published 1896)

Binet, A. (1977b). *On double consciousness*. Washington: University Publications of America. (Original work published 1890)

Blake, W. (1966). *Complete writings*. Oxford: Oxford University Press.

Bliss, E. L. (1980). Multiple personalities. A report of 14 cases with implications for schizophrenia. *Archives of General Psychiatry, 37*, 1388–1397.

Bliss, E. L. (1983). Multiple personalities, related disorders and hypnosis. *American Journal of Clinical Hypnosis, 26*, 114–123.

Bliss, E. L. (1984a). A symptom profile of patients with multiple personalities, including MMPI results. *Journal of Nervous and Mental Disease, 172*, 197–202.

Bliss, E. L. (1984b). Hysteria and hypnosis. *Journal of Nervous and Mental Disease, 172,* 203–206.

Bliss, E. L. (1984c). Spontaneous self-hypnosis in multiple personality disorder. *Psychiatric Clinics of North America, 7,* 135–148.

Bliss, E. L. (1985). Sexual criminality and hypnotizability. *Journal of Nervous and Mental Disease, 173,* 522–526.

Bliss, E. L. (1986). *Multiple personality, allied disorders, and hypnosis.* New York: Oxford University Press.

Bliss, E. L. (1988). Professional skepticism about multiple personality. *Journal of Nervous and Mental Disease, 176,* 533–534.

Bliss, E. L., & Jeppsen, A. (1985). Prevalence of multiple personality among inpatients and outpatients. *American Journal of Psychiatry, 142,* 250–251.

Bliss, E. L., & Larson, E. M. (1985). Sexual criminality and hypnotizability. *Journal of Nervous and Mental Disease, 173,* 522–526.

Boor, M. (1982). The multiple personality epidemic: Additional cases and inferences regarding diagnosis, etiology, dynamics and treatment. *Journal of Nervous and Mental Disease, 170,* 302–304.

Boor, M., & Coons, P. M. (1983). A comprehensive bibliography of literature pertaining to multiple personality. *Psychological Reports, 53,* 295–310.

Bornn, E. M. (1988, October). Multiple personality disorder. *Canadian Nurse,* pp. 16–19.

Bowers, M. K., Brecher-Marer, S., Newton, B. W., Piotrowski, Z., Spyer, T. C., Taylor, W. S., & Watkins, J. G. (1971). Therapy of multiple personality. *International Journal of Clinical and Experimental Hypnosis, 19,* 57–65.

Bowman, E. S., Blix, S., & Coons, P. M. (1985). Multiple personality in adolescence: Relationship to incestual experiences. *Journal of the American Academy of Child Psychiatry, 24,* 109–114.

Bowman, E. S., Coons, P. M., Jones, R. S., & Oldstrom, M. (1987). Religious psychodynamics in multiple personalities: Suggestions for treatment. *American Journal of Psychotherapy, 41,* 542–553.

Brandsma, J. M., & Ludwig, A. M. (1974). A case of multiple personality: Diagnosis and therapy. *International Journal of Clinical and Experimental Hypnosis, 22,* 216–233.

Braun, B. G. (1983a). Neurophysiologic changes due to integration: A preliminary report. *American Journal of Clinical Hypnosis, 26,* 84–92.

Braun, B. G. (1983b). Psychophysiologic phenomena in multiple personality and hypnosis. *American Journal of Clinical Hypnosis, 26,* 124–137.

Braun, B. G. (1984). Hypnosis creates multiple personality: Myth or reality? *International Journal of Clinical and Experimental Hypnosis, 32,* 191–197.

Braun, B. G. (1985). The transgenerational incidence of dissociation and multiple personality disorder: A preliminary report. In R. P. Kluft (Ed.), *Childhood antecedents of multiple personality disorder,* 167–196. Washington, DC: American Psychiatric Press.

Braun, B. G. (1986a). Issues in the psychotherapy of multiple personality disorder. In B. G. Braun (Ed.), *Treatment of multiple personality disorder,* (pp. 1–28). Washington, DC: American Psychiatric Press.

Braun, B. G. (1986b). *Treatment of multiple personality disorder.* Washington, DC: American Psychiatric Press.

Braun, B. G. (1988a). The BASK (behavior, affect, sensation, knowledge) model of dissociation. *Dissociation, 1*(1), 4–23.

Braun, B. G. (1988b). The BASK model of dissociation Clinical applications. *Dissociation, 1*(2), 16–23.

Braun, B. G., & Sachs, R. G. (1985). The development of multiple personality disorder: Predisposing, precipitating, and perpetuating factors. In R. P. Kluft (Ed.), *Childhood Antecedents of Multiple Personality Disorder* (pp. 37–64). Washington, DC: American Psychiatric Press.

Brende, J. O., & Benedict, B. D. (1980). The Vietnam combat delayed stress response syndrome: Hypnotherapy of "dissociative symptoms." *American Journal of Clinical Hypnosis, 23,* 34–40.

Breuer, J., & Freud, S. (1986). *Studies on hysteria.* New York: Pelican Books. (Original work published 1895)

Buck, O. D. (1983). Multiple personality as a borderline state. *Journal of Nervous and Mental Disease, 171,* 62–65.

Caddy, G. P. (1985). Cognitive behavior therapy in the treatment of multiple personality. *Behavior Modification, 9,* 267–292.

Carlson, E. T. (1981). The history of multiple personality in the United States: I. The beginnings. *American Journal of Psychiatry, 138,* 666–668.

Carlson, E. T. (1984). The history of multiple personality in the United States: Mary Reynolds and her subsequent reputation. *Bulletin of the History of Medicine, 58,* 72–82.

Caul, D. (1984). Group and videotape techniques for multiple personality disorder. *Psychiatric Annals, 14,* 46–50.

Caul, D., Sachs, R. G., & Braun, B. G. (1986). Group therapy in treatment of multiple personality disorder. In B. G. Braun (Ed.), *Treatment of multiple personality disorder,* (pp. 143–156). Washington, DC: American Psychiatric Press.

Clark, E. E. (1960). *Indian legends of the Pacific Northwest.* Toronto: McClelland & Stewart.

Clary, W. F., Burstin, K. J., & Carpenter, J. S. (1984). Multiple personality and borderline personality disorder. *Psychiatric Clinics of North America, 7,* 89–99.

Cocores, J. A., Bender, A. L., & McBride, E. (1984). Multiple personality, seizure disorder, and the electroencephalogram. *Journal of Nervous and Mental Disease, 172,* 436–438.

Comstock, C. (1987). Internal self helpers or centers. *Integration, 3*(1), 3–12.

Confer, W. N., & Ables, B. S. (1983). *Multiple personality: Etiology, diagnosis and treatment.* New York: Human Sciences Press.

Congdon, M. H., Hain, J., & Stevenson, I. (1961). A case of multiple personality illustrating the transition from role-playing. *Journal of Nervous and Mental Disease, 132,* 497–504.

Coons, P. M. (1980). Multiple personality: Diagnostic considerations. *Journal of Clinical Psychiatry, 41,* 330–336.

Coons, P. M. (1984). The differential diagnosis of multiple personality. *Psychiatric Clinics of North America, 7,* 51–67.

Coons, P. M. (1985). Children of parents with multiple personality disorder. In R. P. Kluft (Ed.), *Childhood antecedents of multiple personality disorder* (pp. 151–165). Washington, DC: American Psychiatric Press.

Coons, P. M. (1986a). Child abuse and multiple personality disorder: Review of the literature and suggestions for treatment. *Child Abuse and Neglect, 10,* 455–465.

Coons, P. M. (1986b). Dissociative disorders: Diagnosis and treatment. *Indiana Medicine, 79,* 410–415.

Coons, P. M. (1986c). The prevalence of multiple personality disorder. *Newsletter of the International Society for the Study of Multiple Personality and Dissociation, 4*(3), 6–8.

Coons, P. M. (1986d). Treatment progress in 20 patients with multiple personality disorder. *Journal of Nervous and Mental Disease, 174,* 715–721.

Coons, P. M. (1988a). Misuse of forensic hypnosis: A hypnotically elicited false confession with the apparent creation of multiple personality. *International Journal of Clinical and Experimental Hypnosis, 36,* 1–11.

Coons, P. M. (1988b). Psychophysiologic investigation of multiple personality disorder: A review. *Dissociation 1*(1), 47–53.

Coons, P. M., Bowman, E. S., & Milstein, V. (1988). Multiple personality disorder: A clinical investigation of 50 cases. *Journal of Nervous and Mental Disease, 176,* 519–527.

Coons, P. M., & Bradley, K. (1985). Group psychotherapy with multiple personality patients. *Journal of Nervous and Mental Disease, 173,* 515–521.

Coons, P. M., & Fine, C. (1988). Accuracy of the MMPI in identifying multiple personality disorder. In B. G. Braun (Ed.), *Proceedings of the Fifth International Conference on Multiple Personality/Dissociative States* (p. 102). Chicago: Rush-Presbyterian-St. Luke's Medical Center.

Coons, P. M., & Milstein, V. (1984). Rape and post-traumatic stress in multiple personality. *Psychological Reports, 55,* 839–845.

Coons, P. M., & Milstein, V. (1986). Psychosexual disturbances in multiple personality: characteristics, etiology, and treatment. *Journal of Clinical Psychiatry, 47,* 106–110.

Coons, P. M., Milstein, V., & Marley, C. (1982). EEG studies of two multiple personalities and a control. *Archives of General Psychiatry, 39,* 823–825.

Coons, P. M., & Sterne, A. L. (1986). Initial and follow-up psychological testing on a group of patients with multiple personality disorder. *Psychological Reports, 58,* 43–49.

Copeland, C. L., & Kitching, E. H. (1937). A case of profound dissociation of the personality. *Journal of Mental Science, 83,* 719–726.

Crabtree, A. (1985). *Multiple Man: Explorations in possession and multiple personality.* Toronto: Collins.

Crabtree, A. (1986). Explanations of dissociation in the first half of the twentieth century. In J. M. Quen (Ed.), *Split minds split brains* (pp. 85–107). New York: New York University Press.

Curtis, J. C. (1988, February). Exposing multiple personality disorder. *Diagnosis,* pp. 85–87, 90–95.

Cutler, B., & Reed, J. (1975). Multiple personality: A single case study with a 15-year follow-up. *Psychological Medicine, 5,* 18–26.

Damgaard, J., Van Benschoten, S., & Fagan, J. (1985). An updated bibliography of literature pertaining to multiple personality. *Psychological Reports, 57,* 131–137.

Dell, P. F. (1988a). Not reasonable skepticism but extreme skepticism. *Journal of Nervous and Mental Disease, 176,* 537–538.

Dell, P. F. (1988b). Professional skepticism about multiple personality. *Journal of Nervous and Mental Disease, 176,* 528–531.

Derogatis, L. R., Lipman, R. S., Rickels, K., Uhenhuth, E. H., & Covi, L. (1973). SCL-90: An outpatient psychiatric rating scale—preliminary report. *Psychopharmacology Bulletin, 9,* 13–28.

Drew, B. L. (1988). Multiple personality disorder: An historical perspective. *Archives of Psychiatric Nursing, 2,* 227–230.

Dyck, P. B., & Gillette, G. M. (1987). Development of a dissociative symptom inventory. In B. G. Braun (Ed.), *Proceedings of the Fourth International Conference on Multiple Personality/Dissociative States* (p. 143). Chicago: Rush-Presbyterian-St. Luke's Medical Center.

Dysken, M. W., Chang, S. S., Casper, R. C., & Davis, J. M. (1979). Barbiturate-facilitated interviewing. *Biological Psychiatry, 14,* 421–432.

Dysken, M. W., Kooser, J. A., Haraszti, J. S., & Davis, J. M. (1979). Clinical usefulness of sodium amobarbital interviewing. *Archives of General Psychiatry, 36,* 789–794.

Eliade, M. (1964). *Shamanism.* Princeton: Princeton University Press.

Ellenberger, H. (1970). *The discovery of the unconscious.* New York: Basic Books.

Emery, G., Hollon, S. D., & Bedrosian, R. C. (1981). *New directions in cognitive therapy.* New York: Guilford Press.

Fagan, J., & McMahon, P. (1984). Incipient multiple personality in children. *Journal of Nervous and Mental Disease, 172,* 26–36.

Fahy, T. A. (1988). The diagnosis of multiple personality disorder: A critical review. *British Journal of Psychiatry, 153,* 597–606.

Fast, I. (1974). Multiple identities in borderline personality organization. *British Journal of Medical Psychology, 47,* 291–300.

Fine, C. G. (1988). The work of Antoine Despine: The first scientific report on the diagnosis and treatment of a child with multiple personality disorder. *American Journal of Clinical Hypnosis, 31,* 33–39.

Frances, A., & Spiegel, D. (1987). Chronic pain masks depression, multiple personality disorder. *Hospital and Community Psychiatry, 38,* 933–935.

Fraser, G. A., & Lapierre, Y. D. (1986). Lactate-induced panic attacks in dissociative states (multiple personalities). In B. G. Braun (Ed.), *Proceedings of the Third International Conference on Multiple Personality/ Dissociative States* (p. 124). Chicago: Rush-Presbyterian-St. Luke's Medical Center.

Freeman, A. (Ed.) (1983). *Cognitive therapy with couples and groups.* New York: Plenum Press.

French, O., & Chodoff, P. (1987). More on multiple personality disorder (letter). *American Journal of Psychiatry, 144,* 123–125.

Frischholz, M. A. (1985). The relationship among dissociation, hypnosis, and child abuse in the development of multiple personality disorder. In R. P. Kluft (Ed.), *Childhood Antecedents of Multiple Personality Disorder* (pp. 99–126). Washington, DC: American Psychiatric Press.

Goodwin, D. W., Crane, J. B., & Guze, S. B. (1969). Phenomenological aspects of the alcoholic "blackout." *British Journal of Psychiatry, 115,* 1033–1038.

Goodwin, J. (1985). Credibility problems in multiple personality disorder patients and abused children. In R. P. Kluft (Ed.), *Childhood antecedents of multiple personality disorder,* 1–19. Washington: American Psychiatric Press.

Goodwin, J. (1988). Munchausen's syndrome as a dissociative disorder. *Dissociation, 1*(1), 54–60.

Goodwin, J., & Attias, R. (1988). Eating disorder as a multimodal response to child abuse. In B. G. Braun (Ed.), *Proceedings of the Fifth International Conference on Multiple Personality/Dissociative States,* (p. 29). Chicago: Rush-Presbyterian-St. Luke's Medical Center.

Goodwin, J., Cheeves, K., & Connell, V. (1988). Defining a syndrome of severe symptoms in patients with severe incestuous abuse. *Dissociation, 1*(4), 11–16.

Gordon, M. C. (1972). Age and performance differences of male patients on modified Stanford hypnotic susceptibility scales. *International Journal of Clinical and Experimental Hypnosis, 1972,* 152–155.

Gray, G. T., & Braun, B. G. (1986). Report on the 1985 questionnaire multiple personality disorder. In B. G. Braun (Ed.), *Proceedings of the Third International Conference on Multiple Personality/Dissociative States,* (p. 111). Chicago: Rush-Presbyterian-St. Luke's Medical Center.

Greaves, G. B. (1980). Multiple personality. 165 years after Mary Reynolds. *Journal of Nervous and Mental Disease, 168,* 577–596.

Greaves, G. B. (1988). Common errors in the treatment of multiple personality disorder. *Dissociation, 1,* 61–66.

Gruenewald, D. (1971). Hypnotic techniques without hypnosis in the treatment of dual personality. *Journal of Nervous and Mental Disease, 153,* 41–46.

Gruenewald, D. (1977). Multiple personality and splitting phenomena: A reconceptualization. *Journal of Nervous and Mental Disease, 153,* 41–46.

Gruenewald, D. (1984). On the nature of multiple personality: Comparisons with hypnosis. *International Journal of Clinical and Experimental Hypnosis, 32,* 170–190.

Gruenewald, D. (1988). Book review [Review of *Multiple personality, allied disorders, and hypnosis,* by Eugene L. Bliss]. *International Journal of Clinical and Experimental Hypnosis, 36,* 53–56.

Gunderson, J. G., Carpenter, W. T., & Strauss, J. S. (1975). Borderline and schizophrenic patients: A comparative study. *American Journal of Psychiatry, 132,* 1257–1264.

Gunderson, J. G., & Kolb, J. E. (1978). Discriminating features of borderline patients. *American Journal of Psychiatry, 135,* 792–796.

Gunderson, J. G., Kolb, J. E., & Austin, V. (1981). The diagnostic interview for borderlines. *American Journal of Psychiatry, 138,* 896–903.

Gunderson, J. G., & Singer, M. T. (1975). Defining borderline patients: An overview. *American Journal of Psychiatry, 132,* 1–10.

Hall, R. C. W., LeCann, A. F., & Schoolar, J. C. (1978). Amobarbital treatment of multiple personality. *Journal of Nervous and Mental Disease, 166,* 666–670.

Harner, M. J. (Ed.). (1973). *Hallucinogens and shamanism.* New York: Oxford University Press.

Harriman, P. L. (1942a). The experimental induction of a multiple personality. *Psychiatry, 5,* 179–186.

Harriman, P. L. (1942b). The experimental production of some phenomena related to multiple personality. *Journal of Abnormal and Social Psychology, 37,* 244–255.

Harriman, P. L. (1943). A new approach to multiple personalities. *American Journal of Orthopsychiatry, 13,* 638–643.

Haule, J. R. (1986). Pierre Janet and dissociation: The first transference theory and its origins in hypnosis. *American Journal of Clinical Hypnosis, 29,* 86–94.

Hawthorne, J. (1983). *Multiple personality and the disintegration of literary character.* New York: St. Martin's Press.

Heber, S., Fleisher, W. P., Ross, C. A., & Stanwick, R. 1989. Unpublished raw data.

Hicks, R. E. (1985). Discussion: A clinician's perspective. In R. P. Kluft (Ed.), *Childhood antecedents of multiple personality disorder* (pp. 239–258). Washington, DC: American Psychiatric Press.

Hilgard, E. R. (1977). *Divided consciousness: Multiple controls in human thought and action.* New York: Wiley.

Hilgard, E. R. (1984). The hidden observer and multiple personality. *International Journal of Clinical and Experimental Hypnosis, 32,* 248–253.

Hilgard, E. R. (1987). Multiple personality and dissociation. In *Psychology in America: A historical survey* (pp. 303–315). San Diego: Harcourt Brace Jovanovich.

Hilgard, E. R. (1988). Professional skepticism about multiple personality. *Journal of Nervous and Mental Disease, 176,* 532.

Hoch, P. H., & Polatin, P. (1949). Pseudoneurotic forms of schizophrenia. *Psychiatric Quarterly, 23,* 248–276.

Horevitz, R. P., & Braun, B. G. (1984). Are multiple personalities borderline? *Psychiatric Clinics of North America, 7,* 69–87.

Horton, P., & Miller, D. (1972). The etiology of multiple personality. *Comprehensive Psychiatry, 13,* 151–159.

Howland, J. S. (1975). The use of hypnosis in the treatment of a case of multiple personality. *Journal of Nervous and Mental Disease, 161,* 138–142.

James, W. (1983). *The Principles of Psychology.* Cambridge: Harvard University Press. (Original work published 1890)

Janet, P. (1965). *The major symptoms of hysteria.* New York: Hafner. (Original work published 1907)

Janet, P. (1977). *The mental state of hystericals.* Washington, DC: University Publications of America. (Original work published 1901)

Jaynes, J. (1976). *The origin of consciousness in the breakdown of the bicameral mind.* Toronto: University of Toronto Press.

Jones, E. (1953). *Sigmund Freud: Life and work* (Vol. 1). London: Hogarth Press.

Jorn, N. (1982). Repression in a case of multiple personality disorder. *Perspectives in Psychiatric Care, 20,* 105–110.

Jung, C. G. (1977). On the psychology and pathology of so-called occult phenomena. In C. G. Jung, *Psychology and the occult,* (pp. 6–91). Princeton: Princeton University Press. (Original work published 1902)

Kales, A., Soldatos, C. R., Caldwell, A. B., Kales, J. D., Humphrey, F. J., Charney, D. S., & Schweitzer, P. K. (1980). Somnambulism: Clinical characteristics and personality patterns. *Archives of General Psychiatry, 37,* 1406–1410.

Kampman, R. (1976). Hypnotically induced multiple personality: An experimental study. *International Journal of Clinical and Experimental Hypnosis, 24,* 215–227.

Kenny, M. G. (1981). Multiple personality and spirit possession. *Psychiatry, 44,* 337–358.

Kenny, M. G. (1986). *The passion of Ansel Bourne: Multiple personality in American Culture.* Washington, DC: Smithsonian Institution Press.

Kernberg, O. J. (1975). *Borderline conditions and pathological narcissism.* New York: Jason Aronson.

Keyes, D. (1981). *The minds of Billy Milligan.* New York: Random House.

Kline, M. V. (1984). Multiple personality: Facts and artifacts in relation to hypnotherapy. *International Journal of Clinical and Experimental Hypnosis*, *32*, 198–209.

Kluft, R. P. (1982). Varieties of hypnotic interventions in the treatment of multiple personality. *American Journal of Clinical Hypnosis*, *24*, 230–240.

Kluft, R. P. (1983). Hypnotherapeutic crisis intervention in multiple personality. *American Journal of Clinical Hypnosis*, *26*, 73–83.

Kluft, R. P. (1984a). Aspects of the treatment of multiple personality disorder. *Psychiatric Annals*, *14*, 51–55.

Kluft, R. P. (1984b). Multiple personality in childhood. *Psychiatric Clinics of North America*, *7*, 121–134.

Kluft, R. P. (1984c). Treatment of multiple personality disorder. *Psychiatric Clinics of North America*, *7*, 9–29.

Kluft, R. P. (Ed.). (1985a). *Childhood antecedents of multiple personality disorder*. Washington, DC: American Psychiatric Press.

Kluft, R. P. (1985b). Childhood multiple personality disorder: Predictors, clinical findings, and treatment results. In R. P. Kluft (Ed.), *Childhood antecedents of multiple personality disorder* (pp. 167–196). Washington, DC: American Psychiatric Press.

Kluft, R. P. (1985c). Hypnotherapy of childhood multiple personality disorder. *American Journal of Clinical Hypnosis*, *27*, 201–210.

Kluft, R. P. (1985d). Making the diagnosis of multiple personality disorder (MPD). In F. F. Flach (Ed.), *Directions in psychiatry*, *5*(23), 1–10. New York: Hatherleigh.

Kluft, R. P. (1985e). The natural history of multiple personality disorder. In R. P. Kluft (Ed.), *Childhood antecedents of multiple personality disorder* (pp. 197–238). Washington, DC: American Psychiatric Press.

Kluft, R. P. (1985f). The treatment of multiple personality disorder (MPD): Current concepts. In F. F. Flach (Ed.), *Directions in psychiatry*, *5*(24), 1–10. New York: Hatherleigh.

Kluft, R. P. (1985g). Using hypnotic inquiry protocols to monitor treatment progress and stability in multiple personality disorder. *American Journal of Clinical Hypnosis*, *28*, 63–75.

Kluft, R. P. (1986a). High-functioning multiple personality patients. *Journal of Nervous and Mental Disease*, *174*, 722–726.

Kluft, R. P. (1986b). Personality unification in multiple personality disorder: A follow-up study. In B. G. Braun (Ed.), *Treatment of multiple personality disorder* (pp. 29–60). Washington, DC: American Psychiatric Press.

Kluft, R. P. (1986c). Preliminary observations on age regression in multiple personality disorder patients before and after integration. *American Journal of Clinical Hypnosis*, *28*, 147–156.

Kluft, R. P. (1986d). The prevalence of multiple personality [Letter to the editor]. *American Journal of Psychiatry*, *143*, 802–803.

Kluft, R. P. (1986e). Treating children who have multiple personality disorder. In B. G. Braun (Ed.), *Treatment of multiple personality disorder* (pp. 79–105). Washington, DC: American Psychiatric Press.

Kluft, R. P. (1987a). An update on multiple personality disorder. *Hospital and Community Psychiatry, 38*, 363–373.

Kluft, R. P. (1987b). First-rank symptoms as a diagnostic clue to multiple personality disorder. *American Journal of Psychiatry, 144*, 293–298.

Kluft, R. P. (1987c). On the use of hypnosis to find lost objects: a case report of a tandem hypnotic technique. *American Journal of Clinical Hypnosis, 29*, 242–248.

Kluft, R. P. (1987d). The simulation and dissimulation of multiple personality disorder. *American Journal of Clinical Hypnosis, 30*, 104–118.

Kluft, R. P. (1987, October 24). *The process of personality unification in a multiple*. Paper presented at Multiple Personality in the 1980s, Toronto.

Kluft, R. P. (1988a). Editorial: Ubi sumus? quo vademis? *Dissociation, 1*(3), 1–2.

Kluft, R. P. (1988b). On giving consultations to therapists treating multiple personality disorder: Fifteen years' experience—Part I. *Dissociation, 1*(3), 23–29.

Kluft, R. P. (1988c). On giving consultations to therapists treating multiple personality disorder: Fifteen years' experience—Part II. *Dissociation, 1*(3), 30–35.

Kluft, R. P. (1988d). On treating the older patient with multiple personality disorder: "Race against time" or "make haste slowly?" *American Journal of Clinical Hypnosis, 30*, 257–266.

Kluft, R. P. (1988e). The postunification treatment of multiple personality disorder: First findings. *American Journal of Psychotherapy, 42*, 212–228.

Kluft, R. P., Braun, B. G., & Sachs, R. (1984). Multiple personality, intrafamilial abuse, and family psychiatry. *International Journal of Family Psychiatry, 5*, 283–301.

Kluft, R. P., Steinberg, M., & Spitzer, R. L. (1988). DSM-III-R revisions in the dissociative disorders: An exploration of their derivation and rationale. *Dissociation, 1*(1), 39–46.

Krasad, A. (1985). Multiple personality syndrome. *British Journal of Hospital Medicine, 34*, 301–303.

Krippner, S. (1986). Cross-cultural approaches to multiple personality disorder: Therapeutic practices in Brazilian spiritism. *The Humanistic Psychologist, 14*, 176–193.

Larmore, K., Ludwig, A. M., & Cain, R. L. (1977). Multiple personality— An objective case study. *British Journal of Psychiatry, 131*, 35–40.

Lasky, R. (1978). The psychoanalytic treatment of a case of multiple personality. *Psychoanalytic Review, 65*, 355–380.

Laurence, J. R., Nadon, R., Nogrady, H., Perry, C. (1986). Duality, dissociation, and memory creation in highly hypnotizable subjects. *International Journal of Clinical and Experimental Hypnosis, 34*, 295–310.

Leavitt, H. C. (1947). A case of hypnotically produced secondary and tertiary personalities. *Psychoanalytic Review, 34*, 274–295.

Lego, S. (1988). Multiple personality disorder: An interpersonal approach to etiology, treatment, and nursing care. *Archives of Psychiatric Nursing, 2*, 231–235.

Lewis, I. M. (1971). *Ecstatic religion: An anthropological study of spirit possession and shamanism.* Baltimore: Penguin Books.

Lewis, G. R. (1976). Criteria for the discerning of spirits. In J. W. Montgomery (Ed.) *Demon possession* (pp. 346–363). Minneapolis: Bethany House.

Links, P. S. (1988). Symposium: Borderline personality disorder. *Canadian Journal of Psychiatry, 33*(5), 335–374.

Lipton, S. D., & Kezur, E. (1948). Dissociated personality: Status of a case after five years. *Psychiatric Quarterly, 22*, 252–256.

Loewenstein, R. J., Hamilton, J., Alagna, S., Reid, N., & de Vries, M. (1987). Experiential sampling in the study of multiple personality disorder. *American Journal of Psychiatry, 144*, 19–24.

Loewenstein, R. J., Hornstein, N., & Farber, D. (1988). Open trial of clonazepam in the treatment of posttraumatic stress symptoms in multiple personality disorder. *Dissociation, 1*(3), 3–12.

Loewenstein, R. J., & Putnam, F. W. (1988). A comparison study of dissociative symptoms in patients with complex partial seizures, multiple personality disorder, and posttraumatic stress disorder. *Dissociation, 1*(4), 17–23.

Lotterman, A. C. (1985). Prolonged psychotic states in borderline personality disorder. *Psychiatric Quarterly, 57*, 33–46.

Lovitt, R., & Lefkof, G. (1985). Understanding multiple personality with the comprehensive Rorschach system. *Journal of Personality Assessment, 49*, 289–294.

Ludolph, P. S. (1985). How prevalent is multiple personality? and Reply of E. L. Bliss [Letters to the editor]. *American Journal of Psychiatry, 142*, 1526–1527.

Ludwig, A. M., Brandsma, J. M., Wilbur, C. B., Benfeldt, F., & Jameson, D. H. (1972). The objective study of a case of multiple personality, or, are four heads better than one? *Archives of General Psychiatry, 26*, 298–310.

Luria, A. R. (1987). *The mind of a mnemonist.* Cambridge: Harvard University Press. (Original work published 1968)

Luria, A. R. (1987). *The man with a shattered world.* Cambridge: Harvard University Press. (Original work published 1972)

Lynn, S. J., & Rhue, J. W. (1988). Fantasy proneness: Hypnosis, developmental antecedents, and psychopathology. *American Psychologist, 43*, 35–44.

Mai, F. M., & Merskey, H. (1980). Briquet's treatise on hysteria. *Archives of General Psychiatry, 37*, 1401–1405.

Malenbaum, R., & Russell, A. T. (1987). Case report: Multiple personality disorder in an 11 year old boy and his mother. *Journal of the American Academy of Child and Adolescent Psychiatry, 26,* 436–439.

Marcos, L. R., & Trujillo, M. (1978). The sodium amytal interview as a therapeutic modality. *Current Psychiatric Therapies, 18,* 129–136.

Marcum, J. M., Wright, K., & Bissell, W. G. (1986). Chance discovery of multiple personality disorder in a depressed patient by amobarbital interview. *Journal of Nervous and Mental Disease, 174,* 489–492.

Margolis, C. G. (1988). Book review [Review of *Psychiatric Clinics of North America: Vol. 7. Symposium on Multiple Personality,* edited by B. G. Braun]. *International Journal of Clinical and Experimental Hypnosis, 36,* 56–60.

Markowitz, J., & Viederman, M. (1986). A case report of dissociative pseudodementia. *General Hospital Psychiatry, 8,* 87–90.

Marmer, S. S. (1980). Psychoanalysis of multiple personality. *International Journal of Psychoanalysis, 61,* 439–459.

Masterson, J. F. (1976). *Psychotherapy of the borderline adult.* New York: Brunner/Mazel.

Mathew, R. J., Jack, R. A., & West, W. S. (1985). Regional cerebral blood flow in a patient with multiple personality. *American Journal of Psychiatry, 142,* 504–505.

Mayer, R. (1988). *Through divided minds.* New York: Doubleday.

McKee, J. B., & Wittkower, E. D. (1962). A case of double personality with death of the imaginary partner. *Canadian Psychiatric Association Journal, 7,* 134–139.

Meichenbaum, D. (1977). *Cognitive-behavior modification.* New York: Plenum.

Mesulam, M-M. (1981). Dissociative states with abnormal temporal lobe EEG: Multiple personality and the illusion of possession. *Archives of Neurology, 38,* 176–181.

Miller, A. (1984). Hypnotherapy in a case of dissociated incest. *International Journal of Clinical and Experimental Hypnosis, 34,* 13–28.

Millette, C. (1988). Using subparts in a case of multiple personality. In S. R. Lankton, J. K. Zeig (Eds.), *Treatment of special populations with Ericksonian approaches* (pp. 104–119). New York: Brunner/Mazel.

Millon, T. (1977). *Millon clinical multiaxial inventory manual.* Minneapolis: National Computer Systems.

Montgomery, J. W. (Ed.) (1976). *Demon possession.* Minneapolis: Bethany House.

Morgan, A. H., & Hilgard, E. R. (1973). Age differences in susceptibility to hypnosis. *International Journal of Clinical and Experimental Hypnosis, 21,* 78–85.

Naples, M., & Hackett, T. P. (1978). The amytal interview: History and current uses. *Psychosomatics, 19,* 98–105.

Nemiah, J. C. (1980). Obsessive-compulsive disorder. In H. I. Kaplan, A. M. Freedman, B. J. Sadock (Eds.), *Comprehensive textbook of psychiatry* (3rd ed., Vol. 2, pp. 1504–1516). Baltimore: Williams & Wilkins.

Nietzsche, F. (1956). *The birth of tragedy and the genealogy of morals.* New York: Doubleday. (Original work published 1872)

O'Brien, P. (1985). The diagnosis of multiple personality syndromes: Overt, covert, and latent. *Comprehensive Therapy, 11,* 59–66.

O'Connor, J. (1988, September 2). Therapists should consider novel approaches in child abuse treatment cases. *Psychiatric News, 23*(17), 20, 27.

Oesterreich, T. K. (1974). *Possession demoniacal and other.* Secaucus: Citadel Press. (Original work published 1921)

Orne, M. T., Dinges, D. F., & Orne, E. C. (1984). On the differential diagnosis of multiple personality in the forensic context. *International Journal of Clinical and Experimental Hypnosis, 32,* 118–169.

Packard, R. C., & Brown, F. (1986). Multiple headaches in a case of multiple personality disorder. *Headaches, 26,* 99–102.

Paley, A-M. N. (1988). Growing up in chaos: The dissociative response. *American Journal of Psychoanalysis, 48,* 72–83.

Pellegrini, A. J., & Putnam, P. (1984). The amytal interview in the diagnosis of late onset psychosis with cultural features presenting as catatonic stupor. *Journal of Nervous and Mental Disease, 172,* 502–504.

Perry, J. C., & Jacobs, D. (1982). Overview: Clinical applications of the amytal interview in psychiatric emergency settings. *American Journal of Psychiatry, 139,* 552–559.

Prince, M. (1978). *The dissociation of a personality.* New York: Oxford University Press. (Original work published 1905)

Putnam, F. W. (1984a). The psychophysiologic investigation of multiple personality disorder. *Psychiatric Clinics of North America, 7,* 31–39.

Putnam, F. W. (1984b). The study of multiple personality disorder: General strategies and practical considerations. *Psychiatric Annals, 14,* 58–61.

Putnam, F. W. (1985). Dissociation as a response to extreme trauma. In R. P. Kluft (Ed.), *Childhood antecedents of multiple personality disorder* (pp. 65–97). Washington, DC: American Psychiatric Press.

Putnam, F. W. (1986a). The scientific study of multiple personality disorder. In J. M. Quen (Ed.), *Split minds split brains* (pp. 109–125). New York: New York University Press.

Putnam, F. W. (1986b). The treatment of multiple personality: State of the art. In B. G. Braun (Ed.), *Treatment of multiple personality disorder* (pp. 175–198). Washington, DC: American Psychiatric Press.

Putnam, F. W. (1988). The switch process in multiple personality disorder. *Dissociation, 1*(1), 24–32.

Putnam, F. W. (1989). *Diagnosis and treatment of multiple personality disorder.* New York: Guilford.

Putnam, F. W., Guroff, J. J., Silberman, E. K., Barban, L., & Post, R. M. (1986). The clinical phenomenology of multiple personality disorder: Review of 100 recent cases. *Journal of Clinical Psychiatry, 47,* 285–293.

Putnam, F. W., Loewenstein, R. J., Silberman, E. K., Post, R. M. (1984).

Multiple personality in a hospital setting. *Journal of Clinical Psychiatry*, *45*, 172–175.

Quen, J. M. (Ed.) (1986). *Split minds split brains*. New York: New York University Press.

Riley, R. L., & Mead, J. (1988). The development of symptoms of multiple personality disorder in a child of three. *Dissociation 1*(3), 43–46.

Rivera, M. (1987). Multiple personality: An outcome of child abuse. *Canadian Woman Studies, 8*, 18–23.

Rivera, M. (1988). *All of them to speak: Feminism, poststructuralism, and multiple personality*. Unpublished doctoral dissertation. Toronto: University of Toronto.

Robins, L. N., Helzer, J. E., Weissman, M. M., Orvaschel, H., Gruenberg, E., Burke, J. D., & Reiger, D. A. (1984). Lifetime prevalence of psychiatric disorders in three communities. *Archives of General Psychiatry, 41*, 949–958.

Rogo, D. S. (1986a). *Mind over matter: The case for psychokinesis*. Wellingborough: Aquarian Press.

Rogo, D. S. (1986b). *On the track of the poltergeist*. Englewood Cliffs, NJ: Prentice-Hall.

Rosenbaum, M. (1980). The role of the term schizophrenia in the decline of diagnoses of multiple personality. *Archives of General Psychiatry, 37*, 1383–1385.

Rosenbaum, M., & Weaver, G. M. (1980). Dissociated state: Status of a case after 38 years. *Journal of Nervous and Mental Disease, 168*, 597–603.

Rosenzweig, S. (1988). The identity and idiodynamics of the multiple personality "Sally Beauchamp": A confirmatory supplement. *American Psychologist, 43*, 45–48.

Ross, C. A. (1981). Basic research by medical students. *Journal of the Royal Society of Medicine, 74*, 7–10.

Ross, C. A. (1984). Diagnosis of multiple personality during hypnosis: A case report. *International Journal of Clinical and Experimental Hypnosis, 32*, 222–235.

Ross, C. A. (1985). DSM-III: Problems in diagnosing partial forms of multiple personality disorder. *Journal of the Royal Society of Medicine, 75*, 933–936.

Ross, C. A. (1986a). Biological tests for mental illness: Their use and misuse. *Biological Psychiatry, 21*, 431–435.

Ross, C. A. (1986b). The insanity of the insanity defense. *The Medical Post*, July 8, p. 10.

Ross, C. A. (1987). Inpatient treatment of multiple personality disorder. *Canadian Journal of Psychiatry, 32*, 779–781.

Ross, C. A. (1988, January). Multiple personality disorder in Canada. *Psychiatry in Canada*, pp. 11–13.

Ross, C. A., & Anderson, G. (1988). Phenomenological overlap of multiple personality disorder and obsessive-compulsive disorder. *Journal of Nervous and Mental Disease, 176*, 295–299.

Ross, C. A., Anderson, G., Heber, S., & Norton, G. R. (in press). Dissociation and abuse in multiple personality patients, prostitutes, and exotic dancers. *Hospital and Community Psychiatry.*

Ross, C. A., & Fraser, G. A. (1987). Recognizing multiple personality disorder. *Annals of the Royal College of Physicians and Surgeons of Canada, 20,* 357–360.

Ross, C. A., & Gahan, P. (1988a). Cognitive analysis of multiple personality disorder. *American Journal of Psychotherapy, 42,* 229–239.

Ross, C. A., & Gahan, P. (1988b). Techniques in the treatment of multiple personality disorder. *American Journal of Psychotherapy, 42,* 40–52.

Ross, C. A., Heber, S., Anderson, G., Norton, G. R., Anderson, B., del Campo, M., & Pillay, N. (1989). Differentiating multiple personality disorder and complex partial seizures. *General Hospital Psychiatry, 11,* 54–58.

Ross, C. A., Heber, S., Norton, G. R., & Anderson, G. (1989a). Differences between multiple personality disorder and other diagnostic groups on structured interview. *Journal of Nervous and Mental Disease, 179*(8), 487–491.

Ross, C. A., Heber, S., Norton, G. R., & Anderson, G. (1989b). Somatic symptoms in multiple personality disorder. *Psychosomatics, 30*(2), 154–160.

Ross, C. A., & Matas, M. (1987). A clinical trial of buspirone and diazepam in treatment of generalized anxiety disorder. *Canadian Journal of Psychiatry, 32,* 351–355.

Ross, C. A., & Norton, G. R. (1987). Signs and symptoms of multiple personality disorder. *Modern Medicine of Canada, 42,* 392–396.

Ross, C. A., & Norton, G. R. (1988). Multiple personality patients with a past diagnosis of schizophrenia. *Dissociation, 1*(2), 39–42.

Ross, C. A., & Norton, G. R. (1989a). Differences between men and women with multiple personality disorder. *Hospital and Community Psychiatry, 40*(2), 186–188.

Ross, C. A., & Norton, G. R. (1989b). Suicide and parasuicide in multiple personality disorder. *Psychiatry, 52,* 365–371.

Ross, C. A., & Norton, G. R. (in press). Effects of hypnosis on the features of multiple personality disorder. *American Journal of Clinical Hypnosis.*

Ross, C. A., Norton, G. R., & Anderson, G. (1988). The dissociative experiences scale: A replication study. *Dissociation, 1*(3), 21–22.

Ross, C. A., Norton, G. R., & Fraser, G. A. (1989). Evidence against the iatrogenesis of multiple personality disorder. *Dissociation.*

Ross, C. A., Norton, G. R., & Wozney, K. (1989). Multiple personality disorder: An analysis of 236 cases. *Canadian Journal of Psychiatry, 34*(5), 413–418.

Ross, C. A., & Ryan, L. 1988. Unpublished raw data.

Ross, C. A., Siddiqui, A. R., Matas, M. (1987). DSM-III: Problems in diagnosis of paranoia and obsessive-compulsive disorder. *Canadian Journal of Psychiatry, 32,* 351–355.

Ruedrich, S. L., Chu, C-C., & Wadle, C. V. (1985). The amytal interview in the treatment of psychogenic amnesia. *Hospital and Community Psychiatry, 36,* 1045–1046.

Rush, F. (1980). *The best kept secret: Sexual abuse of children.* New York: McGraw-Hill.

Russell, B. (1945). *A history of Western philosophy.* New York: Simon & Schuster.

Ryan, L. (1988). *Prevalence of dissociative disorders and symptoms in a university population.* Unpublished doctoral dissertation. San Francisco: California Institute of Integral Studies.

Ryan, L., & Ross, C. A. (1988). Dissociation in adolescents and college students. In B. G. Braun (Ed.), *Proceedings of the Fifth International Conference on Multiple Personality/Dissociative States* (p. 19). Chicago: Rush-Presbyterian-St. Luke's Medical Center.

Sachs, R. G. (1986). The adjunctive role of social support systems in the treatment of multiple personality disorder. In B. G. Braun (Ed.), *Treatment of multiple personality disorder* (pp. 157–174). Washington, DC: American Psychiatric Press.

Sachs, R. G., Frischholtz, E. J., & Wood, J. I. (1988). Marital and family therapy in the treatment of multiple personality disorder. *Journal of Marital and Family Therapy, 14,* 249–259.

Sanders, S. (1986). The perceptual alteration scale: A scale measuring dissociation. *American Journal of Clinical Hypnosis, 29,* 95–102.

Schafer, D. W. (1981). The recognition and hypnotherapy of patients with unrecognized altered states. *American Journal of Clinical Hypnosis, 23,* 176–183.

Schafer, D. W. (1986). Recognizing multiple personality patients. *American Journal of Psychotherapy, 40,* 500–510.

Schenk, L., & Bear, D. (1981). Multiple personality and related dissociative phenomena in patients with temporal lobe epilepsy. *American Journal of Psychiatry, 138,* 1311–1316.

Schreiber, F. R. (1973). *Sybil.* Chicago: Henry Regnery.

Schultz, R. K., Braun, B. G., & Kluft, R. P. (1985). Creativity and the imaginary companion phenomenon: Prevalence and phenomenology in MPD. In B. G. Braun (Ed.), *Proceedings of the Second Annual International Conference on Multiple Personality/Dissociative States* (p. 103). Chicago: Rush-Presbyterian-St. Luke's Medical Center.

Schwartz, R. (1987, March–April). Our multiple selves. *Networker,* pp. 25–31, 80–83.

Sheehy, M., Goldsmith, L., & Charles, M. A. (1980). A comparative study of borderline patients in a psychiatric outpatient clinic. *American Journal of Psychiatry, 137,* 1374–1379.

Sidis, B., & Goodhart, S. P. (1905). *Multiple personality.* New York: Appleton-Century-Crofts.

Sidtis, J. J. (1986). Can neurological disconnection account for psychiatric dissociation? In J. M. Quen (Ed.), *Split minds split brains* (pp. 127–147). New York: New York University Press.

Silberman, E. K., Putnam, F. W., Weingartner, H., Braun, B. G., & Post, R. M. (1985). Dissociative states in multiple personality disorder: A quantitative study. *Psychiatry Research, 15,* 253–260.

Silbert, M. H., & Pines, A. M. (1981). Sexual child abuse as an antecedent to prostitution. *Child Abuse and Neglect, 5,* 407–411.

Silbert, M. H., & Pines, A. M. (1982). Entrance into prostitution. *Youth and Society, 13,* 471–500.

Silbert, M. H., & Pines, A. M. (1983). Early sexual exploitation as an influence in prostitution. *Social Work, 28,* 285–290.

Silbert, M. H., & Pines, A. M. (1984). Pornography and sexual abuse of women. *Sex Roles, 10,* 857–868.

Sizemore, C., & Pittillo, E. (1977). *I'm Eve.* New York: Doubleday.

Sneiderman, B. (1988, June 20). Sleepwalk defense has precedent. *Winnipeg Free Press,* p. 7.

Spanos, N. P., Weekes, J. R., & Bertrand, L. D. (1985). Multiple personality: A social psychological perspective. *Journal of Abnormal Psychology, 94,* 362–376.

Spanos, N. P., Weekes, J. R., Menary, E., & Bertrand, L. D. (1986). Hypnotic interview and age regression procedures in elicitation of multiple personality symptoms: A simulation study. *Psychiatry, 49,* 298–311.

Spiegel, D. (1984). Multiple personality as a post-traumatic stress disorder. *Psychiatric Clinics of North America, 7,* 101–110.

Spiegel, D. (1986a). Dissociating damage. *American Journal of Clinical Hypnosis, 29,* 123–131.

Spiegel, D. (1986b). Dissociation, double binds, and posttraumatic stress in multiple personality disorder. In B. G. Braun (Ed.), *Treatment of multiple personality disorder* (pp. 61–77). Washington, DC: American Psychiatric Press.

Spiegel, D. (1988). The treatment accorded those who treat patients with multiple personality disorder. *Journal of Nervous and Mental Disease, 176,* 535–536.

Spiegel, D., Hunt, T., & Dondershine, H. E. (1988). Dissociation and hypnotizability in posttraumatic stress disorder. *American Journal of Psychiatry, 145,* 301–305.

Spiegel, D., & Rosenfeld, A. (1984). Spontaneous hypnotic age regression: Case report. *Journal of Clinical Psychiatry, 45,* 522–524.

Spiegel, H., & Spiegel, D. (1978). *Trance and treatment.* New York: Basic Books.

Steinberg, M. (1987). Diagnostically discriminating questions on the structured clinical interview for DSM-III-R dissociative disorders. In B. G. Braun (Ed.), *Proceedings of the Fourth International Conference on Multiple Personality/Dissociative States* (p. 130). Chicago: Rush-Presbyterian-St. Luke's Medical Center.

Steinberg, M., Howland, F., & Cicchetti, D. (1986). The structured clinical interview for DSM-III-R dissociative disorders: A preliminary report. In B. G. Braun (Ed.), *Proceedings of the Third International Conference on Multiple Personality/Dissociative States* (p. 125). Chicago: Rush-Presbyterian-St. Luke's Medical Center.

Stern, C. R. (1984). The etiology of multiple personalities. *Psychiatric Clinics of North America, 7,* 149–159.

Stevenson, I., & Pasricha, S. (1979). A case of secondary personality with xenoglossy. *American Journal of Psychiatry, 136,* 1591–1592.

Stewart, W. A. (1984). Analytic biography of Anna O. In M. Rosenbaum, & M. Muroff (Eds.), *Anna O: Fourteen contemporary reinterpretations* (pp. 50–68). New York: Free Press.

Stoller, R. J. (1973). *Splitting: A case of female masculinity.* New York: Dell.

Sutcliffe, J. P., & Jones, J. (1962). Personal identity, multiple personality, and hypnosis. *International Journal of Clinical and Experimental Hypnosis, 10,* 231–269.

Taylor, W. S., & Martin, M. F. (1944). Multiple personality. *Journal of Abnormal and Social Psychology, 39,* 281–300.

Thigpen, C. H., & Cleckley, H. M. (1957). *The three faces of Eve.* New York: McGraw-Hill.

Thigpen, C. H., & Cleckley, H. M. (1984). On the incidence of multiple personality disorder. *International Journal of Clinical and Experimental Hypnosis, 32,* 63–66.

Torem, M. (1986). Dissociative states presenting as an eating disorder. *American Journal of Clinical Hypnosis, 29,* 137–142.

Torem, M. S. (1987). Ego-state therapy for eating disorders. *American Journal of Clinical Hypnosis, 30,* 94–103.

Torem, M. S. (1988). PTSD presenting as an eating disorder. *Stress Medicine, 4,* 139–142.

van der Hart, O., & van der Velden, K. (1987). The hypnotherapy of Dr. Andries Hoek: Uncovering hypnotherapy before Janet, Breuer, and Freud. *American Journal of Clinical Hypnosis, 29,* 264–271.

Varma, V. K., Bouri, M., & Wig, N. N. (1981). Multiple personality in India: Comparison with hysterical possession state. *American Journal of Psychotherapy, 35,* 113–120.

Veith, I. (1965). *Hysteria: The history of a disease.* Chicago: University of Chicago Press.

Villoldo, A., & Krippner, S. (1986). *Healing states: A journey into the world of spiritual healing and shamanism.* New York: Simon & Schuster.

Vincent, M., & Pickering, M. R. (1988). Multiple personality disorder in childhood. *Canadian Journal of Psychiatry, 33,* 524–529.

Walker, J., Norton, G. R., & Ross, C. A. (in press). *Panic Disorder and agoraphobia: A guide for the practitioner.* Pacific Grove, CA: Brooks/Cole.

Wasson, R. G. (1973). *Soma: Divine mushroom of immortality*. San Diego: Harcourt Brace Jovanovich.

Watkins, J. G. (1984). The Bianchi (L. A. Hillside Strangler) case: Sociopath or multiple personality? *International Journal of Clinical and Experimental Hypnosis, 32,* 67–101.

Weinberg, S. K. (1955). *Incest behavior*. New York: Citadel Press.

Weiss, M., Sutton, P. J., & Utecht, A. J. (1985). Multiple personality in a 10 year old girl. *Journal of the American Academy of Child Psychiatry, 24,* 495–501.

Wilbur, C. B. (1984). Multiple personality and child abuse. *Psychiatric Clinics of North America, 7,* 3–7.

Wilbur, C. B. (1985). The effect of child abuse on the psyche. In R. P. Kluft (Ed.), *Childhood antecedents of multiple personality disorder* (pp. 21–35). Washington, DC: American Psychiatric Press.

Wilbur, C. B. (1986). Psychoanalysis and multiple personality disorder. In B. G. Braun (Ed.), *Treatment of multiple personality disorder* (pp. 133–142). Washington, DC: American Psychiatric Press.

Wilson, W. P. (1976). Hysteria and demons, depression and oppression, good and evil. In J. W. Montgomery (Ed.), *Demon possession* (pp. 223–231). Minneapolis: Bethany House.

Winer, D. (1978). Anger and dissociation: A case study of multiple personality. *Journal of Abnormal Psychology, 87,* 368–372.

Young, W. C. (1986). Restraints in the treatment of a patient with multiple personality. *American Journal of Psychotherapy, 40,* 601–606.

Young, W. C. (1987). Emergence of a multiple personality in a posttraumatic stress disorder of adulthood. *American Journal of Clinical Hypnosis, 29,* 249–254.

Young, W. C. (1988). Psychodynamics and dissociation: All that switches is not split. *Dissociation, 1*(1), 33–38.

Author Index

Subject Index